CU00765039

# George Orwell and Russia

# George Orwell and Russia

Masha Karp

BLOOMSBURY ACADEMIC
LONDON • NEW YORK • OXFORD • NEW DELHI • SYDNEY

BLOOMSBURY ACADEMIC
Bloomsbury Publishing Plc
50 Bedford Square, London, WC1B 3DP, UK
1385 Broadway, New York, NY 10018, USA
29 Earlsfort Terrace, Dublin 2, Ireland

BLOOMSBURY, BLOOMSBURY ACADEMIC and the Diana logo are
trademarks of Bloomsbury Publishing Plc

First published in Great Britain 2023
Reprinted in 2023 (twice)

Copyright © Masha Karp, 2023

Masha Karp has asserted her right under the Copyright, Designs and
Patents Act, 1988, to be identified as Author of this work.

For legal purposes the Acknowledgements on p. xi–xiii constitute an extension of this copyright page.

Cover design by Adriana Brioso
Cover image: Soviet poster by Yakov Guminer, 1931. (© Artyom Smirnov/Russian National Library/
Alamy Stock Photo)

All rights reserved. No part of this publication may be reproduced or transmitted in any form or by any
means, electronic or mechanical, including photocopying, recording, or any information storage or
retrieval system, without prior permission in writing from the publishers.

Bloomsbury Publishing Plc does not have any control over, or responsibility for, any third-party websites
referred to or in this book. All internet addresses given in this book were correct at the time of going
to press. The author and publisher regret any inconvenience caused if addresses have changed or sites
have ceased to exist, but can accept no responsibility for any such changes.

A catalogue record for this book is available from the British Library.

A catalog record for this book is available from the Library of Congress.

Library of Congress Cataloging-in-Publication Data
Names: Karp, Masha, author.
Title: George Orwell and Russia / Masha Karp.
Description: London; New York: Bloomsbury Academic, 2023. | Includes bibliographical references.
Identifiers: LCCN 2022049369 (print) | LCCN 2022049370 (ebook) | ISBN 9781788317139 (hardback) |
ISBN 9781788317122 (paperback) | ISBN 9781788317146 (epub) | ISBN 9781788317153 (pdf) |
ISBN 9781788317160
Subjects: LCSH: Orwell, George, 1903-1950–Political and social views. | Orwell, George, 1903-1950–
Appreciation–Soviet Union. | Literature and society–Soviet Union. | Totalitarianism in literature. |
LCGFT: Literary criticism.
Classification: LCC PR6029.R8 Z7145 2023 (print) | LCC PR6029.R8 (ebook) |
DDC 828/.91209–dc23/eng/20230213
LC record available at https://lccn.loc.gov/2022049369
LC ebook record available at https://lccn.loc.gov/2022049370

ISBN: HB: 978-1-7883-1713-9
PB: 978-1-7883-1712-2
ePDF: 978-1-7883-1715-3
eBook: 978-1-7883-1714-6

Typeset by Deanta Global Publishing Services, Chennai, India
Printed and bound in Great Britain

To find out more about our authors and books visit www .bloomsbury .com and sign up for
our newsletters.

# Contents

# Figures

# Preface

## Reading Orwell in Russia and Britain

'Is it safe to keep this book at home overnight?' – my mother asked me, when in Leningrad of the mid-1970s my friends had given me a copy of the forbidden *Nineteen Eighty-Four* for a couple of days and we both were reading it. Her experience told her that searches and arrests 'invariably happened at night',[1] and although it was now Brezhnev's rather than Stalin's time, the frightening resemblance of the bleak and cruel life in Oceania to our own was overwhelming. 'How did he know?' we wondered. The same question was asked by numerous other readers who were lucky to get hold of Orwell's last novel in the Soviet Union and throughout Eastern Europe between the 1950s and the late 1980s.

Then, with Gorbachev's *perestroika* (restructuring), things started changing, books were no longer banned, but, unfortunately, after seventy years of communist rule, real transformation proved too difficult for Russia – it failed to get totalitarianism out of its system. Under Putin it became obvious that Orwell was relevant yet again. 'How did he know?' – new readers asked in 2022, finding it hard to believe that the Russian state in its sinister absurdity had suddenly launched a brutal war, which was killing thousands of people and razing flourishing cities to the ground but was not allowed to be called war. As Putin turned the clock back, it became clear that not only Oceania's slogans but nearly all the other totalitarian features identified by Orwell returned in roughly the same form as he described them.

It has always seemed a miracle to those on the wrong side of the Iron Curtain that a foreign writer managed 'to convey fully what a totalitarian regime means in terms of the individuals living under it'[2] and to do so in such a way that they not just completely accepted the authenticity of his depiction but marveled at his ability to tell them things they felt but could not always articulate. It seems a miracle today that Orwell's observations of 1948 proved accurate not only in 1984 but also in 2022.

---

[1] Orwell, *Nineteen Eighty-Four* (Harmondsworth, Middlesex: Penguin Books, 1987), 18.
[2] Franz Borkenau to Orwell, 14 September 1949, The OA, UCL, ORWELL/H/1/20/3.

This book was originally conceived as an attempt to explore the nature of this miracle. Orwell did not speak or read Russian, nor did he ever set foot in the Soviet Union, but he could not stop thinking about the country as he was dismayed at its grim trajectory from the revolution against autocracy to a new autocracy. The impact of *Nineteen Eighty-Four* was achieved, as Orwell had hoped, by the fusion of politics and art: by his own unique blend of deep sociological insights into a totalitarian regime – here he was, no doubt, influenced by his friendship with the now nearly forgotten sociologist Franz Borkenau, a pioneer of the theory of totalitarianism – and his poetic imagination, which enabled him to put himself in the position of those who experienced the regime first-hand. 'He felt the Russian tragedy as if it was his own', wrote Victoria Chalikova, the first Orwell scholar in Russia, noting his 'ability to immerse himself completely in the role of a reflective and sensitive victim of political terror'.[3]

And yet it was not just compassion for the victims of totalitarianism that drove Orwell to write about it. Despite his preoccupation with Russia – obvious not only in his fiction but in his essays, his *Tribune* column, his diaries and correspondence – his main concern was about his own country. Orwell saw with remarkable clarity the danger the Soviet system and its 'publicity agents', as he contemptuously called British communists, presented for Britain. 'I have no wish to interfere with the Soviet regime even if I could', he wrote in 1945. 'I merely don't want its methods and habits of thought imitated here.'[4] All his political writing – his journalism, his 'fairy story', his last novel, deliberately set in London – is addressed to his compatriots, to the left-wing British intelligentsia, which, with few exceptions, was infatuated with the 'Russian myth'. 'It is above all necessary to make people see the Russian regime for what it really is', he wrote in the same letter, adding with striking modesty in parentheses '(i.e. what I think it is)'.[5]

Indeed, *Animal Farm* and *Nineteen Eighty-Four* helped to expose the Soviet regime. But very soon after the collapse of the Soviet Union in 1991, understanding Orwell's message started fading – not from Orwell scholarship, which has been developing and expanding, but from contemporary politics and consequently, from the wider culture. As 1991 was the year when I moved to London, I could see how quickly the British media started treating Orwell's politics as outdated. The danger of totalitarianism grew more and more vague and obsolete in people's minds, and in the twenty-first century

3   Victoria Chalikova, '*Vstrecha s Oruellom*' (An Encounter with Orwell) (*Knizhnoe obozrenie*, 20 May 1988).
4   Orwell to Michael Sayers, 11 December 1945, *A Life in Letters*, selected and annotated by Peter Davison (London: Penguin Books, 2011), 275.
5   Ibid.

Orwell's last novel was increasingly read as a warning against technology rather than against the political system behind it.

By 2013, when Orwell's 110th anniversary was celebrated in the UK, the word 'totalitarianism' seemed to have completely fallen out of use. Numerous tributes praised the writer's limpid prose, his exposure of British imperialism and his condemnation of social inequality. He was commended for his early awareness of environmental problems, his unashamed celebration of the English national character and even of English cooking. There was hardly a word in the media about the main aim of the last twelve years of his life – to warn against the appeal of a regime based on lies. Politicians were simply not interested in it anymore.

This was a delusion, and Orwell had warned against it too, only his advice was almost completely ignored.

> For all I know by the time my book is published my view of the Soviet regime may be the generally accepted one. But what use would that be of itself? To exchange one orthodoxy for another is not necessarily an advance. The enemy is the gramophone mind, whether or not one agrees with the record that is being played at the moment.[6]

In the thirty-odd years that I have been living in Britain I have had plenty of opportunities to watch the work of the 'gramophone mind' and the appearances of new orthodoxies, sometimes suspiciously similar to the old ones.

I witnessed the creation of the new 'Russian myth'. It was widely believed here that having said goodbye to the Soviet past, Russia almost overnight became a capitalist democracy like any other – perhaps with its own peculiarities, but at least its 'ideology', so it was claimed, did not differ from that of others as much as communism had. Neither the extreme brutality of its two Chechen wars, nor its war in Georgia in 2008, the annexation of Crimea and invasion of Donbass in 2014, the assassinations of journalists and political opponents at home and abroad, the repressive laws against civil society, nor corruption, which moved across borders and affected Western politicians and commentators, were able to shatter this radiant image. If in Orwell's time the myth was created and supported by the naive idealism and ignorance of the left, now it was an incredible lack of political judgement, coupled with unfettered greed, which impelled groups and individuals of all

---

[6] Orwell, 'The Freedom of the Press', in *The Complete Works of George Orwell*, ed. Peter Davison, 20 vols. (London: Secker & Warburg, 1998), Vol. XVII, 259 – later CW, XVII, 259.

persuasions to grab profits generously offered by the Russian authorities – together, of course, with Russia's skilful propaganda and deep infiltration.

As a newcomer, I was also amazed to discover that those in the West who, like Orwell, sympathized with people living under Soviet totalitarianism and tried to help them either by attracting attention to their plight or by broadcasting and sending books to the 'Soviet bloc', were dismissively called 'cold warriors' – and it was obvious that Orwell escaped this derogatory moniker only because he died in early 1950. And later, when the 'Cold War' was discussed, it often seemed to me that speakers and writers saw no difference between the position of Western democracies, which, with all their numerous faults, still tried to defend liberal values, and the aggressive Soviet Empire, a threat both to its own and other countries' citizens. Moreover, those who attempted to criticize any developments in Yeltsin's and Putin's Russia were routinely reproached with bringing back 'Cold War attitudes', as if saying something disapproving of the Kremlin was necessarily offensive and wrong-headed.

In February 2022, Russia started a full-scale criminal war in Europe and used nuclear blackmail to prevent anybody from interfering. A new era has begun and we do not yet know how it will end. One thing is, however, clear – these disastrous developments have, unfortunately, been made possible by the stubborn refusal 'to see the Russian regime for what it really is'.

\*   \*   \*

I hope this book will arouse the curiosity of those with an interest in Orwell, who may value a Russian perspective on him, and of those with an interest in Russia, who may be stimulated by the opportunity to look at it through Orwell's eyes.

In the first part of the book, I explore the circumstances that determined Orwell's attitude to the USSR before he went to Spain at the end of 1936 (Chapters 1 and 2); examine the changes the Spanish Civil War brought to his perception of Soviet communism (Chapter 3) and consider what helped him to expand and sharpen his understanding of Russia when he came back (Chapters 4 and 5).

The second part describes Orwell's attempts to fight against totalitarianism not only by writing about it, but also by social activism (Chapter 6); his controversial attitude to socialism (Chapter 7); the desperate but doomed attempts of the Soviet authorities to prevent Orwell's books from getting into the country and the effort that went into resisting these attempts (Chapter 8); and finally, the traits that make Oceania so similar to the Soviet Union (Chapter 9) and contemporary Russia (Chapter 10).

# Acknowledgements

Like anyone who writes about Orwell, I am profoundly indebted to the late Peter Davison for compiling and editing the magnificent twenty-volume edition of *The Complete Works of George Orwell*, with its Cumulative Index, which I have opened nearly every day for the last ten years – and each time with admiration and gratitude for this tremendous labour of love.

I am also deeply grateful to The Orwell Society, of which I have been a member since 2013, for all the visits to places related to Orwell, conferences, talks and discussions we have had and for the inimitable sense of community. The help, support and encouragement of Richard and Eleanor Blair, Quentin and Liz Kopp, Dione Venables, Jason Crimp and Anita Coppola, Neil Smith, Leslie Hurst, Ann and Zigurds Kronbergs, Sherry L. Goodman and Joe Luttrell, Ian Bloom, Steve Foulger, Roger Howe, David Milton, Anna Vaninskaya and many others meant a lot to me, as did the inspiring example of renowned Orwell scholars: John Rodden, Jeffrey Meyers, D. J. Taylor and the late Gordon Bowker, all of whom I met thanks to the Society.

I greatly appreciate the interest in my research into Orwell's views on Russia expressed by The Orwell Foundation and its director Jean Seaton as early as 2010 when I was invited by Gavin Freeguard to participate in a public discussion of this subject with John Lloyd. I felt as honoured then as I was in 2022 when the Foundation asked me to contribute a few blogs on Orwell, Ukraine and Russia for their website. I have also been encouraged to explore this subject by the interest and support of many other people, including Julian Bell, Ian Bond, William Horsley, Edward Lucas and Alan Philps.

My enormous gratitude goes to my friends who read the draft versions of this book: first of all to Martin Dewhirst, who read the whole manuscript from beginning to end, as well as to Liz Barnes and Alissa Valles, who read big chunks of it – the book was vastly improved by their comments. I have also received many invaluable suggestions from Stephen Capus, Vera Chalidze, Peter Daniels, John and Nicole Fletcher, Sara Jolly, Jessy Kaner, Andrew McNeillie, Maria Razumovskaya, Natalia Rubinstein, Irina Safyanova and Tatyana Zhakovskaya. I am wholeheartedly grateful to John Crowfoot and Robert Chandler, who understand only too well the difficulty of interpreting Soviet reality to British readers – I could always approach them with all sorts of questions and receive judicious answers. I am also thankful to other professionals who helped me with translations: Dina Newman, Olga Kerziouk, Samantha Kolupov, Ros Schwartz, Anthony Wood and Reuben Wooley.

I was fortunate that Olga Kerziouk could advise me on Esperanto books and experts. As a result, I benefited from the friendliness and generosity of Esperanto scholars and enthusiasts, including Ulrich Lins, Humphrey Tonkin, Bernhard Tuider, the late Bill Chapman, Vinko Markov and Ward de Kock. Esperanto led me to the Siberian town of Omsk, the home of Orwell's landlady's Esperanto correspondent, and I am grateful to Galina Mushinskaya, who used to know this man, and to Natalia Chernyavskaya, a historian from Omsk State Agricultural University, as both supplied essential information about him.

Acquiring facts about the fascinating life and work of the sociologist Franz Borkenau was an exciting process, and I can't sufficiently thank those who helped me along the way – first of all, Franz Borkenau's sons Felix and Peter Borkenau, but also Sue Schmitke, Seumas Spark and Bern Brent in Australia, and Elisabeth Lebensaft and Christoph Mentschl in Austria.

This book would not have been possible without the archives held in many countries of the world and their archivists, who worked hard even during the pandemic. In Britain, I am particularly grateful to Mandy Wise, Dan Mitchell and Rafael C.Siodor of the Orwell Archive at UCL and to the archive's head Sarah Aitchison and her predecessor Gillian Furlong; to Sarah Pymer and Claire Weatherall of the Hull University Archives; Stephen Willis and Danielle Howarth of the Centre for Research Collection at the University of Edinburgh; Jackie Madden of the Bernard Crick Collection in the Birkbeck College Archive; Dr Laura Miller of the Marx Memorial Library, who helped me back in 2014; Dr Helen Wicker of the Kent Archives and K. A. Oram of the Charing & District Local History Society. In the United States, my thanks go to Anatol Shmelev of the Hoover Institution Library and Archives for his longstanding support and advice and also to his colleagues at Hoover: Chris Marino, Katherine Ramirez and Sarah Patton, while in New York I am appreciative of the assistance of Tanya Chebotarev of the Bakhmeteff Archive of Russian and East European Culture at Columbia University. In Russia, I am obliged to Elena Zhemkova, Alexey Makarov and Alena Kozlova from Memorial and to Natalia Volokhonskaya of the Russian State Archive of Social and Political History (RGASPI).

My special thanks are reserved for Gabriel Superfin, a former archivist of the Research Centre for East European Studies in Bremen, Germany, who generously shared with me his infinite knowledge of people involved with the Russian translation and secret dissemination of Orwell's books when they were banned in the USSR; for Catherine Fitzpatrick, who enlightened me on Lyudmila Thorne's tireless efforts to help banned books reach readers in the Soviet Union and directed me to Thorne's unpublished memoir; for Ivan Tolstoy, who provided me with essential facts about some émigré publications;

and for Miriam Frank, who unreservedly shared the information about the Spanish Civil War, which she imbibed as a child from her parents, who had supported the Republican side and knew many of the war's participants – both communists and anarchists.

I am immensely grateful to Bill Hamilton of A.M. Heath and the estate of the late Sonia Brownell Orwell for permission to publish quotes from Orwell's writings as epigraphs; to Franz Borkenau's sons, Felix and Peter, and to Gleb Struve's son, Dimitry, who allowed me to quote from their fathers' letters; to John Saville's estate for permission to quote from material in the John Saville collection in Hull; and to Rick Stapleton of the Bertrand Russell Archives in McMaster University Library for permission to quote from Russell's letter.

This list would surely be incomplete if I did not mention Thomas Stottor, my first editor at I.B. Tauris, who enthusiastically supported the idea of this book at a very early stage, and all the other editors at I.B. Tauris and Bloomsbury – Tomasz Hoskins, Nayiri Kendir and Atifa Jiwa, who have helped me so much in bringing this idea to fruition.

Extracts from *George Orwell and Russia* appeared in *The Orwell Society Journal*:

'The Raven Vanishes', *Journal 9*, Dec 2016, 16–19.
'Lanti and the Soviet Union', *Journal 16*, Spring 2020, 12–16.
'The Unusual Landlady', *Journal 17*, Autumn 2020, 21–25.
'The POUM and *Pravda*', *Journal 18*, Spring 2021, 24–28.
'Mysteries of Russian Archives', *Journal 19*, Autumn 2021, 9–13.
'War is Peace', *Journal 20*, Autumn 2022, 6–9.

and were published on-line by the Orwell Foundation:

'The Ukrainian Translation of *Animal Farm*', 15 March 2022 https://blog. orwellfoundation.com/the-ukrainian-translation-of-animal-farm-excerpt-from-masha-karps-orwell-and-russia/.

'The System of Organised Lying', 29 July 2022 https://orwellprizes. substack.com/p/the-system-of-organised-lying

# Note on translations

Unless stated otherwise, translations from Russian and German are by the author; from Esperanto by Dina Newman; and from French by Ros Schwartz and Samantha Kolupov.

# Glossary

The names of Soviet/Russian security agencies and secret police.

Cheka (1917–1922)    *Chrezvychaynaya Komissia* – The Extraordinary Commission for Combating Counter-Revolution and Sabotage.

FSB (1995–present)    *Federalnaya Sluzhba Bezopasnosti* – Federal Security Service.

GPU (1922–23)    *Gosudarstvennoe Politicheskoye Upravlenie* – The State Political Directorate.

KGB (1954–91)    *Komitet Gosudarstvennoy Bezopasnosti* – Committee For State Security.

MVD (1946–present)    *Ministerstvo Vnutrennikh Del* – Ministry of Internal Affairs.

NKVD (1934–46)    *Narodny Komissariat Vnutrennikh Del* – People's Commissariat for Internal Affairs.

OGPU (1923–34)    *Obyedinennoe Gosudarstvennoe Politicheskoe Upravlenie* – The Joint State Political Directorate.

# Abbreviations

The following short titles are used for some often quoted books:

| | |
|---|---|
| Bowker | Gordon Bowker, *George Orwell*. London: Abacus, 2010. |
| Crick | Bernard Crick, *George Orwell: A Life*. Harmondsworth, Middlesex: Penguin Books, 1982. |
| CW | *The Complete Works of George Orwell*, edited by Peter Davison, 20 volumes. London: Secker & Warburg, 1998. In the notes, CW is followed by a volume number (a Roman numeral) and a page number. |
| Stansky and Abrahams | Peter Stansky and William Abrahams, *Orwell: The Transformation* (London: Paladin Books, Granada Publishing Ltd, 1984). |

The following abbreviations are used for the Archives:

| | |
|---|---|
| Bakhmeteff Archive | Bakhmeteff Archive of Russian and East European Culture, Columbia University, New York. |
| Crick Collection | Bernard Crick Archive, Birkbeck College Archive. |
| Hoover | Hoover Institution Library and Archives, Stanford University, California. |
| HUA | Hull University Archive. |
| MML | Marx Memorial Library. International Memorial Trust. |
| RGASPI | The Russian Archive of Social and Political History, Moscow. |
| The OA, UCL | The Orwell Archive, UCL Library Services, Special Collections. |
| UoE | University of Edinburgh Archive. Arthur Koestler's Papers. Collection-146. |

Part I

# 'I have regarded this regime with plain horror . . .'

# 1

# The first vaccination

*I have never fundamentally altered my attitude towards the Soviet regime since I first began to pay attention to it some time in the nineteen-twenties.*[1]

Orwell, 1946

Paradoxically enough, Orwell first began to pay attention to the Soviet regime in Paris, where he moved in April 1928. He was approaching twenty-five, and the pen-name 'Orwell' had not yet been invented. Before going to Paris, Eric Blair had no real knowledge of what was going on in 'the state of workers and peasants'. Like other fourteen-year-olds at Eton, he had hardly noticed the Russian Revolution of 1917 – it 'made no impression, except on the few whose parents happened to have money invested in Russia'.[2] True, three years later, the situation had changed: answering a question on a school paper: '"Whom do you consider the ten greatest men now living?" Of sixteen boys in the class . . . fifteen included Lenin in their list. This was at a snobbish, expensive public school, and the date was 1920, when the horrors of the Russian revolution were still fresh in everyone's mind'.[3] Orwell explains the choice (and there is no reason to believe that his answer to the question was different from the others) by 'the queer revolutionary feeling of that time' – this was after the Great War – when 'it seemed natural . . . to be "agin the government"'.[4]

After Eton, the young man, who thought himself a socialist, went to serve in the Imperial Police in Burma and returned five years later passionately hating imperialism. Back at home, he took up tramping and writing – the first with a view to learn how 'the lowest of the low'[5] lived and to expiate

---

\*   The title of Part 1 is a quote from: Orwell to Gollancz, 25 March 1947, CW, XIX, 90.

[1]   Orwell's Notes to Randall Swingler's article, 'The Right to Free Expression' (*Polemic*, 5 September–October 1946), CW, XVIII, 443. I am grateful to Bill Hamilton of A.M. Heath and Sonia Brownell Orwell Estate for permission to reproduce Orwell's quotes as epigraphs.

[2]   Orwell, 'My Country Right or Left' (*Folios of New Writing*, No. 2, Autumn 1940), CW, XII, 270.

[3]   Orwell, *The Road to Wigan Pier* (London: Penguin Books, 2001), 130.

[4]   Ibid.

[5]   Ibid., 139.

the guilt he felt for being part of the tyranny; the second in the hope of becoming a professional author. It was mostly poetry and short stories that he wrote. Living in Paris was cheaper; the city had always been attractive for any young artist, and for Eric it had an additional appeal: his favourite Aunt Nellie (Elaine[6] Kate Limouzin), his mother's eccentric sister, had made the same move shortly before him. It was through her that he very soon got an opportunity to discover a world he knew nothing about.

Half-French, half-English, Nellie, like Eric's mother Ida and six other siblings, grew up in Moulmein in Burma in the prosperous family of a rich merchant. By 1904 most of the Limouzin children had left Burma for Britain, where the three sisters – Nora (born 1866), Nellie (1870) and Ida (1875) – plunged into the diverse and sometimes thrilling pastimes their mother's country could offer: they went to theatres and concerts, attended Suffragette meetings and moved in Fabian circles. Nellie was the most bohemian of them – she had a brief career on the music-hall stage and ran a literary salon at her flat in Ladbroke Grove – and also the most radical: a friend of Emmeline Pankhurst, she chained herself to railings in the struggle for women's rights. It was thanks to her that young Eric – to the utmost envy of his childhood friend Jacintha Buddicom[7] – met the author Enid Nesbit, who wrote not only *The Railway Children* but also *The Ballads and Lyrics of Socialism*. Later he got to know Conrad Noel, the 'Red Vicar' of Thaxted, famous for flying a red flag and the flag of Sinn Fein from his church tower. A prominent Christian socialist, Conrad Noel was at some point Aunt Nellie's local curate in Paddington and may have set an example for Eric's future pursuits by visiting the 'spikes' and lodging houses of London's down and outs.[8] In any case, there is no doubt that childless Aunt Nellie adored her precocious nephew and shared many of her interests and enthusiasms with him.

In her early fifties she discovered a new passion – the universal language, Esperanto – and joined a new organization of Esperantists, SAT – *Sennacieca Asocio Tutmonda* (Worldwide Non-National Association) as soon as it was formed in 1921. The aim of this organization, founded by Eugène Lanti, was 'to overturn the capitalist order'[9] with the help of Esperanto. This perfectly suited Aunt Nellie, for, as Lanti's biographer E. Borsboom writes, 'this feminist had become a convinced communist'.[10] Soon she started writing

---

[6]   Sometimes she is also referred to as Hélène or Ellen.
[7]   Jacintha Buddicom, *Eric & Us. A Remembrance of George Orwell, Including a Postscript of Dione Venables* (Chichester: Finlay Publisher, 2006), 15.
[8]   Bowker, 16.
[9]   E. Borsboom, *Vivo de Lanti (A Life of Lanti)* (Paris: SAT, 1976), 23. Here and elsewhere Esperanto is translated by Dina Newman, unless stated otherwise.
[10]  Ibid., 45.

articles for different SAT publications, signing them E.K.L. Her favourite paper was *Sennacieca Revuo* (Non-National Review), which reflected the personality of its editor, Lanti, 'committed to the class-struggle, honest and intelligent' and generally 'the right kind of activist'.[11] The first time she saw him in person was in 1923 at the SAT Congress in Kassel. Now, at the meetings of the communist section, which he had founded, she could enjoy his speeches, delivered slowly in a soft but convincing voice. He also noticed this distinguished-looking Englishwoman and admired her erudition and devotion to the cause. They did not become close immediately, but two years later, in 1925, Elaine Kate Limouzin wrote a letter to her hero suggesting that she move to Paris to live with him as a partner and help him with his SAT work. They discussed their future relationship, promising each other complete freedom – including the freedom to break up 'whenever it would seem convenient or their friendship expires'.[12] The small top floor flat they bought together at 14 Avenue Corbèra, in the12th Arrondissement was, according to their friends, 'in a poor building, in a middling district',[13] and they moved there on 17 February 1926. She was fifty-six; he was forty-seven.

Lanti's real name was Eugène Adam. A farmer's son, he was self-educated and worked first as a skilled furniture-maker and then as a teacher of technical drawing. Initially, under the influence of Pyotr Kropotkin, he was drawn to anarchism with its non-dogmatic nature and its opposition to nationalism. With the start of the First World War, however, Kropotkin disappointed him (and many other anarchists) by announcing that he was a Russian patriot. The war did exactly the opposite to Lanti – his rejection of nationalism only grew stronger, and as an ambulance driver in a combat zone he insisted on helping not only French but also German soldiers.[14] He started learning Esperanto in December 1914, and in October 1917, the Bolshevik revolution happened in Russia. By the time the war ended, tired and disillusioned France was favourably inclined towards Bolshevism – 'the ideology of the Russian revolution exploited simultaneously the urge to destruction, the desire for regeneration and the disgust with the old bourgeois society that was, in the eyes of many, responsible for the disaster of the War'.[15] Lanti certainly was fascinated by it.

---

[11]  Ibid.

[12]  Ibid., 71.

[13]  Crick, 190.

[14]  Esther Schor, *Bridge of Words: Esperanto and the Dream of a Universal Language* (New York: Metropolitan Books, 2016), 144.

[15]  Robert Wohl, *French Communism in the Making, 1914–1924* (Stanford, CA: Stanford University Press, 1966), 115.

In 1919 he attended a meeting of the Esperantist organization 'Liberiga Stelo' ('The Liberation Star') and met like-minded revolutionaries there. It was with their support that in a couple of years he founded SAT. This certainly was a major event in his life, and it was accompanied by a name change from Adam to Lanti – a formal procedure which, in the words of his biographer, was more like a dramatic 'metamorphosis'.[16] An announcement was published in *Sennacieca Revuo* to say that from now on the journal would be edited by Eugène Lanti, because his predecessor Eugène Adam had committed suicide. This was not totally untrue. According to Borsboom, at this point 'a new man was born who had little in common with Adam. . . .. He rejected the last remnants of his Catholicism, moved away from anarchism and set out on an untrodden path, trying to bring together the ideals of communism and Esperanto'.[17]

Besides, Lanti, of course, meant *l'anti* – 'the one who is against', the oppositionist, the contrarian. He started by attacking the 'neutralism' of the existing 'apolitical' Esperantist organization – the Universal Esperanto Association (UEA). Lanti passionately wanted 'to put Esperanto at the service of the class struggle', but – and here was another twist of his argument – this should be 'regardless of party-political preferences'.[18] Having joined the French Communist Party at its inception in 1920, Lanti aimed from the beginning 'to open his organization equally to socialists, communists and anarchists and not allow it to be swayed by the passions and tactical zigzags of the different workers' parties'.[19]

His idealism was even more obvious in the emphasis he put on the 'non-nationalism' of Esperanto, a concept that had acquired almost mystical qualities in his mind:

> By means of our language, a spiritual current must arise that overcomes all national boundaries. This constant intercourse will cultivate in our hearts a feeling that transcends nations. It will serve as a kind of antidote to the ugly nationalist education thrust on us by the state. . . . Using an artificial language as often as possible, we will incorporate in our beings characteristics appropriate for making us true citizens of the world.[20]

---

[16]   Borsboom, *Vivo de Lanti*, 25.
[17]   Ibid., 26.
[18]   Ulrich Lins, *Dangerous Language – Esperanto Under Hitler and Stalin*, trans. Humphrey Tonkin (London: Palgrave Macmillan, 2016), 170.
[19]   Ibid.
[20]   Ibid.

There was no doubt in Lanti's mind that to achieve this bright future, Esperanto should become not just an auxiliary language, as Zamenhof had envisaged, but the primary one, eventually replacing other languages.

'Was Lanti a romantic?' is the question posed by his biographer.[21] He certainly was, but a romantic who possessed enough pragmatism to start a new organization, inspired by his ideas. SAT was founded at the beginning of August 1921 at the 13th World Congress of Esperanto in Prague, where some eighty members of '*Liberiga Stelo*', present at the Congress, supported the idea. The founding resolution, which was approved unanimously, ended with the words: 'Down with neutralist hypocrisy, down with capitalism, long live SAT!'[22]

SAT has indeed lived long – it exists today, although lately its membership has been decreasing (it counted 525 members in 2015–16). But in the 1920s, when 'people of a leftist persuasion' preferred to join SAT rather than other, neutral, Esperanto associations,[23] it continually expanded: in 1922 it had 1,064 members; by 1926 the number had grown to 2,960. In 1927 it rose to 5,216 and in 1929 to 6,500.[24] So when Eric Blair came to visit his aunt and her partner in Paris for the first time in 1928, they ran the affairs of a fairly large international association and – true to Lanti's plan 'to cultivate in our hearts a feeling that transcends nations' – spoke Esperanto at home.[25]

The aversion that Eric Blair, with his outstanding flair for languages, felt for Esperanto is difficult to overstate – after all, he kept it throughout his life and borrowed some of its features for Newspeak in *Nineteen Eighty-Four*. For the young poet enchanted by the beauty of English, who at sixteen had 'discovered the joy of mere words, i.e. the sounds and associations of words' and confessed that 'the lines from *Paradise Lost* . . . sent shivers down [his] spine',[26] Esperanto seemed lifeless, mechanical, dry, arid. Orwell's attitude towards it never changed. In 1944 he wrote: 'If any language is ever adopted as a world-wide "second" language it is immensely unlikely that it will be a manufactured one, and of the existing natural ones English has much the best chance, though not necessarily in its basic form.'[27] The concept behind the 'manufactured' Esperanto was, at least initially, to make the language simple and thus to reduce the number of root words, modifying the meaning through the use of a variety of prefixes and suffixes. Thus, the opposite of

[21]  Borsboom, *Vivo de Lanti*, 26.
[22]  Lins, *Dangerous Language*, 171.
[23]  Ibid., 172.
[24]  Ibid.
[25]  Crick, 190.
[26]  Orwell, 'Why I Write', CW, XVIII, 317.
[27]  Orwell, 'As I Please', 9 (*Tribune*, 28 January 1944), CW, XVI, 82.

*bona* ('good' in Esperanto) is *malbona* ('ungood') and to intensify it one can say *malbonega* ('very ungood'), so Orwell obviously sneered at it by providing Newspeak with 'ungood', 'plusungood' and 'doubleplusungood'.

This, however, was not the only and, luckily, not the main influence of the French Esperantist on the future English author – it was Lanti who first sowed the seeds of doubt about the success of the Russian Revolution in the young man's mind. Thanks to his first-hand experience, Lanti was one of the very few people among the Western left who, in the late 1920s, was fully aware of its disastrous consequences.

\*   \*   \*

Initially, Lanti's ideas seemed to be in complete harmony with the dreams of Esperantists in post-revolutionary Russia, who burned with 'spontaneous desire to put Esperanto at the service of world revolution'.[28] Several attempts were made, both in Russia and in the Comintern, to establish an official body which would work to make these hopes a reality, but they inevitably failed because the Communist Party, even at this very early post-revolutionary stage, had a knee-jerk negative reaction to independent initiatives. Still, in June–July 1921, the Third Comintern Congress in Moscow did discuss the adoption of an auxiliary language and a commission was set up to examine the issue. Unfortunately, a year later, in June 1922, a rumour reached Paris that the idea of an international language for the Comintern had been rejected and the commission looking into it disbanded. On hearing this, Lanti rushed to Russia to see for himself what was happening. So great was his curiosity that he did not mind missing the Second Congress of his own organization, SAT.

He arrived in Petrograd on 9 August 1922, curious and excited by the prospect of visiting the Mecca of World Revolution and left Moscow on 1 September, a sadder and wiser man, largely disappointed by what he saw in Russia. He had proved a keen observer not only of the Esperanto movement in the country but also of the everyday life of its citizens and the policies of its leaders. His observations and reflections found their way into his vigorous essay, 'Three Weeks in Russia', published in instalments in *Sennacieca Revuo* between November 1922 and July 1923.

First of all, he was struck by the poverty, prostitution and bureaucracy that leapt to the eye when he set foot on Russian soil. He was puzzled by the country's adoption of the New Economic Policy (NEP), which allowed private individuals to own small businesses, with the state remaining in control of

[28]   Lins, *Dangerous Language*, 160.

the rest. He spoke frankly about his disappointments. In the introduction to 'Three Weeks in Russia' he insisted on the need to be as honest as possible:

> No political motive can force me to keep silent about the poor impressions I brought back from Russia. *Amicus Plato, ed magis amica veritas.* I love the Russian revolution and I am ready to defend it, and that is why I want to talk about it openly, not like political demagogues. Moreover, the Soviet republic is already powerful enough for the truth to be told about it without any reservations.[29]

Lanti visited the Ministry of Education and the headquarters of the Proletkult.[30] He compared the salaries of different categories of Soviet citizens and talked to a farmer, who told him that communists did not really work and looked 'like well-dressed gentlemen', as well as to an unnamed high-ranking communist, intelligent and multilingual Comrade X, who earnestly discussed the burning issues of the day with his French guest: the glaring difference between Marx's theory of a proletarian revolution and the Bolshevik practice; the failure of revolutions in Germany and Hungary which deferred the desired world revolution to a distant future; and the reasons for the NEP – all this presumably on condition of anonymity, which Lanti observed, unless of course 'Comrade X' was a composite character based on several Russian comrades.

As parts of 'Three Weeks in Russia' were being published in eight issues of Lanti's journal in 1922–3, he received readers' responses to them, and among numerous 'warm and supportive' letters there were some – 'only three', as he touchingly specified – which were 'highly critical' of his reports and stated that they looked as though they came 'from an enemy of communism'.[31] At the end of his essay, Lanti returned to his wish to present the true record of what he saw in Russia that he had promised in the introduction, but this time polemics made him more combative and revealed his true temperament and political stance:

> Should a communist close his eyes if he sees something bad or ugly? Is communism a new religion, full of dogmas which you couldn't possibly discuss without being labelled a heretic? My understanding of communism is different. Moreover, I think that communists who worship Marx's writings as others revere the Bible are not very wise. I have noticed that among us, we have ardent believers of this

[29] Eugéne Lanti, 'Tri Semajnojn en Rusio' (Three Weeks in Russia) (*Sennacieca Revuo*, No. 2 (32), November 1922), 3.
[30] Proletkult (the Russian abbreviation of 'Proletarian Culture') was an organization that aspired to create a new revolutionary working-class aesthetics.
[31] Lanti, 'Tri Semajnojn en Rusio' (*Sennacieca Revuo*, No. 10 (40), July 1923), 9.

type, who expect real life to match the theory. I, on the other hand, see Marxism as a method of analysis that allows one to understand complex and interrelated historical events. For me, a true communist is someone who practises the method rather than holding onto the theory like a religious belief. The doctrine may turn out to contain mistakes, in which case the method itself can be re-adjusted.[32]

He could not help sharing his views on NEP, again honestly looking for its background causes:

> For the first time in history, the proletariat of this vast part of the world fought for power and succeeded in holding on to it. It tried to develop a new type of society: experience, however, showed that a socialist economy was impossible in current conditions. Lenin realized that it was necessary to take a step backwards, and the NEP followed. As soon as they revived some elements of the capitalist system, one could see the resurrection of the whole economy. . . . If you are not a blind follower of theory, you have to admit, whether you like it or not, that applying socialist principles does not bring about the desired results.[33]

Lanti's impressions related to Esperanto were more mixed. He was distressed to find out that the auxiliary language commission had indeed been liquidated. This was confirmed to Lanti by Mátyás Rákosi, later a convinced Stalinist and at that point the secretary of the Comintern's Executive Committee. Rákosi added that the Comintern 'couldn't be bothered with Esperanto' (or any other auxiliary language) because it had 'other, more serious, more pressing tasks'.[34]

This disappointment, however, was offset by much more encouraging news about the position of Esperanto in Russia: since June 1921 Russian Esperantists had had their own official organization – SEU, the Soviet Esperantist Union, which centralized all Esperanto activity in the country. For the next sixteen years – from the Union's foundation to its end – its head was Ernest Drezen, a Latvian by birth, who at the time of Lanti's visit to Moscow held a very high post in the Kremlin: he was deputy to Mikhail Kalinin, head of the All-Russian Central Executive Committee,[35] the nominal head of the Soviet state.

[32] Ibid.

[33] Ibid., 10.

[34] E. Lanti, 'Three Weeks in Russia', trans Mitch Abidor. https://www.marxists.org/archive/lanti/1922/3-weeks.htm.

[35] In 1922, the Committee was renamed the Central Executive Committee of the USSR and in 1938, the Presidium of the Supreme Soviet. Kalinin remained its head until 1946.

Lanti, with his lively mind and eye for detail, described rather sarcastically the bureaucracy of getting into the Kremlin to see his *samideano*[36]: queuing for half an hour to get a pass and showing it three times to different groups of soldiers who were guarding doors in poorly lit corridors leading to the seat of the Soviet government. Drezen was friendly towards his visitor, invited him to dinner at his home and showed him his rich library. He impressed Lanti by his love of Esperanto and the way he spoke about 'our common cause'.[37] And yet the leaders of the two organizations (SEU and SAT), created within two months of each other with broadly similar aims, did not agree even on the day they met. Drezen was unhappy that SAT was not a purely communist organization – 'he did not want to work with anarchists and social democrats' – while Lanti was surprised that SEU had among its members 'not only anarchists but also bourgeoisie of a particular type'.[38]

Lanti felt much more at home at the editorial office of the magazine *La Nova Epoko* (The New Era), founded two months before his arrival, where he met Esperanto activists: Nekrasov, Demidyuk, Polyakov and Futerfas, none of whom was a communist. He felt that this was the real core of the Russian Esperantist movement – their revolutionary spirit was closer to him than Drezen's more cautious, more 'neutralist' approach. Nekrasov and Demidyuk, *La Nova Epoko* founders, soon became his personal friends and correspondents.

The following years were a time of lively cooperation between SEU and SAT, but also of increasingly bitter conflicts, which started playing out in 1928–9, when Eric Blair lived in Paris, and finally led to an irreparable rupture. This was inevitable, as SEU, with Drezen at its head, always toed the party line while the party line kept changing, eventually becoming hostile to any international contacts but passing through several stages on the way.

\* \* \*

Drezen, who in August 1922, according to Lanti, was decisively opposed to the anarchists and social democrats within SAT, had to re-think his position pretty quickly. In November of the same year, after the victory of the fascists in Italy, the Fourth Comintern Congress proclaimed the need to create 'a united front among the working classes' and cooperate 'if necessary, with social democratic organizations'.[39] It was at this point that Drezen replaced his rather sceptical attitude to SAT with a guarded acceptance of it.

[36] *Samideano* – a like-minded person – a usual way for an Esperanto speaker to describe other Esperantists.
[37] Lanti, 'Tri Semajnojn en Rusio' (*Sennacieca Revuo*, No. 3 (33), December 1922), 6.
[38] Ibid.
[39] Lins, *Dangerous Language*, 174.

In 1923, he and five other delegates from SEU attended the Third SAT Congress in Kassel, demonstrating their recognition of an organization that was above party politics. The tension, however, was still there because non-communist political movements within the Soviet Union, even those who considered themselves allies of the communists, could not expect anything but persecution. *La Nova Epoko* magazine, with its non-communist and anarchist contributors, was effectively shut down by Drezen in the second half of 1923, just over a year after its foundation. Its editors tried to insist on the 'pluralism' that reigned in Lanti's SAT in opposition to SEU's 'centralizing tendency'[40] instilled by Drezen, but if they had won, this would have meant that SEU would follow principles different from the rest of the Soviet Union. Drezen, who wanted to preserve his organization at all costs and always chose the safest way, could not allow this to happen.

But Lanti was not interested in conflict either: his slogan at this point was 'unity above all'. He persuaded his friends Nekrasov and Demidyuk to make peace with Drezen and continue their work in SEU. In return Drezen allowed SAT to recruit members in the Soviet Union and abandoned, at least for the time being, his original idea of bringing SAT under the auspices of the Comintern. It was Lanti's diplomacy that also saved *La Nova Epoko*, which in October 1923 became a supplement to *Sennacieca Revuo* – it was published in Leipzig, although its editors remained in Moscow.

Partially thanks to Lanti's readiness for compromise, between 1924 and 1927, SEU-SAT relations were probably at their best, and Esperanto was flourishing in the Soviet Union. Duly obeying the Comintern's 1924 call to increase the flow of information between Soviet workers and 'their comrades in western Europe, still suffering under the yoke of capitalism',[41] Drezen organized a regular exchange of letters in Esperanto. This exchange, he hoped, would convince his communist bosses of the usefulness of the international language – its aim was to increase the number of friends of the Soviet Union abroad and inform Soviet workers about life in capitalist countries. SAT and its periodicals, where letters were published, played an enormous role in this endeavour. The extraordinary success of this scheme is reflected in memoirs and books, including, as shown by Ulrich Lins, Andrey Platonov's unfinished novel *Happy Moscow*. Its central character, Viktor Bozhko, a Soviet worker and enthusiastic Esperantist, 'in whose room hung portraits of Lenin, Stalin and Zamenhof, received letters from different parts of the world almost every day'[42]:

40  Ibid., 176.
41  Ibid., 179.
42  Ibid., 187.

After studying his mail, Bozhko would answer each letter, feeling proud and privileged to be representing the USSR . . . he would sit down and write letters to India, Madagascar and Portugal, calling on people to participate in socialism and to show solidarity with the workers everywhere on this tormented earth, and his lamp would shine on his balding head that was filled with a dream and patience.[43]

Soviet Esperantists started receiving praise for their activities from official sources and achieved further recognition when two postage stamps with texts in Esperanto appeared in 1925. Some western Esperanto speakers visited the USSR and discovered that the international language did indeed help them to establish contacts there. And in August 1926, the Sixth Congress of SAT was held in the Tauride Palace in Leningrad. Out of 400 participants, 140 came from abroad, although the French authorities prevented Lanti himself from travelling to Russia. The honorary president of the Congress was People's Commissar for Education Anatoly Lunacharsky, who acknowledged that 'the Esperantists . . . feel a certain kinship with the great movement for communism'.[44] This was probably the high point of SAT's relations with the Soviet Union – after the Congress in Leningrad, SAT's membership in the USSR grew to almost 2,000, which meant that Soviet Esperantists soon constituted nearly a third of the entire organization.

\* \* \*

This idyll, however, did not last long. Several things happened at once. By 1928 the Soviet Union had ultimately embraced the idea of 'socialism in one country', which was first tentatively put forward by Lenin, and after his death – to Trotsky's indignation – actively promoted by Stalin and Bukharin. It obviously meant that the dream of world revolution, so dear to Lanti's heart, had to be forgotten or at least put on the back-burner. Looking back in 1934, Lanti wrote about his disappointment:

For about at least ten years I thought that the country that brought about the October Revolution was the first bulwark captured by the proletariat from the fortress of capitalism. My hopes turned to Moscow, and I believed that the Comintern would fight exploiters all over the world. . . . But in 1928, under the influence of Stalin, it was proclaimed

---

[43] Andrey Platonov, *Happy Moscow*, trans. Robert and Elizabeth Chandler, et al. (London: The Harvill Press, 2001), 10–11.

[44] Quoted in Lins, 183.

that it was possible to establish 'socialism in one country'. It was obvious to those who paid attention to what was going on that under the guise of revolutionary verbiage, the Comintern was increasingly becoming a tool in the service of Soviet diplomacy. . . . Moscow's main task was not to support the preparation of a world revolution but exclusively promote the national state interests of Stalin's dictatorship.[45]

This was not the only major change in Soviet policy. Stalin was on the rise. In December 1927 his 'left' opponents – Trotsky, Zinoviev and Kamenev – were expelled from the Communist Party, while the idea of the 'intensification of the class struggle' was gathering strength. Social democrats in capitalist countries once again became the communists' worst enemies. This could not have failed to affect Soviet Esperantists' attitudes to SAT and to Lanti, who still insisted that SAT was not 'a political organization' but rather an 'educational, cultural and international',[46] and therefore representative of the different parties under its auspices. The Soviet side could no longer tolerate this, and in August 1928 Drezen issued, for the first time, a threatening ultimatum to Lanti: 'I can say unequivocally: we in the Soviet Union have a dictatorship of the working class; as long as the SAT movement helps us further to educate our workers, we will participate in SAT. There may come a moment when we are compelled to leave SAT or when people of other political tendencies will leave SAT'.[47]

At that point, SEU and SAT managed to find a compromise, but conflict lay ahead. Besides, Lanti's attitude to the Soviet Union was changing. His own misgivings after his 1922 visit to the country were re-enforced in the following years by the letters he regularly received from his younger friend Robert Guiheneuf, who moved there in 1923. Guiheneuf, who had lost both of his parents by the age of twelve, found in Lanti a kind of guiding light. Following Lanti's passions, he learnt Esperanto, joined the Communist Party as soon as it was formed, did undercover work for the Comintern, started learning Russian in 1922 and, the following year, aged twenty-four, went to live in the USSR.

When he first arrived in Moscow, Guiheneuf, like Lanti before him, was shocked to see poverty in the centre of the city. Both noticed that in the early 1920s in the capital 'many walked barefoot, especially the young'.[48] This,

---

[45] *'Herezajo* (Heresy), 1934. Quoted in Borsboom, 135–6.
[46] Records of the SAT 7th Congress in Gothenburg (Sweden), August 1928, quoted in Lins, 206.
[47] Ibid.
[48] Robert Guiheneuf's unpublished memoir quoted in Hervé Guiheneuf, *10 Ans en URSS (1923–1933). L'Itinéraire d'Yvon* (Nantes: Quest Editions, 2001), 28. Translated from French by Samantha Kolupov.

obviously, wasn't the case in Paris. Also like Lanti, Robert immediately got to know the Soviet *nomenklatura*, but, on the whole, his experience was much broader and deeper than that of his teacher, as he stayed in the Soviet Union for ten years. He worked in Moscow and Siberia as both a labourer and a manager in the forestry and aviation industries and grew more and more unhappy with the communist rule. He would probably have returned to France earlier had he not married a Russian woman, and getting his wife and son out of the country proved extremely difficult: he succeeded only in 1933.

Guiheneuf's letters to Lanti, as well as his later memoirs, present a unique record of the transformation of the country under communists, given from the point of view of a Western supporter of the October Revolution. The main theme of his early letters is the disappointment that the *proletarian* revolution did not bring much benefit to Russian workers while their communist rulers seemed to have gained much more. Staying for some time in the spacious and well-furnished apartment of Stanislav Messing – chairman of the Cheka[49] in Moscow and then in Petrograd and a friend of its founder, Dzerzhinsky – Guiheneuf began to wonder whether he was present 'at the birth of a new bourgeoisie'.[50]

In 1924 he told Lanti about the first arrests in his circle; in 1925 he wrote already with some irritation: 'Although I have told you about it several times, it seems you still do not understand what regime we are living under here'.[51] And he went on to explain how scared ordinary Russian people were of the ruthless state that would not stop at ruining their lives and livelihoods:

> Do you know that it takes great courage for communist workers to say IN PRIVATE to their comrades that they are not happy? It is easier and less dangerous for an anarchist to produce propaganda in France than for an unorthodox COMMUNIST WORKER to do that here. Do you understand where we are? ... When we last talked, these comrades, who had taken part in the revolution, told me: 'I am not going to say anything because I have a family, and I'm sure I would find it hard to be sent to Siberia'.[52]

---

[49] *Cheka* was a predecessor of GPU-OGPU-NKVD-KGB-FSB (see p. XV). A kind of secret police, the organization kept changing its names throughout the Soviet and modern Russian history, while preserving its repressive function. The word *chekist(s)* is still used to denote those belonging to the organization.

[50] Robert Guiheneuf to Lanti, 26 September 1923, quoted in Hervé Guiheneuf, 28. This was not just Guiheneuf's view. 'The illegal "Workers' Truth" group started issuing, at the end of 1922, proclamations attacking "the new bourgeoisie", speaking of "the gulf between the party and the workers"' (Robert Conquest, *The Great Terror: A Reassessment* (Oxford: Oxford University Press, 1990), 6.

[51] Lanti quoted this passage from Guiheneuf's letter in his letter to Pierre Monatte; see Hervé Guiheneuf, 54.

[52] Ibid. The original capitalization is preserved.

**Figure 1** SAT Congress in Vienna, 1925. Eugène Lanti (with a parcel) is in the middle; Robert Guiheneuf is to his left; Orwell's 'Aunt Nellie' (Elaine Kate Limouzin) is on the far-right. Courtesy of Vinko Markov, SAT Archive.

There is no doubt that regular information like this influenced Lanti's views on the Soviet Union and communism. Lucien Laurat, a fellow Esperantist and mutual friend of Lanti and Guiheneuf, who returned to France in 1927 after four years' stay in Russia, also gave Lanti a full account of his impressions there that corroborated Guiheneuf's letters. By that time, Lanti had not paid his dues to the French Communist Party for a couple of years, and in 1928 he effectively broke with it. His disillusionment with the USSR made him more combative and more independent in his relations with SEU – he seems to have rejected all the diplomacy he had so successfully applied in the past. This made it easier for SEU to accuse him of an anti-Soviet stance. It must have been one of the most difficult periods in Lanti's life. He had not yet started criticizing the Soviet Union openly – he was, after all, the head of an international organization closely collaborating with it –

and yet the tension was growing. It was at this time that Eric Blair arrived in Paris.

* * *

Not much evidence exists about Blair and Lanti's relations. In fact, there is only one testimony by Lucien Bannier, Lanti's friend since 1919 and his close associate in SAT, who in summer 1983 gave an interview to a CBC (Canadian Broadcasting Corporation) programme: *George Orwell: A Radio Biography*. According to Stephen Wadhams, who made the programme, the interview was given not to him but to his producer, not face to face but over the phone and almost certainly in French.[53] Bannier was ninety at the time:

> Adam [Lanti] was, like me, involved in the October Revolution in Petrograd in 1917. We were both partisans in that revolution. And when I arrived at his aunt's house, Blair was arguing seriously and noisily with his uncle, monsieur Adam. Blair was praising the revolution, the communist system, while Adam had abandoned that idea at least four years before, perhaps even five or six years before. Adam, you see, had gone back to Russia, and there had learned that instead of it being socialism, it was a future prison. Prominent people in the Party in Moscow had not received Adam very well, and he had come back anti-communist. But Eric Blair didn't know of this change in his uncle. And he, Blair, continued to proclaim that the Soviet system was definitive socialism. So they were at each other's throats, despite the presence of the aunt.[54]

Stephen Wadhams admits that his French was not adequate 'for checking for errors or ambiguities in the translation',[55] which probably explains why the description published in English seems to give both the speaker (Bannier) and his friend Lanti a slightly more active role in the October Revolution of 1917 than really was the case. Bannier was obviously talking about their support for the revolution, rather than participation in it, while the sentence 'Adam had gone *back* [emphasis added] to Russia' seems to continue with the idea hinted at in the first sentence: that he had already been there in 1917 – which can't be true. Besides, in his old age, Bannier naturally misremembered

---

[53] Stephen Wadhams's e-mail to the author, 2 January 2020.

[54] *The Orwell Tapes*, conceived and compiled by Stephen Wadhams (Vancouver: Locarno Press, 2017), 65. Previously published as *Remembering Orwell* (Markham, ON: Penguin Books, 1984), 42. Lucien Bannier is mistakenly called Louis Bannier in both editions.

[55] Stephen Wadhams's e-mail to the author, 2 January 2020.

facts and misinterpreted some of his memories. Thus the sentence about 'prominent people in the Party in Moscow' looks like a free rendering of Lanti's meeting with Rákosi or his first meeting with Drezen.

Bannier surely is to be trusted about the central piece of his memoir – the heated argument between Lanti and Blair – after all he witnessed it and was profoundly shocked by it. Did he faithfully reflect Lanti's position? There is no doubt about that: Lanti must have poured out all the anger and frustration he felt not only because of the tense relations with SEU, but mainly because it was unbearably painful for him to lose faith in the revolution, and he could not yet express this pain publicly – this is confirmed by everything he wrote later. It is much more difficult to be sure about Eric Blair's views at the time. Was he really 'praising the revolution, the communist system'? Did he proclaim 'that the Soviet system was definitive socialism'? He may well have done and might have argued 'seriously and noisily', but were these his real convictions?[56] Or was he using the debate as a tool to clarify things for himself, as a way to understand things he wanted to sort out? After all, he was doing it throughout his life. Numerous contradictions, which sometimes seem puzzling in Orwell's journalism, are very often the consequence of his attempts to adopt and develop this or that point of view. It was noticeable already at Eton: one of his contemporaries recalled that when they were 'introduced to Plato and the method of Platonic dialogue, in which Socrates argues like anything with a lot of other people', he thought: 'This man's just like Eric Blair!'[57] A born polemicist, Eric could have been trying to challenge Lanti with endless objections and questions in order to tease out the older man's position and make up his own mind.

Of course, communism in France was in the air, and Eric Blair was intrigued by it. The reports from unnamed informers quoted in his MI5 files, declassified in 2007, show that he was offering his services as a Paris correspondent to *Workers' Life*, the forerunner of the *Daily Worker*.[58] But the intelligence officer, codenamed V.V.[59] did not seem to treat him as a serious suspect. In his letter of 8 February 1929 V. V. wrote: '[Blair] spends his time reading various newspapers, among which is "L'humanite", but he has not so

[56]　Ulrich Lins in his recent article believes they were, that is, that in 1928–9 Orwell shared communist views and supported the Soviet system. See Lins, '*Orwell's Tutor? Eugène Adam (Lanti) und die Ernüchterung der Linken*' (Orwell's Tutor? Eugène Adam (Lanti) and the Sobering of the Left) in: Cyril Robert Brosch; Sabine Fiedler. Jahrbuch der Gesellschaft für Interlinguistik, Leipziger Universitätsverlag, 103–124, 2020.

[57]　*The Orwell Tapes*, 39.

[58]　Orwell's file in the National Archives in Kew (KV2/2699).

[59]　V.V's identity is disclosed as Valentine Vivian (1886–1969) by Darcy Moore in 'Orwell in Paris: Under Surveillance'. https://www.darcymoore.net/2021/07/04/orwell-in-paris-under-surveillance/.

far been seen to mix with Communists in Paris'.[60] Orwell was aware of the
surveillance and mentioned it in *Down and Out in Paris and London*: 'The
Paris police are very hard on communists, especially if they are foreigners,
and I was already under suspicion. Some months before, a detective had seen
me come out of the office of a Communist weekly paper, and I had had a great
deal of trouble with the police.'[61] Whether the trouble with the police was real
or imaginary is not known, but the tone of youthful pride in being involved
in something risky is unmistakable. This fits with the indomitable spirit of
adventure that permeates the Paris part of Orwell's first book, and yet most
of the episodes to do with communists – and with Russians – are treated with
a great deal of humour, if not mockery.

Savouring every detail of the story, Orwell describes a regular in a café:

> The queer thing about Fureux was that, though he was a Communist
> when sober, he turned violently patriotic when drunk. He started the
> evening with good Communist principles, but after four or five litres he
> was a rampant Chauvinist, denouncing spies, challenging all foreigners
> to a fight, and, if he was not stopped, throwing bottles. . . . In the morning
> he reappeared, quiet and civil, and bought a copy of *L'Humanité*.[62]

Another communist, Jules, a waiter, 'had various strange theories (he could
prove to you by figures that it was wrong to work)'.[63] And the most hilarious
episode in the whole book is devoted to Russian communists, or people
pretending to be Russian communists, whom the narrator meets when
Boris, his Russian friend, as impecunious as he is, suggests a wonderful way
of earning some money. They go to a small 'office' of the Moscow paper,
which allegedly wants to recruit the narrator as a correspondent writing
about English politics. The conversation that takes place there reveals the
author's love for Russian literature and also some acquaintance with the style
of communist rhetoric – he hadn't read *L'Humanité* for nothing.

> It was queer, standing in the little secret room with its revolutionary
> posters, listening to a conversation of which I did not understand a word.
> The Russians talked quickly and eagerly, with smiles and shrugs of the
> shoulders. I wondered what it was all about. They would be calling each
> other 'little father', I thought, and 'little dove', and 'Ivan Alexandrovitch',
> like the characters in Russian novels. And the talk would be of revolutions.

[60] Quoted in ibid.
[61] Orwell, *Down and Out in Paris and London* (London: Penguin Books, 2001), 46–7.
[62] Ibid., 98, 100.
[63] Ibid., 107.

The unshaven man would be saying firmly, 'We never argue. Controversy is a bourgeois pastime. Deeds are our arguments.' Then I gathered that it was not this exactly.[64]

The people they deal with turn out to be swindlers, but the narrator does not feel resentful at all; rather, he is uplifted by their resourcefulness.

The fun, however, stops when it comes to Marxism, which suddenly appears in chapter 22 of *Down and Out*, as the narrator tries 'to consider the social significance of a *"plongeur's"* life'.[65] Having described the misery of this life, he deplores the fact that educated, intelligent, cultivated people 'imagine that any liberty conceded to the poor is a threat to their own liberty. Foreseeing some dismal Marxian Utopia as the alternative, the educated man prefers to keep things as they are'.[66] So 'Marxian Utopia' proves not only 'dismal' but also scares people away from necessary change. The author does not go deeper into these issues, but it is obvious that even if the idea of communism did seem thrilling to him, its followers inevitably proved funny and Marxism did not look particularly attractive. It would have been different had he at that time really believed that 'the Soviet system was a definitive socialism'.

Apart from arguments about the Russian Revolution, of which there definitely were more than one, Blair's feelings towards Lanti must have been mixed. On the one hand, he did not like Esperanto and, to quote Bannier, 'had no respect for the Esperantist movement. He didn't believe in the movement or the principles on which the movement was based – absolutely not. In fact, he criticized his Aunt Nellie on this, she who devoted all her life to the movement'.[67] Naturally, he must have blamed Lanti for filling his aunt's head with this nonsense. But there was the other side too: Aunt Nellie and Lanti were the people who helped Eric Blair to become a published author, and he could not help at least acknowledging this. Aunt Nellie found him his first literary agent, and Lanti recommended him to Henri Barbusse, literary editor of the communist *L'Humanité*, who in June 1928 became the founder and editor of the weekly communist journal *Monde*, where he published a couple of Eric's articles.

[64] Ibid., 48–9.
[65] Ibid., 123.
[66] Ibid., 127.
[67] *The Orwell Tapes*, 65.

\*   \*   \*

After Eric left Paris, Lanti's troubles began in earnest. In 1930 SEU dealt SAT a serious financial blow: Moscow stopped the transfer of membership and subscription fees from Russian SAT members, which put Lanti's Association on the brink of bankruptcy. Then the Soviet Esperantists boycotted SAT congresses in London (1930) and Amsterdam (1931) – by that time SAT's activity had been firmly labelled 'counterrevolutionary'.[68] In June 1931, a couple of months before the congress in Amsterdam, Lanti even wrote to Stalin: in his letter he complained that the journal *Sennaciulo*, published by SAT, was blocked by SEU from reaching its subscribers in the USSR and tried to prove that SAT was a truly revolutionary organization. He did not, of course, receive any reply.

Although the Russians had not come to the Amsterdam congress, Lanti had to endure numerous personal attacks from their European supporters, who interrupted his speech by shouting at him: '"charlatan", "fascist", "liar", "bourgeois", "Spinozist", "schismatic" and "cheater"'.[69] Meanwhile, on Comintern orders, SEU took all the correspondence between Soviet workers and workers from capitalist countries under its full control. It started with insisting that it should be moved 'to a higher level – that of collective correspondence',[70] and then went on to censor the letters people continued to write, which made Guiheneuf recommend Lanti 'to write in French so that your letters don't get into the hands of Esperanto censors'.[71]

Abandoned by the Soviet Esperantists and suffering an internal schism, SAT survived just as a small group of supporters of non-nationalism – in 1933 it numbered fewer than 2,000 members. And it was in 1933, at the Stockholm SAT Congress, that Lanti finally announced his resignation from the position of SAT president. This wasn't easy – his life's work and dream lay in ruins, but the decision allowed him to start speaking openly about the USSR. In June 1933, a couple of months before his resignation, he expressed his bitter disappointment in a letter to 'Comrade J.V.M', his correspondent in Amsterdam:

> Now I can write freely because I am sure that you are independent and honest enough not to take advantage of my openness. I have a confession to make. I no longer believe that the Soviet Union remains a revolutionary factor in the struggle of the proletariat for its liberation, nor that Moscow is 'the capital of world revolution'. Trust me, losing this belief was very painful. . . .

---

68   Schor, *Bridge of Words*, 150.
69   Borsboom, *Vivo de Lanti*, quoted in Schorr, 150.
70   Lins, *Dangerous Language*, 198.
71   Robert Guiheneuf to Lanti, 21 June 1932, quoted in Hervé Guiheneuf, 71.

There are no signs of socialism in the Soviet Union; this is state capitalism with a privileged bureaucracy which seizes surplus value even more greedily and shamelessly than private capitalism does. Workers and peasants do not control anything, and the only state apparatus that functions surprisingly well is the GPU[72], as it follows the traditions of the tsarist 'Okhranka'.[73] . . . There is a new official religion in the USSR called 'Marxism-Leninism' and its priests persecute, imprison and kill any heretics.[74]

In this letter, Lanti captures the essential features of the regime, some of which will become well known to the world just over a quarter of the century later in the book written by his partner's nephew: 'The first thing they teach children is to shout: "Long Live Stalin!" in exactly the same way as in Germany they shout, "Heil Hitler!". Stalin's portraits are everywhere. You can't turn your head without seeing a large or small portrait of the leader'.[75] And he comes to a disheartening conclusion: 'One can provide a thousand facts . . . to show that there is really no *essential* (please grasp the exact meaning of the italicized word) difference between the dictatorships of Stalin, Hitler and Mussolini'.[76]

Lanti repeated this conclusion in his pamphlet *Absolutismo*, which was published in 1934 and caused such a storm of protest that he had to explain his arguments once again in a new publication called *Heresy – Lanti's Letter to Dissatisfied Readers of 'Absolutism'*, and then yet again, in even more detail, in his joint work with Guiheneuf '*Is It Socialism that Is Being Built in the Soviet Union?*' Back in France, Guiheneuf used a pseudonym – M. Yvon, as he feared that criticizing the Soviet Union under his own name was too dangerous.

According to Borsboom,[77] Guiheneuf provided the content for the book and Lanti was responsible for its style and form. The book has the following chapters: 'What is socialism?', 'New classes: oligarchy, the patrician class', 'The living conditions of Soviet proletarians', 'How the workers are treated by the new oligarchs and patricians', 'Elections - a great hoax', 'Red militarism', 'New religion, new toxin' and 'So what is being built in the USSR?'. And the discussions its characters hold are summarized like this:

[72] GPU – State Political Directorate (1922–3), then OGPU (1923–34) – Joint State Political Directorate (see p. XV). Cf. 'Nothing is efficient in Oceania except the Thought Police'. Orwell, *Nineteen Eighty-Four*, 158.

[73] Okhranka – pre-revolutionary Russian secret police organization, active between 1881 and 1917.

[74] Letero 11, 30 June 1933 in *Leteroj de E. Lanti* (E. Lanti's Letters) (Paris: SAT, 1940), 65.

[75] Ibid., 66.

[76] Ibid., 66–7.

[77] Borsboom, *Vivo de Lanti*, 136–7.

Having established these undeniable facts, only those who stubbornly close their eyes will not see that the Soviet society being formed now is a completely new form of society which has nothing in common with socialism. The name of a system does not really prove anything, but if a name were required it would be easy to see that many features of Stalin's regime are similar – I am not saying they are the same – to those of the regimes of Hitler and Mussolini, and I come to my conclusion without any hesitation: what reigns in the USSR is RED FASCISM.[78]

Lanti's position was unequivocal, courageous and rare. It was 1935: Boris Souvarine's *Stalin* was published in the same year and André Gide's *Return from the USSR* appeared a couple of years later. After his book with Lanti, Guiheneuf-Yvon wrote two books in French: *What Has Become of the Russian Revolution* (1936)[79] and *The USSR as It Is* (1938),[80] published by Gallimard with a preface by André Gide. In the mid-thirties in France, unlike Britain, there was already a small group of left-wing critics of the Soviet state. Some of them, like Yvon, Souvarine, Laurat, Pascal and Serge, had lived in Russia for some time, others, like Gide and Istrati, just visited it, anarchist Pierre Monatte had never been there, but all of them were dismayed by the communists' failure to bring liberation to working people, despite the promises of the revolution. Lanti definitely belonged to the group and would have been much better known as a Russian regime critic, had he not limited his appeal by writing only in Esperanto. Having finished the joint book with Yvon, he started editing a journal which he titled *Herezulo* (*The Heretic*). It had the same aim as the book – to expose the sham socialism of the USSR. He was involved with this for over a year.

\*    \*    \*

Was Orwell aware of Lanti's split from SEU, his resignation from SAT, his publications and his views on the USSR? He probably was. As far as Lanti's views were concerned, they had been formed long before he started making them public and Eric heard them while still in Paris. And as for the changes in his life, Aunt Nellie must have kept him informed.

Her only surviving letter to him, from 3 June 1933, suggests that the correspondence between them was regular, as she was aware of minute

---

[78] Quoted in Borsboom, 137.
[79] It was translated into English by INTEGER and published in the United States (New York: International Review, 1937).
[80] Marie-Louise Berneri (1918–49), Orwell's anarchist friend, referred to this book in her *Workers in Stalin's Russia* (London: Freedom Press, 1944).

details of her nephew's everyday life. Aunt Nellie also shared her worries about politics: she wrote on the eve of the anti-fascist Congress due to open in Paris and predicted a coming split in the French Socialist Party.[81] In this context there is nothing fanciful about imagining her describing Lanti's troubles and his new pursuits. She obviously thought it absolutely natural to suggest that Eric should translate into English a French book that Lanti was already translating into Esperanto: Paul Gille's *Esquisse d'une Philosophie de la dignité humaine* (Outline of a Philosophy of Human Dignity), which Eric, in a letter to his literary agent Leonard Moore, described as 'a book with an anti-materialist, anti-Marxist slant'.[82] Nothing came of it, but it is clear that Aunt Nellie did not keep Lanti's undertaking secret from her nephew and tried to involve him as well. However tenuous, this is still a proof of family connections continuing after Blair and Lanti parted in 1929.

And one more piece of evidence confirms that Eric Blair probably knew what was going on in Lanti's life. He must have been supplied with regular information about it by Aunt Nellie's friend, Myfanwy Westrope, his employer and landlady, who shared Lanti's views on Russia. When in the late 1950s, Myfanwy gave Nellie's 1934 letter about Eric's planned move to London to a fellow bookseller for safekeeping, she thought it necessary to accompany it with the following note:

> George Orwell probably learned a good deal concerning Russia from E.L.'s husband who, as editor of the *Sennacieca Revuo*, was in close touch with Russian affairs. The latter became a stern opponent of the Stalinist regime, on discovering its true nature – which he designated 'Red Fascism' – and he afterwards edited *Herezulo*, described as 'an independent review for fighting against all dogmas'.[83]

*       *       *

In 1934 Lanti married Aunt Nellie. Unfortunately for her, it did not mean that he was going to live with her happily ever after, but rather that he was planning to abandon her and was trying to provide for her when he would no longer be with her. He was on the point of leaving France. By 1936 he must have been fed up with exposing the Soviet Union and felt that there was something else to life: if he had failed to help others to become citizens of the world, he would at least become one himself. Once he was offered

---

[81]  See Nellie Limouzin to Orwell, 3 June 1933, CW, X, 313–15.
[82]  Orwell to Leonard Moore, 27 January 1934, CW, X, 334.
[83]  Quoted in Editorial Note to 'Booklovers' Corner', CW, X, 355.

early retirement from his post as a technical drawing teacher and received assurances that he could access his pension abroad, he took his chance and set off on a trip around the world.

He left France on 11 June 1936 never to return, and if one feels an impulse to blame Aunt Nellie for her insensitivity when she came to stay in a tiny Wallington cottage with her nephew and his young wife during their honeymoon (they were married on 9 June), it has to be checked: she had nowhere else to go. She had rented this cottage back in early 1936, when she realized that she would have to return to England, and meanwhile leased it to Eric, who moved there in April after his trip to the North.

Lanti went through Spain and Portugal to Japan, from there to Australia and New Zealand, then to South America – Uruguay, Argentina, Brazil, Chile and finally to Mexico, where he settled in 1940. This was the year when his essay-like letters to friends about everything he was concerned about – Esperanto, non-nationalism, the Soviet Union, countries he visited – were published as *Letteroj de Lanti*. He continued to write, but an incurable skin disease had been making his life a misery since 1937, and in January 1947, exhausted by the excruciating pain, he hanged himself.

It is not clear whether he had ever learnt about the crushing of Esperanto and its followers in the Soviet Union. The international language was not denounced, and SEU was not officially suppressed – it simply stopped functioning when, in 1937–8, practically all the leading Soviet Esperantists were arrested and many of them were shot, while others were sent to labour camps. The same fate awaited many hundreds, if not thousands,[84] of ordinary people who had studied Esperanto or were interested in it. The Esperantists were usually accused of Trotskyism (the most common charge in the Soviet Union in those years) and espionage. The latter accusation was based on having 'contacts abroad', which by that time had become a major crime – stamp collectors who maintained correspondence with other countries fell victim to it too.

The thing that would have shocked Lanti, had he ever learnt about it, was that no matter how hard the leaders of SEU tried to display their loyalty to the Soviet regime by fighting against SAT and him personally (and their betrayals certainly hurt), they were still accused of collaborating with him as a Trotskyite, German spy and head of a fascist terrorist organization determined to assassinate Stalin. The time that passed between the dates of arrest and execution is generally indicative of the length of time the interrogators spent

---

[84]  The precise number of victims is not known. Different estimates put it at between several hundreds and five thousand – see Lins, *Dangerous Language – Esperanto and the Decline of Stalinism* (London: Palgrave Macmillan, 2017), 14.

torturing the prisoner to try to force him or her to confess, that is, sign the necessary document.

Drezen was arrested on 17 April and shot on 27 October 1937. His wife, also very active in SEU, was arrested a few weeks later (27 May 1937) and shot a week after him (3 November 1937). Nikolay Nekrasov, one of the founders of *La Nova Epoko*, and a poet, who translated Pushkin, Blok and Mayakovsky into Esperanto, was arrested on 11 February 1938 and shot on 4 October the same year.

Nekrasov's interrogation file contains the following 'confessions': 'as a Lanti supporter who shared his Trotskyist views and as a secret Trotskyist myself, I accepted counter-revolutionary espionage tasks from Lanti and carried them out'; 'we agreed with Lanti's instructions about the need for terror against the leaders of the party and government and a shift towards subversive activity'; 'we were told that Lanti demanded that we "remove" Stalin in the first place'. – 'Question: "What does it mean 'remove'"'? – 'Reply: "To commit a terrorist attack against Stalin"'.[85] József Batta, a Hungarian Esperantist and member of the Austrian Communist Party, was made to go even further and 'confess' that Lanti, who ran an espionage network, had placed SAT members as its agents 'at defence plants, railways, the frontier and postal and telegraph agencies'.[86]

The image of Lanti had obviously acquired enhanced significance in the minds of NKVD interrogators – that of a demon plotting behind the scenes, recruiting politically immature Soviet citizens and ordering them to commit crimes against their own people and leaders; someone similar to Trotsky, or Goldstein from *Nineteen Eighty-Four*, although even Orwell probably would never have thought that this was what fate had in store for the man he knew in his youth in Paris and who was the first to explain to him what was happening in Russia.

[85] Nikolay Nekrasov's interrogation file, 16 February 1938. http://www.e-novosti.info/forumo/nove/topic6633.html.
[86] József Batta's interrogation file, 8 February 1938. http://historio.ru/b2.php.

# 2

# 'We're all Socialists nowadays . . .' [1]

*As to politics, I was only intermittently interested in the subject until about 1935, though I think I can say I was always more or less 'left'. In Wigan Pier I first tried to thrash out my ideas. I felt, as I still do, that there are huge deficiencies in the whole conception of Socialism, and I was still wondering whether there was any other way out.* [2]

Orwell, August 1947

*All people who are morally sound have known since about 1931 that the Russian regime stinks.* [3]

Orwell, April 1940

Orwell's move to London from provincial Southwold in mid-October 1934 immediately brought him into everyday contact with people, who were seriously involved with politics and convinced that socialism was the only way forward. He seemed to find himself 'sandwiched' between two somewhat different groups of socialists: one, more interested in the theory of socialism, consisted of people connected to the magazines *Adelphi* and *The New English Weekly*, while the other was made up of ILP (Independent Labour Party) activists, who gathered around the Westropes, his employers and landlords, recommended by Aunt Nellie. There was, obviously, some overlapping.

As far as the magazines were concerned, 'neither was free of a certain crankiness in the principles and the politics it espoused,' [4] as Orwell's first unofficial biographers Peter Stansky and William Abrahams remark. Both journals passionately promoted not only socialism but also Christianity and the teachings of Lev Tolstoy, while the founder of *The New English Weekly*, A.R. Orage, was a follower of the mystic and philosopher Gurdjieff. *Adelphi* was the first magazine to publish Eric Blair – his reviews in 1930; his early

[1]  Orwell, 'Keep the Aspidistra Flying', in *The Penguin Complete Novels of George Orwell* (London: Penguin Books, 1983), 639.
[2]  Orwell to Richard Usborne, 26 August 1947, *A Life in Letters*, selected and annotated by Peter Davison (London: Penguin Books, 2011), xi.
[3]  Orwell to Humphrey House, 11 April 1940, CW, XII, 141.
[4]  Stansky and Abrahams, 128.

prose, 'The Spike' and 'A Hanging', in 1931; and his poetry up to 1936. He met its editors – John Middleton Murry, Max Plowman and Richard Rees – when he returned from Paris, and Rees, who had edited the magazine since 1930, soon became his closest friend.

Rees obviously didn't mind Eric's taste for satire and forgave him his mockery even when, in his new novel, *Keep the Aspidistra Flying, Adelphi* was called *Antichrist* and described as 'a middle-to high-brow monthly, Socialist in a vehement but ill-defined way'.[5] An Etonian like Eric, just three years older than him, rich, generous and earnest, Richard Rees inherited a baronetcy in 1922 and joined the Labour Party in 1924, honestly hoping to help to change society. Just a couple of headlines featured on one *Adelphi* cover of the May 1933 issue, where Eric Blair's poem 'Summer-like for an instant the autumn sun bursts out'[6] was published, reveal the political direction of the magazine: 'Notes on Democracy and Revolution (Engels, Luxemburg and Marx)'; 'Plain Words to the ILP'; 'If Socialism is to come'; 'May Day and the Derby Conference'; 'Trotsky's History' and so on.

Despite Richard Rees's best efforts to kindle Eric's interest in his creed – 'I spent more than three years trying to convert him to socialism', he admitted later – his friend 'remained unconvinced and not really interested'.[7] Still, they discussed the subject, and their conversations seem to have been faithfully, if derisively, reflected in the satirical mirror of *Keep the Aspidistra Flying*. There Ravelston, the editor of the *Antichrist*, based on Richard Rees, is arguing with Gordon Comstock, the loosely autobiographical protagonist of the novel, about socialism:

'But what's your objection to Socialism, anyway?'

'There's only one objection to Socialism, and that is that nobody wants it.'

'Oh, surely it's rather absurd to say that!'

'That's to say, nobody who could see what Socialism would really mean.'

'But what *would* Socialism mean, according to your idea of it?'

'Oh! Some kind of Aldous Huxley *Brave New World*: only not so amusing. Four hours a day in a model factory, tightening up bolt number 6003. Rations served out in grease-proof paper at the communal kitchen. Community-hikes from Marx Hostel to Lenin Hostel and back. Free

5   Orwell, 'Keep the Aspidistra Flying', 627.
6   Orwell, 'Summer-Like for an Instant . . .' (*The Adelphi*, May 1933), CW, X, 312.
7   Quoted in Stansky and Abrahams, 129.

abortion-clinics on all the corners. All very well in its way, of course. Only we don't want it.'

Ravelston sighed. Once a month, in *Antichrist*, he repudiated this version of Socialism. 'Well, what *do* we want, then?'

'God knows. All we know is what we don't want. That's what's wrong with us nowadays. We're stuck, like Buridan's donkey.'[8]

In his description of Comstock, Orwell certainly exaggerated his own naivety and stubbornness, but he, as much as his protagonist, resisted 'being converted' and generally tried to avoid talking about socialism or contemporary politics with anybody but Richard Rees, whose generosity, kindness and decency meant that he would not be ridiculed. With the ILP people, whom he daily met in the bookshop and the Westropes' sitting room, he would keep silent on these matters.[9]

Two years before he met the Westropes, the Independent Labour Party had taken probably the most decisive and, some thought, the most erroneous step in its entire history – it disaffiliated itself from the Labour Party. The decision was reached after numerous arguments and much soul-searching, as the ILP had been affiliated with the Labour Party since 1906, when the party was born, so to speak, within it and the ILP chairman, Keir Hardie, became the Labour Party's first parliamentary leader.

The ILP, however, had always found the Labour Party too timid and too reformist and was particularly dissatisfied with the political philosophy of gradualism promoted by the Fabian Society and embraced by the Party. In 1928, several ILP leaders developed a platform deliberately opposed to the idea that change should come gradually. It was called 'Socialism in Our Time'.

When the economic crisis broke out, the idea that capitalism was 'tottering and ready to fall'[10] and socialism, therefore, was imminent, gained immediate popularity. In the spring of 1932, Fenner Brockway, then the ILP chairman, in effect proclaimed at the party conference that the ILP should prepare for revolution, while James Maxton, another ILP leader and the author of Lenin's biography, invoked the example of Russia – 'proudly comparing the dispute between the ILP and the Labour Party to that between the Bolsheviks and Mensheviks'.[11]

[8]  Orwell, *Keep the Aspidistra Flying*, 631–2.
[9]  John Kimche, who also worked and lived at the Westropes, recalled: 'Curiously, we never discussed socialism, never discussed current politics', *The Orwell Tapes*, 80.
[10]  Quoted in Paul Corthorn, *In the Shadow of the Dictators: The British Left in the 1930s* (London: I.B. Tauris, 2006), 14.
[11]  Corthorn, *In the Shadow of the Dictators*, 18.

In July 1932, a special conference of the ILP voted to disaffiliate from Labour. The step proved disastrous almost immediately. First, in terms of numbers: in 1932, the ILP had 16,773 members, whereas in 1935, there were just 4,392 – in three years, it lost 75 per cent of its membership. But even more importantly, as part of the Labour Party, the ILP 'had succeeded in occupying the role of left-wing conscience, generating socialist ideas and radical solutions against an obdurate Labour Party leadership', while 'outside the Labour party . . . it rapidly became clear that a vague commitment to revolutionary Marxism and an unchanneled enthusiasm led nowhere'.[12] Aneurin Bevan famously quipped that the disaffiliation would leave the ILP 'pure but impotent' and predicted: 'You will not influence the course of British politics by as much as a hair's breadth.'[13]

Even if true on the whole, the diminished ILP would play its role in relations with other countries, most prominently Spain and also the Soviet Union. Those ILP members who decided to stay within the Labour Party soon joined the Socialist League, a left-wing group of intellectuals founded in October 1932, just a couple of months after the ILP disaffiliation.

In March 1933, with Hitler coming to power in Germany, the ILP formed a united front with the Communist Party of Great Britain (CPGB). This proved an uneasy alliance, and the issue soon became a source of division within the ILP. It also further distanced the ILP from the Labour Party, which would not cooperate with the communists. By 21 March, The National Joint Council, the body that coordinated the work of the Trade Union Congress and the Labour Party, even published a document titled *Democracy versus Dictatorship,* which condemned fascism and communism as similar dictatorships. The document was compiled under the guidance of Walter Citrine, the TUC general secretary and president of the International Federation of Trade Unions, who, after his visit to the USSR in 1925 and attempts to work with the Russian trade unions, had a thorough understanding of the Soviet system.

The Labour Party, on the whole, was convinced that the most robust response to Hitler would be to intensify the fight for socialism. Opinions differed as to how this should proceed. Two documents were produced at about the same time in 1934: *Forward to Socialism,* released in May by the Socialist League, chaired by Stafford Cripps, and *For Socialism and Peace,* published in July by the party's National Executive Committee, its governing body. These were rival programmes, and at the beginning of October 1934, at the Labour Party conference, the Socialist League programme was defeated.

[12]　Ben Pimlott, *Labour and the Left in the 1930s* (Cambridge: Cambridge University Press, 1977), 78.

[13]　Michael Foot, *Aneurin Bevan. A Biography. Volume 1 1897–1945* (London: Faber and Faber, 2008), 144.

When, a couple of weeks later, Eric Blair came to work for the Westropes as a part-time assistant in their Hampstead bookshop called 'Booklovers' Corner' and also became a lodger in their flat on the top floor of the same building, he found himself in a world where all these issues were heatedly discussed.

\* \* \*

Orwell seems to refer to Myfanwy Westrope only once in his writings, when he tells his friend Brenda Salkeld what an unusual landlady she is – 'the non-interfering sort, rare among London landladies',[14] and explains that she did not mind whether he had women in his room at night or not. However, her role in his life certainly was not confined to that.

Myfanwy joined the Independent Labour Party in 1905, when she was twenty, and remained an active member till the end of her days. In 1932 she and her husband moved from Wales to London and bought a bookshop and a flat in Hampstead, which soon became a centre of lively political debates. In her brief outline of Myfanwy's life, Miriam Wynne, the wife of Myfanwy's younger brother Alwyn Wynne, wrote: 'It was here that he [Eric Blair] met with revolutionary socialists as well as members of the ILP. Mrs Westrope herself was a most able exponent of her views, and there were long discussions with very differing factions within the wider socialist movement.'[15]

As a young woman, Myfanwy was involved in the Suffragette movement, but being a pacifist, she tried to avoid militant action. This brought her close to the suffragette and pacifist Sylvia Pankhurst, and during the Great War, Myfanwy contributed to the paper *Woman's Dreadnought* (after 1917 *Workers' Dreadnought*), edited by Sylvia. Myfanwy was so active in the anti-war movement, not least because Frank Westrope, whom she married in 1911, was a conscientious objector and as such was imprisoned between 1917 and 1919. It was in prison that Frank met another conscientious objector – Fenner Brockway, who had been arrested three times during the war for his anti-conscription activities. Brockway remained a friend of the family when he became the ILP secretary and then its chairman.

In May 1926, the Trade Union Congress called a General Strike against the worsening conditions of coal miners – it lasted nine days, and 1.7 million workers took part in it. Myfanwy delivered to the strikers a lecture on 'The Russian Revolution' – she was its enthusiastic supporter, at least partly

[14] Orwell to Brenda Salkeld, 16 February 1935, CW, X, 374.
[15] Miriam Wynne, 'Biographical Details of Mrs Mary Myfanwy Westrope (nee Wynne)'. Mary Myfanwy Westrope file. Hull University Archives (HUA), U DLB-11-124.

because of her friendship with Sylvia Pankhurst, who 'was a key figure in the British socialist response to the Russian revolution'.[16]

In her lecture, Myfanwy told her listeners clearly and intelligibly about the political forces involved in the revolution in Russia: the difference between the Bolsheviks, who wanted to take control of the country immediately; the Mensheviks, who thought that Russia should first have a bourgeois revolution; and the Socialist Revolutionaries who, having started as the Peasants' Party, eventually split between the left and the right, depending on their support for the Bolsheviks or Mensheviks.

A short, hand-written note dated 1972 is attached to Myfanwy's lecture on 'The Russian Revolution' held in the Hull University Archives. The handwriting is recognizably Myfanwy's:

> Nearly 50 years later I am of the opinion that it would have been far better if the Mensheviks had had their way. The Russian people, who are still suffering from shortages[17] after 55 years of so-called Communism and who are less free now than under Tsarism, would have profited by the fast development of industry under Western capitalism and the 2nd World War need not have taken place.[18]

Leaving aside the issue of the Second World War, it is fair to say that Mrs Westrope's understanding of the situation in Russia had definitely moved on since the days she gave her lecture. Naturally, the historical experience of forty years was on her side, but what had originally led her to change her views was something that happened to her personally many years before.

Like many others at the time, she felt a strong desire to visit the land of the revolution she knew so much about – and in 1931 that dream came true. Trips to the Soviet Union were common among the Western intelligentsia in the early 1930s, and the majority of visitors came back full of admiration for what they had seen. Myfanwy Westrope was one of the rare people who returned from the USSR profoundly disappointed. The advantage she had over many other travellers, which enabled her to see a bit more of the real life

---

[16] Ian Bullock, 'Sylvia Pankhurst and the Russian Revolution: The Making of a "Left-Wing" Communist', in *Sylvia Pankhurst. From Artist to Anti-Fascist*, ed. Ian Bullock and Richard Pankhurst (New York: St Martin's Press, 1992), 122. Lenin's work '"Left-Wing" Communism – an Infantile Disorder' (1920) includes a response to Sylvia Pankhurst's views.

[17] A 1972 footnote Myfanwy made to the word 'shortages': 'The former great grain-producing country of Russia has just concluded a deal with USA for the purchase of 1000 million tons of wheat!'

[18] A note attached to 'Lecture on "The Russian Revolution"' given to strikers by Myfanwy Westrope, in May 1926. HUA, U DX135/13.

of the country, was that, apart from official contacts, she got to know some ordinary people there. This became possible owing to a common language she had with them, and it was not Russian, but Esperanto.

Thanks to an Esperanto grammar that her husband had discovered in prison during the First World War, they both quickly became ardent Esperantists and, in 1928,[19] joined Lanti's SAT. As a friend and correspondent of Nellie Limouzin and subscriber to SAT's journal *Sennacieca Revuo*, Myfanwy would have obtained addresses for correspondence and arranged to meet up with the people she wrote to. This advantage, admittedly, also proved to be a cause for worry, as Myfanwy's sister-in-law, Miriam Wynne, hinted in her memoir:

> She corresponded with fellow esperantists all over the world. One such correspondent was Professor Englehart (a professor of English at Omsk University). In April 1931, she was invited to visit Professor Englehart, and she therefore embarked on a visit. She had idealistic ideas at this time of what she envisaged a socialist country should be. She came away sadly disillusioned, and her disquiet grew to a very profound dislike of the Soviet system and a hatred of the methods of the Communist Party. This had a very great influence on her political thinking and her antagonism to the official communist party line.[20]

It was after this disappointing trip, according to Mrs Wynne, that Myfanwy 'became very restless to return to London and become more involved with the political movement'.[21]

Miriam Wynne wrote her outline of Myfanwy's life in 1977 at the request of John Saville, a Marxist historian and co-editor of the *Dictionary of Labour Biography*, who knew Miriam as the wife of his late friend, Alwyn Wynne. Once Saville discovered that Mrs Westrope was Orwell's landlady, he passed on this information to Bernard Crick, who, as Saville knew, was gathering material for his Orwell biography. In his letter to Crick, Saville supplied an important detail, which Mrs Wynne had omitted in her memoir, but must have told him previously: 'She [Myfanwy Westrope] corresponded with a professor of English literature in Omsk – of all places – and in 1931 went to visit him. She came back disillusioned with Soviet Russia, in part the result

---

[19] I am grateful to the late Bill Chapman from the Esperanto Association of Britain (EAB) for supplying me with this information.

[20] Wynne, 'Biographical Details'.

[21] Ibid.

of the fact that the professor apparently disappeared at some point and was heard of no more.'[22]

Naturally enough, Myfanwy Westrope and, consequently, her sister-in-law and John Saville believed that Professor Englehart had been arrested and probably shot. However, as Russian sources[23] reveal, Esperantist Victor Nikolayevich Engelhardt,[24] Professor of English at Omsk Agricultural University, died only in 1957, aged fifty-two, after nearly twenty-five years as head of the University's Foreign Languages Department. It seems Engelhardt had not been arrested but had suddenly stopped his Esperanto activities. In 1929–30, he was very active and published three books on teaching Esperanto. In 1928 and 1929, when he lived in Smolensk and Orenburg, SAT publications printed notices advertising his wish to correspond with Esperantists in other countries, but this was no longer the case in 1930 when he moved to Omsk.

What prevented him from seeing Myfanwy in 1931 or at least carrying on their correspondence? This is not known: it could have been fear (many academics were arrested in Omsk at that time) or some 'advice' either from the OGPU or some Communist Party officials or people 'in the know' that it would not be in his best interests to go ahead with meeting an English social democrat (as Myfanwy would have been classified) at a time when they were labelled 'social-fascists'. He might then have decided not to continue with Esperanto, which almost certainly saved his life in 1937–8 when Esperantists were arrested and shot during the Great Terror.

There is just a tiny indication that Engelhardt had reasons to believe that 'they' (the OGPU-NKVD[25]) knew of his acquaintance with Myfanwy. In 1937 – six years after he failed to meet her and stopped their correspondence – he had to answer the following questions in an official questionnaire, which was due to go on his file in the university: 'Do you have family or friends abroad? Where do they live and what do they do? Why did they leave the USSR?' and although they had not been in touch for ages, he still thought it necessary to write: 'I know an English family of M. F. Westrope. 3 Warwick Mansions, Pond Str. London, NW3; a teacher; they have never lived in the USSR.' He felt he had to admit it because 'concealing' the incriminating information

---

[22] John Saville to Bernard Crick, 12 August 1977, HUA. U DLB-11-124.

[23] 'Sud'by, svyazannye s Omskim GAU' (Lives Affiliated with Omsk Agricultural University), 28 September 2018. https://www.omgau.ru/100let/novosti/sudby-svyazannye-s-omskim-gau-engelgardt-viktor-nikolaevich/.

[24] This is a traditional way of spelling the surname of a Russian aristocratic family of German extraction.

[25] NKVD – *Narodny Komissariat Vnutrennikh Del* (The People's Commissariat of Internal Affairs) replaced the OGPU in 1934. See p. XV.

of this kind, if it was already known to the authorities, would have seemed suspicious or even regarded as a crime.

In any case, although Myfanwy must have been wrong as to what had actually happened to her correspondent, there is no doubt that the Soviet state had in one way or another interfered with his life, that he felt a threat coming from it, and that Myfanwy's 'disquiet' and 'dislike of the Soviet system' caused by this incident were justified.

Having told Bernard Crick about Myfanwy's disappointment at not meeting Engelhardt, John Saville continued:

> Anyway, the point of the story is that by the time Orwell came to lodge with her, which must have been around 1934-35, she was a raving anti-Soviet character who was exceedingly articulate and forceful and according to my information Orwell could not have escaped listening to long diatribes against the Soviet Union from someone who was very political. Moreover, her younger brother was a member of the ILP and at some point – date indeterminate – introduced Orwell to Reg Groves and Hugo Dewar.[26] Groves as you know was one of the leading Trotskyites in the 1930s. However naïve Orwell was in politics, it does seem therefore that he became aware of the existence of the anti-Soviet trend and current perhaps earlier than has previously been accepted.[27]

Crick was extremely grateful, as this was new information for him and, as a biographer, he was particularly distressed that having received a letter from Mrs Westrope in 1973, he 'was slow in looking her up, and by the time [he] did, she was dead'.[28] He concluded that as he had earlier suspected: 'Orwell knew far more about the real Left before going to Wigan than he ever lets on.'[29] It seems, however, that it was not just 'the real Left that Orwell knew far more about . . . than he ever lets on'. He certainly knew a lot about Russia – Myfanwy and Reg Groves together must have supplemented the education he received from Lanti. But before going to Wigan, he was reluctant to share either his knowledge or his thoughts.

*   *   *

Looking back at his life and thinking about being a policeman in Burma and a tramp in England, Orwell concluded that 'these experiences were not

---

[26] Reginald Groves (1908–88) and Hugo Dewar (1908–80) were British Trotskyists.
[27] Saville to Crick, 12 August 1977, HUA. U DLB-11-124.
[28] Crick to Saville, 12 September 1977, HUA. U DLB-11-124.
[29] Ibid.

enough to give me an accurate political orientation. . . . By the end of 1935 I
had still failed to reach a firm decision.'[30] This cautious explanation does not
reveal a lot. However, it seems that being among politically engaged and well-
intentioned people, whose opinions and reasoning he eagerly absorbed, he
found it difficult to fully agree with them. He shared their attitude to the
acute problems of society but not to the solution they unanimously suggested
– he did not like socialism as it appeared in their conversations and 'was still
wondering whether there was any other way out'.[31] He knew that he was 'left',
yet of a different sort. Perhaps the best description of what being 'left' meant
for Orwell belonged to his friend Mabel Fierz, who said years later: 'He was
very much a man who was in sympathy with the downtrodden people in
this world. His socialism was quite individual, a sort of personal feeling of
injustice to the underdog. I think he always felt people should have a fair deal
in life'.[32]

In 1934–5 his internal disagreement with the socialists around him made
him withhold his views from the Westropes and their circle and resist Richard
Rees's intentions to 'convert' him. And yet some occasional glimpses of what
he thought about socialism and politics can be found in his letters to Brenda
Salkeld, with whom he often, almost unreservedly, shared both the details of
his everyday life and his literary and political impressions:

> That night I had been to see Rees . . . but he was at some sort of Socialist
> meeting and they asked me in and I spent three hours with seven or
> eight Socialists harrying me, including a South Wales miner who told
> me – quite good-naturedly, however – that if he were dictator he would
> have me shot immediately.[33]

Although Orwell's tone in this letter is also 'quite good-natured' it is obvious
how sarcastic he was about socialist 'dictators' using violence against
dissenters. This is an extract from a letter of 1935 when he was already
confident enough to enjoy the incident and hoped that Brenda would too.

In another, earlier letter to Brenda, he rants against a former hero of his
youth, George Bernard Shaw: 'Have you seen any more of your friends who
worship Bernard Shaw? Tell them that Shaw is Carlyle & water, . . . that he
has squandered what talents he may have had back in the '80's in inventing
metaphysical reasons for behaving like a scoundrel'.[34] The rant goes on and

[30]   Orwell, 'Why I Write', CW, XVIII, 319.
[31]   Orwell to Usborne, 26 August 1947, *A Life in Letters*, xi.
[32]   *The Orwell Tapes*, 70.
[33]   Orwell to Salkeld, 7 May 1935, CW, X, 386.
[34]   Orwell to Salkeld, 10? March 1933, CW, X, 307.

on; he is accusing Shaw of many – mostly literary – sins, but the comparison with Carlyle is not explained in this letter. Orwell mentions Carlyle many times in his essays, always talking of his power-worship, until in 1945, he simply calls Carlyle 'one of the intellectual fathers of Fascism'.[35] However, it is only in his essay 'Raffles and Miss Blandish' that the affinity between Shaw and Carlyle is actually explained. Having said that 'the interconnection between sadism, masochism, success-worship, power-worship, nationalism and totalitarianism is a huge subject, whose edges have been barely scratched', Orwell suggests that 'the sadistic and masochistic element in Bernard Shaw's work . . . probably has some connection with Shaw's admiration for dictators', and continues:

> The truth is, of course, that the countless English intellectuals who kiss the arse of Stalin are not different from the minority who give their allegiance to Hitler or Mussolini . . . nor from the older generation of intellectuals, Carlyle, Creasey[36] and the rest of them, who bowed down before German militarism. All of them are worshipping power and successful cruelty.[37]

Shaw gave his allegiance to dictators, fascinated by their capacity to 'get things done', that is, by their success. He wrote: 'Mussolini, Kemal, Pilsudski, Hitler and the rest can all depend on me to judge them by their ability to deliver the goods and not by Swinburne's comfortable Victorian notions of freedom. Stalin has delivered the goods to an extent that seemed impossible ten years ago; and I take off my hat to him accordingly.'[38] He wrote this in 1934, and Orwell angrily responded to it in *The Road to Wigan Pier*.

Did Orwell's 1933 charge of 'behaving like a scoundrel' refer, at least in part, to Bernard Shaw's admiration for Stalin and Soviet methods, which he had been publicly proclaiming[39] especially after his 1931 trip to the Soviet Union? It seems probable. There is even a chance that Orwell's anger against Shaw shared with Brenda on 10(?) March 1933 could have been provoked by a letter published by *The Manchester Guardian* on 2 March 1933 (about a week earlier), which was signed by G. B. Shaw and nineteen others who supported

---

[35] Orwell, 'Notes on Nationalism' (*Polemic*, No. 1, 1945), CW, XVII, 151.
[36] Orwell misspelled the name of Edward Creasy (1812-1878), an English historian. It has only one 'e'.
[37] Orwell, 'Raffles and Miss Blandish', 28 August 1944 (*Horizon*, October 1944; *Politics*, November 1944), CW, XVI, 354.
[38] *Stalin-Wells Talk. The Verbatim Record and a Discussion by G. Bernard Shaw, H.G. Wells, J.M. Keynes, Ernst Toller and Others* (London: New Statesman and Nation, 1934), 47.
[39] Shaw's prefaces to some of his later plays (*Too True to Be Good*, 1931; *On the Rocks*, 1933) are an example of that.

the Soviet Union and protested against 'the blind and reckless campaign to discredit it'. The signatories stressed that they wrote from experience and ended their letter with an appeal to 'all men and women of goodwill to take every opportunity of informing themselves of the real facts of the situation'.[40]

There is no knowing about Orwell, but Gareth Jones, a Welsh journalist who had spent March 1933 in the Soviet Union where he saw with his own eyes people dying from the starvation that the collectivization had caused,[41] was absolutely furious on reading this letter:

> I read a translation of it in the *Izvestia*[42] and it appeared farcical to me. Viewed from Moscow it was a mixture of hypocrisy, of gullibility and of such a crass ignorance of the situation that its signatories should be ashamed of venturing to express an opinion about something about which they know so little. I can add here that after Stalin Bernard Shaw is the most hated man in Russia among those who can read newspapers.[43]

That last sentence could seem an exaggeration, but it was not, as Eugene Lyons, an American correspondent in Moscow, confirmed a bit later: 'He [Shaw] judged food conditions by the Metropole[44] menu, collectivization by the model farm, the GPU by the model colony at Bolshevo, socialism by the twittering of attending sycophants. His performance was not amusing to the Russians, I happen to know.'[45] This was particularly obvious, according to Lyons, during Shaw's speech in the Pillar Hall of the House of the Unions[46] on 26 July 1931, the day of his seventy-fifth birthday, which he chose to celebrate in the USSR.

> It was at this gathering that Shaw achieved the apex of cynicism. In any other man it might have been ignorance or stupidity; in Shaw it

---

[40] Letters to the Editor, 'Social Conditions in Russia', 2 March 1933. *The Manchester Guardian*. https://www.garethjones.org/soviet_articles/bernard_shaw.htm.

[41] On Gareth Jones, see www.garethjones.org and Timothy Snyder, *Bloodlands: Europe Between Hitler and Stalin* (New York: Vintage Books, 2011), 21–3, 47, 56.

[42] *Izvestia* (News) was one of the two main official Soviet newspapers, the other being *Pravda* (The Truth).

[43] Gareth Jones, 'Talk "Soviet Russia in March 1933" Given in Chatham House on 30 March 1933', quoted in https://anglorussiannetwork.wordpress.com/topics/travel/gareth-jones-a-man-of-goodwill/.

[44] Metropole (Metropol) was a luxurious hotel in the centre of Moscow with a famous restaurant.

[45] Eugene Lyons, *Assignment in Utopia* (London: George G. Harrap and Co, 1938), 429.

[46] The Pillar Hall of the House of the Unions served as a place for important state events, like Communist Party congresses, state funerals, Moscow show trials, and also as a concert platform for major musical performances.

was cold and calculated taunting of the audience. Shaw could not have failed to know that Russia was suffering acute food shortage. Rations were growing shorter; some foodstuffs have disappeared altogether; scant quotas of milk and butter were reserved for children only and were available only at long intervals; food prices had just been doubled. . . . And in the face of all this, the rosy-cheeked self-satisfied foreigner stood on a platform and mocked the Soviet hardships.

'When my friends learned that I was going to Russia', he said, 'they loaded me with tinned food of all sorts. They thought Russia was starving. But I threw all their food out of the window in Poland before I reached the Soviet frontier'. He laughed like a mischievous schoolboy.

The vision of good English food thrown away in Poland was mockery of the underfed audience. Shaw's listeners gasped.[47]

Unfortunately, it wasn't just Shaw – the gulf between what was actually happening in the Soviet Union in the first half of the 1930s and what the Brits thought about it was enormous. The economic situation in the country was grim. After proclaiming 1929 the year of the 'Great Break', Stalin swiftly moved on to crack down on his remaining political opponents and introduce crash industrialization and collectivization. The latter went under the slogan of 'dekulakization' or 'dispossession of the kulaks',[48] which meant that those peasants who were slightly better off than the others (in fact, mainly the more hard-working ones) were branded 'kulaks', arrested, deprived of their property and either shot or deported to the Far North and Siberia, where they were made to work in labour camps or special settlements. Once the victory over the village was won, all the grain that the peasants produced was taken from them, which led to a terrible famine in Ukraine, the North Caucasus, the Lower Volga and Kazakhstan – at least eight million peasants died as a result in 1932–3.[49]

'Famine Rules Russia' was the headline of an article Gareth Jones published under his own name on 31 March 1933 in the *London Evening Standard,* with the subtitle 'The Five-Year Plan Has Killed the Bread Supply'. Jones spoke openly about the famine and most likely paid for it with his life two years later.[50] But just before his return to Britain, three articles about the famine had appeared in *The Manchester Guardian* on 25, 27 and 28 March

[47] Lyons, *Assignment in Utopia*, 429–30.
[48] Kulak – a derogatory name for a well-to-do peasant; in Russian it is the same word as 'a fist'.
[49] Robert Conquest, *The Harvest of Sorrow: Collectivisation and the Terror-Famine* (Oxford: Oxford University Press, 1986), 306.
[50] See Margaret Siriol Colley, *A Manchukuo Incident* (Newark, Notts: Nigel Linsan Colley, 1999). https://www.garethjones.org/soviet_articles/purpiss_nkvd.htm

1933. They were smuggled out of the Soviet Union in a diplomatic bag and signed 'our correspondent in Russia'. This correspondent was none other than Malcolm Muggeridge, who later (in 1945) became Orwell's friend.

A few times Orwell mentioned the Ukrainian famine in his writing all refer to Britain somehow missing this major event. In 1940 he stressed: 'The Russian revolution . . . all but vanishes from the English consciousness between the death of Lenin and the Ukrainian famine – about 10 years',[51] thus identifying it as a milestone, although not noticed at the time. Later he referred to the famine as something that 'simply passed over the average newspaper-reader's head'[52] and 'escaped the attention of the majority of English Russophiles'.[53]

If crash collectivization was achieved by 'crushing the peasantry',[54] crash industrialization required enslaving the working class: in October 1930, the free movement of labour was banned in the USSR – people could not leave their place of work without permission, and factories were not allowed to employ those who did. This development went unnoticed in Britain, as did the reintroduction of internal passports in December 1932, which imposed a further restriction on the freedom of movement.

This was not yet the 'Great Terror' – just the preparation for it, which included perfecting the techniques of show trials, where cases were founded on 'false confessions extracted by terror'.[55] The most common charge at these trials was that of sabotage or 'wrecking', as it was called, and their official aim was to increase 'vigilance' in society. They started in 1928 with the trial of fifty-five engineers and managers from the town of Shakhty in North Caucasus, which was followed, as Conquest explains, by 'three similar great set-pieces: the so-called Industrial Party of 1930, the Mensheviks in 1931 and the Metro-Vic engineers in 1933'.[56]

Obviously, the trial of six British engineers working in Moscow for the Metropolitan-Vickers company, who were charged with political and military sabotage, was covered in more detail in the UK, and although the government protested against the arrests and even placed a total embargo on trade with the USSR,[57] some British journalists were convinced of the defendants' guilt,

[51] Orwell, *Inside the Whale* (London: Victor Gollancz, 1940), CW, XII, 97.
[52] Orwell, London Letter, 17 August 1941 (*Partisan Review*, November–December 1941), CW, XII, 546.
[53] Orwell, 'Notes on Nationalism', CW, XVII, 147.
[54] Conquest, *The Great Terror: A Reassessment*, 20.
[55] Ibid., 35.
[56] Ibid.
[57] It was lifted when the two main participants of the case were released from prison two months after the trial. See Giles Udy, *Labour and the Gulag. Russia and the Seduction of the British Left* (London: Biteback Publishing, 2017), 453.

because they fully trusted their confessions. Arthur Cummings, the *News Chronicle* correspondent in Russia, who later wrote a book about the trial, even admired the GPU's skill in obtaining them:

> In the intelligent detailed exactitude with which most of the accused persons incriminate themselves and give away others, in the skill with which at just the right moment one prisoner is confronted with the testimony or person of another prisoner and so induced to confess and corroborate, it is something of a masterpiece . . . There is not a police organization in the world which would not regard the final result with admiring envy as an almost perfect artistic achievement or would not be glad to discover the secret of the GPU's technique and in practice imitate the method.[58]

Cummings, whom Orwell years later ironically called, 'the best of friends to the USSR in this country',[59] obviously, did not fully realize what 'the GPU's technique'[60] was.

But it was not just 'the best friends to the USSR' – the British left, on the whole, did not know enough about the extent of terror and hunger in the Soviet Union, and they did not want to know. As early as in 1924, Emma Goldman, a famous Russian-American anarchist, came to London to try to attract the attention of the Labour Party, which was then briefly in power, to the plight of political prisoners in Russia – many of her anarchist friends were imprisoned or exiled just for their views. She wanted, as she explained in her high-flown English, 'to arouse the sensibilities of the fair-minded Englishmen to the purgatory of Russia, to stir them to a concerted protest against the horrors parading as Socialism and Revolution'.[61]

She discussed the matter with Bertrand Russell, whom she had met in Moscow in 1920 and whose book, *The Practice and Theory of Bolshevism*, published in the same year, was the first powerful exposure of the Bolshevik regime. He said he would help her to publish a collection of letters from Russian prisoners (which he did[62]), but he was sure that 'the cruelties would be at least as great under any other party' and was not going to support what

---

[58]  A.J. Cummings, *The Moscow Trial* (London: Victor Gollancz, 1933), quoted in https://spartacus-educational.com/RUSmetro.htm.

[59]  Orwell to Dwight Macdonald, 7 February 1946, CW, XVIII, 93.

[60]  The British engineers were not tortured (if a seventeen-hours-long interrogation is not regarded as torture), but they had Russian acquaintances, who were treated as their hostages. See Udy, 435–53.

[61]  Emma Goldman, *Living My Life* (New York: Dover Publications, 1970), Vol. II, 968.

[62]  *Letters from Russian Prisons.* Published for the International Committee for Political Prisoners (New York: Albert & Charles Boni, 1925).

'might appear as political opposition to the present Soviet Government'.[63] Goldman received a very similar response from Harold Laski, a distinguished Labour intellectual, who wrote to her to say that he could not approve of her putting the atrocities in prisons down 'to the inherent nature of Bolshevism'.[64] Goldman knew that her mission in Britain had failed. It was obvious that the British left saw life through a different lens: for them, attacking Bolsheviks was the exclusive province of the Conservatives (who of course practised it to the full) and, although she was definitely not a Tory, they could not support her – it made things too complicated. She quoted 'a British socialist' as saying: 'It would spell political disaster to my party to declare to its constituents that the Bolsheviks had slain the Revolution'.[65] She also, however, mentioned another reason: 'It was their remoteness from the Russian reality, their lukewarmness to conditions they could not visualize and hence did not feel'.[66]

Sixteen years later Orwell would agree: 'Part of the trouble . . . is that the English intelligentsia have been so conditioned that they simply cannot imagine what a totalitarian government is like'.[67] He meant, in particular, their failure to grasp that 'there is something wrong with the present Russian regime' and referred to Dickens, who 'without the slightest understanding of Socialism etc., would have seen at a glance that there is something wrong with a regime that needs a pyramid of corpses every few years'.[68] He concluded by saying: 'All people who are morally sound have known since about 1931 that the Russian regime stinks'.[69] He must have named 1931 precisely because the collectivization and deportation of 'kulaks' was then at its height.

It was not completely unknown in Britain. In 1931, there was a huge row in the British Parliament over the import of Russian timber, which Conservatives were trying to get the Labour government to ban, because it was felled by the prisoners of forced labour camps – at that time mostly by the deported 'kulaks'.[70] The matter was in the public domain: information about the camps reached Britain as early as the summer of 1930; in January 1931, the controversy was covered in *The Times*; in early March *The Manchester Guardian* reported on the infamous Solovki camps, and the parliamentary debate took place on 25 March. The proposal for a timber embargo was rejected. In their speeches Labour MPs said that conditions in Russian

---

[63] Quoted in Alice Wexler, *Emma Goldman in Exile: From the Russian Revolution to the Spanish Civil War* (Boston: Beacon Press, 1989), 96–7.
[64] Quoted in ibid., 95.
[65] Goldman, *Living My Life*, Vol. II, 968.
[66] Ibid.
[67] Orwell to House, 11 April 1940, CW, XII, 141.
[68] Ibid.
[69] Ibid.
[70] The episode is told in detail in: Udy, *Labour and the Gulag*, 305–422.

prisons were better than in English ones, referred to slave labour practices within the British Empire and enthusiastically upheld the Soviet experiment. It is obvious that in their attitude to the Soviet Union, the British left, with very few exceptions, were guided by ideology and considerations of internal politics rather than 'the moral nose',[71] as Orwell put it. A couple of years later, in 1935, the testimony of a timber camp survivor, Finnish citizen George Kitchin, was published in Britain.[72] After four years of unbearable conditions (1928–32), Kitchin did not live to see his book printed, but he wanted the world to know of his plight, and he spent the last year of his life recording his experiences and making a list of penal camps he knew about with a map of their locations. Not much attention was paid to it.

The Labour Party (together with the left-wing Socialist League) and the Independent Labour Party (with its pro-communist Revolutionary Policy Committee) were full of admiration for the first socialist country and especially for its economic achievement. The Soviet five-year plan led the Labour Party after its electoral defeat in 1931 to commit itself to making 'the creation of a planned economy central to its political programme'.[73] The ILP supported it.

The phenomenon of 'the enchantment' with Russia and its growth has been explained by 'the coincidence of economic disaster in the West with an apparent economic miracle in the Soviet Union'.[74] The same coincidence also defined the impressions of numerous travellers to the Soviet Union – 'political pilgrims',[75] who at the time of the Great Depression, with its economic stagnation and mass unemployment, saw the USSR as a model country immune to capitalist crises and the threat of fascism. This perception was by no means universal – there were, of course, people capable of noticing what was really going on, but they were rare. As Paul Hollander puts it: 'for every André Gide there were ten G.B. Shaws, if not more'.[76]

Later, the blindness of the British left made Orwell furious. However, at the time, if not blind himself, he preferred to keep silent in public. In his letters to Brenda, however, he predicted 'the horrors that will be happening within ten

[71] Orwell to House, 11 April 1940, CW, XII, 141.
[72] George Kitchin, *Prisoner of the OGPU Soviet Prison Camps: Four Years in a Soviet Labour Camp* (London: Longmans, Green and Co., 1935).
[73] Corthorn, 'Labour, the Left, and the Stalinist Purges of the Late 1930s' (*The Historical Journal*, Vol. 48, No. 1, 2005), 182.
[74] Bill Jones, *The Russia Complex: The British Labour Party and the Soviet Union* (Manchester: Manchester University Press, 1977), 11.
[75] Paul Hollander, *Political Pilgrims. Travels of Western Intellectuals to the Soviet Union, China and Cuba 1928–1978* (New York: Harper Colophon Books, 1983).
[76] Ibid., x.

years', including 'some appalling calamity, with revolution and famine'[77] and confessed: 'This age makes me so sick that sometimes I am almost impelled to stop at a corner and start calling down curses from Heaven like Jeremiah or Ezra or somebody'.[78] His outcry: 'I was not born for an age like this'[79] meant that still hoping to be a writer he resented the thought of his personal, artistic, lyrical side being destroyed by the need to fight political evil, which, he must have already guessed, was inevitable and urgent.

He felt acutely the pressure of 'the age', with 'the commissar', 'radio' and 'Austin Seven' – all named in his poem.[80] The aspect that eluded him, which, he knew, was necessary for getting a fuller picture of the situation in Britain, was the life of the working class. So when in 1936 he was offered a chance to explore the dire conditions of miners in the North of England and see with his own eyes how they lived, he grabbed it immediately. When he returned, he felt confident enough to discuss what he thought.

*   *   *

For Richard Rees, who had been trying 'to convert [Orwell] to socialism', this trip seemed to be the turning point: 'He went North. When he came back in the spring of 1936, the conversion had already taken place.'[81] The oversimplification here is obvious and confirmed not just by Orwell's own words written in Spain in June 1937 – 'I have seen wonderful things and at last really believe in Socialism, which I never did before'[82] – but even more profoundly in the book he wrote on coming back – *The Road to Wigan Pier*, full of doubts and anxieties about socialism. No matter how hard he might have tried in the second half of the book to assure his readers that he was playing the devil's advocate, attempting to get 'inside the mind of the ordinary objector to Socialism',[83] there is no doubt that 'the spiritual recoil from Socialism'[84] was his own. Years later, Orwell seemed to admit that the trip to the North was important for him but stressed that it was on the rational level only: 'After having a fairly good look at British industrialism at its worst, i.e. in the mining areas, I came to the conclusion that it is a duty to work for Socialism even if one is not emotionally drawn to it, because the

---

[77]   Orwell to Salkeld, June (?) 1933, CW, X, 317.
[78]   Orwell to Salkeld, Early September? 1934, CW, X, 349.
[79]   Orwell, 'A Happy Vicar I Might Have Been' (*The Adelphi*, December 1936), CW, X, 524–5.
[80]   Ibid.
[81]   Quoted in Stansky and Abrahams, 129.
[82]   Orwell to Cyril Connolly, 8 June 1937, CW. XI, 28.
[83]   Orwell, *The Road to Wigan Pier*, 160.
[84]   Ibid., 174.

continuance of present conditions is simply not tolerable.'[85] Could one call it 'a conversion'?

Rees was closer to the truth when he said:

> There was the extraordinary change in his writing and, in a way, also in his attitude after he'd been to the North and written that book. It was almost as if there had been a fire smouldering in him all his life which suddenly broke into flame at that time. But I can't understand it or explain exactly what happened. I just don't know.[86]

It seems that all the suppressed interest in politics and sociology that had been 'smouldering' in him, did indeed burst into a blaze. This was his first 'sociological' book and, unlike *Down and Out*, where his views about society are expressed sparingly and self-consciously, *The Road to Wigan Pier* is written with the freedom and abandon of someone who now feels entitled to speak openly, because he ardently believes in the need to improve the current conditions of the working class.

Since the publication of *The Road to Wigan Pier*, it has been customary to juxtapose its first and second parts. In the first, Orwell brilliantly fulfilled the task his publisher Victor Gollancz had given to him: his indignation, disgust, anger about the position of miners are palpable on every page, while the second part – which Gollancz had not asked him to write and probably would not have published had he not been bound by a contract – is polemical about almost everything that was taken for granted by socialists at that time. However, the controversies that abound in the second part start much earlier, because the author feels 'torn both ways',[87] as he admits at least twice, when he considers the pros and cons of attempts to help the unemployed or talks about slum clearance and resettling people into Corporation houses – the equivalent of today's social housing.

After every sentence stating some advantage of Corporation housing – 'a bathroom and a bit of garden';[88] 'children start life with better chances'[89] – there is another one beginning with a 'but': 'expensive', 'bleak in winter', 'on the edge of the town'.[90] There are, moreover, additional drawbacks: 'an uncomfortable, almost prison-like atmosphere'; 're-housing ... is being done –

---

85  Orwell to Usborne, *A Life in Letters*, xi.
86  Quoted in Crick, 278.
87  Orwell, *The Road to Wigan Pier*, 77 and 92.
88  Ibid., 63.
89  Ibid., 66.
90  Ibid., 63–5.

perhaps it is unavoidable – in a monstrously inhuman manner':[91] 'You are
not allowed to keep your house and garden as you want them. . . . You are not
allowed to keep poultry or pigeons'.[92] All the benefits handed down to a man
rather than earned by him seem to involve limitations on his freedom, and
Orwell comes to a logical conclusion: 'It is a great achievement to get slum-
dwellers into decent houses, but it is unfortunate that, owing to the peculiar
temper of our time, it is also considered necessary to rob them of the last
vestiges of their liberty.'[93]

Having said all that, he immediately rushes to support the other side of
the argument, as if trying to convince himself and his readers of the opposite:

> Perhaps, however, when it is a case of slum clearance, one must take for
> granted a certain amount of restrictions and inhumanity. . . . A place where
> the children can breathe clean air, and women have a few conveniences
> to save them from drudgery, and the man has a bit of garden to dig in,
> *must* be better than the stinking back-streets of Leeds and Sheffield.

And yet the final verdict is: 'On balance, the Corporation estates are better
than the slums; but only by a small margin'.[94]

This is a perfect example of the workings of Orwell's polemical mind, and
it is clear how difficult it was for him to accept even the most progressive and
reasonable initiative if he felt it to be inhuman or a restriction on personal
liberty. In an autobiographical chapter in Part Two, he says: 'unfortunately I
had not trained myself to be indifferent to the expression of the human face'.[95]
Socialism as a grand system of reorganizing and improving life scared him
precisely by its lack of humanity and individual choice.

*   *   *

In the first part of *The Road to Wigan Pier* Orwell, naturally, does not
mention Russia, but he hardly mentions it in the second part either. There is
not a single positive reference to the country in the book. Russia appears only
when Orwell, trying to define what kind of socialism he would welcome in
Britain, vigorously dismisses the one he dislikes:

---

[91]   Ibid., 65.
[92]   Ibid., 66.
[93]   Ibid., 67.
[94]   Ibid.
[95]   Ibid., 137.

We have reached a stage when the very word 'Socialism' calls up, on the one hand, a picture of aeroplanes, tractors, and huge glittering factories of glass and concrete; on the other, a picture of vegetarians with wilting beards, of Bolshevik commissars (half gangster, half gramophone), of earnest ladies in sandals, shock-headed Marxists chewing polysyllables, escaped Quakers, birth-control fanatics, and Labour Party backstairs crawlers. Socialism, at least in this island, does not smell any longer of revolution and the overthrow of tyrants; it smells of crankishness, machine-worship, and the stupid cult of Russia.[96]

'The stupid cult of Russia' and 'Bolshevik commissars' are rejected straightaway. Soviet socialism is not even considered as a possibility. Orwell's 'Bolshevik commissars' are 'half gangster, half gramophone' – by the 'gangster' half he, no doubt, meant all the horrors Bolsheviks perpetrated during and after the revolution, while the 'gramophone' half was very likely prompted by J. M. Keynes, who said that his picture of H. G. Wells's interview with Stalin was that of 'a man struggling with a gramophone'.[97] This image of the dogmatic, inflexible, repetitious nature of the Soviet, or indeed any, rigid ideology became a favourite with Orwell.

And yet, having discarded 'the stupid cult of Russia' and concentrating only on those aspects which, in his view, made socialism unattractive in Britain: eccentric socialists, machine-worship and the brushing aside of the impoverished middle-class, Orwell, with his incredible insight and, of course, a considerable knowledge of the USSR gained from Lanti, Myfanwy Westrope, Reg Groves and others, spotted in some of the aspirations and habits of British socialists the early signs of the dangers inherent in the Soviet system.

What is mainly remembered about Orwell's attitude to British socialists is his 'semi-frivolous' attack on cranks: 'there is the horrible – the really disquieting – prevalence of cranks wherever Socialists are gathered together'.[98] But behind ridiculing 'crankiness', which Orwell mostly read as 'hopes of adding five years onto the lives of [their] carcase',[99] there was his genuine anxiety that there might be a gaping chasm between these middle-class socialists and working men and women.

'The underlying motive of many Socialists, I believe, is simply a hypertrophied sense of order. . . . The present state of affairs offends them . . . because it is untidy; what they desire, basically, is to reduce the world to

[96]  Ibid., 201.
[97]  *Stalin-Wells Talk*, 30.
[98]  Orwell, *The Road to Wigan Pier*, 161.
[99]  Ibid., 162.

something resembling a chess-board',[100] Orwell starts tentatively, as if he does not yet know that beneath this desire lies a desire for power, a desire to make people obey and thus bring order into their lives. He then mentions 'a lifelong Socialist Bernard Shaw', stressing that for him and others like him, 'poverty and, what's more, the habits of mind created by poverty, are something to be abolished *from above*, by violence if necessary; perhaps even preferably by violence. Hence his worship of "great men" and appetite for dictatorships, Fascist or Communist'.[101]

He sees 'the same' – that is, the same concept 'from above' – 'in a more mealy-mouthed form in Mrs Sidney Webb's autobiography'[102] and concludes: 'The truth is that, to many people calling themselves Socialists, revolution does not mean a movement of the masses with which they hope to associate themselves; it means a set of reforms which "we", the clever ones, are going to impose upon "them", the Lower Orders.'[103]

Beatrice and Sydney Webb, Shaw's fellow Fabians and great admirers of the Soviet Union were 'the sort of socialists who were keener on planning for people than upon people themselves'.[104] No wonder they were very enthusiastic about the role the Communist Party played in the Soviet Union. In the chapter of their book *Soviet Communism: A New Civilisation* titled 'The Vocation of Leadership', they talk enthusiastically of Lenin's need for 'a completely united, highly disciplined and relatively small body of "professional revolutionists"[105] and call its members "super-citizens"'.[106] They did not seem to mind that this idea of 'a party of a new type', as Lenin called it, traced its origin not to Marx and Engels, but to the people of whom Marx and Engels disapproved – radical Russian revolutionaries Pyotr Tkachev and Sergey Nechaev,[107] who passionately supported the idea of a revolutionary vanguard, implying that professional revolutionaries should prepare ordinary people for the revolution and guide them through it.

*The Road to Wigan Pier* is not usually seen by Orwell scholars as a criticism of Soviet socialism. John Newsinger, for example, believes that Orwell 'had

---

[100] Ibid., 166.
[101] Ibid., 166–7.
[102] Ibid., 167.
[103] Ibid.
[104] Jones, *The Russia Complex*, 21.
[105] Sidney and Beatrice Webb, *Soviet Communism: A New Civilisation* (London: Victor Gollancz Ltd, 1937), 342. In the first edition, published by Workers' Educational Association in1935, the title of the book ended with a question mark. In 1937 it was deleted.
[106] Ibid., 339.
[107] Tkachev (1844–86) and Nechaev (1847–82) are often seen as precursors of Bolshevism. Nechaev, who wrote 'The Catechism of a Revolutionary' (1869) was a model for Dostoevsky's Pyotr Verkhovensky in *The Possessed*.

at this time no idea of the enormity of the crimes committed in the name of socialism in the Soviet Union' and argues: 'Looking at *The Road to Wigan Pier*, middle-class, fruit-juice-drinking, nudist vegetarians were, at this time, much more of a problem as far as he was concerned'.[108] Stephen Ingle's view is only slightly different: 'he had in mind not so much Soviet apparatchiks as home-grown socialists such as Bernard Shaw and the Fabians'.[109] This does not seem to be quite the case. It is true, of course, that in 1936 Orwell wrote nothing specifically about 'Stalinism', that is, about this particular stage of the Communist regime in Russia, or about 'Soviet apparatchiks', but it was his knowledge of Russia, combined with his remarkable intuition, that enabled him to recognize in 'home-grown socialists' the wish to reserve a leading position for themselves – so similar to the Bolsheviks' conception of a vanguard party.

From this conception, which lay at the heart of Bolshevism, it logically followed that no discussion of and no alternatives to the decisions already taken by the vanguard could be allowed. 'The Marxist doctrine is omnipotent because it is true',[110] Lenin wrote unflinchingly. This dogmatic approach made his party very much like a church (a Roman Catholic Church, as Orwell would have specified, but indeed almost any church) that seeks to impose its vision on its flock and fights heretics. Orwell felt that this was firmly instilled in the minds of many socialists:

> Sometimes, when I listen to these people talking, and still more when I read their books, I get the impression that, to them, the whole Socialist movement is no more than a kind of exciting heresy-hunt – a leaping to and fro of frenzied witch-doctors to the beat of tom-toms and the tune of 'Fee fi, fo, fum, I smell the blood of a right-wing deviationist![111]

The source of this heresy-hunt culture persecuting 'right-wing deviationists' was obvious. The term was, for example, applied to those who, like Nikolay Bukharin, opposed the drastic methods of Stalin's collectivization.

Another alienating feature Orwell saw in British socialism was the specific, quasi-Marxist language borrowed from Soviet communists and used, often consciously, for constructing an insurmountable barrier between

---

[108] John Newsinger, *Hope Lies in the Proles: George Orwell and the Left* (London: Pluto Press, 2018), 36.

[109] Stephen Ingle, *The Social and Political Thought of George Orwell: A Reassessment* (Abingdon, Oxfordshire: Routledge, 2006), 61.

[110] V.I. Lenin, 'The Three Sources and Three Component Parts of Marxism', trans. George Hanna. https://www.marxists.org/archive/lenin/works/1913/mar/x01.htm.

[111] Orwell, *The Road to Wigan Pier*, 206.

'the vanguard of the working class' – that is, those in a position of power – and everybody else.

> As for the technical jargon of the Communists, it is as far removed from the common speech as the language of a mathematical textbook. I remember hearing a professional Communist speaker address a working-class audience. His speech was the usual bookish stuff, full of long sentences and parentheses and 'Notwithstanding' and 'Be that as it may', besides the usual jargon of 'ideology' and 'class-consciousness' and 'proletarian solidarity' and all the rest of it.[112]

However, the disgust that Orwell must have felt about the language of socialism or the behaviour of socialists seemed to have lost their relevance when the political situation changed. Since 19 July 1936, when a rebellion of fascist generals against the Republican government started the Civil War in Spain, Orwell had been treating the war as a struggle between fascism and socialism. In the light of this, all his objections to socialism, at least for the time being, receded into background: 'To oppose Socialism *now*, when twenty million Englishmen are underfed and Fascism has conquered half Europe, is suicidal.'[113] The task for an individual (presumably, for an individual who, like Orwell, hadn't previously been able to make himself fully support the cause) was clear: 'For the moment, the only possible course for any decent person, however much of a Tory or an anarchist by temperament, is to work for the establishment of Socialism. Nothing else can save us from the misery of the present or the nightmare of the future.'[114]

In the economic sphere, he was convinced, 'no solution except some kind of collectivism is viable'.[115] In Orwell's mind, collectivism was the inevitable consequence of industrialism, but from the very start he saw the dangers it implied:

> The advance of machine technique must lead ultimately to some form of collectivism, but that form need not necessarily be equalitarian; that is, it need not be Socialism. *Pace* the economists, it is quite easy to imagine a world-society, economically collectivist – that is, with the profit principle eliminated – but with all political, military, and educational

[112] Ibid., 163.
[113] Ibid., 204.
[114] Ibid.
[115] Orwell to Usborne, *A Life in Letters*, xi.

power in the hands of a small caste of rulers and their bravos. That or something like it is the objective of Fascism.[116]

Fascism was trying to become 'a world-system' and there was nothing, apart from socialism, he was now sure, that could stop fascism from spreading. That is why he was so shocked by the very idea of likening the two and furious with 'the type of humbug who passes resolutions "against Fascism and Communism", i.e. against rats and rat-poison'.[117] In a review written at about the same time as the ending of *Wigan Pier*, Orwell called the statement 'Communism and Fascism are the same thing' a 'vulgar lie, now so popular'.[118] Little did he know that in less than a year he would discover more similarities between fascism and communism than he would wish for.

And even in August 1936, when he was hastily finishing his book before going to Spain, the Soviet regime made another step towards resembling fascism even more.

\* \* \*

The first show trial of the Great Terror was held between 19 and 24 August. Sixteen prominent political leaders, including Lenin's close associates Zinoviev and Kamenev, were now charged with being accomplices of the Gestapo, conspiring to assassinate Stalin. Trotsky, accused of being the main inspiration behind the conspiracy, was tried *in absentia*, as he had been exiled abroad in 1929. The most absurdly improbable part of the trial was not even the prosecution charges, but the confessions the defendants made under physical and psychological torture. Despite the promises to save their lives, all the defendants were executed the day after the trial ended.

The British left were shocked to learn the news and yet, as Orwell wrote later: 'their opinion was divided, but divided chiefly on the question of whether the accused were guilty. Few people were able to see that whether justified or not the trials were an unspeakable horror'.[119]

Among those who saw it and, moreover, acted quickly was Walter Citrine, who in his capacity as the president of the International Federation of Trade Unions, together with three other people, including the Secretary for the Labour and Socialist International Friedrich Adler, sent a telegram to Moscow on 21 August, demanding 'all legal guarantees' for the accused

---

[116] Orwell, *The Road to Wigan Pier*, 200.
[117] Ibid., 206.
[118] Orwell, 'Review of *The Novel Today* by Philip Henderson' (*New English Weekly*, 31 December 1936), CW, X, 534.
[119] Orwell, 'Arthur Koestler' (11 September 1944, Typescript), CW, XVI, 393.

and a 'defending Counsel . . . independent of the government'.[120] Naturally, this was not granted, but the hysterical reaction of the Soviet press showed that the attack hit the target and stung. Starting on 23 August, *Pravda* published articles about the telegram daily, berating all the four signatories and specifically concentrating on Citrine, who was called 'an Advocate of Fascist Murderers'.[121] *The Daily Herald*, the main Labour Party paper was under the TUC's (i.e. Citrine's) full control and on 2 September its editorial wrote: 'The Communist Party has become Stalin's instrument, accepting "the leader principle" as unquestioningly as do fascists or Nazis'.[122]

Of course, it was not only Citrine. H. N. Brailsford of the ILP, a prolific journalist who had long supported the Soviet Union, wrote that 'there was no scrap of evidence against them [those executed] save confessions so abject that only terror could have extorted them . . . .Civilized justice does not rely on confessions'.[123] Brailsford argued publicly with D. H. Pritt, a former member of the Socialist League, later branded by Orwell a 'hired liar',[124] who attended the hearing and eagerly confirmed that 'the charge was true, the confessions correct, and the prosecution fairly conducted'.[125] The Labour Party as a whole never officially condemned the show trial.

The ILP also seemed puzzled. In his memoirs, its chairman Fenner Brockway describes how he was 'anxious to get at the truth of the matter', made 'a thorough study of the evidence'[126] and found some of the alleged events completely improbable. The National Administrative Council of the ILP demanded an international, impartial investigation and 'in the meantime the party was instructed to refrain from coming to any premature judgement'.[127]

It was only the Spanish Civil War that finally opened the eyes of the ILP members to the true nature of the Soviet Union and its Communist Party. And it did the same for Orwell.

[120] Friedrich Adler, *The Witchcraft Trial in Moscow* (Prism Key Press, 2011), 10.

[121] *Pravda*, 27 August 1936.

[122] Quoted in Corthorn, 'Labour, the Left, and the Stalinist Purges', 186.

[123] Quoted in ibid., 189.

[124] Orwell to House, 11 April 1940, CW, XII, 140.

[125] John Redman, 'The British Stalinists and the Moscow Trials' (*Labour Review*, Vol. 3, No. 2. March–April 1958), 44. https://www.marxists.org/archive/pearce/1958/03/trials .html.

[126] Fenner Brockway, *Inside the Left* (Nothingham: Spokesman, 2010), 259.

[127] Bullock, *Under Siege: The Independent Labour Party in Interwar Britain* (Athabasca, AB: Athabasca University Press, 2017), 281.

# 3

# Stalinism in Spain

*I happened to know, what very few people in England had been allowed to know, that innocent men were being falsely accused.*[1]

Orwell, 1946

*These man-hunts in Spain went on at the same time as the great purges in the USSR and were a sort of a supplement to them.*[2]

Orwell, 1947

Just days before the advent of the most notorious year in Soviet history – 1937, the epitome of the Great Terror – Orwell entered a building decorated with a huge portrait of Lenin. This was the Lenin barracks in revolutionary Barcelona, home of the POUM[3] militia he was going to join. He arrived in Spain on Boxing Day 1936 and left on 23 June 1937. The six months he spent in the country during the Civil War became pivotal to his political thinking. It was at the end of his stay there that he came very close to experiencing the Soviet terror and saw with his own eyes the ruthless, cynical and, what struck him most, mendacious nature of the Soviet-directed communists.

Before Spain, he seems to have had two separate compartments in his mind – one for the USSR, 'the stupid cult'[4] of which annoyed him, the other for British communists, whom he treated like any other party of the left – with scepticism, but amiably. What he did not – and probably could not – know at the time was the extent of the influence the Soviet Union exerted over the CPGB and communist parties in other countries, mostly via the Comintern.

The Nazi threat, which became palpable in 1933, changed Soviet foreign policy: after years of attacking Western social democrats as 'social-fascists' and worse enemies of communists than real fascists, the Comintern suddenly made a U-turn. Its 7th World Congress, held in Moscow in summer

---

[1]  Orwell, 'Why I Write', CW, XVIII, 320.
[2]  Orwell, 'Preface to the Ukrainian Edition of *Animal Farm*', [March 1947], CW, XIX, 87.
[3]  The POUM stood for *Partido Obrero de Unificacion Marxista* – Workers' Party of Marxist Unification.
[4]  Orwell, *The Road to Wigan Pier*, 201.

1935, announced the policy of 'collective security' and endorsed the idea of Popular Fronts of communists and non-communists. These indeed appeared in Spain and in France, but in Britain, the Labour Party leadership was dead set against them: it remembered only too well the previous attempts at communist infiltration based on Lenin's 1921 instructions. However, the Socialist League, headed by Stafford Cripps, who was 'assiduously wooed'[5] by Harry Pollitt, the general secretary of the CPGB, enthusiastically supported the idea of the 'Unity campaign'. As a result, three rather different groups: the British Communist Party, the Socialist League and the ILP, which by that time had come to bitterly regret its isolation, decided to act together and in January 1937 published a 'Unity Manifesto' calling for joint activity 'directed against Fascism, reaction and war and against the National Government'.[6]

By that time an important step to strengthen 'unity' had already been taken. A year earlier, in January 1936, Stafford Cripps asked publisher Victor Gollancz to think of something that could revive the left. This was precisely the task that Gollancz felt up to. Almost immediately he came up with the idea of a Left Book Club. Soon Club subscribers, of left persuasions, started regularly receiving books recommended by a panel of three selectors and published by Gollancz. The panel included Gollancz, who held strong pro-communist views; John Strachey, an influential Marxist writer and a communist, albeit without a party card; and Harold Laski, a political science professor and a member of the Labour Party's National Executive Committee. Gollancz's nose for success did not let him down. By the end of the year the Club had 40,000 enthusiastic members, and the idea of the Communist-Labour Alliance had become popular and even 'fashionable'.[7]

In this context, there is nothing surprising about Orwell's decision, on the eve of his departure to Spain, to approach Harry Pollitt. The Civil War was raging and to cross the border it was considered necessary to obtain supporting papers from a left-wing party – Orwell must have thought that the communists would do as well as any other. His meeting with Pollitt did not go as planned, but immediately exposed the positions of both sides. Later, Orwell described their conversation:

> P after questioning me evidently decided that I was politically unreliable and refused to help me, also tried to frighten me out of going by talking a lot about Anarchist terrorism. Finally he asked whether I would undertake to join the International Brigade. I said I could not undertake

---

5   Fenner Brockway, quoted in Pimlott, 86.
6   Quoted in ibid., 77.
7   Pimlott, *Labour and the Left*, 86.

to join anything until I had seen what was happening. He then refused to help me but advised me to get a safe-conduct from the Spanish Embassy in Paris, which I did.[8]

The CP general secretary must have seen at once that Orwell was not the stuff 'reliable' comrades were made of: too independent, too determined to see for himself rather than trust the party. After this meeting, Orwell got in touch with the ILP. Fenner Brockway and H. N. Brailsford gave him letters addressed to John McNair, the ILP representative in Barcelona, where the ILP had a 'sister party', the POUM. That was how Orwell joined the POUM militia. He did not think much about it – as he claimed afterwards, at that time, he was 'only rather dimly aware of the differences between the political parties.'[9] Later, he defined the POUM as

> one of those dissident Communist parties which have appeared in many countries in the last few years as a result of the opposition to 'Stalinism'; i.e. to the change, real or apparent, in Communist policy.... Numerically it was a small party, with not much influence outside Catalonia, and chiefly important because it contained an unusually high proportion of politically conscious members.[10]

It was POUM's anti-Stalinism that eventually proved fatal. The Party's leader Andrés Nin, one of the founders of the Spanish Communist Party (PCE), had spent nine years (1921–30) in the Soviet Union and was vehemently opposed to Stalin. He managed, after considerable effort, to get permission to return to Spain with his Russian wife Olga Tareeva and their daughters and tried to unite anti-Stalin communists outside the Soviet Union. For this purpose, he founded the Communist Left of Spain, a tiny party affiliated with the Trotsky-led International Left Opposition. However, although Nin had briefly been Trotsky's secretary back in Russia and sided with him in those years, their positions began to differ in the 1930s.

When Trotsky, true to his 'entryism' tactics, suggested that Nin's small and isolated Communist Left should join forces with the Socialist Youth of Spain, Nin broke with him and decided to unite with the Workers and Peasants Bloc led by the Catalan Joaquin Maurin and affiliated with the emerging International Right Opposition. In September 1935 the parties merged to form the POUM, and both Nin and Maurin became its leaders. After the February

[8]   Orwell, 'Notes on the Spanish Militias', CW, XI, 136.
[9]   Ibid.
[10]  Orwell, *Homage to Catalonia* (Harmondsworth, Middlesex: Penguin Books, 1985), 59.

elections of 1936, the POUM, one of the smallest parties in the Popular Front coalition, was represented in the *Cortes* (the Spanish Parliament) by a single deputy – Joaquin Maurin. However, at the very beginning of the Civil War, Maurin was captured by the fascists and detained until 1944, leaving Nin the only leader of the party at the time when Orwell arrived in Barcelona.

\* \* \*

Barcelona was the city of anarchists. Immediately after the fascist rebellion in July 1936, the anarcho-syndicalist union CNT – *Confederación Nacional del Trabajo* (National Federation of Labour) and its political wing, the FAI – *Federación Anarquista Ibérica* (Iberian Anarchist Federation), particularly powerful in Catalonia, called Barcelona's workers to arm themselves and resist the attack of the pro-rebel troops deployed in the city barracks. The street fighting ended with the workers' victory. General Goded, Franco's ally and rival, who arrived by plane from Majorca to take command of the operation, was swiftly arrested and then executed. Thus the anarchists saved Catalonia from the fascists. But this was not all – they started a social revolution, which Spain with its medieval traditions badly needed.

On 21 July, just a couple of days after the fighting, the CNT-FAI formed the Central Committee of Anti-Fascist Militias, which in effect took power in Catalonia and without much ado proceeded to implement revolutionary changes. Soon three-quarters of the Catalan economy were under workers' control. Armed workers led by the CNT-FAI ensured that factories, banks and transport companies, whose owners either were executed or fled, were run by their committees. Peasants seized land from landowners and organized themselves into agricultural communes. Workers' militias were ready to fight the fascist army. Catalonia was ahead of the other parts of the country, but the process was going on everywhere. As historian Anthony Beevor writes: 'The rising of the right had pushed an unplanned revolution into the eager arms of the left.'[11]

Now, this came as a surprise for Orwell – at least he said so in his book. He blamed 'the anti-Fascist press outside Spain' for it: 'The issue has been narrowed down to "Fascism versus democracy" and the revolutionary aspect concealed as much as possible. . . . Outside Spain few people grasped that there was a revolution; inside Spain nobody doubted it.'[12] The 'few people' who knew about the revolution included the ILP, which at that point had just under 3,700

[11] Anthony Beevor, *The Battle for Spain: The Spanish Civil War 1936–1939* (London: Phoenix, 2006), 89.

[12] Orwell, *Homage to Catalonia*, 50–1.

members – its weekly *The New Leader* reported on 'building Socialism' in Catalonia in every issue between August and October 1936. Orwell, of course, may have missed the paper because he was busy writing *The Road to Wigan Pier*. On the other hand, he might have chosen to present it this way for the sake of the dramatic impact of *Homage to Catalonia*. In any case, once he was 'inside', the revolutionary atmosphere of Barcelona fascinated him:

> There was much in it that I did not understand, in some ways I did not even like it, but I recognised it immediately as a state of affairs worth fighting for . . .
>
> Above all, there was a belief in the revolution and the future, a feeling of having suddenly emerged into an era of equality and freedom. Human beings were trying to behave as human beings and not as cogs in the capitalist machine.[13]

The euphoria that Orwell felt on arrival stayed with him for the rest of his life, despite everything that happened later. He was excited by the changes, although initially not knowing much about them. But other more knowledgeable left-wing foreigners were equally impressed by the very real achievements of the Spanish Revolution, which they naturally compared to the one that had taken place in Russia just twenty years earlier.

Among them was anarchist Emma Goldman who, after devoting thirty years to the revolutionary struggle in the United States, spent 1920–1 in Bolshevik, Russia, and fled it in disappointment and despair. 'The Russian experiment has proven the fatality of a political party, usurping the functions of the revolutionary people, of an omnipotent State seeking to impose its will upon the country, of a dictatorship attempting to "organise" the new life' – she wrote in 1925.[14] When the Spanish Revolution started, she was sixty-seven. She rushed to Spain at the first opportunity and found that the anarchists there were incredibly good at keeping order:

> I think it is the first time in history that such stress is being laid on the superior importance of running the machinery of economic and social life as is being done here. And this by the much maligned, chaotic Anarchists who supposedly have 'no program' and whose philosophy is bent on destruction and ruin.[15]

---

[13] Ibid., 8–10.
[14] Goldman, *My Disillusionment in Russia* (ReadaClassic.com, 2011), 14.
[15] Goldman to Stella Ballantine, 19 September 1936, in *Vision on Fire: Emma Goldman on the Spanish revolution*, ed. David Porter (Edinburgh, Oakland, West Virginia: AK Press, 2006), 69–70.

Goldman visited factories and agricultural communes, hospitals, prisons and militias, all successfully run by anarchists, and confirmed in January 1937 that the months spent in Spain were 'the three most exultant months of my entire career'.[16]

Franz Borkenau, a Vienna-born sociologist, was not an anarchist and a much more level-headed person than Goldman, but he was equally excited. 'It was as if we had been landed on a continent different from anything I had seen before',[17] he wrote on arriving in Barcelona in August 1936. Borkenau had spent five years working for the Comintern as a member of the German Communist Party (he broke off with both in 1929) and was particularly focused on analysing the political and social situation in Spain, which he naturally compared to Russia: 'Success or failure of the revolution will depend, to a large extent, upon the ability of the trade unions to manage the expropriated factories. In Russia socialisation meant at first, and for a long time, hardly anything but wholesale disintegration of industry',[18] he remarked. In Catalonia he was very impressed by a self-managed factory he saw, which 'only three weeks after the beginning of the Civil War seems to run as smoothly as if nothing had happened'.[19]

This contradicted the lazy popular perception of anarchists outside Spain, where, since the war started, both the right-wing and the communist press referred to anarchists as 'uncontrollables' or outright terrorists who killed landowners, burned churches and raped nuns. For those on the right, anybody on the Republican side was 'Red' by definition and therefore guilty of terror, but for many on the left, blaming anarchists was a deliberate policy which reflected a fundamental split between anarchists and communists. Orwell described the clash between the two creeds thus: 'The Communist's emphasis is always on centralism and efficiency, the Anarchist's on liberty and equality'.[20] The contrast was immediately obvious when the type of military force necessary to fight Franco was debated: the anarchists insisted on keeping militias formed by different parties, the communists on having a unified army under central command. Franz Borkenau, who in August 1936 attended an anarchist rally to support militias and protest against 'the army principle', summarized the anarchist position: 'They expressly rejected

---

[16] Goldman to John Cooper Powys. 5 January 1937, quoted in David Goodway, *Anarchist Seeds Beneath the Snow* (Oakland, CA: PM Press, 2012), 129.

[17] Franz Borkenau, *The Spanish Cockpit* (London, Sydney: Pluto Press, 1986), 69.

[18] Ibid., 89.

[19] Ibid.

[20] Orwell, *Homage to Catalonia*, 61.

the Russian authoritarian system: Spain ought not to imitate the Russian revolution.'[21]

\* \* \*

So, from the very start, the forces fighting fascists on the Republican side had insurmountable disagreements among themselves. The tiny POUM supported the anarchists: its members, like the anarchists, were adamant that the social revolution that had started so successfully should continue. They promoted the slogan 'the war and the revolution are inseparable' and insisted on keeping the militia system rather than creating a regular army, because, as they claimed, 'either the workers control the armed forces or the armed forces control the workers'.[22]

In Orwell's description 'the war was essentially a triangular struggle'.[23] The anarchists and POUM formed one side of the triangle, the second side was the communists and increasingly – under their influence – the Republican government. They maintained that the revolution could wait, while winning the war was essential but impossible without a regular army under a unified command. The third side of the triangle was Franco's fascists, against whom all the others were fighting.

Orwell admitted that throughout his first four months in Spain (January–April 1937), despite all his sympathy for the anarchists and admiration for their revolution, he had been supporting the communist position: 'the Communists – so it seemed to me – were getting on with the war while we and the Anarchists were standing still.'[24] This support went so far that in April 1937 when Orwell and other Brits from his unit came to Barcelona on leave, he was on the point of leaving the POUM and joining the International Brigades run by the communists. Some of his fellow militiamen (the Trotskyist Harry Milton, for example) tried to talk him out of it, but he would not listen. Eileen Blair, in her letter to her brother, acknowledged the oddness of this move but tried to justify it: 'To join the I.B. with George's history is strange but it is what he thought he was doing in the first place and it's the only way of getting to Madrid.'[25] The seriousness of Orwell's intentions is confirmed by the 'Report on the English Section of the P.O.U.M.' sent to Harry Pollitt by Walter Tapsell, his emissary in Spain:

[21] Borkenau, *The Spanish Cockpit*, 92.
[22] Orwell, *Homage to Catalonia*, 60.
[23] Ibid., 54.
[24] Ibid., 62.
[25] Eileen Blair to Dr Laurence O'Shaughnessy, 1 May 1937, CW, XI, 21.

The leading personality and most respected man in the contingent at present is Eric Blair. . . . He has little political understanding and says that he is not interested in party politics and came to Spain as an Anti-Fascist to fight Fascism. . . . In a conversation with the writer on 30th [April] Blair enquired whether his association with the P.O.U.M. would be likely to prejudice his chances of enlisting with the International Brigade. He wishes to fight on the Madrid front and states that in a few days he will formally apply to us for enlistment when his discharge from the P.O.U.M. has been regularised.[26]

The fact that Orwell enquired about the possibility of his association with the POUM threatening his chances of joining the International Brigade shows that in April 1937, he already had some understanding of party politics. This can also be seen from the way he reacted to Harry Pollitt's scorching review of *The Road to Wigan Pier* in the *Daily Worker* in March 1937: 'Yes, Pollitt's review was pretty bad, tho' of course good for publicity. I suppose he must have heard I was serving in the Poum militia'.[27] Actually, Orwell could have known about the tensions between the communists and the POUM even earlier.

From mid-December 1936, the ILP paper *The New Leader* had been covering the 'political offensive' against the POUM, which originated in Moscow and was conducted by the Comintern, the Spanish Communist Party and the Catalonian PSUC.[28] It included 'denouncing them as in effect pro-Fascist and supporters of Hitler and Mussolini'.[29] From the very start of this campaign, Fenner Brockway, the ILP general secretary and its paper's editor, and John McNair, who had been living in Barcelona since August 1936, stood by their 'sister party' and tried to give their readers a detailed account of the charges against it. *The New Leader* was regularly, if belatedly, delivered to the ILP contingent on the Aragon front – in fact, many of its members complained of 'their lack of reading matter of any kind except *The New Leader*'[30] – so there is no doubt Orwell and his fellow militiamen read and discussed the paper.

[26] Walter Tapsell, 'Report on the English Section of the P.O.U.M.' *Marx Memorial Library*, Box C/13/7a.

[27] Orwell to Eileen, 5 (?) April 1937. CW, XI, 16.

[28] PSUC – *Partit Socialista Unificat de Catalunya* (The Unified Socialist Party of Catalonia). Despite its name, the PSUC was a Communist Party and under Comintern control.

[29] Fenner Brockway, 'Workers' Control in Barcelona' (*The New Leader*, 18 December 1936). According to John McNair, 'the campaign of calumny' against the POUM started as early as September 1936 (*The New Leader*, 17 December 1936). *The New Leader* devoted a lot of space to this campaign, especially in issues of 1 and 8 January, 12 March 1937 and others.

[30] Tapsell, 'Report On the English Section', MML Box C/13/7a.

The anti-POUM campaign was also taken quite seriously in John McNair's office in Barcelona, where Eileen started working as a secretary in mid-February 1937 and where she also helped the American Charles Orr to edit the POUM's English-language bulletin *Spanish Revolution*. Just before Eileen's arrival, Charles's wife, nineteen-year-old Lois wrote to her family: 'The campaign of the PSUC and the Communist International against POUM has intensified. They use the Moscow trial[31] as evidence that the POUM should be physically exterminated. They have claimed that more and more openly in their papers: that we should be liquidated as counterrevolutionaries and fascist agents. Can you imagine that?'[32]

Orwell at that point did not feel anything like the indignation expressed by Lois Orr. Before May 1937, he had been sceptical of the POUM and everything it did and said. He disagreed with its position on the war and revolution and, having spent much of his time at the front in political discussions, admitted: 'the political side of the war bored me and I *naturally* [emphasis added] reacted against the viewpoint of which I heard most, i.e. the POUM-ILP viewpoint'.[33] This, of course, would hardly be natural for most people, who rather tend to agree with the viewpoint of which they hear most, but for Orwell, with his independent and polemical mind, it, surely, was: he could not help questioning 'the wisdom of the party', the party of which he knew most, that is, the POUM. Besides, he still treated the Spanish War as primarily a struggle against fascism and was upset that on the Aragon front, he 'had not done [his] fair share of the fighting',[34] while the communist International Brigades were fighting and moreover, fighting in Madrid, the most important place of all.

Enlisting with the Brigades was a logical step forward for him, while the communists' attacks on the POUM must have looked like petty squabbles between parties fighting on the same side. He lightmindedly dismissed the warnings which scared and outraged less naïve people. His shock and outrage came later. As he put it in *Homage to Catalonia*, 'the things that most enlightened me had not yet happened'.[35] But they were not long in coming.

---

[31] Lois meant the Second Moscow Trial (Pyatakov-Radek Trial), which took place in January 1937.

[32] Lois Orr to her family, 4–12 February 1937 in *Letters from Barcelona: An American Woman in Revolution and Civil War*, ed. Gerd-Rainer Horn (London: Palgrave Macmillan, 2009), 128.

[33] Orwell, *Homage to Catalonia*, 57.

[34] Ibid, 70.

[35] Ibid.

\* \* \*

The Soviet Union intervened in the Spanish Civil War two and a half months after it started. The first supply of weapons for the Republicans arrived on 4 October 1936. Stalin was slow to come to the Republic's assistance: it took him some time to decide how to use the Spanish conflict to his own advantage. He started by joining the Non-Intervention Committee set up by France and Great Britain, which got twenty-seven countries on board. However, Hitler and Mussolini, having signed the Non-Intervention Agreement, breached it almost immediately by openly sending military aid to Franco. Stalin was still thinking. Soviet defector Walter Krivitsky, whose account Orwell thought 'genuine',[36] explained what was behind it:

> [Stalin's] idea was – and this was common knowledge among us who served him – to include Spain in the sphere of the Kremlin's influence. Such domination would secure his ties with Paris and London, and thus strengthen, on the other hand, his bargaining position with Berlin. ... He would be a force to be reckoned with, an ally to be coveted.[37]

Stalin's ambitions in Spain became clearer in retrospect. The editors of *Spain Betrayed* describe them thus: 'in exchange for military aid, Stalin demanded the transformation of the Republic into a prototype for the so-called People's Democracies of postwar Eastern and Central Europe.'[38] The same comparison had been made even earlier by one of the POUM leaders, Julián Gorkin, in his 1961 essay titled '*Espana, primer ensayo de democracia popular*' ('Spain: First Attempt at a People's Democracy').[39] However, at the time of the conflict Stalin's aims were not so easy to understand. Orwell wrote in 1942:

> As to the Russians, their motives in the Spanish war are completely inscrutable. Did they, as the pinks believed, intervene in Spain in order to defend democracy and thwart the Nazis? Then why did they intervene on such a niggardly scale and finally leave Spain in the lurch? Or did they, as the Catholics maintained, intervene in order to force the revolution in Spain? Then why did they do all in their power to crush the

[36] Orwell to MacDonald, 15 April 1947, CW, XIX, 128.
[37] W.G. Krivitsky, *In Stalin's Secret Service* (New York: Harper and Brothers Publishers, 1939), 76.
[38] Ronald Radosh, Mary R. Habeck and Grigory Sevostianov, eds., *Spain Betrayed. The Soviet Union in the Spanish Civil War* (New Haven and London: Yale University Press, 2001), XVII–XVIII.
[39] Quoted in Stéphane Courtois and Jean-Louis Panné, 'The Shadow of the NKVD in Spain', in *The Black Book of Communism: Crimes, Terror, Repression*, ed. Stéphane Courtois et al. (Cambridge, MA and London, England: Harvard University Press, 1999), 336.

Spanish revolutionary movements, defend private property and hand power to the middle class as against the working class? Or did they, as the Trotskyists suggested, intervene simply in order to *prevent* a Spanish revolution? Then why not have backed Franco? Indeed their actions are more easily explained if one assumes that they were acting on several contradictory motives.[40]

The main reason behind these contradictions was that Stalin was not yet sure which side he would take in the inevitable future world war. He could supply enough weapons to the Republic to stifle the fascist rebellion, but he was not sure he needed to, as he did not exclude a future alliance with Hitler. At the same time, he courted Britain and France and did not want to scare them by raising the spectre of world revolution – that is why he tried to suppress any mention of the revolutionary changes in Spain. But it would not do to antagonize Western communists either – therefore he could not openly refuse to support the Spanish working class. Besides, he had to pretend that the Soviet Union remained true to the non-intervention policy – the shipment of weapons to Spain was never overt. And finally, he had a private and passionate wish to settle scores with his political opponents – Trotskyists, anarchists and, in fact, anybody who had ever expressed dissatisfaction with his policies. The last thing that bothered him was the fate of the Spanish people. Or any other people, for that matter.

Contrary to what Frankoists were saying, there was no Russian army in Spain – something Orwell never ceased to stress. Anthony Beevor gives the following figures for Soviet personnel who served in the Spanish Civil War: 'never more than 800 were present at any one time. The total appears to have been a maximum of 2,150, of whom 600 were non-combatants, including interpreters. There were, in addition, between 20 and 40 members of the NKVD and between 20 and 25 diplomats'.[41] This list does not, however, include Spaniards and non-Soviet foreigners working for the NKVD, individually or in groups. In Catalonia – the prime target of the communists – two groups were formed under NKVD control as early as September 1936: a *Grupo de Información* (Information Group) inside the Catalan Secret Services, which soon employed fifty people, and the *Servicio Extranjero* (Foreign Service) inside the PSUC. The task of the Foreign Service was 'to control all foreign communists arriving in Barcelona to fight in Spain'.[42]

One of the people working for this group was a British communist, Hugh O'Donnell. He arrived in Spain in August 1936 as the head of the British

[40] Orwell, 'Looking Back on the Spanish War', CW, XIII, 508.
[41] Beevor, *The Battle for Spain*, 183.
[42] Courtois and Panné, 'The Shadow of the NKVD in Spain', 337–8.

Medical Unit run by the Communist Party of Great Britain. However, quite soon Harry Pollitt started receiving letters from people working with O'Donnell in Spain (including, for example, British writer Sylvia Townsend Warner[43]), who complained of O'Donnell's neglect of his duties, lack of tact when dealing with Spaniards, lack of communication with his comrades, drunkenness and profiteering on the exchange of BMU money on the 'Black Exchange'. Responding to requests to remove O'Donnell, Pollitt sent a telegram ordering him to return to Britain.

Instead of obeying the recall, O'Donnell explained that he was carrying out much more important tasks than those given to him by the general secretary of the British Communist Party:

> Comrade Fedeli[44] had the impression that you were not fully informed of the responsible work I was doing as member of the P.S.U.C . . .. I should explain that the nature of my work cannot be fully explained in a letter and that much of it is of a character which can only be undertaken by a party comrade who has had previous experience in this work.[45]

The 'nature' and the 'character' of work were also implied in the letter Pollitt received from Walter Tapsell, the same man he sent to Barcelona to gather information on the ILP contingent. The diligent Tapsell sent back a lengthy piece called 'Case of Comrade O'Donnell', where he stated: 'As already reported, O'Donnell's funds come from another source and another job to that which [he] is officially supposed to be doing. The job was *secret*, should remain *secret*, and its nature I have not enquired to. It also accounts for the fact that he appears to give little attention to his official responsibilities.'[46] This was meant to explain to Pollitt that Hugh O'Donnell was working not so much for London, but rather for the NKVD base in Albacete or simply for Moscow. As an NKVD agent, under the codename Sean O'Brien, he played his part in suppressing the POUM and its allies. It is difficult to imagine that he had much time or strength left to spend on the British Medical Unit.[47]

[43]  Report by Sylvia Townsend Warner and Valentine Ackland. MML, Box C/7/1.
[44]  Armando Fedeli (1888–1965) was an Italian communist and one of the heads of the Foreign Service.
[45]  Hugh O'Donnell to Pollitt, 18 March 1937. MML, Box C/12/3.
[46]  Tapsell, 'Case of Comrade O'Donnell', April 1937. MML, Box C/12/3.
[47]  By August 1938 O'Donnell had left the BMU, concentrating on his work for Comrade Fedeli. *Anonymous Report*, RGASPI, f 495, op.183, d.6, l.37-38.

\* \* \*

The 'fraternal military aid' did not come to Spain for free. The weapons had to be paid for in gold and the gold was to be held in Moscow. In 1936 Spain had the fourth largest gold reserves in the world, and in July the Spanish government started transferring it to France for the purchase of arms. However, in September 1936, the remaining three-quarters of the gold reserves and other precious metals, 510 tonnes altogether, were taken to Moscow. By 1938, according to Soviet calculations, the level of the current account in gold was exhausted. This, as Anthony Beevor explains, was the result of Soviet 'creative accounting'.[48]

Soviet military aid attracted Spaniards to the Communist Party. The Soviet Union was the only country (apart from Mexico with its much more limited assistance) that supplied the Republicans with weapons and thus gained enormous popularity among their supporters. Orwell wrote: 'The Russian arms and the magnificent defence of Madrid by troops mainly under Communist control had made the Communists the heroes of Spain. As someone put it, every Russian aeroplane that flew over our heads was Communist propaganda.'[49] Party membership increased dramatically. Besides, the military aid worked as leverage that allowed Moscow to dictate terms to the Republican government. Some Republican leaders openly admitted this quite soon. Julián Zugazagoitia, Minister of the Interior and afterwards Secretary of the Ministry of Defence, said in an interview quoted by Orwell: 'We have received aid from Russia, so we have had to permit things we did not like'.[50] Irving Pflaum, an American correspondent in Spain and author of one of the first denunciations of Russia's role in the Civil War, wrote in 1939:

> Soviet assistance . . . was never large enough to guarantee victory, though the USSR had the resources to make short work of the rebellion. In effect, its injection simply helped to maintain the stalemate that the conservative British government obviously desired, and to squelch socialist and anarcho-syndicalist experiments in socialisation. Russia doled out its help carefully, teasingly and maneuvered it in line with special Soviet objectives.[51]

[48] Beevor, *The Battle for Spain*, 173.
[49] Orwell, *Homage to Catalonia*, 62.
[50] Quoted in Orwell's letter to the Editor, *The Manchester Guardian*, 5 August 1938, CW, XI, 185.
[51] Irving Pflaum, 'Russia's Role in Spain' (*The American Mercury*, May 1939), 10.

One of these objectives was to deliver arms to the Republican troops, controlled by the communists, and to avoid arming the anarchist militias. The lack of weapons on the Aragon front, so familiar to Orwell when he was there, was thus easily explained. Walter Krivitsky testified that having loaded a boat with 'fifty pursuit planes and bombers' that he had, with a huge effort, bought for the Republicans, he was ordered by Moscow

> not to permit the boat to deliver its cargo in Barcelona. Under no circumstances were those planes to pass through Catalonia, which had its own government. . . . This Catalonian government was dominated by revolutionists of anti-Stalinist persuasion. They were not trusted by Moscow . . .. In the meantime, Loyalist Spain was fighting desperately and was woefully short of planes.[52]

Even the Soviet Consul-General in Barcelona, Vladimir Antonov-Ovseyenko, wrote to Moscow as early as in November 1936 that Catalonia urgently needed weapons: 'There are no tanks on this front, no modern aircraft at all. The troops have been staying in wet trenches for over two months. Drastic inspirational remedies are needed to rouse them . . . and nothing would be better than supporting them with modern aviation. Under present conditions, their success is highly doubtful.'[53]

Antonov-Ovseyenko, once described as 'more Catalan than the Catalans', was ordered to return to Moscow and shot dead within a couple of months. The weapons he asked for were never sent to Catalonia. For Orwell, this refusal to send weapons to the Aragon front proved that the communists did not really care about winning the war. He soon realized that even 'the often-repeated slogan: "the war first and the revolution afterwards" . . . was eyewash',[54] because the aim of the communists was not to postpone the revolution but to stop it in its tracks, 'to check every revolutionary tendency'.[55]

Other communist lies were particularly striking when compared to the propaganda within the Soviet Union. In Spain the communists proclaimed they were fighting for 'a democratic and parliamentary republic of a new type'.[56] Emma Goldman commented sarcastically: 'Their sudden discovery of Democracy as a beautiful bride is nothing else but the deliberate intention

---

[52]  Krivitsky, *In Stalin's Secret Service*, 91.
[53]  *Donesenie V.Antonova-Ovseenko po voennym voprosam* (The Report on Military Issues by V. Antonov-Ovseyenko), 18 November 1936. http://www.milresource.ru/Rybalkin-Doc-1a.htm.
[54]  Orwell, *Homage to Catalonia*, 66.
[55]  Ibid., 67.
[56]  Quoted in: Pierre Broué and Emile Témime, *The Revolution and the Civil War in Spain*, trans. T. White (Chicago, IL: Haymarket Books, 2008), 230.

of the Soviet Government to destroy the Revolution in Spain, and they are losing no time to achieve this.'[57]

The communist attitude to collectivization in Spain, where they adamantly defended the right of individual peasants not to be collectivized, blatantly contradicted their own rhetoric and behaviour in the USSR, where just six years earlier those reluctant to join collective farms had been deported or sent straight to the Gulag. Borkenau's description of what he saw in the Valencia region in August 1936 summarizes the absurdity of the situation: 'When I went to the communist headquarters and entered the secretary's room, my eye was caught by an enormous picture of Stalin and a smaller one of Kiroff. Besides these there were two posters with the slogans: "Respect the property of the small peasant" and "Respect the property of the small industrialist".'[58] Around the same time, Mikhail Koltsov[59] was assuring the readers of *Pravda* that communes created 'by orders and threats . . . disintegrate immediately',[60] and proclaimed: 'No one is permitted to impose their will on Aragonese peasants'.[61] If his readers had any questions about Russian peasants, they did not dare to ask them.

The direct target of this attack against 'forced collectivisation' were the anarchists. They could not respond in kind: although strong initially, especially in Catalonia, they had to make compromises that significantly weakened them. The Central Committee of the Anti-Fascist Militias in Catalonia was dissolved as soon as anarchists, contrary to their principles, joined the Generalitat. Still they were numerous and remained strong in Catalonia – no matter how much the communists wanted to crush them, they could not yet do so. There was, however, a much easier target – the POUM.

\* \* \*

The decision to settle accounts with the POUM must have been taken by the communists very early on. Just five days after the Popular Front's victory at the February 1936 elections, the Comintern Secretariat called on the Spanish Communist Party to begin 'an energetic struggle against the Trotskyite counter-revolutionary sect'.[62] One of the first entries in Mikhail Koltsov's

[57]  Goldman to Max Nettlau, 9 May 1937, *Vision on Fire*, 135.
[58]  Borkenau, *The Spanish Cockpit*, 117.
[59]  Mikhail Koltsov (1898–1940) was a journalist and agent, nicknamed 'Stalin's eyes and ears in Spain'.
[60]  *Pravda*, 16 August 1936.
[61]  *Pravda*, 1 September 1936.
[62]  Courtois and Panné, 'The Shadow of the NKVD in Spain', 338.

*Spanish Diary,* written on 9 August 1936, is full of animosity towards the party: 'The POUM is playing a role of provocation and demoralisation . . . demanding a broad and immediate social revolution in Spain and speaking with repugnant demagoguery against the Soviet Union'.[63]

What Koltsov called 'repugnant demagoguery' was the criticism of the USSR that naturally increased when the show trial of Kamenev, Zinoviev and others started in Moscow ten days later. This was a rare case when the POUM unanimously stood behind its leader: Andrés Nin had known some of the accused when he was living in Russia and obviously could not believe that they were 'fascist agents'. The charge, however, was very soon transferred to the POUM too – as they were a 'Trotskyist' party.

Franz Borkenau, who during his second trip to Spain in winter 1937 was himself arrested on suspicion of being a Trotskyist, explained:

> The communists have got into the habit of denouncing as a Trotskyist everybody who disagrees with them about anything. For in communist mentality, every disagreement in political matters is a major crime, and every political criminal is a Trotskyist. A Trotskyist, in communist vocabulary, is synonymous with a man who deserves to be killed.[64]

Applying the term to the POUM was especially easy because it was based on Nin's brief association with Trotsky in the 1920s; despite the two men's very public split ten years later it was still convenient to use. Orwell ridiculed the logic of it, saying: 'By the same line of argument it could be shown that the English Communist Party is really a Fascist organisation, because of Mr John Strachey's one-time association with Sir Oswald Mosley'.[65] The communists, however, did not try very hard to make their arguments convincing — any argument would work if reinforced by terror, and if Trotsky was a fascist, anybody who was labelled Trotskyist was a fascist too.

Since the beginning of 1937, the intense preparation for the attack on the POUM had been gathering strength. In the report of military adviser A. V. Mokrousov on Catalonia written by the beginning of February 1937, the last item in the list of immediate objectives reads: 'To achieve the liquidation of the POUM by diplomatic means'.[66] The endnote added in 2019 informs

---

[63]  Koltsov, *Ispaniya v ogne (Spain on Fire)* (Moscow: Political Literature Publishers, 1987), Vol. I, 17.

[64]  Borkenau, *The Spanish Cockpit*, 240.

[65]  Orwell, *Homage to Catalonia*, 170.

[66]  *RKKA I Grazhdanskaya voina v Ispanii* (RKKA and the Civil War in Spain) *1936–1939. Informational Reports of the Soviet Military Intelligence*, Vol. 1 (Moscow: Rosspen, 2019), 301.

readers that in the summer of 1937 the POUM was liquidated 'through the use of force'.[67]

\* \* \*

Force was first used in the afternoon of 3 May 1937, when following the weeks of tension between communists and anarchists, the Republican Assault Guards sent by the Generalitat attacked the telephone exchange held by the anarchists. The Assault Guards were met with fire. This acted as a signal: in different parts of the city people started shooting and building barricades out of stones torn from the pavements — the lessons of the revolutionary days of July 1936 were not forgotten. Only now the conflict was within the Republican forces. The POUM instinctively supported the anarchists, and Orwell, puzzled and distressed, spent the next three days on the roof of the Poliorama cinema in Las Ramblas, protecting the POUM buildings against possible attacks. In *Homage to Catalonia* he remarked: 'it was one of the most unbearable periods of my whole life. I think few experiences could be more sickening, more disillusioning, or, finally, more nerve-racking than those evil days of street warfare'.[68] The worst part of it surely was that having come to Spain to fight for the Republican government against fascists, he suddenly found himself opposing the government troops.

'The civil war within the civil war' lasted for five days and left 500 dead (400 according to other sources) and 1,000 wounded. The Generalitat asked the government for help, and on 7 May 5,000 Assault Guards and *carabineros* reached Barcelona to restore law and order. The shooting nearly stopped and the barricades began to be dismantled, but there was no doubt that these several days of clashes had strengthened the communists.

On 9 May José Díaz, the general secretary of the Spanish Communist Party, declared at a public meeting:

> Our principal enemies are the fascists. However, these not only include the fascists themselves but also the agents who work for them . . . Some call them Trotskyists, which is the name used by many disguised fascists who use revolutionary language in order to sow confusion. I therefore ask: If everyone knows this, if the government knows it, why does it not treat them like fascists and exterminate them pitilessly?[69]

[67]  Ibid., 513.
[68]  Ibid., 125.
[69]  Quoted in Burnett Bolloten, *The Grand Camouflage: The Communist Conspiracy in the Spanish Civil War* (London: Hollis and Carter, 1961), 307–8.

With one blow, the communists managed to hit both the 'Trotskyists', by announcing that it was the POUM that had instigated the May clashes, and the Republican government, by claiming that it had not been fighting the 'disguised fascists'. Was all this a deliberate provocation by the communists in order to suppress the POUM and depose Caballero? Orwell did not believe it. However, a detailed report written in French by a Comintern representative in Spain (possibly André Marty) at the end of March 1937 and forwarded to Stalin seems, in an indirect way, to prove him wrong. The report complains about Prime Minister Largo Caballero's intransigence and his 'attempts to isolate the Communists'[70] and ends with the call 'not to wait passively for a "natural" unleashing of the hidden government crisis, but to hasten it and, if necessary, provoke it, in order to obtain a solution for these problems'.[71]

The NKVD was quick to obtain solutions for any problems – soon it announced the discovery of '*very interesting documents proving the connection of the Spanish Trotskyists with Franco*'.[72] Among them was a coded message addressed 'To the Generalissimo'. It was allegedly composed by a fascist agent writing to Franco about his meeting with Nin (hidden under the letter 'N'!). The document was an elaborate forgery, masterminded by Alexander Orlov, by that time Head of the NKVD in Spain. Orlov was so convinced of his impunity that he wrote to Moscow on 23 May 1937: 'We have . . . composed the enclosed document, which indicates the cooperation of the POUM leadership with the Spanish Falange organisation — and through it, with Franco and Germany. . . . We expect this affair to be very effective in exposing the role the POUM has played in the Barcelona uprising.'[73] Many people, including Orwell, did not have the slightest doubt even in 1937 that the 'discovery' was fabricated, and yet thanks to communist propaganda and, in particular, to Mikhail Koltsov's personal efforts, the story was picked up by the world press and helped to support the charge that the POUM had collaborated with the fascists.

The impact of these early developments (the worst was still to come!) on Orwell is hard to exaggerate. He was outraged that political differences between the POUM and communists could have led the latter to accuse another party on the Republican side of being 'a gang of disguised fascists': 'This implied that scores of thousands of working-class people, including eight or ten thousand soldiers who were freezing in the front-line trenches and hundreds of foreigners who had come to Spain to fight against Fascism,

---

[70]   Radosh et al., *Spain Betrayed*, 190.
[71]   Ibid., 194.
[72]   Ibid., 196.
[73]   Costello and Tsarev, *Deadly Illusions*, 288–9.

often sacrificing their livelihood and their nationality by doing so, were simply traitors in the pay of the enemy.[74]

The shock of it made Orwell take three important decisions. First, he would not join the International Brigades. He was not the man to abandon a losing side, especially when he was absolutely convinced of the honesty of those who fought fascism under the POUM banner. Moreover, he now wished he had joined the POUM, despite all his previous criticism of its line.

Second, as an eyewitness to the momentous developments of recent days, he felt he had to write about them. Hardly had the clashes in Barcelona stopped on 9 May, than he suggested to his publisher Victor Gollancz that he should submit a book on his Spanish experience by early 1938. The powerful need to present a true picture of events, against 'the most appalling lies' of English newspapers, is evident in his words: 'I greatly hope I will come out of this alive if only to write a book about it.'[75] The third decision, which obviously contradicted the wish to stay alive, was to return to the front to fight.

On 15 May the communist minister Uribe 'demanded on Moscow's orders that the POUM be suppressed and its leaders arrested'.[76] Largo Caballero refused to comply. The anarchists and a few old socialist colleagues supported him, but the rest of his cabinet, still concerned about the delivery of Soviet arms, went along with the communists. On 17 May, Largo Caballero resigned and Juan Negrín became the next prime minister of the Republic. This was something that Moscow had long been waiting for. Ousting Caballero allowed Stalin 'to seize full control'.[77] Julián Gorkin described the immediate change in the atmosphere:

> A few days after Juan Negrín's government had been formed, Orlov was already acting as though Spain was some sort of a Communist satellite. He turned up at the headquarters of the security offices and asked for Colonel Antonio Ortega, whom he now considered to be one of his subordinates, and demanded warrants for the arrests of members of the POUM Executive Committee.[78]

One of Negrín's first orders was to ban the POUM's newspaper *La Batalla*, which deprived the party of an opportunity to respond to the charges. This was the start of the full-blown terror against the POUM.

---

[74]  Orwell, *Homage to Catalonia*, 63.
[75]  Orwell to Gollancz, 9 May 1937, CW, XI, 22.
[76]  Beevor, *The Battle for Spain*, 302.
[77]  Krivitsky, *In Stalin's Secret Service*, 108.
[78]  Quoted in Courtois and Panné, 341.

*    *    *

On 16 June the POUM was declared illegal and its leaders were arrested. On Orlov's orders, Nin, the party's general secretary, was singled out, interrogated in secrecy and almost certainly tortured. Orlov hoped to make him admit charges of collaboration with the fascists, which were chiefly based on his own forgery, but Nin would not break. In Orlov's eyes he was therefore unsuitable for the Moscow-style show trial planned by the NKVD and had to be killed. But Republican Spain was not yet a Soviet province and killing the leader of a political party in custody could not be done openly, so Orlov staged a show to shift the blame from the NKVD and simultaneously slander the man who would not be broken. A rumour was spread that Nin had been 'rescued' by the Gestapo. Nin's disappearance profoundly embarrassed the Republican government – Prime Minister Negrín called the whole incident a 'dirty business', and President Azaña, when informed of the 'rescue' version, inquired sceptically: 'Was that not a little like a novel?'[79] Still, they would not admit any responsibility or challenge the NKVD.

The full truth, suspected from the first days of Nin's disappearance, came out only in the early 1990s, when Orlov's reports emerged from the NKVD archives, but the suspicion that Nin was no longer alive arose in Barcelona almost immediately. Orwell heard it when he returned to Barcelona a month after he had been wounded by a fascist sniper. He spent that month convalescing in hospitals and sanatoriums and then gathering papers for his discharge from the army. Apart from the rumour of Nin's death, he also learnt of the arrests of many POUM members, including personal friends such as his commander Georges Kopp. Soon came the news about the death of the twenty-two-year-old Bob Smillie, who was arrested on his way back home and, thrown into jail in Valencia. This death epitomized for Orwell all the injustice of the persecution of the POUM: a young, brave, honest man, who gave up everything to help the Spanish Republic fight fascism, was falsely accused and ended his life in a Republican jail without trial.

Orwell's own life was also in danger. On 17 or 18 June, when he was travelling from one hospital to another collecting his discharge certificates, Eileen's room at the Hotel Continental in Barcelona was searched by the Spanish police, under orders from the NKVD. Luckily, Eileen was not arrested and even managed to keep the passports and cheque book under the mattress she was lying on, due to the courtesy (unimaginable in Russia) of the policemen, who did not dare to ask a foreign señora to get out of bed. All the other papers were confiscated. Their list available today in the

---

[79]    Costello and Tsarev, *Deadly Illusions*, 290.

Russian Archive of Social and Political History (RGASPI)[80] provides some information about the Blairs and also about NKVD methods of staging cases. It begins like this:

List of Eileen Blair's documents
>   10 July 1937
> 1. Correspondence between Eileen and Eric Blair.
> 2. Printed documents: newspaper cuttings, manifestos, brochures, newspapers, art cards etc.
> 3. Correspondence of George Orwell (alias Eric Blair) regarding his book *The Road to Wigan Pier*.

Telegrams and photos are mentioned in passing, but Item 5, titled 'Various documents', has twenty-five separate entries and supplies some interesting biographical details.

A 'letter of recommendation from the FAI Propaganda Department proposing that Eric Blair be admitted to the union' proves that at some point Orwell was at least considering joining the anarchists; a letter from Moscow is, most likely, the letter from Sergei Dinamov, the editor of *International Literature*, which Orwell mentions in his reply to Dinamov's second letter of 2 July 1937,[81] and a postcard from Richard Rees[82] to Eileen, dated 19 April 1937, informs her of his work in the American hospital near Tarancon. There are also about a dozen entries naming letters and notes, mostly from members of the ILP contingent (John McNair, Douglas Moyle, Arthur Clinton et al) addressed either to Eric or to Eileen, and finally, papers hinting at Georges Kopp's interest in Eileen: his letter to her, his poem to her and a jocular note in Spanish apparently asking city patrols to leave her alone.

Out of all these documents, only one seems to have survived today[83] – the last entry on the list: a letter from David Wickes to Eileen Blair, sent from Albacete on 5 June 1937. But this one was obviously honoured with special attention – it was translated into German, the language widely used by the Comintern and by numerous German agents in Spain, and prepared for sending to two different addresses: there are two type-written copies of

[80]  RGASPI, f.545, op.6, d.107, l.22. Translated from French by Ros Schwartz. The full list is published in English in *The Orwell Society Journal*, 19, 2021.

[81]  Orwell to Sergei Dinamov, 2 July 1937 in *The Lost Orwell*, 99–100.

[82]  There is no surname on the postcard, but the details provided there are corroborated by Rees's autobiographical book *A Theory of My Time* (London: Secker and Warburg, 1963), 96.

[83]  So far, despite numerous attempts to find them, neither Orwell's correspondence, nor his diaries have been discovered in the Russian Archives. It is not even known whether they still exist.

the letter in the archive. At the top of one there is a hand-written scribble in German reading 'To Valencia (Fritz)',[84] at the top of the other it says, also in German: 'To Albacete'.[85] Valencia, the seat of the Republican government, was also the seat of the Tribunal for Espionage and High Treason; while Albacete, the NKVD base, soon became the headquarters of the SIM (*Servicio de Investigación Militar*) – the Military Investigation Service, run by the NKVD. 'Fritz' (aka 'Fritz Schimmel' or 'Fritz Valencia') was a codename of Wilhelm Tebarth, one of the prominent German communists who, together with his friend, another German communist, Hubert von Ranke (codename 'Moritz'), worked for the NKVD in Spain.[86]

The fact that David Wickes's letter was singled out and presumably sent to both Valencia and Albacete meant that the NKVD attached a special importance to it – which also must have helped it to reach us. But why? Probably because the documents found in Eileen's hotel room were from the very beginning meant to be the basis for trumped-up charges against Orwell. Although 'the law was what the police chose to make it',[87] the police – especially at a lower level – still had to pretend that their case was built on the evidence they discovered, and it seems that the list of entries in 'Various documents' was prepared and arranged with a view of charging 'the suspect'. Whether this was done convincingly or not is another matter. A summary of the 'Report on the Confiscated POUM materials' held the following information about Eric Blair:

> B. played a leading role in the Front Committee of the ILP, Lenin Division. B. took an active part in the May uprising. From previous correspondence, it can be assumed that subversive work was carried out in Albacete. It should also be noted that a notepad with records of various positions of the PSUC formations on the Aragon front was found among B.'s effects.[88]

Although the first sentence is true – Orwell was indeed an officer and in charge of the ILP contingent during its commander Bob Edwards' leave, the second is already dubious. The only evidence obtained during the search that

---

[84]  RGASPI, f.545, op.6, d.107, l.26.

[85]  RGASPI, f.545, op 6, d.107, l.6.

[86]  See Werner Abel, *Der Tod Hans Beimlers und die Reaktionen der KPD-Abwehr in Spanien* (Hans Beimler's Death and the Reaction of the German Communist Party in Spain). http://www.kfsr.info/2017/07/der-tod-hans-beimlers-und-die-reaktionen-der-kpd -abwehr-in-spanien-von-werner-abel/

[87]  Orwell, *Homage to Catalonia*, 201.

[88]  *Bericht vom Beschlagnahmten POUM-Material, Zusammenfassung* (Report on the Confiscated POUM material, Summary), RGASPI, f.495, op.183, d.5, l. 17–18.

in the view of the police could prove that Orwell 'took an active part in the May uprising' was Orwell's note to Eileen, 'telling her that he looked for her, that he is returning to his post at the Local Committee opposite the Hotel Falcon and that he took his "bomb" and asking her to keep out of danger. (PROBABLY WRITTEN DURING THE EVENTS OF MAY)'.[89] Capitals in the list seem to testify that the police thought that the note was a good enough evidence. As if answering this allegation, Orwell wrote, in *Homage to Catalonia*: 'Certainly I had carried arms during the May fighting, but so had (at a guess) forty or fifty thousand people'.[90]

Further conclusions look even more bizarre: Orwell could not have been involved, by any stretch of the imagination, in 'the subversive work carried out in Albacete', where the NKVD base was located. But this was what the desperate NKVD agents, faced with the task of building a case, tried to demonstrate by presenting 'previous correspondence'.

The first example of it was 'Eric B.to Eileen B. letter', which contained the words: 'Richard should already be in Albacete. He said he'd write to you soon'. It was obviously extracted from the rest of the Blairs' correspondence to back up 'the Albacete theory'. It is not clear whether the 'Richard' mentioned there was Richard Rees, but, in any case, it was obviously decided to keep this letter together with Rees's postcard.

David Wickes's letter from Albacete was apparently treated as the most important 'clue', although it does not contain anything extraordinary. Wickes, aged thirty-six, like other men who knew Eileen in Barcelona, seems to have been infatuated with her – indeed, his letter begins: 'I like and admire you'.[91] Then he complains of his roommates ('things get lost'[92]) and praises the food and exercises. It is the middle paragraph that, presumably had the potential to serve the agents as evidence of 'subversive work carried out in Albacete': 'I cannot write about the military and political situation, nor about my own activities. I have carried out my plans'.[93]

David Leslie Wickes, who went to Barcelona supported by the ILP but very soon moved to Albacete and joined the International Brigade, was most likely an agent himself.[94] Whether those who hoped to use Wickes's letter

[89]  RGASPI, f.545, op.6, d.107, l. 23.
[90]  Orwell, *Homage to Catalonia*, 201.
[91]  RGASPI, f. 545, op.6, d.107, l. 26.
[92]  Ibid.
[93]  Ibid.
[94]  The likelihood of it is mentioned in Bowker's *George Orwell*, 220, and in Boris Volodarsky, *Stalin's Agent* (Oxford: Oxford University Press, 2015), 494. Tapsell's report, 'Case of David Leslie Wickes' (MML Box C/13/13), states that on coming to Barcelona 'the chap contacted the Catalonian Party [i.e. PSUC] Foreigners Dept.', that is, the Foreign Service which worked under the NKVD.

to incriminate the Blairs expected him to play along is not known,[95] but evidently those higher up in the NKVD hierarchy felt that the evidence for the 'subversive work in Albacete' was insufficient and it was not included into Orwell's final indictment.

The same fate awaited the last piece of evidence against him – 'a notepad with records of the various positions of the PSUC formations on the Aragon front'. The notepad must have been part of what is listed among the confiscated papers as 'Various papers with drawings and scribblings'. Presumably, this was what Orwell calls 'my diaries'. It is hard to believe that 'various positions of the PSUC formations' took centre-stage there.

Still, Blair, with his 'leading position', had to be charged and the NKVD conceived a different plan – they decided to use materials seized from Charles Doran, one of Orwell's many friends in the English contingent, during the search in his room. Charles Doran was also first said to have 'connections with Albacete'[96] but the charge, as in Blair's case, was dropped later.

It may have proved unnecessary because the search of Doran's belongings produced a real scoop: the police found his letter to John Strachey written in Glasgow on 29 December 1936, where Doran expressed his indignation with the *Daily Worker*'s campaign against Trotsky and protested against Radek's indictment.[97] This obviously 'exposed' him as a Trotskyist. Doran, however, had never concealed his beliefs, and Walter Tapsell in his April report 'On the English Section' listed him among those who should not be allowed to join the International Brigade because of their Trotskyist views.[98]

Connecting Doran to Blair opened the possibility of directly accusing the latter of Trotskyism. The necessary piece of the puzzle, also found in Doran's room, was supplied by a letter from John McNair to Blair asking him to write for the ILP. NKVD agents were instructed to identify foreign organizations assisting the POUM:[99] the ILP fit the bill perfectly. Eric and Eileen Blair's final indictment 'Report to the Tribunal for Espionage and High Treason, Valencia', dated 13 July 1937 came to the conclusion that 'Eric Blair and his wife Eileen Blair . . . are confirmed Trotskyists . . . they must be considered liaison officers of the ILP with POUM'.[100]

The Spanish police, guided by the NKVD, was obviously given orders to identify any 'ring-leaders', who could later be accused at a show trial, so

[95] In the Blairs' final indictment, David Wickes is named as their 'contact' in Albacete; see 'Report to Tribunal for Espionage and High Treason', 13 July 1937. CW, XI, 31.
[96] Report on the Confiscated POUM material. RGASPI, f.495, op.183, d.5, l.16.
[97] RGASPI, f.545, op.6, d.125, l.96.
[98] Tapsell, 'On the English Section', MML Box C/13/7a.
[99] There is a special section in the Report on the Confiscated POUM material devoted to them. RGASPI, f.495, op.183, d.5, l.19.
[100] Report to Tribunal for Espionage and High Treason, 13 July 1937. CW, XI, 31.

their task was not only to prepare charges against individuals but to expose a plot, a conspiracy – as had been done for the Moscow trials. In Doran's indictment, Blair's name is mentioned twice. Written on the same day (13 July 1937) as the indictment of the Blairs, it states: 'In his material, you can often find the names KOPP and MACNAIR, as in Blair's material' and 'D., as well as Blair and MacNair, has written for the ILP'.[101] Luckily, Orwell, McNair and Doran managed to escape from Spain at the end of June, before these reports were compiled.

If they had stayed in Spain their fate would have, most likely, been the same as that of Georges Kopp, who – the only one of the four named in the document above – was arrested, spent eighteen months in Spanish prisons and had to endure repeated interrogation and torture. Physically, he was a much stronger man than Orwell, but the imprisonment seriously undermined his health. Given Orwell's poor health, it is difficult to imagine that he would have survived prison.

\* \* \*

On 23 June, Orwell and Eileen, together with John McNair and fellow militiaman Stafford Cottman, took a train to France. In Perpignan they met with Fenner Brockway, who was travelling to Spain because he was worried about the fate of POUM leaders and ILP comrades. After Brockway, two more ILP leaders, both MPs, travelled to Spain as part of foreign delegations trying to ensure the release or at least a trial of POUM and ILP prisoners – James Maxton in August and John McGovern in November 1937. In 1938 McGovern published a pamphlet titled *Terror in Spain*.

Orwell, no longer a witness of Spanish developments, now relied on the evidence of others for a clear picture of 'the Moscow technique of dealing with political prisoners'.[102] In *Homage to Catalonia* he quoted the Spanish Minister of Justice, Manuel de Irujo, as saying that 'the [Spanish] police had become "quasi-independent" and was in reality under the control of foreign Communist elements'.[103] At that time, Orlov and his men controlled not only the police but also the SIM, which 'in the first eight months of [its] existence . . . was a sinister tool in [their] hands'.[104] The Republican government could not do very much, as the lists of the victims were compiled by the NKVD.

In 1947, when Orwell wrote 'These man-hunts in Spain went on at the same time as the great purges in the USSR and were a sort of supplement to

[101] RGASPI, f. 545, op. 6, d. 125, l. 95.
[102] Brockway, *Inside the Left*, 317.
[103] Orwell, *Homage to Catalonia*, 168.
[104] Beevor, *The Battle for Spain*, 340–1.

them,[105] he could not, of course, have known that, in December 1936, Nikolay Yezhov, the new head of the NKVD, 'set up an "Administration of Special Tasks" . . . with "mobile groups" to carry out assassinations abroad ordered by Stalin. Its main field of action during the next two years was Spain'.[106] The chief 'special task' of the Administration was 'liquidation of the Trotskyist leadership',[107] primarily foreigners critical of Stalin.

In many cases, these foreigners were kidnapped and murdered. Rumour had it that they were taken secretly to the Soviet Union; today, however, it seems much more probable that they were killed in a building with a secret crematorium which 'enabled the NKVD to dispose of its victims without leaving any traces of their remains'.[108] The construction and security of the crematorium was under the command of Stanislav Vaupshasov, 'the Soviet Union's most abundantly decorated intelligence hero'.[109]

It has never been established what exactly happened to Mark Rein, the son of the Russian Menshevik Rafael Abramovich – he simply vanished in Barcelona even before the May events, on 9 April 1937. The Italian anarchist philosopher Camillo Berneri and his friend Francesco Barbieri were abducted on 7 May and their bodies were found the next day in the centre of Barcelona.[110] All those who were in any way connected to Trotsky were Soviet targets: Hans Freund, Trotsky's ardent young supporter, and Erwin Wolf, Trotsky's secretary, just 'disappeared' – the former on 2 August and the latter on 13 September 1937. The case of Austrian communist Kurt Landau was different, although his fate was the same.

A prominent political activist, Landau had broken with Trotsky and was publicly critical of him. Still, he was also profoundly shocked by the Moscow Trial of August 1936 and tried to organize a joint protest against Stalin in Paris. On his arrival in Barcelona in November 1936, he joined the POUM. He contributed to *La Batalla* and coordinated the POUM's international relations. His strong anti-Stalinism and profound naiveté are apparent in his letter of July 1937:

> In spite of this bloody hard situation I feel at home like a fish in water. . . . A fight to death has been declared between us and the Stalinists.

[105] Orwell, 'Preface to the Ukrainian Edition of *Animal Farm*', CW, XIX, 87.
[106] Christopher Andrew and Oleg Gordievsky, *KGB. The Inside Story of its Foreign Operations from Lenin to Gorbachev* (London, Sydney, Auckland, Toronto: Hodder & Stoughton, 1990), 121–2.
[107] Ibid., 121.
[108] Christopher Andrew and Vasili Mitrokhin, *The Mitrokhin Archive. The KGB in Europe and the West* (London: Penguin Books, 2000), 97.
[109] Ibid.
[110] Berneri had written prophetically: 'Today we fight Burgos, tomorrow we must fight Moscow for our freedom', quoted in Courtois and Panné, 340.

СОВЕТСКИЙ РАЗВЕДЧИК

С. А. ВАУПШАСОВ
1899—1976
5 к ПОЧТА СССР 1990

**Figure 2** A stamp in honour of Stanislav Vaupshasov, senior Soviet military adviser during the Spanish Civil War. The stamp was issued in 1990 as part of a series celebrating five famous spies of Stalin's time (Abel, Philby, Kudrya, Molody, Vaupshasov).

They are 10 times stronger than us, but until now they have had to deal with broken men [in the Soviet Union], a single intellectual [Trotsky] and some little groups. But here we have the possibility of developing, not just a little faction fight or a literary joust against them, but a class struggle of workers against Stalinism . . . the class struggle of the revolutionary working class and the Stalinist counter-revolution. It is on our tough bones that Stalin will break at least a few teeth. The POUM represents the only considerable political force on which Marxism can lean.[111]

Landau wrote this letter in hiding – first in the CNT headquarters and then in a POUM safe house. His wife, Katia Landau (née Julia Lipschutz), Eileen Blair's acquaintance, was arrested on 17 June; the NKVD tried in vain to learn her husband's whereabouts from her. Other people who knew Landau were arrested and tortured, but nobody betrayed him. In August, Orlov reported to the Centre:

> *Liternoe delo*[112] of Kurt Landau turned out to be the most difficult of all previous cases. . . . He went deep underground and . . . we have not so far been able to find him. Landau is without doubt a central figure in the underground organisation of the POUM. . . . In spite of the tense situation I think that, taking Landau's importance into account, we should not hesitate and that we should also carry out this *liter* in such a way as you instructed us.[113]

The last sentence reveals that Orlov was carrying out instructions from the Centre and, as Costello and Tsarev point out in their book, 'that meant Stalin'.[114]

Kurt Landau's hiding place was eventually discovered. He was kidnapped on 23 September 1937 and never seen again. Katia, who was then still in prison, was told of her husband's disappearance and demanded a judicial enquiry from the Spanish authorities. When she did not receive any information, she went on a hunger strike and persuaded 500 inmates in the women's prison to join her. Trying to prevent the hunger strike from spreading and the Landau case from gaining more notoriety, Minister of Justice Manuel de Irujo personally visited her in prison on 22 November. He also agreed to see John McGovern and his French colleague, who were on a mission to enquire into the affairs of the Republican government, allowed them to visit Katia and even gave them a permit to enter any prison they wished. The day after McGovern's visit to the hospital where she was held, Katia was released – only to be re-arrested a week later when Irujo lost his

---

[111] Quoted in Hans Shafranek, *Kurt Landau*. https://www.marxists.org/history/etol/revhist /backiss/vol4/no1-2/schafra.htm.

[112] '*Liternoe delo*' or '*liter*' in the NKVD jargon stood for assassination; the word 'liter' means a 'special letter' in Russian.

[113] Orlov to Centre, 25 August 1937, quoted in Costello and Tsarev, *Deadly Illusions* (London: Century, 1993), 286.

[114] Costello and Tsarev, *Deadly Illusions*, 286.

post as the Minister of Justice. This was a sign of the obvious tension between the government and 'foreign Communist elements', that is, the NKVD.

Katia was arrested for the second time when John McGovern was already back in Britain, but he saw this tension for himself when, after visiting several government prisons, he tried to use the permit signed by Irujo (still the minister then) and the Director of Prisons to enter one of the NKVD secret prisons, which the Spanish called *chekas*.[115] In the *cheka* Calle Vallmajor Prison in Barcelona he and his colleague were met by the official, who

> looked at our credentials with evident contempt. He informed us that he did not take any orders from the Director of Prisons or the Minister of Justice as they were not his bosses. We enquired who was his boss, and he gave us an address to the Cheka headquarters . . .
>
> We proceeded to the Cheka headquarters. . . . In due course there appeared two young men, neither of whom was Spanish. Our interpreter who has a wide knowledge of languages and countries, was convinced from their manner of speech that one was Russian and the other German. The Russian informed us that we could neither see inside the prison nor interview the prisoners.[116]

McGovern, who had been planning to leave Barcelona immediately, decided to wait and see 'who would win this battle – the Government or the Cheka'.[117] He waited a couple of days hoping that Irujo would be able to prevail and the British delegation would be allowed into the secret prison. This did not happen. 'The Ministers', McGovern concluded, 'were willing but powerless. The Cheka was unwilling and it had the power'.[118]

No visitors were allowed into *chekas* because the NKVD was using the methods it had always used. The threat of torture hung over everybody who fell into their hands. Emma Goldman spoke ironically about Stalin's 'aid' to the Republic: 'The world was still to learn that in addition to the arms, though never quite profuse, Stalin sent his Communist "blessing": his G.P.U. and Cheka methods to extort confessions'.[119] When planning her second trip to Spain in September 1937, Goldman was fully aware of the danger she faced

---

[115] *Cheka* – from the name of the Soviet secret police; see p. XV.

[116] McGovern, *Terror in Spain: How the Communist International has Destroyed Working-Class Unity, Undermined the Fight Against Franco, and Suppressed the Social Revolution* (London: ILP, 1938), 13.

[117] Ibid.

[118] Ibid.

[119] Goldman, 'Betrayal of the Spanish Workers' (*Spain and the World*, 21 January 1938).

as an outspoken critic of the communists and tried to prepare for it. She wrote to a friend a couple of days before her departure:

> Well, dear Roger, I am going into the cage of mad dogs. Whatever they will do to me, I want you and my other friends to know that I hope to die as I live. True one never knows what one will do under duress. I can only hope that I will be strong enough neither to 'confess' nor to 'recant' nor to grovel in the dust for my life. I have prepared a statement which has gone to Stella[120] and other of my comrades to give to the public if anything should happen to me. I have done that because I do not want the same miserable lies hurled against me by the Spanish Communists as those sent out broadcast against the unfortunate victims of the Moscow regime.[121]

Goldman managed to escape the NKVD and Katia Landau was freed a month after her second arrest (altogether she spent about six months in prison), thanks to the intervention of prominent Austrian and French socialists.[122] Katia fled to Paris and published a pamphlet called *Stalinism in Spain*, which Orwell was proud to own. In 1945, making a note of his pamphlet collection for his literary executor, he mentioned it as an example of one or two pamphlets that 'must be great rarities'.[123] Apart from presenting the general picture of the terror and describing her own experience in prisons, Katia also collected recollections of friends. What is obvious from all these accounts is that the methods of torture used in the *chekas* were exactly the same as those practised by Stalin's investigators before and after 1937.

The Spanish *chekas* did not make any special efforts to conceal who had set them up. On the contrary, they apparently wanted their prisoners to be aware of it. A description of the prison at 24 Puerta del Angel supports this:

> Down we went; a floor below it was already a little less hospitable – filthy and bare cellars, with grills before the windows, no daylight, air, beds, mattresses or coverings. But a large portrait of Stalin right in front of the door of our cell compensated us for a certain lack of comfort. We no longer doubted that we were, as had so often been repeated to us, in the hands of the Spanish state police, but what seemed to be

---

[120] Stella Ballantine was Goldman's niece.

[121] Goldman to Roger Baldwin, 12 September 1937, *Vision on Fire*, 152.

[122] One of them was Marceau Pivert, the man who together with Eileen convinced Orwell of the need to get out of the Hotel Continental on 20 June 1937 (Orwell to Doran, 2 August 1937, CW, XI, 64).

[123] Orwell, Notes for My Literary Executor, 31 March 1945, CW, XVII, 115.

rather strange was that in this curious state police, strangers of every nationality played a dominant role, often without speaking a single word of Spanish.[124]

The American couple Charles and Lois Orr were held in another *cheka* and their memoirs, written after their release and departure from Barcelona, confirm that the Russian, or NKVD, presence there, was obvious:

> There were Russians upstairs, directing the translating of our documents. When they took our fingerprints (five copies) or asked us questions or finally let some of us speak with our consuls, a Russian was always present, as translator, they said, though we could see no reason for translators when we spoke with our consuls.[125]

Orwell's commander and friend Georges Kopp had a particular predicament when in prison. Russian was his native language, as he had moved to Belgium from St Petersburg at the age of nine. During the eighteen months he spent in jail with NKVD officers interrogating him, he knew he should never betray the fact that he did not need an interpreter, because his Russian would have immediately confirmed for the NKVD that he was a 'Trotskyist'. Kopp was tortured in prison – in prisons, to be more precise, as there were about a dozen of them altogether. His interrogators were trying to make him 'confess' that the POUM was a nest of spies and traitors. Although luckily Orwell, who was tried *in absentia* at the POUM trial in autumn 1938, managed to avoid a personal prison or camp ordeal, his writer's sensibility helped him to imagine the feelings of the inmates. Lois Orr described what she felt when in a Barcelona *cheka* a Russian with 'excellent English' explained to her the gravity of her situation. He 'frightened [her] to death' as he explained where the five forms bearing her fingerprints would go:

> One goes to Moscow, one to the FBI in Washington, one to the Valencia government, one to the Generality police, and one we keep here. You will never be able to escape from your crimes.
>
> I did not know what my crimes were, but a terrifying feeling of utter helplessness overcame me at the thought of such a far-reaching organisation determined to incriminate me. I was only one person, alone, in face of such power.[126]

[124] Katia Landau, 'Stalinism in Spain' (*Revolutionary History*, Vol. 1, No. 2, Summer 1988). https://www.marxists.org/history/etol/document/spain/spain08.htm.
[125] *Letters from Barcelona*, 188.
[126] Ibid., 190.

Lois says that 'the Russian succeeded in producing abject fear'[127] in her, and Orwell's understanding of this fear is evident from the extraordinarily precise descriptions of helplessness experienced by Winston Smith in the cellars of the Ministry of Love. Numerous remarks about 'the concentration camp' made in Orwell's letters of summer and autumn 1938 show that he was training himself to live with the idea that 'the concentration camp looms ahead'.[128] On several occasions in his life, he felt this threat as very real. This does not necessarily mean that it *was* real but it certainly proves that his awareness of the possibility of a lawless, brutal attack, acquired in Spain, stayed with him forever.

His biographer Gordon Bowker recorded an episode imparted to him by Orwell's former pupil Tony Hyams, who bumped into the Blairs on board a ship in September 1938 when they were travelling to Morocco: 'Orwell was quite pleased to see him but seemed preoccupied. He told Hyams that, having fought in Spain, he was now terrified that, passing through Spanish Morocco to reach Marrakech he might be arrested and end up in a concentration camp.'[129] This, and his later suspicion that the young communist David Holbrook, who in autumn of 1946 came to remote Jura as a boyfriend of young Richard's nanny Susan Watson, 'had been sent by a Communist Party',[130] might be dismissed as paranoia, but this kind of paranoia was typical – in varying degrees – of practically everybody who had had any experience of Soviet methods, as it was based in real life. After all, Trotsky *was* assassinated in far-away Mexico; the Swedish diplomat Raoul Wallenberg *was* kidnapped in Budapest on 17 January 1945 by the counter-intelligence unit within the Red Army and never seen again.

There is no doubt that Orwell's understanding of the fear a human being feels when faced with a huge, ruthless, inhuman power was born in Spain, where he suddenly found himself under the arbitrary rules of an oppressive regime. Years later, when Orwell wrote a preface to the Ukrainian edition of *Animal Farm*, he found it necessary to explain to his Soviet readers that the workers and intelligentsia 'in a country like England', 'in which to hold and to voice minority views does not involve any mortal danger',[131] simply could not imagine that this might not be the case elsewhere. And in *Homage to Catalonia* he attempted to reveal to his English readers the difference

[127] Ibid.
[128] Orwell to John Sceats, 24 November 1938, XI, 237. For the threat of a concentration camp, see also letters to Jack Common (XI, 149 and 212), Geoffrey Gorer (XI, 321) and others.
[129] *Bowker*, 243.
[130] *The Orwell Tapes*, 218.
[131] Orwell, 'Preface to the Ukrainian edition of *Animal Farm*', CW, XIX, 88.

between their own country and the regime of political terror that reigned in Barcelona in June 1937: 'The jails were places that could only be described as dungeons. In England you would have to go back to the eighteenth century to find anything comparable.'[132] 'It was no use hanging on to the English notion that you are safe so long as you keep the law. Practically, the law was what the police chose to make it.'[133] 'In Spain there is – at any rate in practice – no *habeas corpus*, and you can be kept in jail for months at a stretch without even being charged, let alone tried.'[134]

In a long 1944 essay on Koestler, while acknowledging the contribution continental Europeans made to contemporary English literature, Orwell points out that in England

> there has been nothing resembling . . . *Darkness at Noon* because there is almost no English writer to whom it has happened to see totalitarianism from inside. . . . England is lacking, therefore, in what one might call concentration camp literature. The special world created by secret police forces, censorship of opinion, torture and frame-up trials is, of course, known about and to some extent disapproved of, but it has made very little emotional impact. . . . To understand such things one has to be able to imagine oneself as the victim, and for an Englishman to write *Darkness at Noon* would be as unlikely an accident as for a slave-trader to write *Uncle Tom's Cabin*.[135]

Orwell's encounter with the communist practices in Spain allowed him to identify with a person living under a totalitarian regime – he became that 'Englishman' who was 'able to imagine [himself] as the victim'.

[132] Orwell, *Homage to Catalonia*, 206.
[133] Ibid., 201.
[134] Ibid., 174.
[135] Orwell, 'Arthur Koestler', CW, XVI, 393.

# 4

# The totalitarian enemy

*'Totalitarian' is a new word and not well defined, but in general the
country is considered to be totalitarian when it is governed by a one-party
dictatorship which does not permit legal opposition and crushes freedom of
speech and the press . . . .[1]*

Orwell, 1946

In Spain, Orwell saw totalitarianism 'from inside'[2] and could never forget
it. It changed his attitude not so much to the Soviet Union itself as to the
role it played in the world and the danger it presented for other countries.
Ten years later, in 1947, he wrote that his experience of 'man-hunts' in Spain
was 'a valuable object lesson: it taught me how easily totalitarian propaganda
can control the opinion of enlightened people in democratic countries.'[3] His
first impulse on leaving Spain was to share his new understanding of Soviet
participation in the conflict but he soon realized how difficult it would be to
publish anything critical of communism in 'enlightened' Britain. His letter
to Rayner Heppenstall of 31 July 1937 – the first detailed letter he wrote on
returning to Wallington after his escape from Spain – reflects the strength of
his feelings both about the situation there and in Britain:

> Though we ourselves got out all right nearly all our friends and
> acquaintances are in jail and likely to be there indefinitely, not actually
> charged with anything but suspected of 'Trotskyism'. The most terrible
> things were happening even when I left, wholesale arrests, wounded men
> dragged out of hospitals and thrown into jail, people crammed together
> in filthy dens where they have hardly room to lie down, prisoners beaten
> and half starved etc., etc. Meanwhile it is impossible to get a word about
> this mentioned in the English press.[4]

[1]  Orwell's Notes to Swingler's article, CW, XVIII, 442.
[2]  Orwell, 'Arthur Koestler', CW, XVI, 393.
[3]  Orwell, 'Preface to the Ukrainian Edition of *Animal Farm*', CW, XIX, 87.
[4]  Orwell to Rayner Heppenstall, 31 July 1937, CW, XI, 53.

He then described the refusal of the *New Statesman* to publish his article about the suppression of the POUM and another decision not to publish the commissioned review of Borkenau's book *The Spanish Cockpit*. The magazine's editor, Kingsley Martin, wrote to Orwell that his review 'too far controverts the political policy of the paper'[5] – in the conflict within Republican forces, the *New Statesman* sided with the communists. So did Orwell's publisher Victor Gollancz who, although bound by a contract, refused to publish Orwell's book on Spain 'though not a word of it was written yet'.[6]

This hostile reaction to what he – an eyewitness – could say about the dramatic turn of events in Spain, which, he was adamant, people in Britain should know about, shattered him. He poured out his indignation in letters to friends (Heppenstall, Doran, Gorer, Davet, Connolly, Common), telling them again and again about Martin and Gollancz. Finally, he gave vent to his anger in an appropriately named article, 'Spilling the Spanish Beans':

> in England, in spite of the intense interest the Spanish war has aroused, there are very few people who have even heard of the enormous struggle that is going on behind the Government lines. Of course, this is no accident. There has been a quite deliberate conspiracy (I could give detailed instances) to prevent the Spanish situation from being understood. People who ought to know better have lent themselves to the deception on the ground that if you tell the truth about Spain it will be used as Fascist propaganda.[7]

In a later article, where he attacked the seemingly valid argument that telling the truth about the part played by the Communist Party would only 'prejudice public opinion against the Spanish Government and so aid Franco', he added contemptuously: 'I do not agree with this view, because I hold an outmoded opinion that in the long run it does not pay to tell lies'.[8]

This was the beginning of the rift between Orwell and the pro-communist left which lasted till the end of his life. 'Communism is now a counter-revolutionary force. . . . Communists everywhere are in alliance with bourgeois reformism and using the whole of their powerful machinery to crush or discredit any party that shows signs of revolutionary tendencies',[9]

[5]   Kingsley Martin to Orwell, 29 July 1937, in: Crick, 341.
[6]   Orwell to Heppenstall, CW, XI, 53.
[7]   Orwell, 'Spilling the Spanish Beans' (*New English Weekly*, 29 July and 2 September 1937), CW, XI, 46.
[8]   Orwell, '"Trotskyist" Publications' (*Time and Tide*, 5 February 1938), CW, XI, 114.
[9]   Orwell, 'Spilling the Spanish Beans', CW, XI, 46.

he wrote bluntly in 'Spilling the Spanish Beans'. And he had no illusions as to where it was coming from:

> The Communists, of course, deny that any direct pressure has been exerted by the Russian Government. But this, even if true, is hardly relevant, for the Communist Parties of all countries can be taken as carrying out Russian policy; and it is certain that the Spanish Communist Party, plus the right-wing Socialists whom they control, plus the Communist Press of the whole world, have used all their immense and ever-increasing influence upon the side of counter-revolution.[10]

He said this again in a more succinct form in his review of Borkenau's book *The Spanish Cockpit* – the review that Kingsley Martin would not publish: 'The most important fact that has emerged from the whole business is that the Communist Party is now (presumably for the sake of Russian foreign policy) an anti-revolutionary force. So far from pushing the Spanish Government further towards the Left, the Communist influence has pulled it to the Right'.[11]

This thought was as striking as it was new to him. Less than a year before, he was fuming in *Wigan Pier* against those who pointed at similarities between communism and fascism. Now he wrote: 'If Fascism means suppression of political liberty and free speech, imprisonment without trial etc., then the present regime in Spain *is* Fascism, so in apparently fighting against Fascism you come straight back to Fascism'.[12] Accepting this, he developed the idea further and came to the conclusion that 'Fascism and so-called democracy are Tweedledum and Tweedledee'[13] and 'you can't fight Fascism in the name of democracy, because what we call democracy in a capitalist country . . . in time of difficulty . . . turns immediately into Fascism'.[14]

Orwell was projecting the Spanish situation onto the British one, which was, of course, different, but this projection reflected his new perception of the Soviet role in the conflict. Now he clearly saw that 'the unity of all democratic forces' in the face of fascism, promoted so eagerly by the Socialist League,[15] or the Communist-Labour alliance popularized by the Left Book Club, were advancing the interests of the USSR: 'Of course, all the Popular

[10] Ibid., 44.
[11] Orwell, 'Review of *The Spanish Cockpit* by Franz Borkenau' (*Time and Tide*, 31 July 1937), CW, XI, 51–52.
[12] Orwell to Amy Charlesworth, 30 August 1937, CW, XI, 76.
[13] Ibid.
[14] Ibid.
[15] The Socialist League dissolved itself in May 1937 after being disaffiliated by the Labour Party in January.

Front stuff that is now being pushed by the Communist press and party, Gollancz and his paid hacks etc, etc only boils down to saying that they are in favour of British Fascism (prospective), as against German Fascism.'[16] He tried to imagine what British Fascism ('not of course called Fascism') would be like: 'You will have Fascism with Communists participating in it, and, if we are in alliance with the U.S.S.R., taking a leading part in it. This is what happened in Spain'.[17]

He held on to this position for the next two years. It was based on his belief that only workers, who 'keep the power in their own hands',[18] can stand up to fascism, whereas 'democratic' government could not be trusted. That is why he so vehemently opposed the idea of Britain fighting Germany in the imminent conflict. In summer 1937, he saw everything through the prism of the Spanish Civil War: he felt betrayed by the communists, betrayed by the Republican government and desperate about the fate of his comrades who failed to escape the clutches of the NKVD-controlled Spanish police.

\* \* \*

On arriving in Wallington at the very beginning of July, Orwell discovered a letter dated 31 May from Sergei Dinamov, editor-in-chief of the magazine *Internatsionalnaya Literatura* (International Literature), published in Moscow. This was already the second letter from Dinamov – in the earlier one, which most likely was 'a letter from Moscow' seized from Eileen's hotel room in Barcelona,[19] the Russian editor asked Orwell to write something for *International Literature*. In his second letter, Dinamov requested a copy of *The Road to Wigan Pier*, which he would like to have reviewed or even translated – he had read some reviews of the book and thought the magazine's readers might find it interesting. Orwell's response was typically comradely and honest:

> I would like to be frank with you, however, and therefore I must tell you that in Spain I was serving in the militia of the POUM, which as you [no] doubt know, has been bitterly denounced by the Communist Party and was recently suppressed by the Government; also that after what I have seen I am more in agreement with the policy of the POUM than with that of the Communist Party. I tell you this because it may be that your

[16] Orwell to Geoffrey Gorer, 15 September 1937, CW, XI, 80.
[17] Ibid.
[18] Orwell to Charlesworth, CW, XI, 76.
[19] See Chapter 3.

paper would not care to have contributions from a POUM member and I do not wish to introduce myself to you under false pretences.[20]

Arlen Blyum, a Russian historian of Soviet censorship, who first published this letter in translation, rightly suggested that Orwell must have been trying to avoid getting the editor into trouble. Still, one can imagine how frightening it was for the editorial board of *International Literature* to receive this letter in July 1937. It was obvious to them that they could easily be accused of, however unknowingly, committing a crime – they had approached a 'Trotskyist'! In these circumstances, the only way out was to write to the NKVD and ask their advice. This was done by Dinamov's deputy, Timofey Rokotov, on 28 July 1937:

To the Foreign Section, NKVD.

The editors of the journal *International Literature* have received a letter from England, from the writer George Orwell, which for your information I am sending you in translation in connection with the fact that the reply of this writer reveals that he is a member of the Trotskyist organisation POUM.

I request your instructions whether it is necessary to make any reply to him at all, and, if so, in what spirit?

May I remind you that I have not so far received an answer to the letter of R. Rolland [I] sent on to you.

Editor of the journal *International Literature*
(T. Rokotov)[21]

Judging by the editor's mention of Romain Rolland, seeking NKVD advice on editorial policy was not unique to the magazine's correspondence with Orwell, but rather a common practice. This time the 'instruction' was to reply to Orwell and the following letter was sent from Moscow to Wallington on 25 August:

Mr George Orwell

The Editorial Office of the *International Literature* has received your letter, in which you answer our letter dated May 31st. You are right to be frank with us, you are right to inform us of your service in the militia of the POUM. Our magazine, indeed, has nothing to do with POUM-members; this organisation, as the long experience of the Spanish

---

[20] Orwell to Sergei Dinamov, 2 July 1937, *The Lost Orwell*, 99–100.

[21] RGALI. f. 1397, op. 1, d. 867, l. 29, published in Arlen Blyum, 'George Orwell in the Soviet Union: A Documentary Chronicle on the Centenary of His Birth', trans. I.P. Foote (Oxford University Press, *The Library*, Vol. 4, No. 4, December 2003), 404–5.

**Figure 3** Sergei Dinamov, editor-in-chief of the *Internatsionalnaya Literatura* (International Literature) magazine. He corresponded with Orwell in 1937, was arrested in 1938 and shot in 1939. The prison photo was held in the FSB Archive and released to the human rights NGO Memorial in the early 1990s. Courtesy of the Memorial Archive.

    people's struggle against insurgents and fascist interventions has shown, is a part of Franco's 'fifth column' which is acting in the rear [of] the heroic army of Republican Spain.

*International Literature*

T. Rokotov [22]

That was the end of Sergei Dinamov's attempt to publish Orwell. It was soon followed by the end of his career, his liberty and then by the end of his life – he was arrested just over a year later, on 26 September 1938, and shot on 16 April 1939. The same fate was in store for Timofey Rokotov – he was shot in

[22]  Crick, 346.

1945. And *The Road to Wigan Pier* had to wait to be published in Russia for nearly eighty years.

*   *   *

It was a stroke of luck that Kingsley Martin asked Orwell to review *The Spanish Cockpit* by Franz Borkenau rather than any other book. Orwell liked everything about it: the political judgement close to his own and the 'calm and lucid'[23] style. At the beginning of his glowing review, he said: 'Dr Borkenau has performed a feat which is very difficult at this moment for anyone who knows what is going on in Spain; he has written a book about the Spanish war without losing his temper.'[24] He probably could not say the same thing about himself, but his was a different book. As he said later, he could not have written it if he 'had not been angry.'[25]

What must have particularly impressed Orwell about *The Spanish Cockpit* was that Borkenau saw the significance of the conflict between anarchists and communists *before* the final act of the drama. Unlike Orwell, Borkenau had no personal experience of Barcelona in May 1937 – he had left Spain at the end of February. All the conclusions he drew about the conflict, all the predictions he made about the situation in Spain, were the result of his being a sociologist ('social scientist', as he specified), and this was extraordinarily interesting for Orwell.

In his review, Orwell also noted that Borkenau paid special attention to the suppression of truth in the Spanish conflict and stressed that 'the Press [was] not even allowed to mention'[26] the anarchist-communist conflict. He quoted approvingly a long paragraph from *The Spanish Cockpit*, which ended with the statement, 'The concealment of the main political facts from the public and the maintenance of this deception by means of censorship and terrorism carries with it far-reaching detrimental effects which will be felt in the future even more than at present.'[27]

It does not seem so surprising then, that when Borkenau read Orwell's review published in *Time and Tide*, a much smaller and less prominent magazine than the *New Statesman*, he immediately wrote to Orwell:

> Your review, if I may be allowed to say so, stands out by its grasping and emphasising of precisely the one point which in my opinion is the central

[23]   Orwell, 'Review of *The Spanish Cockpit*', CW, XI, 51.
[24]   Ibid.
[25]   Orwell, 'Why I Write', CW, XVIII, 319.
[26]   Quoted in Orwell, CW, XI, 52.
[27]   Ibid.

point of the whole matter: the struggle between the revolutionary and the non-revolutionary principle, with the communists standing at the extreme right of the movement . . .. Unfortunately, with all the praise bestowed upon the book and by the people of very different opinions, this essential conclusion has been hushed up. That is why I am so grateful for your review, which has brought this matter emphatically into the foreground.[28]

In the same letter, Borkenau suggested that they should meet, specifically asking Orwell to update him on the situation in Spain. This started a friendship which meant a lot for both of them. Less than a year later, when *Homage to Catalonia* was published, *Controversy: a socialist monthly forum*, a tiny publication issued by the ILP, sent it to Borkenau for review. Impressed by the book, Borkenau wrote to the author stressing their affinity:

> If it is not immodest on my part to say so, I suppose your account is carrying on just at the point where mine is breaking off and the two together will form a picture of the revolutionary phase of the Spanish war . . .. To me your book is a further confirmation of my conviction that it is possible to be perfectly honest with one's facts quite irrespective of one political convictions.[29]

In the review that was signed *Historicus*, Borkenau also emphasized Orwell's truthfulness, especially in his description of the May events in Barcelona.[30] This insistence on honesty and truth brought the two very different men together. Unable to remain in Nazi Germany after 1933 as half-Jewish and a former communist, Borkenau first came to London in 1934, then spent the academic year 1934–5 teaching in Panama and settled in London in 1936. Since 1934 he had been writing in English. Orwell, who, according to his biographer Gordon Bowker, had an 'intuitive grasp of social patterns and processes' and a 'sociological imagination'[31] could not help admiring Borkenau's capacity for social analysis, unusual in Britain at that time – no wonder that a couple of years later he called his new friend 'one of the most valuable gifts that Hitler made to England'.[32] He avidly read Borkenau's articles and books, trusted his

[28] Borkenau to Orwell, 6 August 1937. The OA, UCL. Orwell/H/1/20/1.
[29] Borkenau to Orwell, 11 June 1938. The OA, UCL. Orwell/H/1/20/2.
[30] Historicus, 'Spain: Sham and Truth'. Review of *The Civil War in Spain* by Frank Jellinek and *Homage to Catalonia* by George Orwell. *Controversy*, No. 22, July 1938. https://wdc .contentdm.oclc.org/digital/collection/scw/id/16668/rec/29.
[31] Bowker, xii.
[32] Orwell, 'Review of *The Totalitarian Enemy* by F. Borkenau' (*Time and Tide*, 4 May 1940), CW, XII, 160.

**Figure 4** Sociologist Franz Borkenau. Date Unknown. Courtesy of his sons Felix and Peter Borkenau.

judgement on politics and learnt a great deal from him about the ways and methods of Soviet communists – a subject Borkenau knew inside out.

Born in Vienna in 1900, Franz Borkenau went to Leipzig University in Germany, joined the German Communist Party in 1921 and soon became the leader of all German communist students. He was then a 'sincere Marxist' who dreamt of world revolution.[33] In 1924 he started working for the

---

[33] Quoted from a letter of Richard Löwenthal, 1986, in: William D Jones, 'Toward a Theory of Totalitarianism: Franz Borkenau's *Pareto*' (*Journal of the History of Ideas*, Vol. 53, No. 3, 1992), 457.

Comintern – more precisely, for its research section, which operated from the building of the Soviet Embassy in Berlin and sent confidential reports on international developments to Comintern headquarters in Moscow. In the process, Borkenau, whose task was to study social democratic movements in Europe based on their own publications, learnt to read in ten languages, including Russian. At that time, toeing the party line in reports had not yet been absolutely necessary, but when the section was transferred to Moscow,[34] Borkenau realized that independence of opinion would no longer be allowed and decided to stay in Berlin, where he worked for another year for the Comintern's West European Bureau.

In 1928, however, he realized that he could no longer agree with the Comintern's position. As his friend Richard Löwenthal put it, he refused 'to accept a policy which treated the Social Democrats as "the main enemy" while the Nazi danger was rising'.[35] This led in 1929 to Borkenau's expulsion from the German Communist Party and his break with the Comintern. Commenting on Borkenau's reversion 'to a belief in liberalism and democracy', Orwell remarked: 'This is a development about as uncommon as being converted from Catholicism to Protestantism, but a sociologist could hardly have a better background'.[36]

In the 1930s, Borkenau indeed devoted himself to sociological research and, in particular, became one of the pioneers of the theory of totalitarianism. Even before he travelled to Spain, in his book *Pareto* (1936) Borkenau first stated: 'Bolshevism and Fascism can only really be treated as slightly different specimens of the same species of dictatorship'.[37]

Meanwhile in the Soviet Union, totalitarianism entered its most fearsome stage.

\*   \*   \*

The Great Terror of 1936–8 was the epitome of the wide-scale political repressions which had been carried out continuously between 1918 and 1953. It stands out, first of all, because of the sheer number of people arrested, tortured, and shot or sent to concentration camps and also because of

---

[34] The head of this section, Eugen Varga (1879–1964) moved to the USSR in 1927 and soon became Stalin's economic adviser.

[35] Löwenthal's Preface to Franz Borkenau's *End and Beginning* (New York: Columbia University Press, 1981), ix.

[36] Orwell, 'Review of *The Communist International* by Franz Borkenau' (*New English Weekly*, 22 September 1938), CW, XI, 202.

[37] Borkenau quoted in: Jones, 'Toward a Theory of Totalitarianism', 463.

sentencing by extra-judicial commissions or *troikas*,[38] often in the absence of the accused, without any defence or right of appeal. The sentencing was carried out in accordance with quotas issued by the NKVD, which prescribed a certain number of people to be shot in each region of the country, and a certain number to be sent to the Gulag. During a period of sixteen months (August 1937 to November 1938), over one and a half million people were arrested by the NKVD. About half of the arrested were sentenced to death, others to forced labour in concentration camps; 800,000 people were executed with a shot to the head. On average there were 50,000 executions a month, or 1,700 per day for nearly 500 days.[39]

Another prominent feature of the Great Terror was that, unlike other periods, in 1936–8 all sections of the population were targeted simultaneously: the 'old Bolsheviks', who brought about the revolution of 1917, together with 'counter-revolutionary elements' and former members of non-Bolshevik revolutionary parties (socialist revolutionaries, anarchists, etc.); the top leadership of the Red Army; the intelligentsia; religious believers; members of some national minorities (German, Polish, Latvian, etc.); wives of 'traitors to the Fatherland'; and those who had contacts abroad.

The scale of these repressions was not known in the West until much later, but the Moscow show trials, which presented the tip of the iceberg in more senses than one, did attract attention. They were evidence of Stalin's political struggle against his rivals and his desire to eliminate the old Bolshevik party and replace it with younger and obedient officials. The third Moscow trial held in March 1938 was known as the 'Bukharin-Rykov Trial' or, officially, the 'Trial of the Anti-Soviet "Block of Rightists and Trotskyists"'. It had taken over a year to prepare, and its outcome reaffirmed Stalin's complete domination.

This trial scared the British left more than its predecessors. The first Moscow trial in August 1936 was treated with apprehension; the second ('Radek-Pyatakov' trial) – in January 1937 – saw the British left 'inevitably less vocal . . . than it had been the previous August',[40] because of the constraints of the Unity Campaign, which required all its participants to curtail their criticism of the USSR. But by March 1938, with the campaign's collapse and the Socialist League's dissolution, while the terror was growing in the Soviet

---

[38] The *troika* means 'made up of three', this was the name of sentencing commissions, which consisted of the head of the local branch of the NKVD, the head of the local party committee and the local procurator.

[39] Nicholas Werth, 'Mass Crimes Under Stalin', *SciencesPo*. https://www.sciencespo.fr/mass -violence-war-massacre-resistance/fr/document/les-crimes-de-masse-sous-staline -1930-1953.html#title5.

[40] Corthorn, *In the Shadow of the Dictators*, 136.

Union and reaching the highest ranks of the Red Army by summer 1937, attitudes had changed. Borkenau wrote in his letter to Orwell: 'the killing of Tukhachevski,[41] ... in my opinion, was the turning point in Russia's prestige'.[42]

The third trial stunned even such an apologist of the Soviet regime as Harold Laski. A friend who met him as the news of the trial was breaking, recorded in his diary: 'Laski very disturbed. Said he could not believe allegations. Getting very worried about the Soviet Union. Even said he regretted learning Russian'.[43]

The ILP, which had been the most critical of the Communist position in Spain and had effectively broken with the CPGB over it, spoke most vehemently against the trials. *The Times* published an appeal to Stalin called 'End this Regime of Blood', signed by Fenner Brockway and four ILP MPs, which was also delivered to Ivan Maisky, the Soviet ambassador in London. They wrote:

> Recent developments in the USSR have shocked us. Because of our faith in Soviet Russia and the support which we had given it, we are compelled now to voice our protest. The workers of Britain can never be convinced that the majority of the Bolshevik leaders, the most intimate associates and co-workers of Lenin, men who gave their all to the cause of the workers, have become, as if overnight, champions of capitalism, spies and agents of the Imperialist powers and tools of Fascist reaction . . .
>
> The very nature of the 'confessions', the manner and technique of the trials, their preparation, the inconceivable character of the alleged crimes, not only failed to convince – they have the opposite effect. . . . This is not working- class justice. It is barbarous injustice. It is an insult and injury to all international working-class ideals and interests.[44]

When in June 1938 Orwell joined the ILP and publicly explained his motives for doing so in the party's newspaper *The New Leader*, he did not mention either this letter or the party's attempts to release ILP and POUM members from Spanish prisons. Still, there is no doubt that the ILP position on the terror in the USSR and in Spain meant a lot for him.

Joining the ILP was a public gesture. Meanwhile, privately, Orwell started avidly reading books and pamphlets about the Soviet Union. The pamphlets in his collection, which he must have read in 1937–8, included the recently

---

41  Mikhail Tukhachevsky, a Soviet military leader, one of the five Marshals of the USSR, was executed on 12 June 1937.
42  Borkenau to Orwell, 11 June 1938. The OA, UCL. Orwell/H/1/20/2.
43  Patrick Gordon Walker's diary, quoted in Corthorn, *In the Shadow of the Dictators*, 177.
44  *The Times*, 10 March 1938, quoted in Udy, *Labour and the Gulag*, 432–433.

published brochures on the Moscow trials: 'Summary of the Final Report of the Commission of Enquiry into the Charges Made Against Trotsky' (the so-called 'Dewey Report'); 'Why Did They Confess?' ('A Study of The Radek-Piatakov Trial'), with an introduction by James Burnham, written on 15 April 1937; Boris Souvarine's 'Cauchemar en URSS' (1937) and some others.

Souvarine's 48-page pamphlet was among the first Orwell read when he came back from Spain and it definitely left its imprint on him not only because of its passionate protest against Stalin's 'extermination of the Bolshevik "old guard"',[45] many of whom Souvarine knew personally,[46] but also – despite the scale of the tragedy – for its almost satirical approach to the absurdity of the trials:

> The presiding judge at the tribunal does not show the least professional curiosity . . . and does not raise an eyebrow when the accused admit to having stolen the Kremlin towers. The prosecutor spews a torrent of insults and opprobrium over the accused, without attempting to prove anything. . . . The defendants have dismissed the counsel for the defence preferring to represent themselves, and have entered as their plea every crime imaginable, or rather unimaginable, denouncing one another, admitting everything and more.[47]

But the most important aspect of the pamphlet for Orwell was Souvarine's answer to the question on everybody's mind: 'Why did they confess?':

> The explanation can be summed up in a word: the Terror . . . One shouldn't forget that between the trials, day-to-day repression never stopped; thousands of individuals have been executed each year without publicity, hundreds of thousands and millions locked up in prisons, 'detention centres', sent to concentration camps or deported, banished, transplanted to unhospitable climes. . . . Thousands of others, at relative liberty, have undergone interrogations by the GPU, trembling for their wives, their children, their elderly parents.[48]

---

[45]　B. Souvarine, *Cauchemar en URSS* (Paris: La Revue de Paris, 1 July 1937), 1. Translated by Ros Schwarz.

[46]　Born in Kiev in 1895 as Boris Lifschits, Souvarine was bilingual: he grew up in Paris, joined the Comintern in 1919, spent three years (1921–4) in Russia, but had to return to France after losing his position in the Comintern as a supporter of Trotsky.

[47]　Souvarine, *Cauchemar en URSS*, 5.

[48]　Ibid., 37.

Having started with this general description, Souvarine then goes deeper: being Bolsheviks, he argues, the accused did not care for the truth:

> The amoral morality of the 'Party above all else', has become a fundamental immoralism, prescribing a continual stream of lies, in all circumstances, in line with the Party's interest, understood in a particular manner and of which Stalin alone is the interpreter. To speak the truth would be to step away from the Party, hence from the state, to go from one world to another and, in denying Bolshevism, to deny one's own raison d'être.[49]

This explanation obviously impressed Orwell, and he remembered it later when he read Koestler's *Darkness at Noon,* which he called 'an expanded imaginative version of Souvarine's pamphlet'.[50]

Much of Souvarine's evidence of Stalin's terror came from the people he knew in Russia; in particular, from the writer Isaak Babel, who regularly came to Paris in the 1930s to visit his estranged wife and daughter before he fell victim to it himself.[51]

*       *       *

By June 1938 Orwell had read probably one of his first books about Russia – Andre Gide's *Return from the USSR,*[52] to which he unexpectedly referred a couple of years later when writing about Dickens. Discussing 'the American chapters of *Martin Chuzzlewit*', Orwell sees in them 'the reaction of a generous mind against cant. If Dickens were alive today he would make a trip to Soviet Russia and come back with a book rather like Gide's *Retour de l'URSS*'.[53]

Gide's book is friendly, generous, compassionate towards the USSR and yet, just like Dickens in Orwell's imagination, he is shocked when he is deceived: 'There are no more classes in the USSR – granted. But there are poor. There are too many of them – far too many. I had hoped not to see any – or, to speak more accurately, it was in order *not* to see any that I had come to the USSR'.[54] Gide notices how important compliance and conformism have become in the USSR, how 'the smallest protest, the least criticism is liable

[49]  Ibid., 39.
[50]  Orwell, 'Review of *Darkness at Noon* by Arthur Koestler' (*The New Statesman and Nation*, 4 January 1941), CW, XII, 357.
[51]  Souvarine, 'Last Conversations with Isaak Babel' (*Dissent*, Summer 1982).
[52]  Orwell to Yvonne Davet, 7 June 1938, CW, XI, 157.
[53]  Orwell, *Charles Dickens* (London: Gollancz, 1940), CW, XII, 35.
[54]  André Gide, *Return from the USSR* (New York: Alfred A. Knopf, Borzoi Books, reprint by Lightning Source Ltd), 40.

to the severest penalties, and in fact is immediately stifled'.[55] 'I doubt', he adds, 'whether in any other country in the world, even Hitler's Germany, thought has been less free, more bowed down, more fearful (terrorized), more vassalized'.[56] This leads him to reflections on the impossibility of truly great art and literature in a country where free thought is stifled – a theme that soon became particularly significant for Orwell.

The first book on Russia that Orwell reviewed was Eugene Lyons's *Assignment in Utopia* (1938), which he must have read at about the same time as *Return from the USSR*. This vivid and detailed description of life under communist rule taught him a lot. His memory retained numerous emotionally charged descriptions of Soviet life which later made their way into *Animal Farm* and, even more prominently, into *Nineteen Eighty-Four*. Orwell seems to have saved the salient details in his mind for future use, while the review he wrote of *Assignment in Utopia* tackles more general issues.

It starts with a brilliant parody of absurd charges and confessions heard at the Moscow trials. Being in a way a precursor of *Animal Farm*, the parody provides English readers with a complete explanation of how far-fetched and indeed ludicrous the accusations were ('A high official of the Post Office admits to having brazenly embezzled postal orders to the tune of £5,000,000, and also to having committed lèse-majesté by drawing moustaches on postage stamps'.[57]).

Only gradually does Orwell get to Lyons's book. He is cautious because 'any hostile criticism of the present Russian regime is liable to be taken as propaganda *against Socialism*; all Socialists are aware of this, and it does not make for honest discussion'.[58] Lyons, Orwell confirms, is honest and trustworthy – he went to the USSR as a true believer in socialism and spent six years there (1928–34) as a United Press Agency correspondent, trying to make the country as attractive as possible for his readers in the States, while being himself plagued by doubt and disillusionment, and then finally deciding to tell the truth. Only after establishing that the book is not *against Socialism*, that its author started with high hopes and his disillusionment was genuine, Orwell actually gets to the heart of the matter and states quite bluntly: 'The system that Mr Lyons describes does not seem to be very different from Fascism'.[59]

The features that characterize 'the system' mentioned by Orwell include: workers being deprived 'even of the elementary right to strike', internal

[55]  Ibid, 42.
[56]  Ibid.
[57]  Orwell, 'Review of *Assignment in Utopia* by Eugene Lyons' (*New English Weekly*, 9 June 1938), CW, XI, 159.
[58]  Ibid.
[59]  Ibid., 160.

passports, the omnipresence of the GPU, complete absence of freedom of speech and of the press, 'periodical waves of terror', 'the "liquidation" of kulaks or Nepmen', 'monstrous state trials', 'incredible confessions' and children saying 'I repudiate my father as a Trotskyist serpent'.[60] However, as though trying hard to remain objective, Orwell mildly reproaches the author for showing 'signs of being embittered by his experiences' and probably exaggerating 'the amount of discontent prevailing among the Russians themselves'.[61]

Read today, with the knowledge of what happened to the country, the book does not seem at all bitter but rather unusually full of compassion for the people who happened to live under a regime 'not very different from fascism'. As someone born within the Russian Empire (Uzlyany, Belarus), Lyons, although he grew up in Manhattan and spoke no Russian when he arrived in the USSR, soon learnt to 'see the physical and social landscape through Russian eyes'.[62] He quotes a woman who asked him, as an interpreter for a group of Americans, how they liked life in the USSR and on hearing that the visitors found it 'interesting', she burst out: 'Interesting! Sure, it's interesting to watch a house on fire. But we're *in* it! Tell them that, citizen!'[63]

Lyons left the country before the Great Terror actually started, but everyday life had already been difficult for ordinary people since the 'Year of the Great Break' – 1929, the end of NEP. It was then that the campaign targeting 'the kulaks' started. Lyons explains that these so-called 'kulaks' were usually 'the most efficient farmers'[64] or those 'who failed conspicuously to fall into line with the Soviet policies'.[65] It was their fate, their ruthless arrests and deportations that caused Lyons's greatest doubt and then disillusionment.

Orwell mentioned Lyons's book in his 1946 article 'What Is Socialism?' along with Koestler's *Darkness at Noon* and Gide's *Return from the USSR* as books that convey 'a fear that the original aims of the Socialist movement are becoming blurred',[66] so he obviously did not forget it. And yet, answering in 1947 a question from Dwight Macdonald about important books on the USSR, he failed to name *Assignment in Utopia* – maybe because its detailed descriptions of everyday life under totalitarianism had so firmly become part of his own image of it.

---

[60]  Ibid.
[61]  Ibid.
[62]  Ibid., 219.
[63]  Ibid., 227.
[64]  Ibid., 288.
[65]  Ibid., 276.
[66]  Orwell, 'What Is Socialism?' (*Manchester Evening News*, 31 January 1946), CW, XVIII, 61.

*      *      *

The book that Orwell does name and even single out in this letter to Macdonald as the 'book that taught [him] more than any other about the general course of the revolution'[67] is *The Communist International* by Franz Borkenau, which he read and reviewed in September 1938, just a couple of months after Lyons's book. What made *The Communist International* 'profoundly interesting'[68] for Orwell was the same quality that he admired in *The Spanish Cockpit*, which, he claimed, was 'a book different in *kind* from nearly all that have appeared on either side'.[69] There is no doubt that once again he was fascinated by Borkenau's sociological approach. Here it was used to explain how different the Russian revolutionary movement was from its Western counterparts and to expose the harm that Moscow-led Comintern guidance did to the Western left. For Orwell it was a revelation.

Borkenau starts by drawing particular attention to Lenin's idea of the party as 'the organization of professional revolutionaries, strictly selected, bound to absolute obedience towards the superiors of the organization, ready for any sacrifice, severed from every link with the outside world, classless in the most emphatic sense of the word, knowing neither satisfaction nor moral obligation outside the good of their organization'.[70] Borkenau traces this idea back to Nechaev[71] and the nineteenth-century revolutionary group *Narodnaya Volya* (People's Will) and asserts that it is 'a specific creation of the Russian soil . . . Having conquered Russia with his organization of professional revolutionaries, [Lenin] attempted to transfer the same methods to the West. The history of this attempt is the history of the Communist International' – and, according to Borkenau, 'an instance of a clash of cultures'.[72]

The situations in the West and Russia at the beginning of the twentieth century were radically different: many Western countries had had bourgeois revolutions hundreds of years earlier; they had a large and mature working class and an active 'labour movement'. None of these features was present in Russia, which, therefore, was unable to lend itself easily to Marxist interpretation. This did not, however, stop Lenin. He suggested that 'an organization of professional revolutionaries', that is, his party, should be '*linked* with the working-classes'.[73] Rosa Luxemburg, as Borkenau reminds his

[67]   Orwell to Dwight Macdonald, 15 April 1947, CW, XIX, 128.
[68]   Orwell, 'Review of *The Communist International*', CW, XI, 204.
[69]   Ibid., 202.
[70]   Borkenau, *The Communist International*, 26.
[71]   See Chapter 2.
[72]   Borkenau, *The Communist International*, 26.
[73]   Ibid., 45.

readers, protested against this idea as early as in 1904, writing in the German Marxist theoretical review *Neue Zeit*: 'In fact . . . the Social-democratic Party is not *linked* with the organisations of the working class, it is itself the movement of the working class'.[74]

Rosa Luxemburg, Borkenau deplores, 'would have been one person to withstand the influence of Russians' [in the Comintern],[75] but she was murdered on 15 January 1919 just before the Comintern was formed. On 21 January 1919 the decision was made in Moscow to hold the Comintern's founding congress, and it took place in March of the same year. The principles of the new organization were laid down: 'essential among them was the principle of the Soviet dictatorship and the duty of severing in every country all ties with both patriots and pacifists'.[76]

This was the beginning. In the years to follow the Comintern kept changing the tactics it prescribed for communists in different countries in accordance with the Soviet leaders' policies for this or that period. In his review of *The Communist International* Orwell presented Borkenau's conclusions:

> In the twenty years history of the Comintern Dr Borkenau traces three more or less separate periods. In the first period, the immediate post war years, there is a genuine revolutionary ferment in Europe, and in consequence the Comintern is an organisation sincerely aiming at world revolution and not entirely under Russian influence. In the second phase it becomes an instrument in Stalin's struggles first against the Trotsky-Zinoviev group, later against the Bukharin-Rykov group. In the third phase, the one we're in now, it becomes more or less openly an instrument of Russian foreign policy.[77]

As well as these three periods there were 'the alternate swings of Comintern policy to "left" and "right"'.[78] So Borkenau distinguishes 'six phases of Comintern policy, three of a "left" and three of a "right" character' and stresses that 'every turn to the left or to the right exceeds the previous one in vehemence'.[79]

Taking the 'left' turns first it is interesting to note that, in 1920 and 1921, the social-democrats are simply 'social-patriots', 'social-traitors', and the like. During the left period of 1924-5 they are already regarded as a bourgeois party, 'the third party of the bourgeoisie'. But during the

---

74  Luxemburg, quoted in ibid.
75  Borkenau, *The Communist International*, 148.
76  Ibid., 163.
77  Orwell, CW, XI, 202.
78  Ibid.
79  Borkenau, *The Communist International*, 415.

extreme rages of the left tack of 1929-34 they have been promoted to the rank of 'social-Fascists' and both the German and French communists unite in practice with the real Fascists of their respective countries in order to defeat 'social-Fascism'.[80]

It was precisely this last turn that made Borkenau's own break with the Comintern inevitable. But there is not a scrap of personal drama in his description. He writes dispassionately, giving more space to Germany because it was in Germany that the communists' tactics 'had their share in bringing about the success of Hitler; in other countries the action of the communists had no such historical importance'.[81] The German communists imagined that the overthrow of democracy 'meant actual revolution',[82] in the course of which, as they proclaimed, it would be equally easy to get rid of the Nazis – and this led to disaster. The Nazi victory proved Borkenau right, while his personal frustration was overshadowed by the scale of the world catastrophe.

The turns or swings to the right, Borkenau states, started in 1922-3, when 'united front' tactics were developed. There was still hope for world revolution although there was no more chance of it happening. Then in 1925-6, the unique roles of the communist parties in the West were partially abandoned – Zinoviev, the head of the Comintern at the time, even proclaimed that 'in Britain revolution may come, not through the door of the Communist Party but through that of the trade-unions'.[83] And then the 'collective security' strategy adopted in 1935 basically meant that revolutionary intentions were completely and officially renounced.

This was publicly confirmed by Stalin, who in his interview with American correspondent Roy Howard, published in *Pravda* on 5 March 1936, called the idea that the Soviet Union had had 'plans and intentions for bringing about world revolution "the product of a misunderstanding"' and then, answering the question of the puzzled journalist, whether this 'misunderstanding' was 'tragic', replied that it was 'a comical one. Or perhaps tragicomic'.[84]

These constant policy shifts had numerous consequences. Borkenau stressed that as these tactics had 'an importance quite incomparable with what they mean in any other movement' and were 'the chief measure of

[80] Ibid.
[81] Ibid., 347.
[82] Ibid., 343.
[83] Ibid., 414.
[84] Interview Between J. Stalin and Roy Howard. Marxists Internet Archive. https://www.marxists.org/reference/archive/stalin/works/1936/03/01.htm/.

orthodoxy,[85] any deviations from the current position were, of course, condemned and punished. But even more strikingly, 'theories had to be created every time in order to prove that the new tactics were within the scope of the accepted dogmas'.[86] Orwell remembered these succinct formulas less than a year later, in August 1939, when the Nazi-Soviet pact was signed. This was a *volte-face* obvious not only to those following the developments in the Soviet Union or the Comintern but to the whole world. Writing his first 'literary-sociological essay'[87] 'Inside the Whale', under the palpable influence of Borkenau, Orwell enriched the sharp observation of the sociologist with the vision and the language of the artist:

> Alliances, changes of front, etc. which only make sense as part of the game of power politics have to be explained and justified in terms of international Socialism. Every time Stalin swaps partners, 'Marxism' has to be hammered into a new shape. This entails sudden and violent changes of 'line', purges, denunciations, systematic destruction of party literature, etc., etc. Every Communist is in fact liable at any moment to have to alter his most fundamental convictions or leave the party. The unquestionable dogma of Monday may become the damnable heresy of Tuesday, and so on.[88]

The totalitarian change of tactics and the consequences it entails would soon become the pivotal theme in *Nineteen Eighty-Four*. It is, therefore, not surprising that Orwell was so grateful to the author of *The Communist International*, whose originality he noted with admiration at the end of his review: 'It is a most encouraging thing to hear a human voice when fifty thousand gramophones are playing the same tune.'[89]

\*   \*   \*

At the end of November 1938, Orwell, distressed by yet another bout of the bronchitis, which had attacked him after six months in a sanatorium and another three in the warm climate of Morocco, wrote to a friend: 'What with all this illness I've decided to count 1938 as a blank year and sort of cross it off the calendar.'[90] And yet his new novel *Coming Up for*

85  Borkenau, *The Communist International*, 230.
86  Ibid.
87  Orwell to Leonard Moore, 14 July 1939 [4 July?], CW, XI, 365.
88  Orwell, *Inside the Whale* (London: Gollancz, 1940), CW, XII, 101.
89  Ibid.
90  Orwell to Sceats, 24 November 1938, CW, XI, 237.

*Air*, the draft of which he had nearly finished by the end of 1938, and the two reviews published in January 1939 show how thoroughly he had grasped – in one short year – the essence of a totalitarian system. Before *Animal Farm*, where he 'tried with full consciousness of what [he] was doing to fuse political purpose and artistic purpose into one whole',[91] he attempted, maybe not so consciously, to do it at least twice: in *Homage to Catalonia*, where his artistic purpose struggles against the constraints of a documentary narrative, and in *Coming Up for Air*, where politics bursts out of the traditional novel form. One image from this novel, where the traits of Nazi and Soviet regimes are brought together, forecasts the atmosphere of *Nineteen Eighty-Four*:

> The world we're going down into, the kind of hate-world, slogan-world. The coloured shirts, the barbed wire, the rubber truncheons. The secret cells where the electric light burns night and day, and the detectives watching you while you sleep. And the processions and the posters with enormous faces, and the crowds of a million people all cheering for the Leader till they deafen themselves into thinking that they really worship him, and all the time, underneath, they hate him so that they want to puke.[92]

Just as his letters of this time are full of the imminent threat of the concentration camp, so this image of the 'world we're going down into' never leaves him and is present in his book reviews too.

One of these is a review of Bertrand Russell's *Power: A New Social Analysis*. Orwell admired Russell's early book on Russia, *The Practice and Theory of Bolshevism* (1920), because 'he . . . was able to foretell in general terms a good deal that happened later'.[93] In his 1939 review he praises Russell for the same quality for which he praised Borkenau – the free thinking that remains independent whatever others say: 'Few people during the past thirty years have been so consistently impervious to the fashionable bunk of the moment'.[94] And yet Orwell's polemical mind immediately grasps the weak point in Russell's line of reasoning and his over-optimistic prognosis that power can be 'tamed'.

[91]  Orwell, 'Why I Write', CW, XVIII, 320.
[92]  Orwell, *Coming Up for Air* (London: Penguin Books, 1962), 149.
[93]  Orwell to Macdonald, 15 April 1947, CW, XIX, 128.
[94]  Orwell, 'Review of *Power: A New Social Analysis* by Bertrand Russell' (*The Adelphi*, January 1939), CW, XI, 312.

Underlying this is the idea that common sense always wins in the end. And yet the peculiar horror of the present moment is that we cannot be sure that this is so. It is quite possible that we are descending into an age in which two and two will make five when the Leader says so. Mr. Russell points out that the huge system of organised lying upon which the dictators depend keeps their followers out of contact with reality and therefore tends to put them at a disadvantage as against those who know the facts. This is true so far as it goes, but . . . it is quite easy to imagine a state in which the ruling caste deceive their followers without deceiving themselves. Dare anyone be sure that something of the kind is not coming into existence already? One has only to think of the sinister possibilities of the radio, State-controlled education and so forth, to realise that 'the truth is great and will prevail'[95] is a prayer rather than an axiom.[96]

Here, for the first time, Orwell names the key features of the regime based on lies. He mentions 'the huge system of organized lying' which he will describe in *Animal Farm* and *Nineteen Eighty-Four*; the centralized indoctrination ('the sinister possibilities of the radio, State-controlled education and so forth'), which this system imposes, and the figure of the Leader, whose authority is undisputable, and therefore any absurdity he pronounces like 'two plus two will make five' is taken as the ultimate wisdom.

Although Russell in his book writes about the tyranny of Hitler, the formula used by Orwell refers to the Soviet Union – he discovered it just six months earlier in Lyons's *Assignment in Utopia*. Its origin was local and crystal clear to the people living in the country: it was a numerical embodiment of the slogan 'The Five-Year Plan in Four Years'. Lyons described how overwhelmed he was to see it 'posted and shouted throughout the land'.

The formula . . . seemed to me at once bold and preposterous – the daring and the paradox and tragic absurdity of the Soviet scene, its mystical simplicity, its defiance of logic, all reduced to nose-thumbing arithmetic . . . 2 + 2 = 5: in electric lights on Moscow housefronts, in foot-high letters on billboards, spelled planned error, hyperbole, perverse optimism; something childishly headstrong and stirringly imaginative. . . .

---

[95]  Coventry Patmore, 'The Unknown Eros', quoted by Orwell in ibid.
[96]  Orwell, 'Review of *Power*', 311–312.

**Figure 5** Soviet Poster '2+2 = 5' by Yakov Guminer, 1931. It reads: 'The arithmetic of an alternative industrial-economic plan: 2+2, plus workers' enthusiasm = 5'. Wikimedia Commons.

The preliminary triumphs, which evoked the slogan 2 + 2 = 5, were in many ways disastrous. They corroborated the taskmasters' inherited conviction that any miracles could be worked through this sorcery of naked force.[97]

---

[97]  Lyons, *Assignment in Utopia*, 240.

The 'sorcery of naked force' will be of course later presented by Orwell in conjunction with this very formula, which has already entered his consciousness as the symbol of 'the age we are descending into'.

In another review – of Nicholas de Basily's book *Russia under Soviet Rule. Twenty Years of Bolshevik Experiment* (1938) – published at about the same time, Orwell continues the theme of indoctrination and its influence on human beings. He is a bit sceptical about the book's author – 'an exile, of course, [who] . . . is attacking the Bolshevik experiment from a liberal-capitalist point of view'.[98] Still, Orwell mostly accepts de Basily's analysis of the Russian economy and 'the intellectual, moral and political developments – the ever-tightening party dictatorship, the muzzled press, the purges, the oriental worship of Stalin'.[99] Where he takes issue with the author is in his optimism, his hope 'that the spirit of freedom is bound to revive sooner or later'.[100]

> The terrifying thing about the modern dictatorships is that they are something entirely unprecedented. Their end cannot be foreseen. In the past every tyranny was sooner or later overthrown, or at least resisted, because of 'human nature', which as a matter of course desired liberty. But we cannot be at all certain that 'human nature' is constant. It may be just as possible to produce a breed of men who do not wish for liberty as to produce a breed of hornless cows. The Inquisition failed, but then the Inquisition had not the resources of the modern state. The radio, press censorship, standardised education and the secret police have altered everything. Mass-suggestion is a science of the last twenty years, and we do not yet know how successful it will be.[101]

This genuine concern about 'human nature' under oppressive regimes will become the main theme of Orwell's most important novel. At the beginning of 1939, he felt that there was just one way to resist the oppression: 'no system except democracy can be trusted to save us from unspeakable horrors'.[102] This was his general assertion, but in the review of de Basily's book he also speaks directly about Russia and its leaders:

[98] Orwell, 'Review of *Russia Under the Soviet Rule* by N. de Basily' (*New English Weekly*, 12 January 1939), CW, XI, 315. Nicholas de Basily (1883–1963) was a Russian diplomat, who prepared the text of the tsar's abdication in 1917.

[99] Ibid., 316.

[100] Ibid.

[101] Ibid., 317.

[102] Orwell, 'Review of *Power*', 311.

It is noticeable that Mr de Basily does not attribute all the shortcomings of the present Russian régime to Stalin's personal wickedness. He thinks that they were inherent from the very start in the aims and nature of the Bolshevik party. It is probably a good thing for Lenin's reputation that he died so early. Trotsky, in exile, denounces the Russian dictatorship, but he is probably as much responsible for it as any man now living, and there is no certainty that as a dictator he would be preferable to Stalin, though undoubtedly he has a much more interesting mind. The essential act is the rejection of democracy – that is, of the underlying values of democracy; once you have decided upon that, Stalin – or at any rate something *like* Stalin – is already on the way.[103]

In this review, Orwell used the word 'democracy' both as a 'system' and as the 'underlying values of democracy' – after his Spanish experience the first still seemed to him capable of turning into fascism. He was still against the war with Hitler's Germany, as he was sure it would only bring the communists to power. He supported Chamberlain's Munich agreement of September 1938. And yet, he knew that war was inevitable and hoped to remain 'both anti-war and anti-fascist' and 'to put up a fight'[104] against German or British fascism. However, August 1939 changed everything.

\*    \*    \*

On 23 August 1939, the Soviet Union signed a Non-Aggression Pact with Nazi Germany. Western communists and fellow-travellers were profoundly shocked by this turn of events. Some of them were ready to remain loyal to the Soviet Union under any circumstances, but others, including Orwell's publisher Victor Gollancz and even the general secretary of the British Communist Party Harry Pollitt, voiced their protest, although the CPGB itself did not dare to disobey – it was easier to change the general secretary.

Orwell must have been less surprised than many – he hadn't quite excluded the possibility of the USSR 'joining up' with Germany,[105] but the developments affected him deeply, and he completely discarded his scepticism about the war against Hitler. On 9 September 1939, six days after war was declared, he applied to the Ministry of Labour and National Service to help the war effort. At the same time, the Soviet-Nazi agreement made him think even harder about the impact of the Soviet Union on the Brits.

[103] Orwell, 'Review of *Russia Under the Soviet Rule*', 317.
[104] Orwell to Herbert Read, 5 March 1939, CW, XI, 340.
[105] Orwell, 'Review of *Union Now* by Clarence K Streit' (*The Adelphi*, July 1939), CW, XI, 360.

The genre of 'semi-sociological literary criticism'[106] which he chose for 'Inside the Whale' gave him yet another opportunity to fuse artistic and political purpose and to use Borkenau's sociological methods. The main hero of 'Inside the Whale' is Henry Miller, whom he sees as 'Jonah in the whale's belly',[107] that is, a passive observer of the evil events happening around him rather than an active fighter against them. Yet Miller, Orwell insists, unlike many others, sees very clearly what is going on: 'In his case the whale happens to be transparent. Only he feels no impulse to alter or control the process that he is undergoing.'[108]

Miller's social passivity is attractive to Orwell as a contrast to the socially active writers of the 1930s: Auden, Spender, McNeice, Isherwood, Lehman and others, who fell under the 'almost irresistible fascination'[109] of the Communist Party. This was the beginning of the 1930s, the time of the economic crisis, when '"disillusionment" was immensely widespread' and it was the Communist Party that gave these young writers 'something to believe in. Here was a Church, an army, an orthodoxy, a discipline. Here was a Fatherland and – at any rate since 1935 or thereabouts – a Fuehrer. . . . Patriotism, religion, empire, military glory – all in one word, Russia. Father, king, leader, hero, saviour – all in one word, Stalin'.[110]

This was one reason for the attraction of communism. The other was that these young, 'soft' British writers had no idea what was really happening in the Soviet Union and were unable to imagine it. Unlike Henry Miller, who, with all his indifference, cynicism and irresponsibility, could see the world around him, they seemed to be rather blind, especially as far as their ideal was concerned: 'To people of that kind such things as purges, secret police, summary executions, imprisonment without trial etc., etc., are too remote to be terrifying. They can swallow totalitarianism *because* they have no experience of anything except liberalism.'[111]

Of course, Orwell's own shock in Spain, where he realized that not every country in the world had *habeas corpus*, was also the result 'of the softness and security of life in England'.[112] However, in contrast to him, the British intelligentsia 'who contributed to the cult of Russia'[113] had generally had quite limited exposure to reality:

[106] Orwell to Gorer, 3 April 1940, CW, XII, 137.
[107] Orwell, 'Inside the Whale', CW, XII, 107.
[108] Ibid.
[109] Ibid., 101.
[110] Ibid., 102–3.
[111] Ibid., 103.
[112] Ibid.
[113] Ibid., 104.

It is the same pattern all the time: public school, university, a few trips abroad, then London. Hunger, hardship, solitude, exile, war, prison, persecution, manual labour – hardly even words. No wonder that the huge tribe known as 'the right left people' found it so easy to condone the purge-and-Ogpu side of the Russian régime and the horrors of the first Five-Year Plan. They were so gloriously incapable of understanding what it all meant.[114]

As Orwell was finishing his essay when Nazi Germany and the Soviet Union having signed the pact started dividing the world, desperate, tragic notes appeared in his conclusion:

> Until recently . . . it was generally imagined that Socialism could preserve and even enlarge the atmosphere of liberalism. It is now beginning to be realized how false this idea was. Almost certainly we are moving into an age of totalitarian dictatorships – an age in which freedom of thought will be at first a deadly sin and later on a meaningless abstraction. The autonomous individual is going to be stamped out of existence.[115]

It would take Orwell nine years to develop his novel about 'the autonomous individual' unable to survive under a totalitarian dictatorship, but he first articulated the danger in 'Inside the Whale'. And in the same essay, in the same breath, so to speak, he made another prediction – no less distressing for him – the death of literature:

> Literature, as we know it is an individual thing, demanding mental honesty and a minimum of censorship. And this is even truer of prose than of verse. It is probably not a coincidence that the best writers of the thirties have been poets. The atmosphere of orthodoxy is always damaging to prose, and above all it is completely ruinous to the novel, the most anarchical of all forms of literature. . . . The novel is practically a Protestant form of art; it is a product of the free mind, of the autonomous individual.[116]

The development of this idea would follow in other articles, culminating in 'The Prevention of Literature', one of Orwell's finest essays of the late 1940s, but in his original plan for *Nineteen Eighty-Four* the protagonist was

---

[114] Ibid.
[115] Ibid., 110.
[116] Ibid., 105.

to be a writer – so close to each other were for him the destruction of the individual and of literature, and so personally he took the consequences of the 'totalitarian dictatorship'.

\* \* \*

A couple of months later a response to the Nazi-Soviet pact was published by Franz Borkenau. Orwell reviewed his new book *The Totalitarian Enemy* in May 1940. *The Totalitarian Enemy* was written at extraordinary speed – 250 pages took Borkenau just two months. The great advantage of this rush was that it was indeed an immediate reaction to the pact and to the joint, German and Soviet, invasion of Poland. The sudden friendship and alliance of the USSR and Germany confirmed for Borkenau what he had been saying all along, at least since 1936, when he wrote *Pareto*: 'The German-Russian pact has . . . convinced many of those who were reluctant to believe it that Russia and Germany, in the main, do not represent two antagonistic types of social régime, but one and the same type. It is no longer heresy to describe the Nazi régime as "Brown Bolshevism" and Stalin's régime as "Red Fascism".'[117]

Borkenau names the features the two regimes have in common: one-party rule, one man's 'will and whim'[118] governing the party and the country, state control over everything, complete disregard for individual liberty, messianic ambitions . . . Although Orwell started his review by claiming that 'this is not one of Dr Borkenau's best books'[119] and concluded it with: 'in spite of some brilliant passages, [this book] seems to have been hastily written and has faults of arrangement',[120] he still thought very highly of what Borkenau had to say.

He fully agreed with the author of *The Totalitarian Enemy* about 'the more and more striking resemblance between the German and Russian régimes' and 'the eye-opener' of 'the Hitler-Stalin pact'.[121] He mocked both British conservatives and socialists, 'Blimps and Left Book Club readers', as he called them, for misunderstanding the nature of Nazism, because both of them had 'so to speak, a vested interest in ignoring the real facts. Quite naturally the propertied classes wanted to believe that Hitler would protect them against Bolshevism, and equally naturally the Socialists hated having to admit that the man who had slaughtered their comrades was a Socialist himself'.[122]

[117] Franz Borkenau, *The Totalitarian Enemy* (London: Faber and Faber Ltd, 1940), 13.
[118] Ibid., 24.
[119] Orwell, 'Review of *The Totalitarian Enemy*', CW, XII, 158.
[120] Ibid., 160.
[121] Ibid., 158.
[122] Ibid.

Building on Borkenau's description of Germany and Russia as countries
with state-controlled economics (based on collectivism) and led by a small
group of rulers (oligarchy), Orwell brought out their similarity in a term he
coined: 'The two régimes, having started from opposite ends, are rapidly
evolving towards the same system – a form of oligarchical collectivism'.[123] He
obviously felt the term was fitting because about seven years later he used it
in *Nineteen Eighty-Four*, in the title of Goldstein's book *Theory and Practice
of Oligarchical Collectivism*.

Orwell had always found it more important to fight the Soviet
totalitarianism rather than the German one, as Nazism – especially since
the start of the war – had been almost universally condemned, whereas the
invariable infatuation of the British left with communism presented, he was
sure, a very real danger for Britain. Borkenau's comparison of the two, no
doubt, helped Orwell to see the difference between them clearer.

> Russia is infinitely more totalitarian than Germany. Massacres of
> important party leaders and their personal following have occurred in
> Germany occasionally, but in Russia they have been a constant feature
> of the régime. . . . Many of the original leaders of the Nazis are still in
> power, whereas Stalin had to slaughter the whole of the old guard of
> Bolshevism. . . .
>
> Whatever sufferings the Nazis may have brought upon the German
> masses, they bear no comparison with the disasters that accompanied
> the first Five-year plan in Russia when whole villages died of hunger and
> millions of recalcitrant peasants were deported to die in the Arctic. . . .
> Russia is the totalitarian country *par excellence*; Communism the purest
> and most logical form of totalitarianism.[124]

Borkenau thoroughly analysed both the economics and ideology of Nazism
and Bolshevism, paying special attention to the phenomenon he somewhat
clumsily called 'scapegoatism', that is, the search for somebody to blame as an
intrinsic feature of any totalitarian regime. He was sure that, in this respect
too, the Russian regime had moved much further than the German:

> In Germany only one group is consistently treated as a scapegoat: the
> Jews. The other groups persecuted by the régime are not mere scapegoats
> (though they may be occasionally used as such) but its real adversaries.
> But in Russia, charges of Trotskyism, Fascism, and conspiracy with

---

[123] Ibid., 159.
[124] Borkenau, *The Totalitarian Enemy*, 227.

foreign countries have been bandied about against all and sundry, leading to the physical destruction of the greater part of the higher Civil Service and of the military commands. Scapegoatism is all-pervading in Russia.[125]

'Enemy of the people' was the label almost indiscriminately applied to anybody whom the Soviet regime wanted to destroy. In his review, Orwell stressed that neither of the two totalitarian regimes really cared about the actual nature of this or that enemy. It was not even so much about ideology, but mostly about power struggle, that is why both Nazism and Bolshevism were ready to attack any group of population in their countries. Orwell started his sarcastic analysis with the Nazis:

> If the first step is to smash the Socialist to the tune of anti-Marxist slogans – well and good, smash the Socialists. If the next step is to smash the capitalists to the tune of Marxist slogans – well and good, smash the capitalists. It is all-in wrestling, and the only rule is to win. Russia since 1928 shows distinctly similar reversals of policy, always tending to keep the ruling clique in power. As for the hate-campaigns in which totalitarian régimes ceaselessly indulge, they are real enough while they last, but are simply dictated by the needs of the moment. Jews, Poles, Trotskyists, English, French, Czechs, Democrats, Fascists, Marxists – almost anyone can figure as Public Enemy No 1. Hatred can be turned in any direction at a moment's notice like a plumber's blow-flame.[126]

One of the most conspicuous features of all Orwell's writings about Borkenau is his almost subconscious translation of Borkenau's sociological concepts into images and then developing these images. The last simile, slightly modified, re-appears in *Nineteen Eighty-Four* when the 'Two Minutes Hate' is depicted:

> A hideous ecstasy of fear and vindictiveness, a desire to kill, to torture, to smash faces in with a sledge-hammer, seemed to flow through the whole group of people like an electric current, turning one even against one's will into a grimacing, screaming lunatic. And yet the rage that one felt was an abstract, undirected emotion which *could be switched from one object to another like the flame of a blowlamp* [emphasis added].[127]

---

[125] Ibid., 228–9.
[126] Orwell, 'Review of *The Totalitarian Enemy*', CW, XII, 159.
[127] Orwell, *Nineteen Eighty-Four*, 15.

Apart from the blowlamp, this description of the 'Two Minutes Hate'
resurrects yet another image: that of smashing 'faces in with a sledge-
hammer', which originated in *Coming Up for Air* as 'smashing people's faces
in with a spanner'[128] – both reveal that Orwell had been thinking about
the psychological impact of the state's struggle against 'Public Enemies' for
many years. The concept of this induced hate experienced by the crowd
had crystallized in his mind long before he came to write *Nineteen Eighty-
Four* – it reflected the totalitarian reality. It seems probable that Orwell
had absorbed Eugene Lyons's faithful depiction of crowd reactions to the
Trial of the Industrial Party, which took place in Moscow in 1930, and let
his imagination work on it. *'Planned hysteria* [emphasis added] reached its
highest pitch in the Ramzin affair'[129] – this is how Lyons starts the chapter
titled 'Death to Wreckers' and continues:

> More than half a million workers from the factories and offices of Moscow
> marched through the snows in the grayish dusk on November 25. They
> marched under banners inscribed, 'Death to the agents of imperialism!',
> 'Kill the wreckers!', 'No mercy to these class enemies!' Hour after hour as
> night engulfed the city the gigantic parade rolled past the Nobles' Club
> and its shouts of 'Death! death! death!' could be heard in the columned
> ballroom where the trial was underway since three in the afternoon.[130]

\*    \*    \*

When about eight months later, in January 1941, Orwell reviewed Arthur
Koestler's *Darkness at Noon*, he switched from the sociological 'bird's-eye'
view of Soviet totalitarianism presented by Borkenau to the psychological
approach of a novelist, who inevitably came to similar conclusions. Koestler's
novel was an example of what Orwell would later call the 'literature of
disillusionment about the Soviet Union'.[131] Like Borkenau, Koestler was born
in Vienna but joined the German Communist Party after Borkenau had
already left it – at the very end of 1931. He spent the following year in the
Soviet Union, wrote a book, *Red Days and White Nights,* glorifying Soviet
achievements, and then worked in the Comintern's anti-fascist propaganda
unit.

[128] Orwell, *Coming Up for Air*, 148.
[129] Lyons, *Assignment in Utopia*, 370.
[130] Ibid., 372.
[131] Orwell, 'Arthur Koestler', CW, XVI, 393.

His disillusionment was gradual and determined by two events – the same that led him to write *Darkness at Noon*. The first one was his ninety-day confinement in 1936 in one of Franco's prison in Seville, where he witnessed almost daily executions of his comrades and expected to be executed himself at any moment. This made him suddenly fully appreciate the value of human life. The second was the fate of his childhood friend, and later lover, Eva Striker, who in 1932 lived with her husband, the physicist Alexander Weissberg, in Kharkov – it was there that Koestler stayed for several months while writing his book.

In May 1936, when Eva was Director of Design at the famous Dulevo porcelain factory near Moscow, she was arrested and initially charged with 'having inserted swastikas into the pattern on the teacups which she had designed for mass production'[132] and then – after she was transferred from the Lubyanka to a prison in Leningrad – with plotting to assassinate Stalin. After months of solitary confinement punctuated by interrogations, threats and pressure from her tormentors, which made her attempt suicide, she was released in September 1937 and expelled from the Soviet Union as an 'undesirable alien'. Koestler was shocked to realize to what extent Eva's experience in a Soviet prison was similar to his own in a fascist one. This uncanny similarity was reflected in the opening pages of *Darkness at Noon*, where Rubashov, on waking up, can't immediately figure out what prison he is in – one run by the NKVD or by the Gestapo.

*Darkness at Noon*, however, went further. 'Brilliant as this book is as a novel, and a piece of prison literature', argued Orwell in his review, 'it is probably most valuable as an interpretation of the Moscow "confessions" by someone with an inner knowledge of totalitarian methods'.[133] The psychology of Rubashov, who admitted committing crimes he had not committed and was shot after his 'confession', was the most interesting aspect of the book for Orwell, the reviewer, and also the one that proved most relevant for his own work.

'If one writes about the Moscow trials one must answer the question, "Why did the accused confess?", and which answer one makes is a political decision',[134] claimed Orwell in his 1944 essay on Koestler. There he offered three possible explanations for the 'confessions': (1) the accused were guilty; (2) they were tortured; and (3) 'they were actuated by despair, mental bankruptcy and the habit of loyalty to the party'.[135] He decisively dismissed

[132] Arthur Koestler, *The God that Failed: Six Studies in Communism* (London: Hamish Hamilton, 1950), 78.
[133] Orwell, 'Review of *Darkness at Noon*', CW, XII, 359.
[134] Orwell, CW, XVI, 397.
[135] Ibid., 396.

the first one; unmistakably chose the second for his own, *Nineteen Eighty-Four*, version of an incarceration in a totalitarian country; and accepted the possibility of the third one, that is, of Koestler's suggestion, supported by Souvarine's pamphlet, that the Bolsheviks had been corrupted by Bolshevism.

In *Darkness at Noon*, it is Rubashov's first investigator, Ivanov, who tells him that his confession would be 'the last service required of him by the party'.[136] Orwell's comment on it echoed Souvarine's pamphlet: 'Rubashov ultimately confesses because he cannot find in his own mind any reason for not doing so. Justice and objective truth have long ceased to have any meaning for him. For decades he has been simply the creature of the Party, and what the Party now demands is that he shall confess to non-existent crimes'.[137]

As Koestler's book was the only novel out of all the works on Russia Orwell reviewed, it probably made him think harder than the others about human psychology. Less than a year earlier, in 'Inside the Whale' he had written that freedom of thought was impossible in the 'age of totalitarian dictatorships',[138] but in his talk 'Literature and Totalitarianism',[139] broadcast by the BBC for the first time in May 1941, he took yet another step towards exposing the phenomenon of thought control:

> Totalitarianism has abolished freedom of thought to an extent unheard of in any previous age. And it is important to realise that its control of thought is not only negative, but positive. It not only forbids you to express - even to *think* - certain thoughts but it dictates what you *shall* think, it creates an ideology for you, it tries to govern your emotional life as well as setting up a code of conduct. And as far as possible it isolates you from the outside world, it shuts you up in an artificial universe in which you have no standards of comparison. The totalitarian state tries, at any rate, to control the thoughts and emotions of its subjects at least as completely as it controls their actions.[140]

In the talk, Orwell's main preoccupation was with the position of the writer under totalitarianism. But for his own future novel, the logic of 'positive control' - that is, instilling in ordinary people what they ought to think - was perhaps even more important.

---

[136] Orwell, 'Review of *Darkness at Noon*', CW, XII, 358.

[137] Orwell, CW, XVI, 396.

[138] Orwell, 'Inside the Whale', CW, XII, 110.

[139] Orwell, 'Literature and Totalitarianism'. The shortened version of the talk was published in *The Listener*. See CW, XII, 501–5.

[140] Ibid., 503.

In *Darkness at Noon*, he was particularly interested in the difference between the two investigators interrogating Rubashov: Ivanov, a contemporary of his prisoner, who is suddenly removed from the proceedings and shot, and a younger man, Gletkin, 'the good Party man', whom Orwell calls 'an almost perfect specimen of a human gramophone'.[141] Gletkin, who has grown up after the revolution, is completely ignorant of two things: the outside world and the past, which, Orwell stresses, 'leaves him not only without pity but without imagination or inconvenient knowledge'.[142] He is a product of Soviet propaganda and therefore 'no distinction between guilt and innocence exists in his mind. . . . As he sees it, anyone capable of thinking a disrespectful thought about Stalin would, as a matter of course, attempt to assassinate him. Therefore, though no attempt at assassination has perhaps been made, it can be held to have been made'.[143] This is, of course, a direct, if perhaps not the only, source of the concept of 'thoughtcrime' and the word Orwell coined for it in Newspeak.

\*    \*    \*

One of the most striking consequences of the Nazi-Soviet pact on the human level was the behaviour of Orwell's publisher Victor Gollancz. Once he realized that supporting Communists would from now on mean supporting the Nazis, which he could not do, he started looking for ways to change his reputation. Keeping close to Orwell, whose anti-communist *Homage to Catalonia* he had recently rejected, seemed to him an appropriate thing to do. By winter 1941 Gollancz was busy collecting a book of essays under the unambiguous title *Betrayal of the Left*, where apart from his own numerous essays, he published two of Orwell's: 'Patriots and Revolutionaries' and 'Fascism and Democracy'. The latter, especially, contained one of Orwell's most thorough denunciations of the pernicious dependence of the British communists on Russia, as

> they were forced not only to change their most fundamental opinions with each shift of Russian policy, but to insult every instinct and every tradition of the people they were trying to lead. . . . Instead of pointing out that Russia was a backward country which we might learn from but could not be expected to imitate, the Communists were obliged to

---

[141] Orwell, CW, XII, 358.
[142] Ibid.
[143] Ibid.

pretend that 'the purges', 'liquidations', etc. were healthy symptoms which any right-minded person would like to see transferred to England.[144]

A new 'shift of Russian policy' took place very soon and was not initiated by Russia – on 22 June 1941, Hitler invaded the Soviet Union and many communists in Britain 'were forced' – yet again! – 'to change their most fundamental opinions'.[145] On 3 July Orwell recorded in his diary:

> One could not have a better example of the moral and emotional shallowness of our time, than the fact that we're now all more or less pro-Stalin. This disgusting murderer is temporarily on our side, and so the purges, etc., are suddenly forgotten. So also with Franco, Mussolini, etc., should they ultimately come over to us.[146]

Victor Gollancz was profoundly relieved that he did not need to quarrel with the Soviet Union anymore – in his new book *Russia and Ourselves*, he, as an experienced demagogue, simply gave another – pro-Soviet – slant to everything he said in *Betrayal of the Left*. Sir Walter Citrine, who had been so critical of the Moscow trials and the general lack of freedom in the Soviet Union, also tried to strike a positive note in his new book *In Russia Now*, while G. D. H. Cole, an economist, libertarian socialist and former member of the Socialist League, who in 1939 opposed Stalin's dictatorship, now stated in his book *Europe, Russia and the Future*: 'Much better to be ruled by Stalin than by the destructive and monopolistic cliques which dominate Western capitalism'.[147] Britain, which had been fighting Hitler all alone for nearly two years, was delighted to welcome an ally.

Orwell, who in 1941–3 was too busy with his work for the BBC to argue with pro-Soviet writers, could not resist responding to Harold Laski's book *Reflections on the Revolution of Our Time* the moment he became freer. In his review, he dealt specifically with Laski's attitude to the Soviet Union:

> Needless to say, Professor Laski is very unwilling to admit a resemblance between the German and Russian systems. There is much in the Soviet régime that he does not like, and he says so with the boldness that will

[144] Orwell, 'Fascism and Democracy' (*The Left News*, February, 1941), CW, XII, 380.
[145] Ibid.
[146] Orwell, *War-Time Diary*, 3 July 1941, *The Orwell Diaries*, ed. Peter Davison (London: Penguin Books, 2010), 317.
[147] G. D. H. Cole, *Europe, Russia and the Future* (London: Victor Gollancz Ltd, 1941), 104.

get him into serious trouble with the left. . . . But he does defend the purges, the GPU, and the crushing of intellectual liberty.[148]

*The Observer* published it in October 1943. However, just five months later, in March 1944, Orwell's review of Laski's new book *Faith, Reason and Civilisation*, was rejected – 'evidently because of its anti-Stalin implications'.[149] 'This', Orwell explained to his American editor and friend Dwight Macdonald, 'will give you an idea of the kind of thing you can't print in England nowadays'.[150]

---

[148] Orwell, 'Review of *Reflections on the Revolution of Our Time* by Harold J. Laski' (*The Observer*, 10 October 1943), CW, XV, 271.
[149] Orwell to Macdonald, 23 July 1944, CW, XVI, 298.
[150] Ibid.

# 5

# The Russian myth

*Nor was I ever . . . – supposing I had had the power – anxious to interfere with the USSR's internal affairs. I merely object to Russian interference here.* [1]

Orwell, 1946

By July 1944, Orwell knew exactly 'what kind of thing you can't print in England nowadays'[2] – *Animal Farm*. It took him just three months to write his fairy story, about six to find a publisher who would agree to bring it out and twelve months of waiting till it actually happened. His best book to date, his masterpiece could not reach its readers sooner, because of the unwillingness of publishers to produce anything that attacked Britain's 'great ally', the Soviet Union.

In his letter to Macdonald, Orwell named two reasons for it: 'Editors will print nothing anti-Russian because of the supposed Russomania of the general public and also because of the complaints which the Soviet government is constantly raising about the British press.'[3] There was also the third one: 'the servility of the so-called intellectuals',[4] which a bit later he expanded to: 'the servility with which the greater part of the English intelligentsia have swallowed and repeated Russian propaganda from 1941 onwards'.[5] In fact, all three reasons were intertwined, because, to a large extent, both 'the supposed Russomania of the general public' and 'the servility . . . of the English intelligentsia' were actively fuelled by Soviet agents.

This does not mean that there was no genuine admiration for the courage and resilience of Russian soldiers. The battles of Stalingrad (summer 1942–winter 1943) and Kursk (summer 1943) changed the character of the war on the Eastern front, and the Brits were certainly impressed by the Red Army and grateful to it. Fredric Warburg, who eventually published *Animal Farm* – and reaped the fruit of its success – revealed years later that his own wife had

[1]  Orwell's Notes to Swingler's article, CW, XVIII, 443.
[2]  Orwell to Macdonald, 23 July 1944, CW, XVI, 298.
[3]  Ibid.
[4]  Orwell, London Letter, 17 April 1944 (*Partisan Review*, Summer 1944), CW, XVI, 159.
[5]  Orwell, 'The Freedom of the Press', CW, XVII, 255.

threatened to divorce him, if he published Orwell's satire, as she could not bear the thought of ingratitude towards the Russians, 'who had done most of the fighting since 1941'.[6]

Dwight Macdonald, writing in the November 1944 issue of *politics* about the problem identified by Orwell, tried to analyse the psychology of the growing pro-Soviet sentiment in Britain and explained it by 'the universal feeling that the Red Army "saved" England – as it probably did – coupled with admiration for Russian military strength. And from such admiration it is a short step to the conclusion that a nation which performs so effectively on the battlefield must be pretty wonderful behind the lines'.[7]

Creating the feeling that the Soviet Union was 'pretty wonderful behind the lines' required, however, a special effort – facts which contradicted it were simply 'kept out of the Press'[8] and those that confirmed it were enthusiastically supported. In Britain the whole process was supervised and guided by one dedicated man – the remarkably active and successful Soviet mole Peter Smollett, who, between 1941 and 1945, held the position of Head of the Soviet Relations Division in the Ministry of Information. He was exposed in print only after his death in 1980, first in Chapman Pincher's book,[9] then in others, and finally, his work for the Soviet Union was confirmed by the Mitrokhin Archive – the notes copied by KGB archivist Vasili Mitrokhin and successfully retrieved from his house by MI6 in 1992. Even Smollett's codename was revealed – ABO.[10]

A friend and colleague of Kim Philby and Guy Burgess, Smollett remained less well known than other Soviet spies. This was partly because, unlike them, he was neither British nor a member of the privileged class (born Harry Peter Smolka, an Austrian Jew, he anglicized his name in 1938), and partly because his role in actual spying was rather inconspicuous: the information he supplied was passed on via Philby, Burgess and Blunt. After Burgess's defection to the Soviet Union in 1951, some documents he left behind 'were identified as Smollett's from the typewriter on which he had typed them which had a defective letter "m"'.[11] As an informer, he probably was not very prominent, but as an agent of influence he was second to none.

[6]   Fredrick Warburg, *All Authors Are Equal* (London: Hutchinson & Co, 1973), 49.
[7]   Quoted in Editorial note, CW, XVI, 299.
[8]   Orwell's Notes to Swingler's article, CW, XVIII, 441.
[9]   Chapman Pincher, *Their Trade Is Treachery* (London: Sidgwick & Jackson, 1981), 114.
[10]  Andrew and Mitrokhin, *The Mitrokhin Archive*, 158.
[11]  Charmian Brinson, '"Nothing Short of a Scandal"? Harry Peter Smolka and the British Ministry of Information', (*Journal for Intelligence, Propaganda and Security Studies*, Vol. 10. No. 1, 2016), 15.

Recruited in the early 1930s, he moved to Britain in 1933 and established his reputation as a journalist with a series of articles about the Soviet Arctic, later published as a bestselling book. Nobody seemed to be particularly bothered by the obvious propaganda nature of the book, where the Gulag was described as 'an idealistic experiment in social reform'.[12] Smollett then tried and failed to enter the British secret services but succeeded, in 1939, in getting a job with the newly formed Ministry of Information. His journalistic background, combined with a never-failing vivacity – George Weidenfeld saw him as 'ebullient' and 'buccaneering'[13] – enabled Smollett to make many friends in high places, including David Astor, who considered him for the post of Editor of the *Observer*,[14] and Brendan Bracken, the owner of the *Financial Times* and a close friend of Churchill's. In 1940 Bracken became the PM's parliamentary private secretary and, in July 1941, the Minister of Information. So, when the Soviet Relations Branch (later Division) was created in the Ministry in late August 1941, 'after some debate and a brief search',[15] Smollett was put in charge of it.

Not that the British establishment was completely unaware of the dangers posed by the propaganda aspect of the alliance with the USSR. As early as September 1941, Churchill asked Bracken 'to consider what action was required to counter the present tendency of the British public to forget the dangers of Communism in their enthusiasm over the resistance of Russia'.[16] Even if Bracken had considered this request, he showed no particular vigilance in carrying it out. The first thing he did after Smollett's appointment to the Soviet Relations Branch was to make him his personal liaison with the Soviet Embassy in London, so granting the Soviet agent a unique opportunity to visit the Embassy regularly and contact there his handler, Anatoly Gorsky, and, of course, the ambassador, Ivan Maisky.

Smollett very soon monopolized control over all information about Russia – in November 1941, the Ministry of Information adopted a policy which said: 'no statement about Russia or action to present Russia in England should be taken by [the Ministry] without Mr Smollett approving it from the angle of its suitability in the eyes of the Russian Embassy'.[17] True, the

---

[12]  Andrew and Gordievsky, *KGB*, 266.

[13]  George Weidenfeld, *Remembering Good Friends. An Autobiography* (London: HarperCollins, 1995), 145.

[14]  Richard Cockett, *David Astor and the Observer* (London: Andre Deutch, 1991), 102.

[15]  Steven Merritt Miner, *Stalin's Holy War: Religion, Nationalism and Alliance Politics, 1941–1945* (Chapel Hill and London: The University of North Carolina Press, 2003), 247.

[16]  Policy Committee Notes, 4 September 1941, quoted in ibid., 249.

[17]  Decisions of a Ministry of Information meeting of 11 November 1941, quoted in ibid, 249.

document also stated that Mr Smollett was not entitled 'to approve any action to be taken without securing the approval of Mr Parker [the Head of the Ministry Home Division] as to its suitability from the Home angle',[18] but Smollett was extraordinarily clever in bypassing bans and circumventing official instructions, especially when he could play one British institution against another.

'His influence and tentacles were extensive', writes Richard Davenport-Hines in his recent book *Enemies Within*. 'He was not merely a Soviet informer, but a master at misdirection by hints, distractions, suppressions and diversions'.[19] Smollett's self-declared tactics was 'to "steal the thunder" of radical left propaganda . . . by outdoing them in pro-Russian publicity while at the same time keeping this publicity on such lines as we think most desirable'.[20] This approach impressed the Brits but it also 'suited the NKVD policy perfectly', as it 'preferred to have the Soviet case put by apparently impartial British speakers rather than by open Communists'.[21] Thus, pro-Soviet organizations like the Russia Today Society, the Friends of the Soviet Union and the newspaper *Russia Today* were excluded from propaganda exercises, which allowed Smollett to display his 'even-handedness' – against this background, his refusal to engage White Russian émigrés or indeed anybody else who would be critical of Stalin looked absolutely fair in British eyes.

Smollett organized 'Anglo-Soviet Weeks' with rallies and exhibitions all over Britain (where, of course, no criticism of the USSR was permitted); supported the 'Society for Cultural Relations with the USSR', directly controlled by Moscow; and helped to circulate its publication – the *Anglo-Soviet Journal*.[22]

In August 1942, London decided to publish its own paper, called *Britansky Soyuznik* (The British Ally) to promote Britain in the USSR, and Smollett rushed to supervise this too.[23] It was he who in 1943 organized the visit of the Archbishop of York to Russia, trying to convince Russia's allies that the country was experiencing a religious revival. It was also thought particularly important to assure the citizens of Eastern Europe and the Balkans of this revival, in the hope that this would allay their fears about the imminent advance of the Red Army. Smollett commissioned the whole

[18]  Miner, *Stalin's Holy War*, 247.
[19]  Richard Davenport-Hines, *Enemies Within. Communists, the Cambridge Spies and the Making of Modern Britain* (London: William Collins, 2019), 278.
[20]  H.P. Smollett, 'Policy on Russian Propaganda' (early October 1941), quoted in Andrew and Gordievsky, 267.
[21]  Andrew and Gordievsky, *KGB*, 267.
[22]  Miner, *Stalin's Holy War*, 248.
[23]  Ibid., 250.

series of programmes, which the BBC duly broadcast both in English and in the mother tongues of Orthodox believers.[24] At the BBC he had a reliable supporter – Guy Burgess, who was employed there as a producer between 1941 and 1944. This rather subtle work went hand in hand with numerous day-to-day activities, neatly summarized by Andrew and Mitrokhin:

> By 1943 Smollett was using his position to organise pro-Soviet propaganda on a prodigious scale. A vast meeting at the Albert Hall in February to celebrate the twenty-fifth anniversary of the Red Army included songs of praise by a massed choir, readings by John Gielgud and Laurence Olivier, and was attended by leading politicians from all parties. The film *USSR At War* was shown to factory audiences of one and a quarter million. In September 1943 alone, the Ministry of Information organised meetings on the Soviet Union for 34 public venues, 35 factories, 100 voluntary societies, 28 civil defence groups, 9 schools and a prison; the BBC in the same month broadcast 30 programmes with a substantial Soviet content.[25]

This was the situation in 1943. The next year, 1944, apart from a similar frenzy of activity, was marked in Smollett's life by three events. First, the British Government awarded him an OBE; then, between April and June, as part of his duties for the MOI he visited the Soviet Union (Ambassador Maisky, who wrote to Moscow to obtain permission for Smollett to visit Leningrad and Kiev, felt it necessary to stress: 'He is not at all hostile to us'[26]); and finally, on his return he was approached by a London publisher who wanted his opinion about a short book he was going to print, called *Animal Farm*. Although this last event was probably much less important for him than others, it became the one that Smollett has remained chiefly remembered for.

\*  \*  \*

'The Freedom of the Press' – Orwell's most powerful essay on the 'servility of the English intelligentsia' – starts with the story of *Animal Farm* being rejected by four publishers. 'Only one of these had any ideological motive',[27] Orwell wrote, referring obviously to Victor Gollancz, of whose pro-

---

[24] Ibid., 271.

[25] Andrew and Mitrokhin, *The Mitrokhin Archive*, 158.

[26] Maisky's letter to F. Molochkov, 18 May 1944, quoted in Oksana Zakharova, *Kak v SSSR prinimali vysokikh gostey* (Entertaining Visiting Dignitaries in the Soviet Union) (Tsentpoligraf, 2018), Appendix 3.

[27] Orwell, CW, XVII, 253.

communist stance he had always been aware. The second was Nicholson & Watson, who, as Orwell informed his literary agent, had also – like Gollancz – said that it was 'bad taste to attack the head of an allied government in that manner, etc.'[28] The reply of T. S. Eliot, then the director of Faber and Faber, was much more sophisticated, although still negative, but Orwell's deepest shock came when Jonathan Cape, who, having agreed in May to publish *Animal Farm,* announced in June that he had changed his mind, because of 'the reaction that [he] had received from an important official in the Ministry of Information'.[29] In a letter to Orwell's agent, Leonard Moore, Cape confessed that the official's opinion had 'given him seriously to think' and took care to explain what his thoughts were:

> If the fable were addressed generally to dictators and dictatorships at large then publication would be all right, but the fable does follow, as I see now, so completely the progress and development of the Russian Soviets and their two dictators, that it can apply only to Russia, to the exclusion of other dictatorships. Another thing: it would be less offensive if the predominant caste in the fable were not pigs. I think the choice of pigs as the ruling caste will no doubt give offence to many people, and particularly to anyone who is a bit touchy, as undoubtedly the Russians are.[30]

Quoting this extract in 'The Freedom of the Press', Orwell supplied it with a footnote: 'It is not quite clear whether this suggested modification [re: the choice of pigs as the ruling caste] is Mr . . . 's own idea, or originated with the Ministry of Information, but it seems to have the official ring about it'.[31] According to Crick's biography, the MOI official was also Jonathan Cape's friend, who 'followed up their conversation with a personal letter strongly imploring Cape not to publish a book that would so damage good relations with Russia'.[32] There is very little doubt today that the friend who was so concerned about 'good relations with Russia' was Peter Smollett. The 'touchiness' of the Russians had always been his favourite argument,[33] so Orwell's guess about 'the official ring' was most likely correct.

---

[28] Orwell to Moore, 15 April 1944, CW, XVI, 155.
[29] Jonathan Cape to Moore, 19 June 1944, in Crick, 455.
[30] Ibid., 456.
[31] Orwell, CW, XVII, 254.
[32] Crick, 455. Crick relied on the letter of Veronica Wedgewood, who in 1944 used to work for Jonathan Cape. Crick's Collection, GB 1832 CRCK6/2/24.
[33] Smollett to Dew (FO) quoted in Brinson, 14.

He must also have guessed that the 'MOI official' was Smollett, whom he had met, and the astuteness which enabled Orwell to see through him seems striking. Unlike his literary friends deceived by Smollett's brilliance, or the British establishment, impressed by his diligence, or MI5, which was unable to find sufficient evidence to expose him, Orwell was sure of the man's duplicity. He confidently included Smollett in the list of 135 crypto-communists and fellow-travellers, which he compiled for himself and his friend Richard Rees, and wrote against his name: 'Almost certainly agent of some kind. Said to be careerist. Very dishonest'.[34] And when in May 1949 he updated the list for the Information Research Department,[35] he added even more certainty to his assessment: 'gives strong impression of being some kind of Russian agent. Very slimy person'.[36] And yet, the IRD, like other British institutions, was not sufficiently interested even to look into the case.

However, on first reading Jonathan Cape's letter, Orwell seemed to be less shocked by the 'veiled censorship' exercised by the MOI than by the behaviour of the publisher, who asked the MOI for guidance:

> The MOI does not, of course, dictate a party line or issue an index expurgatorius. It merely 'advises'. Publishers take manuscripts to the MOI, and the MOI 'suggests' that this or that is undesirable, or premature, or 'would serve no good purpose'. And though there is no definite prohibition, no clear statement that this or that must not be printed, official policy is never flouted. Circus dogs jump when the trainer cracks his whip, but the really well-trained dog is the one that turns his somersault when there is no whip.[37]

This confirmed the thought he had earlier expressed in his London Letter: 'The servility of the so-called intellectuals is astonishing'.[38] He meant, of course, left-wing intellectuals – it was their blind loyalty to the 'disgusting murderer . . . temporarily on our side',[39] that caused his anger and frustration. Without telling the story of *Animal Farm* rejections he wrote in the same London Letter:

> It is now next door to impossible to get anything overtly anti-Russian printed. Anti-Russian books do appear but mostly from Catholic

[34] Orwell's List of Crypto-Communists and Fellow-Travellers, CW, XX, 255.
[35] See Chapter 6.
[36] *The Lost Orwell*, 147–8.
[37] Orwell, As I Please, 32 (*Tribune*, 7 July 1944), CW, XVI, 277.
[38] Orwell, London Letter, 17 April 1944, CW, XVI, 159.
[39] Orwell, *War-Time Diary*, 3 July 1941, *The Orwell Diaries*, 317.

publishing firms and always from a religious or frankly reactionary angle. 'Trotskyism', using the word in a wide sense,[40] is even more effectively silenced than in the 1935-39 period. The Stalinists themselves don't seem to have regained their influence in the press, but apart from the general Russophile feeling of the intelligentsia, all the appeasers, e.g., Professor E. H. Carr, have switched their allegiance from Hitler to Stalin.[41]

Passionately wishing *Animal Farm* to appear in print and feeling certain that 'what it says wants saying, unfashionable though it is nowadays',[42] Orwell did not consider approaching right-wing publishers, although he realized that 'the extreme Tories will seize on anything anti-Russian, and don't necessarily mind if it comes from Trotskyist instead of right-wing sources'.[43] Instead, he tried to talk sense into colleagues on the left – the earnest, educated people, who honestly believed that capitalism should be replaced with socialism and the working class liberated. His essay 'The Freedom of the Press' was addressed to them.

It was due to be published as a preface to *Animal Farm* 'and a space was left for it, as the pagination of the proof shows'.[44] However, in August 1945, as the fable was finally about to be published, Orwell changed his mind and discarded the preface, which then got lost and resurfaced only in 1971.[45] The date when it was written is not known, but the feelings conveyed there are close to the anger and frustration he expressed in print in April–July 1944, when he was going through the ordeal of receiving refusals from publishers.

In the essay, Orwell gradually builds the case against the left, who felt it was their duty to support the Soviet Union whatever happened, and comes to the conclusion that this behaviour betrays a totalitarian mindset and leads to 'the general weakening of the western liberal tradition'.[46] Stressing the difference between official and voluntary censorship, he says that in Britain, '*official* censorship has not been particularly irksome',[47] even during the war, when it would have been understandable, while voluntary censorship flourished and became particularly aggressive in the war years:

[40] By 'Trotskyism in a wide sense' Orwell means 'anti-Stalinism'.
[41] Orwell, CW, XVI, 159.
[42] Orwell to Moore, 15 April 1944, CW, XVI, 156.
[43] Orwell, As I Please, 28 (*Tribune*, 9 June 1944), CW, XVI, 253.
[44] Editorial Note, CW, XVII, 252.
[45] It was first published in the *TLS* on 15 September 1972 and in the *NY Times* magazine on 8 October 1972.
[46] Orwell, CW, XVII, 259.
[47] Ibid., 254.

At any given moment there is an orthodoxy, a body of ideas which it is assumed that all right-thinking people will accept without question. It is not exactly forbidden to say this, that or the other, but it is 'not done' to say it, just as in mid Victorian times it was not done to mention trousers in the presence of a lady. . . .

At this moment what is demanded by the prevailing orthodoxy is an uncritical admiration of Soviet Russia.[48]

Orwell stresses that this attitude did not just suddenly appear with the start of the war. The English intelligentsia had for a long time 'felt that to cast any doubt on the wisdom of Stalin was a kind of blasphemy'.[49] That is why it was ready to 'justify the endless executions in the purges of 1936-38',[50] conceal the famine in Ukraine and not allow publishing a word in defence of 'the factions on the Republican side'[51] libelled by the Russians. But during the war it came to accept and publicize the Soviet viewpoint 'with complete disregard to historical truth or intellectual decency'.[52] Orwell gives several examples of the latter, starting with the following: 'The BBC celebrated the 25th anniversary of the Red Army without mentioning Trotsky. This was about as accurate as commemorating the battle of Trafalgar without mentioning Nelson, but it evoked no protest from the English intelligentsia.'[53]

No doubt Orwell suspected that the behaviour of the BBC was the result of deep Soviet infiltration, but in this essay his anger was directed primarily against those in Britain who were ready to swallow Soviet propaganda. Behind their 'timidity and dishonesty' was, he was sure, a wish to conform, 'a cowardly desire to keep in with the bulk of the intelligentsia, whose patriotism is directed towards the USSR rather than towards Britain'.[54] He dismissed contemptuously the usual arguments behind the intention to stifle a differing opinion, which he parodied as: 'What you said might possibly be true, but it was "inopportune" and "played into the hands of" this or that reactionary interest'.[55] This tendency to swallow what they are told among intelligentsia, that is, people who should have more, not less, 'tolerance and decency'[56] than others, but who were ready to 'tolerate not only censorship, but the deliberate

---

[48]  Ibid., 254–5.
[49]  Ibid., 257.
[50]  Ibid.
[51]  Ibid., 256.
[52]  Ibid., 255.
[53]  Ibid.
[54]  Ibid., 260.
[55]  Ibid., 257.
[56]  Ibid., 258.

falsification of history'[57] seriously worried Orwell. Remarkably, arguing his point, he saw that the problem was not limited by the 'admiration of Soviet Russia':

> Quite possibly that particular fashion will not last. For all I know, by the time this book is published my view of the Soviet regime may be the generally-accepted one. But what use would that be in itself? To exchange one orthodoxy for another is not necessarily an advance. The enemy is a gramophone mind, whether or not one agrees with the record that is being played at the moment.[58]

He ended the essay with a mighty hit: 'In our country . . . it is the liberals who fear liberty and the intellectuals who want to do dirt on the intellect: it is to draw attention to that fact that I have written this preface.'[59]

Nevertheless, the preface was discarded. Maybe he felt that preceding *Animal Farm* with an openly polemical piece would distract attention from the fable, the publication of which he had been anticipating for so long. Or he might have suddenly felt reluctant to base his criticism of the 'gramophone minds' on his personal story. In any case this certainly was not his only, even if his most powerful, attack on them – similar thoughts were scattered in his other writings.

*       *       *

*Animal Farm* was published on 17 August 1945 and was, as is well known, a resounding success. Orwell, obviously pleased, wrote to Dwight Macdonald: 'The comic thing is that after all this fuss the book got almost no hostile reception when it came out. The fact is people are fed up with this Russian nonsense and it's just a question of who is first to say, "The Emperor has no clothes on".'[60] However, even this perfectly friendly reception revealed both the timidity of the British intelligentsia and its lack of understanding of what was going on in the USSR. Gleb Struve, a Russian émigré who was then teaching in the School of Slavonic Studies at London University, wrote to Orwell to say that he was very 'amused by the *pudeur* of those reviewers who had praised the book but avoided mentioning its real target'.[61] Indeed, Orwell's friend Tosco Fyvel called *Animal Farm a* 'gentle satire on a certain

[57]  Ibid., 259.
[58]  Ibid.
[59]  Ibid., 260.
[60]  Orwell to Macdonald, 3 January 1946, CW, XVIII, 11.
[61]  Struve to Orwell, 28 August 1945, The OA, UCL, Orwell/H/2/85

State and on the illusions of an age which may already be behind us'.[62] This received an immediate response from another – younger – friend of Orwell's, Julian Symons:

> Should we not expect, in *Tribune* at least, acknowledgment of the fact that it is a satire not at all gentle upon a particular State – Soviet Russia? . . . It seems to me that . . . a reviewer should have the courage to identify Napoleon with Stalin, and Snowball with Trotsky, and express an opinion favourable or unfavourable to the author, upon a political ground.[63]

Funnily enough, the reviewer who expressed an opinion 'unfavourable to the author upon a political ground' was Cyril Connolly, Orwell's oldest friend. He praised the book to the skies as a work of literature, saying that it was 'deliciously written, with something of the feeling, the penetration and the verbal economy of Orwell's master, Swift',[64] but he criticized it for 'the particular bitterness of the disappointed revolutionary'.[65] Russia, in Connolly's view, was

> an immensely powerful managerial despotism – far more powerful than its Czarist predecessor – where, on the whole, despite a police system which we should find intolerable, the masses are happy, and where great strides in material progress have been made (i.e. independence of women, equality of sexes, autonomy of racial and cultural minorities, utilisation of science to improve the standard of living, religious toleration etc.).[66]

This extraordinary arrogance – 'a police system which *we* should find intolerable' (though, presumably, it must be perfectly acceptable for the Russians) – together with the naïve trust in Russian propaganda, which always stressed that in the USSR there was complete unity between the people and the authorities, brought Connolly to his final and presumably, in his view, undeniable argument: if Stalin and his regime had not been loved, why would the Russian people have risen in arms to fight the invader? 'And if in truth Stalin is loved, then he and his regime cannot be quite what they appear to Mr Orwell (indeed Napoleon's final brutality to Boxer – if Boxer symbolises

---

[62]  Tosco Fyvel (*Tribune*, 24 August 1945), CW, XVII, 253.
[63]  Julian Symons (*Tribune*, 7 September 1945), CW, XVII, 253.
[64]  C. C. (Cyril Connolly) (*Horizon*, September 1945) in Meyers, 200.
[65]  Ibid.
[66]  Ibid.

the proletariat, is not paralleled by any incident in Stalin's career . . .)'.[67] The reviewer's ignorance or, as Orwell put it elsewhere, 'indifference to reality': 'a remarkable capacity for not even hearing'[68] about concentration camps or general lack of civil rights for the proletariat in the Soviet Union would have been surprising, had it not been very common in Orwell's lifetime – and much later too.

*   *   *

Meanwhile, Orwell was gathering more and more information about the Soviet Union. First of all, from Gleb Struve, the son of the well-known Russian politician and philosopher Pyotr Struve. As a young man, Gleb Struve fought against the Bolsheviks in the White Army, then fled to Britain, where he went to Balliol College, Oxford and in 1932, after Prince Mirsky's departure for the Soviet Union, replaced him as a Russian lecturer at the School of Slavonic Studies in London. In 1944 Struve published a new and enlarged edition of his earlier, 1935, book under a new title: *25 years of Soviet Russian Literature*.[69] It was this book that he sent to Orwell with a 'kind inscription'[70] – which implies that the author sent it not simply to *Tribune*'s literary editor, but to the man whom he read and admired.

Orwell's by now famous letter with thanks for the gift was open and friendly to the extent that he mentioned both of his works in progress: *Nineteen Eighty-Four* and *Animal Farm*. He admitted that he had never previously heard of the Russian writer Evgeny Zamyatin's novel *We* and explained: 'I am interested in that kind of book, and even keep making notes for one myself that may get written sooner or later'.[71] He obviously couldn't help adding cryptically: 'I'm writing a little squib which might amuse you when it comes out, but it is so not O.K. politically that I don't feel certain in advance that anyone will publish it. Perhaps that gives you a hint of its subject'.[72] There is no doubt that Struve got the message.

Orwell's very first letter to Struve established a good, trusting relationship between them – both knew that at least in one respect they were close. So, when in November 1944 Struve read in *Tribune* Orwell's reflections on falsifying history,[73] he wrote to the author to give a wonderful example of

[67]   Ibid., 200–1.
[68]   Orwell, 'Notes on Nationalism', CW, XVII, 147.
[69]   Gleb Struve, *25 Years of Soviet Russian Literature (1918–1943)* (London: George Routledge and Sons, 1944).
[70]   Orwell to Struve, 17 February 1944, CW, XVI, 99.
[71]   Ibid.
[72]   Ibid.
[73]   Orwell, As I please, 48 (*Tribune*, 17 November 1944), CW, XVI, 465.

the way the falsification happened in the Soviet Union. A rather significant anniversary – five years of the Soviet-Nazi pact signed in August 1939 – was deliberately omitted in the two chronological tables: 'Principal Dates in the History of the USSR' and 'Principal Dates in Modern History' published in the 'Reference Calendar for 1944'. The pact was, as Struve put it, 'simply struck out of history'.[74] Having told Orwell about it, Struve added: 'Should you wish to use this information in print, I would ask you to withhold my name'.[75] As a Russian lecturer at the University, Struve at this point evidently did not feel free enough to be associated with criticism of Stalin's Russia.

Another column in *Tribune*[76] provoked a response from Frank Barber, the assistant editor of the *Leeds Weekly Citizen*, who brought to Orwell's attention another, even more common, example of Soviet falsification – when a person rather than a recent event was 'struck out of history'. Alexander Barmine, a former Soviet diplomat, who decided not to return to the USSR in summer 1937, wrote a book called *One Who Survived: The Life Story of a Russian under the Soviets*, which was due to be published in the United States by Doubleday, Doran, but was suppressed by the publisher – in the same way and at the same time as Trotsky's *Life of Stalin* and the book by the former *New York Times* Moscow correspondent C. E. R. Gedye *My Year in the USSR*[77] were suppressed by Harper. There is no doubt that this was done to avoid annoying the Soviet Union, which became the United States' ally after the US joined the war on 7 December 1941. Frank Barber told Orwell that even earlier, in 1938, his paper, the *Leeds Weekly Citizen*, published Barmine's letter to the League for the Rights of Man in Paris, where Barmine told his story

> and expressed his horror at the Moscow Trials and some other developments in Russia. Six months later we received a letter from a reader saying he had sent our story to Moscow and asked for explanation. He told us that he received no reply to his first letter, but when he wrote again, he received a denial that Barmine ever existed! On this information our reader practically accused us of lying.[78]

Orwell was sincerely grateful to his correspondent:

> I was very interested in your note about Barmine. In my small way I have been fighting for years against the systematic faking of history which now

[74] Struve to Orwell, 28 November 1944, CW, XVI, 476.
[75] Ibid.
[76] Orwell, As I Please, 50. (*Tribune*, 1 December 1944), CW, XVI, 489.
[77] This book was never published.
[78] Frank Barber to Orwell, 8 December 1944, CW, XVI, 491.

goes on. . . . My attention was first drawn to this deliberate falsification of history by my experiences in the Spanish civil war. One can't make too much noise about it while the man in the street identifies the cause of socialism with the USSR, but I believe one can make a perceptible difference by seeing that the true facts get into print, even if it is only in some obscure place.[79]

Even these obscure places were, of course, not always available. In September 1945 Orwell wrote to Barber to express his regret that the latter had left the *Leeds Weekly Citizen*, 'as it is so important that there would be some Labour papers which are not taken in by Russian propaganda'.[80]

\*   \*   \*

Struve and Barber attracted Orwell's attention to the falsification of recent history. The issue of the so-called Displaced Persons (DPs) – those who during the war had been forcefully removed from their native land to work as slave labourers for the Germans – was something that the world was dealing with in 1945–6 but the press was not yet sufficiently alert to it. Orwell, who saw DPs – Russians, Ukrainians, Poles and Italians – when he was in Germany in spring of 1945, was one of the first journalists to send a report about them. On 15 April he published an article in *Observer*, where he made a passing reference to the potential problem of their unhappiness about going home. In January 1946, in his powerful essay 'The Prevention of Literature', he returned to the DPs' predicament and also mentioned 'very large numbers of Soviet Russians [who] – mostly, no doubt, from non-political motives – had changed sides and were fighting for the Germans'.[81]

In fact, on the territories liberated from the Nazis, there were at least three categories of Soviet citizens: DPs, POWs and those who fought together with the Nazis against the USSR in the Russian Liberation Army (Vlasov's Army), which numbered 120,000–130,000 people. On returning to the USSR, all of them could expect harsh treatment at the hands of the NKVD: not only those who had joined the Nazis – they were mostly shot, but even DPs and POWs, who had never changed sides, were also considered traitors and sent to the Gulag.[82]

[79] Orwell to Barber, 15 December 1944, CW, XVI, 498.
[80] Orwell to Barber, 3 September 1945, CW, XVII, 278.
[81] Orwell, 'The Prevention of Literature' (*Polemic*, January 1946; *The Atlantic Monthly*, March 1947), CW, XVII, 373.
[82] Reliable statistics for each category are difficult to obtain. In 2021 Moscow 'Memorial' quoted a figure of 226,127 former POWs who, on coming home, were dealt with by the NKVD. This is 14.5% of all the POWs who came back.

Unfortunately, the Brits, unlike the Americans, would not protest against forcible repatriations. Moreover – bound by the Yalta agreements, reluctant to quarrel with Stalin and afraid that, if they didn't comply with the Soviet demands, their own POWs might suffer – they often used force and deception to send Soviet citizens home. Later, this complex issue was scrupulously explored in a number of books.[83] In the Introduction to one of them, Nicholas Bethell's *The Last Secret*, historian Hugh Trevor-Roper singled out Orwell as 'one of the few writers to declare in print that Russian prisoners and "displaced persons" . . . were being "repatriated" against their will. He was promptly attacked for doing so'.[84]

The issue of forcible repatriation was just one point – although quite significant – where Orwell crossed swords with communist Randall Swingler, who in his article 'The Right to Free Expression', published in *Polemic*, launched a vicious attack on 'The Prevention of Literature'. Appropriately for the magazine's name, Orwell was allowed to respond, that is, to make annotations printed in very small type in the margins of Swingler's article.

Replying to Swingler's blunt accusation of distorting facts, Orwell remembered his visit to a POW camp not far from Munich, where in May 1945 he saw former Soviet citizens who 'were being sorted by asking the simple question, "Do you want to go back to Russia or not?" A respectable proportion – I have no exact figures, of course – answered "not", and these were regarded as Germans and kept in the camp while the others were released'.[85] This was, of course, a fairer solution than many others.

Orwell stressed that the press did not seem to be interested in these people, and even General Eisenhower's order to stop the forcible repatriation of Russian DPs received little attention, while it was obvious that

> at least some thousands . . . must previously have been repatriated against their will. Most recently there have been occasional reports of mass attempts at suicide by Russians who were about to be deported. Clearly, this kind of thing points to the existence of at least *some* disaffection – much more than existed in Britain during the war for instance.[86]

---

[83] See: Nicholas Bethell, *The Last Secret: Forcible Repatriation to Russia 1944–7* (London: Andre Deutsch, 1974); Nikolai Tolstoy, *Victims of Yalta* (London: Hodder & Stoughton, 1977).

[84] Hugh Trevor-Roper, *Introduction* to Bethell, X.

[85] Orwell's Notes to Swingler's article, CW, XVIII, 440.

[86] Ibid.

Orwell also exposed as a complete fabrication Swingler's assertion that 'the Russians found in German uniforms were simply slave labourers kept obedient by terrorism', by inquiring sarcastically: 'Supposing that one can usefully employ prisoners in this way, and then trust them with weapons in their hands, why was this done to Russian prisoners and not to British or Americans? And how many British or American prisoners or DPs have refused to return home?'[87]

Orwell was cautious yet firm in his assessments: 'I did not and do not suggest that there is very widespread opposition to the Stalin regime. . . . What I protest against is the dishonesty of those who wish to conceal or explain away *all* evidence of disaffection and then present us with the spectacle of a completely united nation as an argument in favour of terrorism.'[88]

Gleb Struve, who saw Orwell soon after his return from the continent, confirmed: 'It was even then not necessary to open his eyes to the evil of Stalinist totalitarianism, but a visit to the Displaced Persons camp gave him valuable information'.[89] Apart from the unwillingness of the Soviet people to return home, it seems that the 'valuable information' referred also to the scale and geography of the Soviet concentration camps. Orwell mentioned these newly discovered, and as yet unconfirmed, details for the first time in his London Letter, where he reflected on people's capacity to ignore facts: 'If it could be proven tomorrow that the Russian concentration camps in the Arctic actually exist, and that they contain 18 million prisoners, as some observers claim, I doubt whether this would make much impression on the Russophile section of the public.'[90]

The end of the war increased the 'trickle' of information about the Soviet Union coming to Britain. In the same London Letter, Orwell acknowledged that 'there [had] been more contact than before between Britain and Russia' thanks to 'the British prisoners liberated by the Red Army in eastern Germany', 'the crews of the ships that [went] to Archangel' and the air crews which were . . . operating in the USSR'.[91] He found all this – and particularly stories of the DPs – extremely important for understanding the real Russia, rather than living with 'a mythos' created by Soviet propaganda and its agents in Britain. Two years later he wrote to Arthur Koestler: 'I have been saying

---

[87]  Ibid., 440–441.
[88]  Ibid., 441.
[89]  Struve, 'Telling the Russians', trans. Susan Saunders Vosper in *Orwell Remembered*, compiled by Audrey Coppard and Bernard Crick (London: Ariel Books, BBC, 1984), 260.
[90]  Orwell, London Letter, 5 June 1945 (*Partisan Review*, Summer 1945), CW, XVII, 163.
[91]  Ibid.

ever since 1945 that the DPs were a godsent opportunity for breaking down the wall between Russia and the west'.[92]

\*   \*   \*

The reason behind Orwell and Struve's meeting just after the war was Orwell's interest in Zamyatin – naturally, having read about *We* in Struve's book, he now wanted to read the novel, but it was not at all easy. Zamyatin wrote his 'most malicious novel'[93] in 1919–20, and could not publish it in Russia, where it had to wait nearly sixty-eight years for its publication in 1988.[94] It was, however, translated into English and published by E. P. Dutton in New York in 1924. By the time Orwell wanted to read it, the original American edition was out of print. So, Struve, as he recalled later, 'procured for Orwell a French translation[95] of *We* from Zamyatin's widow, and it was after reading it in French that he wrote his article for *Tribune* and became so keen on seeing it published in England'.[96]

Orwell's review of *We* that appeared in *Tribune* at the very beginning of 1946 was called 'Freedom and Happiness'. He quoted from Zamyatin's utopia: 'the guiding principle of the State is that happiness and freedom are incompatible' and explained that the State in the novel took it upon itself to grant man happiness 'by removing his freedom'.[97] Happiness in Zamyatin's *We* meant 'a rationalized, mechanised, painless world',[98] just as in Huxley's *Brave New World* – Orwell, in fact, suspected that Huxley's utopia, which was published in 1932, eight years after the publication of Zamyatin's English translation, 'must be partly derived from [*We*]'.[99] In both novels, 'the primitive human spirit'[100] rebels against mechanized happiness as it strives for freedom. Orwell knew that the book was forbidden in Soviet Russia, as 'ideologically undesirable', and he acknowledged that, unlike Huxley's novel, Zamyatin's had 'a political point',[101] but at the end of his review he also suggested another interpretation:

---

[92]  Orwell to Koestler, 20 September 1947, CW, XIX, 207.
[93]  Evgeny Zamyatin to Korney Chukovsky, 19 July 1921, quoted in J.A.E. Curtis, *The Englishman from Lebedian: A Life of Evgeny Zamiatin* (Brighton: Academic Studies Press, 2013), 112.
[94]  Several chapters were published in Russian in an émigré paper in 1927 and the full Russian edition appeared in 1952 in New York.
[95]  It was published by Gallimard in 1929.
[96]  Struve to Ian Angus, 28 October 1963. Crick Collection, CRCK6/2/26.
[97]  Orwell, 'Freedom and Happiness' (*Tribune*, 4 January 1946), CW, XVIII, 14.
[98]  Ibid.
[99]  Ibid.
[100]  Ibid.
[101]  Ibid.

It may well be, however, that Zamyatin did not intend the Soviet regime to be the special target of his satire. Writing at about the time of Lenin's death, he cannot have had the Stalin dictatorship in mind, and conditions in Russia in 1923[102] were not such that anyone would revolt against them on the ground that life was becoming too safe and comfortable. What Zamyatin seems to be aiming at is not any particular country but the implied aims of industrial civilization.[103]

Three weeks later – also in *Tribune* – Gleb Struve disagreed with Orwell about Zamyatin's target:

> There is no doubt that Zamyatin had in mind, in his Utopian satire, the Soviet Union which, even in 1922, was a single-party dictatorship, and it was because it was understood to be aimed at the Soviet State that the book was refused publication. . . . Conditions of life in Zamyatin's "Single State" may differ in important particulars from those actually prevailing in the USSR at the time the book was written, but the aspects on which Zamyatin dwelt were those which seemed to him to be the inevitable logical outcome of modern totalitarianism . . . . [The book] is important just because it is even more *prophetic* than topical.[104]

Struve's view was indeed very close to what was said twenty-four years earlier by Alexander Voronsky, a subtle and discerning Soviet literary critic, who admired earlier works by Zamyatin but immediately opposed *We*, precisely because he understood the target of the writer's attack only too well. In his review, he remarked: 'This is no utopia; it is a fictional squib about the present day, with an attempted prognosis of the future to boot'.[105] In a private letter to Zamyatin, he was even more direct: 'It's early days to be firing such satires at us.'[106]

But the writer's dismay was precisely the result of the 'early days' of the revolution. Zamyatin started as a Bolshevik – he joined the party in 1905 (two years after the Russian social democrats had split into Bolsheviks and Mensheviks). This was the time of the First Russian Revolution, and

[102] It was then thought that the book was written in 1923–4.
[103] Orwell, CW, XVIII, 16.
[104] Struve's response to 'Freedom and Happiness' (*Tribune*, 25 January 1946), CW, XVIII, 16.
[105] Alexander Voronsky, '*Literaturnye siluety*' (Literary Profiles). 3. Evgeny Zamyatin', trans. Reuben Wooley, http://zamyatin.lit-info.ru/zamyatin/kritika/voronskij-literaturnye-siluety-zamyatin.html.
[106] Voronsky, 'Evgeny Zamyatin', quoted and translated by Curtis in *The Englishman from Lebedian*, 126.

he actively participated in it. In February 1917 he passionately supported the deposition of the Tsar. But less than a year later, in January 1918, he, like many others, was appalled by the Bolsheviks' forcible dispersal of the democratically elected Constituent Assembly. According to his biographer, Zamyatin felt 'instant hostility to the Leninist leadership and to the Bolshevik policies and methods' and made 'blatant personal attacks on Lenin'.[107] So it is not so surprising that already in 1919–20 Zamyatin managed to forecast many horrible consequences of the Bolshevik regime.

The omnipotent state – even perhaps originally inspired by the intention of creating universal happiness – regulates everything in its citizens' lives and stamps out their individual features. They all wear identical uniforms with badges bearing their numbers, as they have no names – what is this, if not the archetype of a concentration camp?! The greatest holiday in this state is the annual 'Day of Unanimity', when citizens unanimously elect their leader – the Benefactor – at the elections so different from the 'lawless, disorganised elections the Ancients used to have where – don't laugh – they didn't even know the results ahead of time'.[108]

The central political point of Zamyatin's novel is the conflict between 'I' and 'we', the individual and the state, and it is hardly surprising that the criticism of the novel was also political: Voronsky, 'a romantic dogmatist',[109] unhesitatingly chose the side of 'we'.

> The individualistic can only be harmful, philistine and reactionary. We communists must be fanatics within our great social struggle. This means ruthlessly crushing all that comes from a small, animalistic heart, anything personal, as, at least for the time being, that will only damage and disrupt the struggle, and hinder our victory. We shall only win when we are all as one.[110]

Orwell, naturally, was on the side of the individual, and it was the transformation of a person, who has to be 'cured' to become like others, that must have intrigued Orwell sufficiently to influence his own novel.

---

[107] Curtis, *The Englishman from Lebedian*, 88.
[108] Yevgeny Zamyatin, *We*, trans. Bela Shayevich (Edinburgh: Canongate, 2020), 154.
[109] Varlam Shalamov, Alexander Konstantinovich Voronsky. https://shalamov.ru/library/32/4.html
[110] Voronsky, 'Evgeny Zamyatin', trans. Wooley.

\*   \*   \*

According to Bernard Crick and Peter Davison, Orwell made notes for *The Last Man of Europe* (the projected title of the future *Nineteen Eighty-Four*) in September 1943, or at least before January 1944 – long before he read Zamyatin. There are already numerous features in his original detailed plan that survived till the book's final version: 'the party slogans (War is peace, Ignorance is strength, Freedom is slavery)', 'The Two Minutes Hate', 'Dual standard of thought' (later to become 'doublethink'); 'Newspeak', 'Leader-worship', 'The system of organized lying', 'Sexual code', 'the love-affair with Y' and 'torture and confession'.[111] Orwell's protagonist even at this early stage was supposed to keep a diary – the diary-keeping of Zamyatin's D-503 seems to be a coincidence or rather a common device used by both authors.

Other similarities between the two novels are, most likely, Orwell's borrowings from Zamyatin – not so numerous, but quite significant: Winston and Julia have their trysts above Mr Charrington's junk-shop, just as D-503 and his beloved I-330 have theirs in the 'Ancient House', which is preserved to show how 'the Ancients' lived; in Oceania, citizens are constantly watched by telescreens and the Thought Police, while in the One State, for the convenience of their 'guardians', they simply live in glass apartments (mentioning this in his review, Orwell remarks parenthetically: 'this was written before television was invented',[112] which might mean that he had already thought of telescreens by that time); the theme of conspiracy against the regime is present in both novels, although it is treated in different ways; both Winston Smith and D-503 betray the women they love and finally – just as D-503 undergoes the removal of his imagination, torture subdues Winston Smith's rebellious spirit and makes him relinquish the idea of objective reality, acknowledge that the Party is always right and replace his love for Julia with love for Big Brother. Both protagonists are 'cured' and made to comply with the official doctrine.

However, the differences between *We* and *Nineteen Eighty-Four* are more profound than their similarities. The one that first leaps to the eye is the difference in style. Struve quotes Mirsky, who 'aptly compared' Zamyatin's peculiar style 'to Cubism in painting'.[113] The whole of *We* is written as a diary, which makes D-503's narrative abrupt, disjointed and not always immediately comprehensible, not to mention the fact that the first-person narration, a priori, makes it difficult to present a full picture. Orwell, on the other hand, uses the straightforward form of a traditional novel, which allows him a clearer layout for his book and more subtle psychological portrayals of his

---

[111] Orwell's Notes for 'The Last Man in Europe', CW, XV, 367–369.
[112] Orwell, CW, XVIII, 14.
[113] Gleb Struve, *25 Years*, 20.

characters. In the futuristic worlds of both books, Winston Smith and Julia seem much more credible than D-503 and his mysterious I-330. But even more importantly, Zamyatin's book is a prophetic conjecture based on his deep and often brilliant understanding of an emerging phenomenon. The Bolsheviks' belief in their own infallibility ('One State Science cannot make mistakes'[114]), for example, allowed him to imagine how their state would function in the future, while Orwell, who wrote his novel nearly thirty years later, knew from his own and other people's experiences what totalitarian regimes were really like. He could therefore be more precise and convincing about the origins of the existing totalitarianism, its essence and its impact on its victims. There is much less 'science fiction' in Orwell's book. Instead of Zamyatin's 'removal of imagination' as the way to 'cure' the rebels, Orwell has 'torture and confession' already in his original plan, obviously referring to the confessions at Stalin's show trials. Whereas Zamyatin had to rely on his – quite extraordinary – imagination, nearly all the 'dystopian' elements of *Nineteen Eighty-Four* can be traced back to the Soviet totalitarian reality.

\* \* \*

Orwell proved close to Zamyatin in yet another aspect – both writers were concerned about the position of literature in a totalitarian country. Zamyatin expressed his anxiety in an essay called 'I am afraid', where he insisted that

> true literature can only exist when it is created not by efficient and dependable functionaries, but by madmen, hermits, heretics, daydreamers, rebels, sceptics. . . . I am afraid that we will have no true literature until we cure ourselves of this new kind of Catholicism, which no less than the old one fears every heretical word. And if this illness turns out to be incurable, then I am afraid that Russian literature will have only one future – its past.[115]

Orwell had not read this article of Zamyatin's, but he had certainly read Gleb Struve's book, where Struve writes about the writer's freedom and refers to Max Eastman's *Artists in Uniform*:[116]

---

[114] Zamyatin, *We*, 25.
[115] Zamyatin, 'I Am Afraid', translated by Curtis and partially quoted in *The Englishman from Lebedian*, 106.
[116] Max Eastman, *Artists in Uniform: A Study of Literature and Bureaucratism* (London: George Allen &Unwin Ltd), 1934.

Mr Eastman, of course, is fundamentally right in his contention that artists have to wear 'uniform' in the Soviet Union and are under compulsion to 'toe the line' – the general line of the Soviet government whatever this line may be at any given moment. The point is that the line itself changes, that it may be now broader now narrower, and thus allow of greater or lesser degrees of freedom for the artist both in the choice of his theme and in its treatment. The whole history of literature in Russia since the revolution is an illustration of this point.[117]

Orwell also read Max Eastman and certainly his chapter about Zamyatin, where Eastman writes: 'His heresy consists essentially in . . . believing in the value of heresy as such'.[118] Some passages in Orwell's essay, 'The Prevention of Literature', dealing with the difficult position of a truthful writer (and not only in totalitarian countries), seem to echo Zamyatin's words, so that his essay could almost have an alternative title 'The Value of Heresy':

> Everything in our age conspires to turn the writer, and every other kind of artist as well, into a minor official, working on themes handed to him from above and never telling what seems to him the whole of the truth. . . . In the past, at any rate throughout the Protestant centuries, the idea of rebellion and the idea of intellectual integrity were mixed up. A heretic – political, moral, religious, or aesthetic – was one who refused to outrage his own conscience.[119]

Two conclusions are confidently drawn by Orwell in this essay. One deals with 'the poisonous effect of the Russian *mythos* on English intellectual life', the result of which is that 'known facts are suppressed and distorted'[120] and names one of the key features of totalitarianism, the feature that actually defines it: 'the organised lying'.[121]

The second conclusion of the essay involves the writer himself. Orwell insists that totalitarianism destroys literature, especially prose and, in this respect, there is not much difference between a mere journalist and an imaginative writer:

[117] Struve, *25 Years*, 256.
[118] Eastman, *Artists in Uniform*, 85. Cf. Voronsky: 'Zamyatin loves this word "heretic"' (Voronsky, 'Evgeny Zamyatin')
[119] Orwell, 'The Prevention of Literature', CW, XVII, 372.
[120] Ibid., 373.
[121] Ibid., 379.

The journalist is unfree, and is conscious of unfreedom, when he is forced to write lies or suppress what seems to him important news: the imaginative writer is unfree when he has to falsify his subjective feelings, which from his point of view are facts. . . . If he is forced to do so, the only result is that his creative faculties dry up. Even the single taboo can have an all-round crippling effect upon the mind, because there is always the danger that any thought which is freely followed up may lead to the forbidden thought.[122]

Orwell first wrote about the dangers for freedom of thought in his 1940 essay, 'Inside the Whale', where he predicted that it would be impossible for 'an autonomous individual' and for imaginative literature to survive under totalitarianism. In the 'Prevention of Literature' he concentrates on imaginative literature: he mentions the deterioration of the novel in the totalitarian countries – Germany, Italy, Russia – and the 'literary prostitutes like Ilya Ehrenburg or Alexey Tolstoy',[123] but he could not of course know the full scale of the persecution of writers in the Soviet Union or the full impact the regime had on their personalities and faculties.

\* \* \*

Against this background, it is even more difficult to accept that a British poet, not exposed to any kind of duress, would see nothing wrong in enthusiastically championing the USSR and spreading communist lies. However, Randall Swingler, who attacked Orwell in his article 'The Right to Free Expression', was exactly the type of an English communist or 'fellow traveller' that Orwell described in his essay. During the twenty months between September 1939 and June 1941, the period of the Soviet-Nazi friendship, he obediently changed his position in accordance with the change of the party line. Swingler's biographer, Andy Croft, sympathizes with him: 'The change of line brought Swingler to the edge of an emotional and intellectual crisis. He was in profound disagreement with his party. But he did not hesitate to endorse the new line in public. . . . It was a matter of discipline and loyalty for Swingler.'[124] He threw himself into anti-war propaganda, wrote anti-war articles and songs, but, in full keeping with Orwell's depiction, 'on June 22,1941, he had to start believing once again that Nazism was the most hideous evil the world

[122] Ibid., 375.
[123] Ibid.
[124] Andy Croft, *The Years of Anger: The Life of Randall Swingler* (London and New York: Routledge, 2020), 112.

had ever seen'.[125] Swingler must have recognized himself in this portrait and was furious.

Swingler's attack on Orwell in *Polemic* was particularly spiteful because he claimed that it was caused not by 'political controversy' but by his concern 'with Orwell's method of using language and argument'.[126] The idea behind it was to doubt the writer's credibility, turn him into an 'unreliable witness'. He criticized Orwell for being 'singularly independent of factual evidence', called his testimony (about the Russians fighting for Nazism) 'dubious'[127] and basically accused him of lying – lying about the Russians changing sides during the war, about Communists publishing 'garbled versions' of original books, about writers persecuted in the USSR, only then coming to his final conclusion: '[Orwell's] defence of intellectual liberty has become synonymous with full-scale attack on the USSR.'[128] Here Swingler was right – for Orwell, indeed, the British intelligentsia supporting the Soviet totalitarian regime was not intellectually free. But at this particular point, Swingler naturally sprang to the defence of the Soviet Union, reverting to the most banal pro-Soviet arguments. He said that Orwell's criticism of the USSR was inappropriate and advised him to follow the example of well-known Soviet supporters in Britain: 'people who appear to have taken very considerable trouble to verify their facts and have spent some time in the country, such as Beatrice and Sydney Webb or the Dean of Canterbury, or Alexander Werth, or Pat Sloan'.[129]

These of course were the people who Orwell called 'paid and unpaid apologists of totalitarianism' in Britain.[130] The manipulation of contemporary information, Orwell insisted, had been going on for at least four years, when

> news items unfavourable to the USSR were kept out of the Press and the public seriously misled, particularly with regard to the Russian attitude towards ourselves. . . . The public was told little or nothing about the frankly hostile Russian attitude, the playing-down of the British war effort in the Soviet Press, the non-mention of British and American aid in food and war materials, and the refusal to allow free movement to British military attachés and correspondents. Similarly, great efforts were made in the Press to erase the memory of the Russo-German pact.[131]

[125] Orwell, CW, XVII, 376.
[126] Swingler, 'The Right to Free Expression', CW, XVIII, 436.
[127] Ibid., 434–5.
[128] Ibid., 436.
[129] Ibid., 437.
[130] Orwell's Notes to Swingler's article, 443.
[131] Ibid., 441.

It was these obvious lies that helped to create 'the Russian myth', regularly presented in the form of 'glowing prospectuses'[132] by the very people whom Swingler praised for 'verifying the facts'.

*　*　*

In his comments, Orwell remarked that Swingler in his article 'left more or less undiscussed' the main question raised in 'The Prevention of Literature': 'whether it is possible to produce worth-while literature' under tight party control.[133] The question was unambiguously answered by the Soviet Union, where on 14 August 1946, just a couple of months before the publication of Swingler's piece annotated by Orwell, the Communist Party Central Committee issued a decree directed against two literary journals, *Zvezda* and *Leningrad*, attacking, in particular, two of the most talented writers of the time: the satirist Mikhail Zoshchenko and the poet Anna Akhmatova, both living in Leningrad. On 16 August, Andrey Zhdanov, Stalin's 'cultural commissar', went to Leningrad and gave a speech which marked the start of a new period of the party's heavy-handed interference in literary life. Akhmatova and Zoshchenko were vilified, defamed and expelled from the Writers' Union, which on a professional level meant a nearly complete ban on publishing them, and on a practical level, the loss of the food ration cards which they received as Union members.

The campaign unleashed against Zoshchenko and Akhmatova was the first in a series of subsequent party attacks on the arts and sciences. It felt like a clampdown on the institutions and individuals who had managed to survive after the purges of the late 1930s. In literature and the arts, campaigns were conducted under various slogans: 'for socialist realism', 'against formalism', 'against kowtowing to the West', etc., but their real aim was to bring the intelligentsia into line and isolate it from the rest of the world. Paradoxically, during the war against the Nazis, with all its pain and suffering, many people in the Soviet Union felt freer than in the pre-war years of the state's indiscriminate terror and started to hope that the victory – achieved together with the Allies – might somehow soften the Soviet regime. The final pages of Pasternak's *Doctor Zhivago* bear evidence to that. This hope now had to be stifled.

Among the several factors that determined the choice of victims was Stalin's personal antipathy to Zoshchenko, based perhaps on his jealousy of the satirist's fame. Zoshchenko's hilarious short stories – poking fun at ordinary

---

[132]  Ibid., 443.
[133]  Ibid., 440.

Soviet citizens, often narrow-minded, hardened in battles with neighbours in communal flats and not particularly overburdened by morals – were not only immensely popular with a mass readership, but also highly esteemed by such perceptive judges as the poet Mandelstam, who wrote: 'I demand monuments to Zoshchenko in all the cities and towns of the Soviet Union, or at least just one like that to Grandpa Krylov in the Summer Gardens'.[134] The name of the famous nineteenth-century fabulist Ivan Krylov mentioned here was no accident – Zoshchenko was renowned for the amazing vernacular, spoken by his characters, that exposed both the comedy and the tragedy of their everyday existence.

Zoshchenko first got into serious trouble with the authorities in 1944, when his autobiographical novel *Before Sunrise* was lambasted by the journal *Bolshevik*, but the literary work selected as a target for the attack by Zhdanov in 1946 was an innocent children's story, 'The Adventures of a Monkey', republished in *Zvezda* after it had appeared four times elsewhere. It was this story that Zhdanov pounced on in his speech, calling Zoshchenko a 'philistine and vulgarian' who was in 'the habit of jeering at Soviet life, ways and people', whose works were 'steeped in the venom of bestial enmity towards the Soviet order' and who had forever remained 'a preacher of ideological emptiness and vulgarity, an unprincipled and brazen-faced literary hooligan'.[135]

Orwell did not know these details, but he responded to Zhdanov's report in his *As I Please* column in early January 1947. He saw the attack as another attempt of the party to gain full control over literature. Having dismissed Zhdanov as a man who has – 'to judge from his speeches – about as much knowledge of literature as I have of aerodynamics', he proceeded in satirical mode to express compassion for him, as he must be

> truly shocked by the defection of certain Soviet writers, which appears to him as an incomprehensible piece of treachery, like a military mutiny in the middle of a battle. The purpose of literature is to glorify the Soviet Union; surely that must be obvious to everyone? But instead of carrying out their plain duty these misguided writers keep straying away from the paths of propaganda, producing non-political works, and even, in

---

[134] Osip Mandelstam, *Collected Works in Three Volumes*, ed. G.P. Struve and B.A. Filipoff (New York: Inter-Language Literary Associates, 1971), Vol. II, 191.

[135] Report on the Journals *Zvezda* and *Leningrad* in Andrei Zhdanov. On Literature, music and Philosophy, https://www.marxists.org/subject/art/lit_crit/zhdanov/lit-music -philosophy.htm and The *Zvezda* Affair, http://soviethistory.msu.edu/1947-2/zhdanov /zhdanov-texts/the-zvezda-affair/

the case of Zoshchenko, allowing a satirical note to creep into their writing.[136]

Coming back to his own voice, Orwell, yet again, repeated the deep conviction he had previously expressed in 'The Prevention of Literature': 'The thing that politicians are seemingly unable to understand is that you cannot produce a vigorous literature by terrorising everyone into conformity. A writer's inventive faculties will not work unless he is allowed to say approximately what he feels.'[137]

Sadly, this was exactly what happened to Zoshchenko – in the twelve years remaining to him, he did some writing and translating but never reached the heights of his 'inventive facilities'. The decree of 1946 was not revoked after Zhdanov's death in 1948 or even after Stalin's death in 1953. Moreover, 1954 set in motion 'the second round' of attacks on Zoshchenko, triggered by the unfortunate visit to Leningrad of a delegation of British students,[138] who naively thought that after Stalin's death things had changed dramatically and asked the persecuted writers about their attitude to Zhdanov's speech. Zoshchenko said that he could not agree with it. This caused a new barrage of criticism in the papers and the reversal of the decision to publish some of his stories which was made after his membership in the Writers' Union had been restored in autumn 1953. At a plenary meeting of Leningrad writers, to which Zoshchenko was summoned, he said: 'A satirist should be morally pure and I am humiliated like the lowest son of a bitch! How can I carry on working?'[139] And he could not – he was destroyed as a writer and died in 1958, before he turned sixty-three. The decree that dealt him his death blow was repealed thirty years later.

The attention paid by Orwell to the decree and to Zhdanov's speech was, no doubt, a manifestation of his remarkable capacity to imagine the consequences of social developments at the human level, the capacity that is so obvious in *Nineteen Eighty-Four*. In 1946, not having much information about Zoshchenko, he still felt for the unknown writer and hoped that 'Zoshchenko and the others at least have the satisfaction of understanding what is happening to them'.[140]

---

[136] Orwell, *As I Please*, 68 (*Tribune*, 3 January 1947), CW, XIX, 6.
[137] Ibid.
[138] Among these twenty students from different UK universities were Harold Shukman, a future historian and the only Russian speaker there; Fred Jarvis, then the president of the National Union of Students, and Richard J Cook, who left his memoirs about the event, published in *Vospominania o Mikhaile Zoshchenko* (Reminiscences of Mikhail Zoshchenko) (St Petersburg: Khudozhestvennaya literatura, 1995), 324–32.
[139] Sarnov, *Stalin and Writers*, Vol. II, 509.
[140] Orwell, *As I Please*, 68, CW, XIX, 7.

\*   \*   \*

Orwell's own understanding of what was happening in the Soviet Union was expanding – by now he was able not only to analyse but also to predict social developments. In the finale of 'The Prevention of Literature' he comes back to 'the Russian myth', to which a large part of the British intelligentsia has succumbed, to make the following observation:

> When one sees highly educated men looking on indifferently at oppression and persecution, one wonders which to despise more, their cynicism or their short-sightedness. Many scientists, for example, are uncritical admirers of the USSR. They appear to think that the destruction of liberty is of no importance so long as their own line of work is for the moment unaffected. . . . They do not see that *any* attack on intellectual liberty, and on the concept of objective truth, threatens in the long run every department of thought.[141]

This was published in January 1946, and in August 1948, the scientific world was struck by an official onslaught on science and scientists who dared to think in a way different from that prescribed by the party. The infamous session of the Lenin All-Union Academy of Agricultural Sciences (VASKhNIL) took place in Moscow between 31 July and 7 August and arbitrarily suppressed the development of genetics, which had been rapidly and successfully growing in the USSR under the guidance of the outstanding geneticist and botanist Nikolay Vavilov. He was VASKhNIL's director between 1924 and 1935 and worked enthusiastically to help improve Soviet food production.

Vavilov's work was widely known outside the USSR: many British and American geneticists came to Leningrad to admire his unique collection of plant seeds, corresponded with him and expected him to preside over the Seventh International Congress of Genetics, held in Edinburgh in 1939. Instead, an empty chair stood on the stage to mark his absence: Vavilov and twenty-eight of his colleagues had not been allowed out of the country. By that time, Vavilov had already lost many of his official positions, which had been taken one after another by the half-educated, but politically astute, Trofim Lysenko, preferred by Stalin, partly because Stalin in his youth had read Lamarck, whom Lysenko's theories relied on.

In August 1940 Vavilov was arrested, and two and a half years later, in January 1943, the remarkable scientist who had been planning to feed the world died in prison from starvation. Several colleagues of Vavilov were also arrested and shot in the early 1940s. And yet genetics in the USSR was

---

[141] Orwell, CW, XVII, 379.

not yet quite finished – there were still other biologists who hoped that the obvious inadequacy of Lysenko's theories would attract the attention of the international community and the issue would still be solved through scientific discussion.

Orwell first heard about the Soviet genetics controversy 'in the speech given by John Baker at the PEN conference in 1944 and afterwards read about it at greater length in Baker's book *Science and the Planned State*'.[142] In both his speech and his book, Baker, the Oxford biologist who in 1940, together with Michael Polanyi, had founded the Society for Freedom in Science, ardently denounced the planned state and totalitarianism as pernicious for the development of science, 'for even with the best will in the world, the political bosses cannot distinguish between the genuine investigator on the one hand and the bluffer and self-advertiser on the other'.[143] This was an obvious allusion to Lysenko, whose story, Baker argued, 'provides a vivid illustration of the degradation of science under a totalitarian regime'.[144] Baker's colleague, eugenicist C. P. Blacker, explained later how Baker had obtained his rich first-hand knowledge of what was going on in the USSR: 'Baker's wife is Russian and it was she who translated the documents on which Baker founded his case'.[145]

Orwell singled John Baker out when he wrote to Koestler about the future anti-totalitarian league they hoped to organize together: 'He is evidently one of the people we should circularize when we have a draft proposal ready. He could probably also be useful in telling us about other scientists who are not totalitarian-minded, which is important, because as a body they are much more subject to totalitarian habits of thought than writers and have more popular prestige'.[146] Indeed, many British geneticists, who naturally opposed Lysenko's views, were reluctant to bring scientific discussion onto the political plane, mostly for fear that it would only 'play into the hands' of the enemies of the first socialist state. Soon, however, Orwell was sent an article, 'A Revolution in Russian Science', written by a geneticist who clearly was 'not totalitarian-minded' and, most importantly, was eager 'to deal with [Lysenkoism] at all levels, from the purely academic to the purely political'.[147]

[142] Orwell to Dr C.D. Darlington, 19 March 1947, *The Lost Orwell*, 130.

[143] John R. Baker, 'Science, Culture and Freedom', in *Freedom of Expression: A Symposium*, ed. Hermon Ould (London, New York: Hutchinson International Authors, 1945), 118.

[144] Ibid., 119.

[145] C. P. Blacker to Darlington, 17 December 1948, quoted in Oren Solomon Harman, 'C. D. Darlington and the British and American Reaction to Lysenko and the Soviet Conception of Science' (*Journal of the History of Biology*, Vol. 36, No. 2, 2003), 332. In fact, Baker's wife Liena (Helen) (1897–1993) was born in Russia of English parents and must have been fully bilingual.

[146] Orwell to Koestler, 31 March 1946, CW, XVIII, 214.

[147] Darlington to Michael Polanyi, 14 March 1947, quoted in Harman, 320.

This was Cyril Dean Darlington, who had been friends with Vavilov and who, once the news of Vavilov's death was confirmed, co-authored, together with Sidney Harland, his obituary in *Nature*.[148] However, when he tried to publish a piece called 'Science and Politics in the Soviet Union' in the *Fortnightly Review*, its editor declined it, explaining that he was 'anxious to publish the article although fearful of being thought a stumbling block to better relations between the countries'.[149] After a couple of other rejections, Orwell, who immediately recognized the similarity between Darlington's situation and his own with *Animal Farm*, advised the scientist to send his article to *Polemic* and, when *Polemic* had to close, helped to publish it in *The Nineteenth Century and After*, under the title 'The Retreat from Science in Soviet Russia'.[150]

In less than a year, the retreat from science was confirmed by the triumph of Lysenko at the VASKhNIL session in Moscow. On the last day of the proceedings, he announced that his paper and therefore his views had been approved by the Central Committee. Years later, it was discovered that Stalin had acted as his personal editor.[151] Lysenko's victory served as a signal, on the one hand, to persecute geneticists, who lost their jobs, saw their research halted and laboratories closed, and on the other, to start 'similar campaigns in other sciences – physiology, cytology, physical chemistry, and physics'.[152] Physics, however, where the scheduled conference was due 'to condemn the theory of relativity and quantum mechanics', survived, probably because Beria, responsible for 'the Soviet atomic bomb project',[153] persuaded Stalin not to jeopardize it.

The fact that physics was spared also supported Orwell's idea, first expressed in 1942, when he spoke about the safeguards against the endless totalitarian violation of the truth: 'you . . . can't violate it in ways that impair military efficiency',[154] and then powerfully developed in 'The Prevention of Literature':

> At this stage of history, even the most autocratic ruler is forced to take
> account of physical reality, partly because of the lingering-on of liberal

[148] Obituary of Professor N. I. Vavilov, Foreign Member Royal Society (*Nature* 156, 24 November 1945), 621.

[149] John Armitage to Darlington, 6 January 1947, quoted in Harman, 320.

[150] Darlington, 'The Retreat from Science in Soviet Russia' (*The Nineteenth Century and After* 142, October 1947).

[151] Kirill O. Rossianov, 'Stalin as Lysenko's Editor: Reshaping Political Discourse in Soviet Science' (*Russian History*, Vol. 21, No. 1, 1994), 49–63.

[152] Ibid., 61.

[153] Ibid.

[154] Orwell, 'Looking Back on the Spanish War', CW, XIII, 505.

habits of thought, partly because of the need to prepare for war. So long as physical reality cannot be altogether ignored, so long as two and two have to make four when you are, for example, drawing the blueprint of an aeroplane, the scientist has his function, and can even be allowed a measure of liberty. His awakening will come later, when the totalitarian state is firmly established.[155]

The small islands of scientific communities creating nuclear weapons for a future war were left in relative peace, while the totalitarian state of the Soviet Union was successfully fighting the concept of objective truth on other battlefields. The ten years between 1943, when a Soviet victory over the Nazis started looming on the horizon, and 1953, when Stalin died, were the years of the most aggressive offensive against free thinking in all spheres of life. The best writers, composers, actors, scholars and scientists fell victim to its ruthless campaigns. And this was at the time when, to Orwell's outrage, the majority of the British intelligentsia still believed in the need to support 'the Soviet experiment'.

[155] Orwell, 'The Prevention of Literature', CW, XVII, 380.

# Part II

# 'Don't let it happen.

# It depends on you.'

# 6

# Opposing the Soviet menace

*From Stettin in the Baltic to Trieste in the Adriatic an iron curtain has descended across the Continent. . . . The Communist parties, which were very small in all these Eastern States of Europe, have been raised to pre-eminence and power far beyond their numbers and are seeking everywhere to obtain totalitarian control.[1]*

Winston Churchill, 1946

*Isn't it funny how surprised everyone seems over this Czechoslovakia business? Many people seem really angry with Russia, as though at some time there had been reason to expect different behaviour on the Russians' part.[2]*

Orwell to Dwight Macdonald, 1948

In 1945, when the Nazis were defeated, the need to build a new, just world, where nightmares like the recent war would never be allowed to happen, was felt by many people in many countries. To Orwell, 1945 brought both a tragedy – the sudden death of his wife, Eileen, in March – and a triumph – the enormous success of *Animal Farm*, finally published on 17 August. There was also something else to be proud of: 'The fact that after six years of war we can hold a general election in a quite orderly way and throw out a Prime Minister who has enjoyed almost dictatorial powers, shows that we *have* gained something by not losing the war',[3] he wrote in his London Letter in mid-August. Hopes for the new Labour government, which promised to introduce long overdue changes in the country, were, however, dampened by the widespread fear of the new weapon – the atom bomb, first used by the United States against Japan on 6 and 9 August. Its invention, Orwell predicted, would either make it likely that 'we all are to be blown to pieces by it within the next five years' or that 'a permanent state of "cold war"'[4]

---

\*  The title of Part 2 is a quote from Orwell's Statement on *Nineteen Eighty-Four*, CW, XX, 134.

[1]  Winston Churchill, 'The Sinews of Peace' (*Fulton Speech*, 5 March 1946). https://winstonchurchill.org/resources/speeches/1946-1963-elder-statesman/the-sinews-of-peace/.

[2]  Orwell to Macdonald, 7 March 1948, CW, XIX, 282.

[3]  London Letter, 15–16 August 1945 (*Partisan Review*, Fall, 1945), CW, XVII, 245.

[4]  Orwell, 'You and the Atom Bomb' (*Tribune*, 19 October 1945), CW, XVII, 319.

would soon become the norm. Orwell, who first coined the phrase 'cold war', defined it as 'a peace that is no peace'.[5] It was only later that it came to mean the geopolitical tension between the United States and the Soviet Union. This new state of affairs that emerged immediately after the war made Orwell busier than he had ever been, not only with his writing – in just over a year since Eileen's death he wrote well over a hundred articles and reviews, including his best essays, 'The Prevention of Literature', 'Politics and the English Language', 'Why I Write' and others – but also with political and social activism.

\*   \*   \*

Some of the tasks he set himself at that time might seem less significant than others, but in fact all of them – big and small – were about establishing the truth. This was especially obvious at the time of the Nuremberg Trials, held between 20 November 1945 and 1 October 1946. In early 1946 the Revolutionary Communist Party (British Trotskyists) made an attempt to verify the allegations put forward against Trotsky at Stalin's show trials of 1936 and 1937. The party circulated a letter titled 'Nuremberg and the Moscow Trials', which questioned the charges of Trotsky's and other defendants' collaboration with the Nazi government and the Gestapo. In particular, Trotsky was said to have met Rudolf Hess – 'the only Nazi named in the Moscow indictment'.[6] Although these charges had been decisively dismissed by the Dewey Commission, initiated in March 1937 by the American Committee for the Defence of Trotsky, it would be even more convincing, the letter claimed, to see the records of the Gestapo, now in the hands of the Allied Powers in Nuremberg, and to interrogate Hess, who was there in the dock.

This letter was sent to Orwell, who not only signed it immediately but tried to circulate it further. Eventually, about a dozen of signatories endorsed it, with H. G Wells and three of Orwell's friends – Arthur Koestler, Paul Potts and Julian Symons among them. On 25 February the letter was published in *Socialist Appeal* (a newspaper of British Trotskyists) and then, on 16 March, in the Scottish socialist newspaper *Forward*, where Orwell first saw it.

An interesting sequel to this episode was the publication of a short piece *about* the letter, called 'Trotsky and Hess' in the journal *Time and Tide*, where Orwell had contributed during the war, which makes it possible that

---

[5]   Ibid., 321.
[6]   'Nuremberg and the Moscow Trials', a letter of the Revolutionary Communist Party, CW, XVIII, 113.

it appeared there thanks to him. Moreover, the final sentences of the piece with their distinct irony make one wonder whether it might even have been written by Orwell: 'Mr Pritt and others have been insistent that Soviet judicial procedure at the trials was beyond reproach. An excellent opportunity now offers to vindicate this opinion. It will be a great pity if advantage is not taken of it.'[7]

The advantage was not taken. With the Soviet team at Nuremberg pursuing Stalin's agenda, the Allied Powers failed to use this unique opportunity. Likewise, they failed to use the Nuremberg Trials to reveal the truth about the Katyn massacre – the execution by the NKVD of 22,000 Polish officers and intelligentsia. They were imprisoned after the Soviet invasion of Poland in September 1939 and then shot in April and May 1940. Since the discovery of mass graves in Katyn forest by the Nazis in April 1943, the Soviet Union kept claiming that the Poles had been killed by the Nazis. The Soviets even hoped to bring this claim to Nuremberg but could not build their case convincingly and the International Military Tribunal did not accept it. By that time enough evidence had already been collected to prove the culpability of the USSR, but no attempt was made to bring it to justice. For over forty years after Nuremberg, the British and other Western governments did not have the courage to name the real perpetrators of the killings. They admitted that the Soviet Union had been responsible for them only in 1988 – just two years before Russia itself did.

Orwell and Koestler, however, tried to bring the tragedy to the attention of the world as early as in spring 1946, when they discussed the possibility of publishing the testimony of Polish writer and painter Józef Czapski, who, together with just 78 other POWs, miraculously survived the executions in the Starobielsk camp where nearly 4,000 officers were shot. Orwell met Czapski in Paris in March 1945 and in December of the same year Czapski approached him with a request to find an English publisher for his forty-page-long *Wspomnienia Starobielskia* (Memories of Starobielsk), which had already been translated into Italian and French. At the beginning of March 1946, Orwell wrote to Arthur Koestler:

It's funny you should send me Czapsky's pamphlet, which I have been trying for some time to get someone to translate and publish. Warburg would not do it because he said it was an awkward length, and latterly I gave it to the Anarchist (Freedom Press) group. I don't know what decision they've come to. I met Czapsky in Paris and had lunch with him. There is no doubt that he is not only authentic but a rather

---

[7] 'Trotsky and Hess', editorial note, CW, XVIII, 132.

exceptional person, though whether he's any good as a painter I don't know.[8]

Despite all the efforts of both friends, their attempts to publish Czapski's short memoir in English fell through. The second, longer, part of his memoirs, *The Inhuman Land,* appeared in Britain in 1951 and was republished several times, but *Memoirs of Starobielsk* had to wait for over seventy-five years to be finally translated into English in full and published in the United States.[9]

Just a bit later, in 1947–8, Orwell tried as desperately, and as unsuccessfully, to have other books translated and published in Britain: Mandelstam's essays, Zamyatin's prose and Victor Serge's memoirs. The publishing world did not seem to have any appetite for that.

＊　　＊　　＊

In August 1945 Orwell became a vice chairman of the Freedom Defence Committee, a mostly anarchist group (its chairman was Herbert Read and secretary George Woodcock), which was founded on 3 March 1945 with the aim to 'uphold the essential liberty of individuals and organisations, and to defend those who are persecuted for exercising their rights to freedom of speech, writing and action'.[10] In May, Orwell signed a letter of protest against the imprisonment of three editors of the magazine *War Commentary* (one of them was his friend Vernon Richards) and in December, when anarchist and pacifist newspaper-sellers were arrested for obstruction at Speakers' Corner in Hyde Park, published an article 'Freedom of the Park'. He even appeared twice on a public platform at the events organized by the FDC, which was quite unusual for him. One of the reasons why he must have felt the acute need to support the newly formed committee was his anger at realizing that the organization previously responsible for reacting to cases like this – the National Council for Civil Liberties (NCCL) – had become 'a Communist front'.[11]

Disappointed also by the British intellectuals' 'growing indifference to tyranny and injustice abroad',[12] he was particularly enthusiastic about Arthur

[8]　Orwell to Koestler, 5 March 1946, CW, XVIII, 137.
[9]　Józef Czapski, *Memories of Starobielsk. Essays Between Art and History,* ed. and trans. from the Polish by Alissa Valles (New York: NYRB, 2022).
[10]　Nicholas Walter, 'Orwell and Anarchism', in *George Orwell at Home (and among the Anarchists)* (London: Freedom Press, 1998), 71.
[11]　Ibid.
[12]　Orwell, 'Freedom of the Park' (*Tribune,* 7 December 1945), CW, XVII, 418.

Koestler's proposal to create a new 'League for the Rights of Man',[13] a broader international organization 'to defend the individual against the arbitrary action of the state',[14] the demand for which was growing even more urgent as Soviet totalitarianism had been spreading over Eastern Europe. At Koestler's invitation, Orwell, with his nineteen-month-old, adopted son Richard, came for Christmas to Bwlch Ocyn cottage in Wales, where Koestler and his fiancée Mamaine Paget then lived, and spent most of his time there discussing the possibilities of creating a new international body. When he returned to London, he sent Koestler the first draft of the League's manifesto, which he must have been working on for several days after his return.

His starting point was that 'totalitarians' underestimated the concept of liberty: 'Both Communists and Fascists', he stressed, 'have reiterated that liberty without social security is valueless, and it has been forgotten that without liberty there can be no security'.[15] Orwell himself had never stopped thinking about the need for the 'synthesis between political freedom on the one hand and economic planning and control on the other',[16] which in this context meant bringing liberty and security together. Having specified the main functions the state should have to provide security, he then continued to name the tasks of the League:

> It will fight for the defence of the Individual against arbitrary arrest, imprisonment without trial, punishment under retrospective laws, arbitrary displacement or restriction of movement or of the right to nominate and vote for candidates of his own choice.[17]

Importantly, it would not matter whether infringements 'occur in the British Empire or in Russian occupied territory'.[18] Apart from this practical work, the League would need to have a 'theoretical platform', which would be created by the 'exchange of ideas in the League's quarterly and later monthly magazine, between individuals and groups in various countries pursuing similar aims'.[19]

In Britain, however, the draft stated, 'a considerable part of the intelligentsia has set itself almost consciously to break down the desire for liberty and to hold

---

[13] Suggested names for it were also: 'Magna Carta League', 'Renaissance – A League for the Defence and Development of Democracy' and 'League for the Freedom and Dignity of Man'.
[14] Draft of the Manifesto, UoE, Arthur Koestler's Papers, Coll-146 MS 2345-2.4-12.
[15] Ibid.
[16] Ibid.
[17] Ibid.
[18] Ibid.
[19] Ibid.

totalitarian methods up to admiration'.[20] Instead of reacting with indignation to 'tyrannous practices abroad or at home', many adhered to the concept of 'political realism' (today it would be called *Realpolitik)*, which Orwell defined as the 'tendency to subordinate ethical values to opportunistic expediency'.[21] He concluded his preamble with: 'It is therefore felt that the time has come to form a new organisation to do the work which such bodies as the League for the Rights of Man were supposed to do and failed to do'.[22]

Orwell was convinced that the old League, like the NCCL, had been 'stalinised',[23] as he wrote to Dwight Macdonald, when telling him about Koestler's project. In his next letter to Koestler he explained: 'I'm certain that some years before the war it had become a Stalinist organisation, as I distinctly remember that it refused to intervene in favour of the Trotskyists in Spain; nor so far as I remember did it do anything about the Moscow trials'.[24] As he was writing this letter, it must have been clear to him that there was little hope that the old League, which still existed in France, would be anti-totalitarian. The triumphant success of the Communist Party at the 1945 French elections had affected the country's intellectuals, and Orwell complained to his friend: 'The French publisher who had signed a contract to translate *Animal Farm* has got cold feet and says it is impossible "for political reasons". It's really sad to think a thing like that happening in France, of all countries in the world'.[25]

There was no doubt in Orwell's mind that the organization he wanted to create should be anti-totalitarian, which in 1946 could only mean anti-communist and anti-Soviet (or anti-Russian, as it was common to say then, as the country was still casually called Russia, rather than the Soviet Union). In his manifesto draft he specified: 'Since Nazism collapsed, the one great power with a totalitarian structure is the USSR, and it is chiefly in the form of uncritical admiration for the USSR that totalitarian ideas established themselves in the western countries'.[26] In his letter of 10 January 1946 he told Koestler of his meeting with two British journalists, whom the friends had planned to inform about their intention to create the new League:

> I saw Barbara Ward and Tom Hopkinson today and told them about our project. They were both a little timid, chiefly I think because they realise

---

[20]  Ibid.
[21]  Ibid.
[22]  Ibid.
[23]  Orwell to Macdonald, 3 January 1946, CW, XVIII, 8.
[24]  Orwell to Koestler, 10 January 1946, CW, XVIII, 28.
[25]  Ibid.
[26]  Ibid.

that an organisation of this type would in practice be anti-Russian, or would be compelled to become anti-Russian, and they are going through an acute phase of anti-Americanism. However they are anxious to hear more and certainly are not hostile to the idea.[27]

Orwell also sent a copy of the draft to Michael Foot, then the *Tribune*'s editor, who broadly approved it,[28] and Koestler got in touch with Bertrand Russell, his neighbour in Wales. Although Russell thought that it was almost too late to start the movement when the world was on the brink of an atomic war, he got interested and suggested organizing a conference of about a dozen influential people, which he was happy to join. Possible participants in this conference included Orwell, Koestler, Russell, Foot, Gollancz, some continental writers with anti-communist views: an Austrian, Manès Sperber, a Frenchman, André Malraux, an Italian, Ignazio Silone, and 'an American', whom Orwell was due to bring along.

Orwell and Koestler hoped that Rodney Phillips, a wealthy Australian publisher of the new magazine *Polemic*, would help them financially. And they did not doubt that *Polemic*'s editor, Humphrey (Hugh) Slater would be on their side. However, Slater and Phillips saw the situation differently: they were surprised and not really happy when the rumour reached them that some group had designs on their journal, envisaged, they insisted, as 'purely theoretical'. Slater wrote a long letter to Koestler, explaining that 'in a political sense [he] was in favour of the project',[29] but theirs was a completely different undertaking.

So the idea of an Easter conference collapsed, but Koestler would not give up. He felt passionately that 'if those of us who see clearly the disaster into which we are drifting don't speak out there will be no excuse for us'.[30] Soon after Churchill's speech about the Iron Curtain he, together with his fiancée, Mamaine, drafted a new document, which as his biographer puts it, was due 'to accompany (or replace – the intention is not clear), Orwell's original manifesto'.[31] Supposed 'to be signed by at least a hundred leading personalities', it stated that 'despite mutual suspicion and tension between Western powers and the USSR . . . a stable *modus vivendi* can and should be found' between

[27]  Ibid, 27–8. Barbara Ward was a writer on politics and assistant editor of the *Economist*; Tom Hopkinson was an author and journalist, founder and editor of *Picture Post*.
[28]  See Orwell to Koestler, 11 February 1946, CW, XVIII, 105; 27 February 1946, CW, XVIII, 133.
[29]  Humphrey Slater to Koestler, 19 March 1946, UoE, MS2346,2,108r.
[30]  Koestler to Bertrand Russell, 6 May 1946, UoE, MS2346.2.90.
[31]  Michael Scammell, *Koestler: The Indispensable Intellectual* (London: Faber and Faber, 2010), 267.

them. And the pre-condition for it should be '*psychological disarmament*',[32] which implied 'the free exchange of newspapers and periodicals between the two blocs, . . . the abolition of travel restrictions, and the free circulation of ideas across frontiers'.[33]

Some of the ideas of Koestler's petition were rather utopian, and Russell called this suggestion 'unworkable'. The disagreement, obvious from their correspondence, was not so much about the petition, but about the attitude to the task – Koestler's and Russell's personalities proved incompatible. Russell was annoyed by Koestler's lack of attention to detail and argued that 'men who are writers do better work as individuals than by collaborating in groups'.[34] Koestler, on the other hand, insisted, that 'the so-called intellectuals have to try to influence the politicians by concerted action, as a chorus and not as solo voices. Otherwise they will not have sufficient impact'.[35] Unfortunately, the argument about the petition got mixed up with personal matters, and the whole plan for the new League for the Rights of Man was abandoned. However, there is no doubt that it was out of its seed that the Congress for Cultural Freedom, founded five months after Orwell's death, eventually grew.

On 28 June 1950, the final day of the Congress's inaugural conference in Berlin, Koestler, with his impetuous temper, addressed the crowd of 15,000 people, who had gathered to protest against the invasion of South Korea by North Korean troops, supported by the Soviet Union. Having read out the 'Freedom Manifesto', of which he was the main author, Koestler, defiant as ever, finished by triumphantly proclaiming in German: 'Friends, freedom has seized the initiative!'[36] Another of his dreams also came true: the conference in Berlin was indeed attended by 'at least a hundred leading personalities from all over the world', as he had hoped in his 'Draft for the Petition'. They were illustrious intellectuals, who represented democratic and non-Communist Left: apart from Russell, Silone, Sperber, who were among the possible participants of the frustrated conference of 1946, Berlin also hosted James Burnham, John Dewey, Sidney Hook from America; Benedetto Croce and Altiero Spinelli from Italy, Karl Jaspers from Switzerland (originally from Germany), A. J. Ayer and Hugh Trevor-Roper from Britain and Raymond Aron from France.

---

[32] Koestler, Draft for the Petition, UoE, MS2345.2.53-68.
[33] Scammell, *Koestler*, 267.
[34] Russell to Koestler, 13 May 1946, UoE, MS2346.
[35] Koestler to Russell, 6 May 1946.
[36] Scammell, *Koestler*, 359; Peter Coleman, *The Liberal Conspiracy. The Congress for Cultural Freedom and the Struggle for the Mind of Postwar Europe* (New York: The Free Press, 1989), 1.

And another plan of Koestler's and Orwell's came to fruition: one of the main activities of the Congress for the next seventeen years of its existence was publishing magazines – *Der Monat* in Germany, *Encounter* and *Soviet Survey* in Britain, *Preuves* in France, *Tempo Presente* in Italy, *Quadrant* in Australia and others – and trying to deliver them, if not directly to the USSR, then at least, to 'the territories occupied and controlled by her'.[37]

It was Orwell's idea of 'a series of intellectual magazines that would not shy away from polemics'[38] that particularly impressed a young American journalist, recently demobilized from the US Army and based in Berlin, who in the bitter winter of 1946–7 travelled to London to visit Orwell. They spent hours in Orwell's freezing flat in Canonbury talking about the past and present horrors of totalitarianism, and the writer told the young man about the failed plans for an international organization and showed him his draft of the manifesto. The American's name was Melvin J. Lasky. Soon, inspired by Orwell's vision, he became editor of *Der Monat* (1948) and then *Encounter* (1958) magazines and one of the organizers of the 1950 Berlin Conference, which gave birth to the Congress.

However, on Easter Sunday 1946, Koestler's friend, the writer Margaret Storm Jameson, wrote to him to say that, if his petition was intended for publication in the newspapers, 'it must be written without anti-Soviet bias, while at present the bias stands out a mile'.[39] 'I do not believe', she continued, 'that it is yet [she underlined the word] time for a hundred leading *clercs*[40] to appear in public holding their noses against the stink of censorship rising from Russia'.[41] Koestler – and maybe even more so, Orwell – thought differently, but faced with an obvious failure, Koestler had to acknowledge that his attempt was perhaps premature. Writing about the 'postponement' of the Easter Conference to his friend Manès Sperber, he explained it by 'the usual business of people quarrelling' and added: 'This probably means that the time is not quite ripe yet'.[42] In the next four years, however, the situation changed dramatically.

---

[37]  Koestler, Draft for the Petition.
[38]  See Marko Martin, *Orwell, Koestler und all die anderen: Melvin J. Lasky und Der Monat* (Orwell, Koestler and all the others. Melvin J. Lasky and *Der Monat*) (Asendorf: MUT-Verlag, 1999), 19–20; Giles Scott-Smith, '"A Radical Democratic Political Offensive": Melvin J. Lasky, '*Der Monat*, and the Congress for Cultural Freedom' (*Journal of Contemporary History*, Vol. 35, No. 2, April 2000), 263–280.
[39]  Margaret Storm Jameson to Koestler, 21 April 1946, UoE, MS2345.2.111.
[40]  Intellectuals (Fr.). The word comes from the title of Julien Benda's book *La Trahison des Clercs* (The Treason of the Intellectuals).
[41]  Storm Jameson to Koestler, 21 April 1946.
[42]  Koestler to Sperber, 22 March 1946, UoE, MS 2345.2.110.

* * *

When on 5 March 1946, Winston Churchill, then the Leader of the Opposition, gave his 'Iron Curtain' speech in the American town of Fulton, Missouri, not many people in the world realized the aggressive nature of the Soviet expansion into Eastern Europe. Historian David Caute observed that among fellow-travellers 'the dominant attitude was one of guilt and a sense of gratitude to Russia for her immense sacrifices. Clearly the USSR could not tolerate for a second time a ring of hostile states on her borders',[43] but even for less sympathetic people the effects of the Soviet occupation of Eastern Europe were not immediately seen. It was assumed that in 1944–1945 the region still had 'genuine democracy', then 'bogus democracy' came to replace it and it was only in 1947–1948 that there came 'an abrupt policy shift and a full-fledged takeover'.[44]

Thanks to the opening of the archives in the early 1990s, it became obvious that 'this early liberal period was, in reality, not quite so liberal as it sometimes appeared in retrospect'.[45] Anne Applebaum describes 'certain key elements of the Soviet system' imported 'into every nation occupied by the Red Army from the very beginning'.[46] They were: 'selective violence' by secret police forces; relentless propaganda promoted by 'the era's most powerful form of mass media: the radio'[47]; the ban on independent organizations – that is, on civil society; and mass ethnic cleansing – deportations of large groups of people.[48] The rest came later, but these four features were present in all East European countries from the start.

The year 1947 saw a powerful leap in the USSR setting itself and its allies against its opponents in the West. By the autumn of that year the Cominform (the Communist Information Bureau) was created.[49] Its formation was triggered by President Truman's proposal to start the Marshall Plan – a programme meant to assist in rebuilding European economies, as 'the seeds of totalitarian regimes are nurtured by misery and want'.[50] Originally, the Soviet Union was due to be a recipient of American help too, but this was angrily dismissed by Molotov at the debates in June 1947. Consequently, East European countries, whose policies after the occupation by the Red

---

[43]  David Caute, *The Fellow-Travellers: A Postscript to the Enlightenment* (London: Weidenfeld and Nicolson Ltd, 1973), 275.

[44]  Anne Applebaum, *Iron Curtain: The Crushing of Eastern Europe 1944–56* (London: Allen Lane, 2012), xxx.

[45]  Ibid.

[46]  Ibid., xxxi.

[47]  Orwell predicted the 'sinister possibilities of the radio' back in 1938 (CW, XI, 312).

[48]  Applebaum, *Iron Curtain*, xxxii.

[49]  The Comintern, which might be called its predecessor, had been dissolved on 15 May 1943.

[50]  Truman Doctrine Speech, quoted in: Applebaum, *Iron Curtain*, 233.

Army had to be aligned with those of the USSR, were not allowed to join the programme either, no matter how much they might have wanted to participate in it. Instead, their leaders were offered Zhdanov's speech at the Cominform's founding meeting in Poland, where he spoke specifically about the 'American plan for the enslavement of Europe'.[51] The 'hostile' atmosphere, it was suggested, demanded that East European countries should rally around the Soviet Union, and therefore communist parties should take the dominant position everywhere, not allowing any opposition to deter them.

Czechoslovakia had been holding out longer than others. In his 1947 speech in Poland, Zhdanov acknowledged 'the complete victory of the working class over the bourgeoisie in every East European land except Czechoslovakia, where the power contest still remains undecided'.[52] As Czechoslovak general elections were approaching, it was clear that the communists were heading for defeat – the population was increasingly unhappy with the police becoming a tool in the hands of their party, with the imminent collectivization and demands for workers to increase their output for the same wages. The conflict between communists and non-communists in the government reached its climax by the end of February. Twelve non-communist ministers resigned in protest against the extension of police powers, hoping that President Beneš, who had been the president of the government-in-exile during the war years, would not accept their resignations. Indeed, a week earlier he had promised to resist the communist takeover. And yet, as the communists were organizing mass demonstrations, Prime-Minister Klement Gottwald supported them and the armed militia and police took over Prague, Beneš faltered and the resignations were accepted. The communists won.

For about a week a lingering hope of restoring democracy was pinned on the country's foreign minister, Jan Masaryk, the son of Czechoslovakia's 'founding father' and also a former member of the government-in-exile, but on 10 March he was found dead, lying in the courtyard in his pyjamas under his bathroom window. The official version claimed that it was a suicide, but later investigations concluded that Masaryk had been murdered by the Russian NKVD.[53] The investigation of 2019–21, however, returned an open verdict yet again.

[51] Andrey Zhdanov, 'New Aspects of World Conflict: The International Situation', 22 September 1947. https://soviethistory.msu.edu/1947-2/cold-war/cold-war-texts/zhdanov-on-the-international-situation/

[52] Robert C. Grogin, *Natural Enemies: The United States and the Soviet Union in the Cold War 1917–1991* (Lanham, MD: Lexington Books, 2001), 134.

[53] A Russian journalist's story seemed to corroborate the latter version. https://english.radio.cz/masaryk-murder-mystery-back-headlines-russian-journalist-speaks-out-8612711.

Orwell's remark in his letter to Macdonald about the suppression of democracy in Czechoslovakia (written before Masaryk's death) – 'Many people seem really angry with Russia, as though at some time there had been reason to expect different behaviour on the Russians' part'[54] – confirms that he had not been under any illusions as far as the Soviet Union was concerned. Moreover, apart from increasingly concentrating on his last novel with its warning against following the Soviet ways and methods, he kept working on a variety of articles exposing the danger of the Soviet Union and its Western apologists.

In the witty editorial of *Polemic* 3, written but not signed by him, Orwell mocks Professor J. D. Bernal – a physicist and sociologist of science, who for years had been an admirer of the Soviet Union. After Orwell's death, he was awarded the Stalin Peace Prize (1953) – no doubt, for his unfailing support – and kept his position of president of the World Peace Council, founded by the USSR, between 1959 and 1965. Orwell's attack on Bernal was triggered by an editorial in 'the Communist-controlled' journal *Modern Quarterly* which had berated the *Polemic* for its alleged 'persistent attempts to confuse moral issues, to break down the distinction between right and wrong'.[55]

Orwell singled out Bernal's essay 'Belief and Action' published in the same issue of the *Modern Quarterly* as the anti-*Polemic* editorial, because he was sure that it reflected the journal's own approach to right and wrong. Had the Professor's language, 'at once pompous and slovenly', been translated into plain English, Orwell argued, his essay would simply say that 'almost any moral standard can and should be scrapped when political expediency demands it'.[56] Bernal claimed that 'new social relations' required 'a radical change in morality', and although 'many of the old virtues . . . need no changing, *those based on excessive concern with individual rectitude need reorienting in the direction of social responsibility*'[57] [Orwell's emphasis]. This, Orwell sneered, meant 'that public spirit and common decency pull in opposite directions' and 'we must alter our conception of right and wrong from year to year, and if necessary from minute to minute'.[58] Or just keep up with the pace of changes adopted by Moscow radio.

He also could not deny himself a pleasure of ridiculing Professor Bernal's calls for more cooperation with the USSR:

---

54 Orwell to Macdonald, 7 March 1948. CW, XIX, 282.
55 Editorial. *Polemic*, 3 May 1946, CW, XVIII, 263.
56 Ibid., 265.
57 Ibid., 264.
58 Ibid.

What exactly does Professor Bernal mean by 'fellowship' and 'ever closer understanding' between Britain and USSR? Does he mean, for instance, that independent British observers in large numbers should be allowed to travel freely through Soviet territory and send home uncensored reports? Or that Soviet citizens should be encouraged to read British newspapers, listen to the BBC and view the institutions of this country with a friendly eye? Obviously he doesn't mean that. All he can mean, therefore, is that Russian propaganda in this country should be intensified, and that critics of the Soviet regime (darkly referred to as 'subtle disseminators of mutual suspicion') should be silenced.[59]

Orwell refused to be silenced. As long as he had enough physical strength to use not only for writing his novel, which obviously was of primary importance for him, he would fight those who, he felt, were trying to bring totalitarian attitudes to Britain. In his London Letter published in the Summer 1946 issue of *Partisan Review* he wrote about '"underground" Communist MPs[60] – that is, MPs elected as Labour men, but secretly members of the CP or reliably sympathetic to it'.[61] He thought there were about 20 or 30 people like that out of 300 Labour parliamentarians.

Their tactic, needless to say, is to clamour inside and outside parliament for a policy of appeasement towards the USSR, and at the same time to try to group the Left elements in the country round them by playing on domestic discontent . . . . Considering that the USSR is and must be implacably hostile to a Social Democratic government of the British type, it is clear that a combination of open Communists like Arthur Horner at the head of big trade unions, 'underground' Communists like Zilliacus in Parliament, and 'sympathisers' like Priestley in the popular press could be very dangerous.[62]

Orwell was pleased to inform his American readers that 'the popular enthusiasm [for Communism] of a year or two ago [had] worn very thin'. Still he was afraid that 'as an organised body [the "underground" Communists] might be able to do enormous mischief'.[63]

[59]  Ibid., 265.
[60]  Later Orwell used the term 'crypto-Communists'.
[61]  London Letter, early May 1946? (*Partisan Review*, Summer 1946), CW, XVIII, 286.
[62]  Ibid., 287.
[63]  Ibid.

Konni Zilliacus, a Labour MP and one of the main targets of Orwell's attack, read this London Letter six months later and immediately sent to *Tribune* an angry reply. In this reply he called Orwell's article 'despicable' and stated: 'I'm not a member of the CP, never have been a member of the CP, and would consider it a disgraceful thing to do, to be secretly a member of any party or organisation, membership of which was not compatible with membership of the Labour Party'.[64] Orwell hit back immediately: 'He *says* he is not a "crypto-Communist." But of course he does! What else could he say? . . . The whole effectiveness of Mr Zilliacus and his associates depends on their *not* being branded as Communists'.[65] He added that he did not care whether Zilliacus had 'a Communist Party ticket or any direct connexion with the CP', but he was sure that 'he and others like him are pursuing a policy barely distinguishable from that of the CP, that they are in effect the publicity agents of the USSR in this country, and that when Soviet and British interests appear to them to clash, they will support the Soviet interest'.[66]

The most obvious examples of this support displayed by Zilliacus and his group were for Orwell 'their persistent efforts to persuade the public of this country that the puppet regimes of Eastern Europe are democracies'.[67] Zilliacus responded to that by writing in his next letter that 'the Communists of 1946 are very different from those of 1917, and are becoming . . . more and more identified with the working-class and influenced by the national characteristics of their respective countries'.[68] This was of course an official Soviet line used to soften the impression of the USSR subjugating these countries to its creed by sheer force. The polemics, which included other participants as well, lasted in *Tribune* for four weeks, till 7 February. Orwell held firmly to his position and predicted that 'in all issues of importance Mr Zilliacus [would] continue to support and justify Soviet policy, whatever that policy may be and whatever changes it may go through'.[69] Indeed, in three years' time Zilliacus, who had been consistently against Ernest Bevin's foreign policy, was expelled from the Labour Party together with another Soviet sympathizer, D. H. Pritt, and three more MPs over their opposition to the creation of NATO.

[64]  Konni Zilliacus, 'Communists and Democrats' (*Tribune*, 17 January 1947), CW, XVIII, 290.
[65]  Orwell's response to Zilliacus (*Tribune*, 17 January 1947), CW, XVIII, 290–291.
[66]  Ibid., 291.
[67]  Ibid.
[68]  Zilliacus's second letter (*Tribune*, 24 January 1947), CW, XVIII, 293.
[69]  Orwell's second response (*Tribune*, 31 January 1947), CW, XVIII, 294.

\* \* \*

The brutal suppression of the last vestige of democracy in Eastern Europe during the Czechoslovak coup in February 1948 made the Western world fully realize the threat and make an effort to defend its political system. A year earlier, on 12 March 1947 the Truman doctrine was announced, which committed the United States to providing economic, political and military support to democratic nations, while trying to contain Soviet expansionism and its totalitarian ways. On 17 March 1948, President Truman spoke to the Congress: 'The issue is as old as recorded history', he said. 'It is tyranny against freedom'.[70] His determination helped to speed up the adoption of the Marshall Plan, which did indeed bring restoration to the European economy. It also affected the French and Italian communist parties, which had quickly lost the support they enjoyed immediately after the war, because, following Moscow guidance, they opposed the Marshall Plan – their position, understandably, failed to prove popular with the people of their countries.

An urgent problem was, however, presented by Germany, whose economic situation was desperate. To help it, the United States, Britain and France decided to unite their three zones, introduce a Deutschmark and thus create West Germany. Stalin, who had in 1945 hoped that eventually Germany would be united under Communist rule, protested by attempting to get control over the whole of Berlin, although the former capital, like the rest of Germany, had also been divided into four zones. To put pressure on the allies, he could not think of anything better than blockading their parts of the city.

On 24 June 1948 Soviet troops and tanks blocked road and rail access to Berlin for citizens of Britain, France and the United States. Simultaneously, they cut off the electric current and all deliveries of food and fuel, so that two and a half million West Berliners remained trapped with the prospect of starvation and freezing. The military governor of the US zone in Germany, General Lucius Clay, who as early as April had warned the Pentagon: 'When Berlin falls, Western Germany will be next. If we mean . . . to hold Europe against communism, we must not budge',[71] started organizing a massive airlift to supply the city with food and fuel. Soon American and British pilots made about 1,500 flights each day, bringing in 4,500 tonnes of cargo. Stalin did not risk shooting the planes down, as he realized that this might start a war. At that point the Soviet atom bomb was not yet ready – it was first tested in July 1949. It took just under a year of unprecedented

[70] Quoted in: Martin Gilbert, *Descent into Barbarism: A History of the XX Century (1933–1951)* (London: HarperCollins, 1999), 813.
[71] Quoted in Grogin, *Natural Enemies*, 150.

Western resistance to Stalin, for him to realize his defeat and to lift the blockade on 12 May 1949.

The outcome of the blockade, however, was not at all clear when, in August 1948, just two months after it started, Orwell wrote to Melvin Lasky in Berlin: 'It must be ghastly being in Berlin now. I trust you won't all have to fly with the MVD on your heels'.[72] In the last sentence he obviously hinted at his own flight from Spain with the NKVD on his heels – the names of the sinister organization kept changing but not the essence of what it did.

Melvin Lasky, who visited Orwell in the winter of 1946–7, had by that time become editor of a German monthly magazine simply called *Der Monat*. This happened thanks to the extraordinary audacity he displayed in October 1947, when he crossed over to Berlin's Eastern sector and came uninvited to the Congress of German writers held there under the auspices of the Soviet authorities. In his unscheduled appearance on the podium he made an extraordinary speech. 'I was congratulating the German writers on escaping the clutches of the Gestapo and Nazi censorship and calling attention to the fact that the Russians also had the secret police and reserved cells for their writers'[73] – he recalled over fifty years later.

The Russians were furious. The communist German writer Anna Seghers 'left her seat in the front row and rushed out of the auditorium to get Colonel Alexander Dymschitz',[74] the head of the Soviet delegation. Lasky spoke about the writers persecuted by the Soviet regime, including its most recent victims – Akhmatova and Zoshchenko – and, most likely, closely following Orwell's passage in 'The Prevention of Literature', stressed the role of writers as rebels in society.[75] Despite indignant screams from the communists, he was allowed to finish his address, because the German novelist Guenter Birkenfeld, who was chairing the session, insisted that it would only be fair as on the previous day the audience had listened to a long speech of the Soviet writer Vsevolod Vishnevsky, who enticed them to the Soviet side and accused Anglo-Saxon writers of being 'a menace to peace lovers everywhere'.[76]

Since the very start of its post-war conflict with the Western world, the Soviet Union insisted that it was committed to the 'struggle for peace', while the term 'cold war' was generally reserved by Soviet propagandists for the activities of its adversaries, involved in 'war-mongering'. Naturally, after years

[72]  Orwell to Melvin Lasky, 31 August 1948, CW, XIX, 426.
[73]  Lasky's interview to the author, on 23–24 June 2000, Berlin.
[74]  *New York Times*, 8 October 1947 quoted in: S.A. Longstaff, '"Missionary in a Dark Continent": *Der Monat* and Germany's Intellectual Regeneration, 1947–1950' (*History of European Ideas*, Vol. 19, No. 1–3, 1994), 93.
[75]  Boris Shub, *The Choice* (New York: Duell, Sloan and Pearce, 1950), 77–83.
[76]  Longstaff, 'Missionary in a Dark Continent', 95.

of suffering, the word 'peace' seemed profoundly attractive both to Soviet citizens and to Westerners. In Germany, the propagandists also tried to stress that they were 'patrons of German art, music and literature' and imply that 'Russians and Germans together had to defend culture against the forces of the dollar'.[77] Americans, on the contrary, were then much less effective in the art of propaganda: it took them 'more than two years to install a major broadcasting outlet in Berlin, whence the inhabitants of the Soviet zone could be reached', while the Russians seized the powerful Radio Berlin as soon as they entered the capital.[78]

When General Clay (the future organizer of the Berlin Airlift) heard about a huge row caused by Melvin Lasky's intervention in East Berlin, he was on the point of expelling Lasky from the city, but the brilliant journalist managed to convince him of the need to have an American publication in post-war Germany which would complement in ideas and culture what the Marshall Plan was already doing in the economy. 'Its *formula*', wrote the inspired Lasky in his proposal, 'would be to address, and to stimulate, the German-reading intelligentsia of Germany and elsewhere with the world-views of American writers and thinkers'.[79] The international aspect, which included the 'recognition of the common cultural values shared among the European intelligentsia', was very important for Lasky, as was his resolve 'not only to face up to the fascist past but also to defend those values against the immediate communist threat'.[80] The US Office of the Military Government in Germany (OMGUS) received this proposal in December 1947 and agreed to finance the new review,[81] while Lasky, thanks to General Clay, was given full independence as its chief editor.

The first issue of *Der Monat* appeared in October 1948. It had 112 pages and carried articles by Europeans – Koestler, Crossman, Spender and Sartre – and by Americans – Kazin and Greenberg. The topic of the issue – 'The Fate of the West' – was discussed by Russell, Borkenau and Toynbee; George Orwell was listed as 'the journal's London correspondent'.[82] Lasky sent him a copy of this issue as soon as it was published and Orwell, although admitting that he couldn't 'read a word of German, except the words everyone knows', added, no doubt, sincerely: 'it looks most impressive and I do hope it will be

---

[77] Ibid.
[78] Ibid., 94.
[79] Quoted in: Scott-Smith, 'A Radical Democratic Political Offensive'.
[80] Ibid.
[81] *Der Monat* was funded by OMGUS for six years; then it became one of the journals financed by the Congress for Cultural Freedom, while Lasky in 1958 moved to London to become a co-editor of another Congress journal, *Encounter*.
[82] Scott-Smith, 'A Radical Democratic Political Offensive'.

a success'.[83] He tried to contribute to Lasky's endeavour by offering to write something on Koestler's new books and suggesting that Lasky should publish an extract from *Homage to Catalonia*, but neither of these plans materialized: Orwell was too busy with retyping *Nineteen Eighty-Four* and too weak, while his agent Leonard Moore failed to find a copy of *Homage*. Nothing, however, could stop Lasky.

In December 1948 he published in translation Orwell's essay 'The Labour Government After Three Years' and then serialized in *Der Monat* translations of both *Animal Farm* (February–April 1949) and *Nineteen Eighty-Four* (November 1949–March 1950). Lasky was also instrumental in helping to publish and distribute *Animal Farm* in Russian by forwarding the Deutschmarks Orwell earned in *Der Monat* to its publisher, *Possev*, based in Germany.[84] Orwell was right when he wrote to his agent that 'the editor of *Der Monat* . . . would be sympathetic to this idea'.[85]

One of the things Orwell paid attention to while looking at the first issue of *Der Monat* was the name that was dear to him: 'I am glad to see you have Borkenau writing for you and I would like to have his address',[86] he wrote to Lasky.

It is worth noting that Orwell was personally friendly with and politically close to all the three people who gathered in August 1949 'in a Frankfurt hotel to develop a plan for an international conference of anti-Communist Leftists to be held in 1950 in Berlin'.[87] They were Franz Borkenau, Melvin Lasky and Ruth Fischer – the latter Orwell had met just a couple of months earlier, when she visited him in the Cranham sanatorium. Both Borkenau and Fischer were former communists, well-acquainted with the Russian – most brutal – incarnation of the creed. Fischer was a former general secretary of the German Communist Party, from which she was expelled as a Trotskyist, and the author of the book *Stalin and German Communism*, which Orwell enjoyed reading.[88] He also enjoyed making Fischer's acquaintance, because, as he wrote to a friend, 'it was fun meeting somebody who had known Radek & Bukharin and others intimately'.[89] Lasky started as an American Trotskyist, but later worked in the American magazine *New Leader*, where he was very much under the influence of its editor, a Russian Menshevik and a friend of

[83]   Orwell to Lasky, 29 October 1948, CW, XIX, 458.
[84]   See Chapter 8.
[85]   Orwell to Moore, 21 July 1949, CW, XX, 150.
[86]   Orwell to Lasky, 29 October 1948, CW, XIX, 459.
[87]   Coleman, *The Liberal Conspiracy*, 15.
[88]   Orwell to Ruth Fischer, 21 April 1949, XX, 93.
[89]   Orwell to Tosco Fyvel, 20 June 1949, CW, XX, 138.

Kerensky, Sol Levitas.[90] And it wasn't confined to the organizers – the non-communism of the Congress for Cultural Freedom, as a whole, had mostly grown out of its members' strong opposition to Soviet totalitarianism, which many of them had experienced first-hand. At the same time, most of them were opponents of political conservatism.

The reputation of the Congress was damaged in 1967, when it was revealed that since 1950 it had been secretly financed by the CIA.[91] The shock was mostly caused by the word 'secretly', although when the Congress was being created this definitely was the best possible way to fund it without annually asking permission of the US Congress. Further damage to its reputation was done in the early 2000s when Frances Stonor Saunders's book with its charged title, *Who Paid the Piper?*,[92] effectively reduced all the rich and diverse activities of the Congress to the issue of its funding and made it seem that the brilliant cultural figures involved with it had simply obeyed CIA orders. Hugh Wilford's book, which appeared a couple of years later, had a polemical question mark in its subtitle, *The CIA, the British Left and the Cold War: Calling the Tune?*[93] and went much deeper in exploring the relations between the left in Britain and America, concluding that: 'Far from feeling themselves to be the victims of aggressive ideological colonisation, many on the British left positively welcomed the US intervention because they naturally shared its values and goals'.[94]

There is obviously no telling how Orwell's political views would have developed had he not died at the age of forty-six and whether he would have supported the Congress for Cultural Freedom, which he did not live to see, or whether, had he known about it, he would have seriously minded its being funded by the CIA. Still, Hugh Wilford's definition of him as 'the archetype of the anti-Stalinist man of letters, who formed the centre of reasonably distinct community of non-communist left *literati* in Britain',[95] and John Newsinger's acknowledgement that Orwell was 'involved with this [cultural] US dimension and ready "to cooperate with US organisations"'[96] make his

---

[90] On 25 May 1948 Levitas wrote to Orwell that his magazine *The New Leader* was 'the only publication of the "left" in this great, big country of ours which had combatted totalitarianism for the last 25 years' (CW, XIX, 388).

[91] See Coleman, *Liberal Conspiracy*, 46–50, 219–35.

[92] Frances Stonor Saunders, *Who Paid the Piper?* (London: Granta Books, 1999) and its American edition: *The Cultural Cold War: The CIA and the World of Arts and Letters* (New York: The New Press, 2000).

[93] Hugh Wilford, *The CIA, the British Left and the Cold War: Calling the Tune?* (London and Portland, OR: Frank Cass, 2003).

[94] Ibid., 2.

[95] Ibid., 8.

[96] Newsinger, *Hope Lies in the Proles*, 128.

support of the Congress fairly likely, as far as the 1950s are concerned. Surely, his approach could have changed later.

\* \* \*

In 1947, however, Orwell's position in the growing conflict between the USSR and the United States was unambiguous. During that year he returned to this issue at least three times. In March 1947 he wrote to Victor Gollancz politely asking him to terminate the contract originally made just before Orwell's departure for Spain. He pointed out that after the publisher's refusal to accept *Animal Farm*, it was clear that the two of them disagreed politically over a 'difficulty' which was 'likely to arise again'.[97] Having received Gollancz's 'kind and considerate' response, which had not, however, provided him with a definite answer, Orwell wrote again, being a bit blunter about it:

> You know what the difficulty is, i.e., Russia. For quite 15 years I have regarded this regime with plain horror, and though, of course, I would change my opinion, if I saw reason, I don't think my feelings are likely to change so long as the Communist Party remains in power . . . I don't, God knows, want a war to break out, but if one were compelled to choose between Russia and America – and I suppose that is the choice one might have to make – I would always choose America.[98]

Even before this letter to Gollancz, Orwell had written and sent to the United States his insightful essay 'Burnham's View of the Contemporary World Struggle'. There he dismissed Burnham's suggestion that it was the 'national pride' that made the Brits refuse 'the fusion of Britain with the United States',[99] and stressed that 'anti-American feeling is strongest among those, who are also anti-imperialist and anti-military' and 'see that to be tied to America probably means preserving capitalism in Britain'[100] – that is, among the left.

This is followed by a wonderful 'overheard' dialogue, which starts: 'How I hate the Americans! Sometimes they make me feel almost pro-Russian'. Then, when urged to choose between America and Russia, the same person says: 'I refuse to choose. They're just a pair of gangsters'. And finally, he/she admits: 'Oh, well, of course, if one *had* to choose, there's no question about

[97] Orwell to Gollancz, 14 March 1947, CW, XIX, 78.
[98] Orwell to Gollancz, 25 March 1947, CW, XIX, 90.
[99] Orwell, 'Burnham's View of the Contemporary World Struggle' (*The New Leader NY*, 29 March 1947), CW, XIX, 103.
[100] Ibid.

it – America'.[101] According to Orwell, this choice was the choice of necessity, like the one socialists in Britain had during the war when they supported Churchill, because obviously 'Churchill was preferrable to Hitler'.[102] Orwell regretted that there was not enough interest for other possibilities, for example, for his favourite vision of the Socialist United States of Europe.

He was not alone in his search for other possibilities: the left wing of the Labour Party was also hoping at that time to find the 'Third Force' policy that would be both anti-communist and yet actively pro-socialist. This position was gradually eroded, 'forcing British leftists to "choose sides"'.[103] Explaining the choice facing the left in the late 1940s, Hugh Wilford stresses that 'even the most obdurate left-wingers'[104] welcomed, for example, the Marshall Plan. Orwell shared this view: although America was not at all an ideal state and definitely not a socialist one, in his equation 'Churchill was preferrable to Hitler', the Soviet Union felt rather like Hitler.

And finally, Orwell returned to the issue of the choice between America and Russia, which 'may be forced on us'[105] in his article 'In Defence of Comrade Zilliacus', which was written for *Tribune* but not published by it. There he said again: 'everyone knows in his heart that he should choose America'.[106] Moreover, criticizing *Tribune*'s ambiguous position on foreign policy, which seemed to reveal how reluctant the paper was to admit its support of the country's foreign secretary, Ernest Bevin, as this would inevitably make it unpopular with 'the Communists, the fellow-travellers and the fellow-travellers of fellow-travellers', Orwell explained what, in his view, lay at the bottom of this phenomenon:

To be anti-American nowadays is to shout with the mob. Of course it is only a minor mob, but it is a vocal one. . . . At any given moment there is always an orthodoxy, a parrot cry which must be repeated and in the more active section of the Left the orthodoxy of the moment is anti-Americanism. . . . To speak favourably of America, to recall that the Americans helped us in 1940 when the Russians were supplying the Germans with oil and setting on their Communist parties to sabotage the war effort, is to be branded as a "reactionary". And I suspect that

[101] Ibid.
[102] Ibid.
[103] Wilford, *The CIA, the British Left and the Cold War*, 21–2.
[104] Ibid., 22.
[105] Orwell, 'In Defence of Comrade Zilliacus', August–September (?) 1947, CW, XIX, 182.
[106] Ibid.

when *Tribune* joins in the chorus it is more from fear of this label than from genuine conviction.[107]

The left kept the orthodoxy of anti-Americanism for many years to come. 'The mob' has grown enormous and much more vocal. And it was anti-Americanism that made many of the British left support Russia even in 2000s to 2020s, when there was no longer any communism there.

But even assessing Orwell's approach historically, John Newsinger is sure that his position can be explained by 'the debilitating effect of Orwell's exaggerated fear of the Soviet Union'. Orwell was, Newsinger states, 'right about the Soviet Union . . . and the regimes . . . imposed throughout Eastern Europe, but he was completely wrong about the threat that the Soviet Union, devastated as it was by war, posed. This led to him ignoring the realities of US imperialism'.[108] This presumably means that the Soviet Union did not constitute a threat for Britain, while US imperialism did.

There is no subjunctive mood in history and it can't be known what might have occurred, had the West not confronted Soviet attacks of different kinds and capitulated in the 'battle for hearts and minds' – apart from the evidence of 2022, which shows what happens when a totalitarian regime is not resisted. It is also not quite clear how being 'right about the Soviet Union' might co-exist with being 'completely wrong about the threat that the Soviet Union . . . posed'. Since the end of the war in 1945, the Soviet Union had been hostile to the West – its aggressiveness was openly displayed in Orwell's lifetime by the Berlin blockade and later by the Korean War and Cuban Missile Crisis. The fact that the country was 'devastated . . . by war' did not eliminate the threat of its using a nuclear bomb it was known to be working on. And of course the devastation of the Soviet Union had nothing to do with Soviet infiltration and generously funded anti-Western propaganda, which seemed to have hit an all-time high in 1949.

\* \* \*

The year 1949 started with an attempt by the French magazine *Les Lettres Françaises*, financed by the Soviet Union and the French Communist Party, to prove in court that there were no concentration camps in the USSR, and that the Soviet defector Victor Kravchenko, who denounced them in his book *I Chose Freedom* was lying at the bidding of the Americans. Later, the Soviet Union staged two huge international peace conferences: in New York in March and

---

[107] Ibid., 181–2.
[108] Newsinger, *Hope Lies in the Proles*, 106–7.

in Paris in April, which were due to convince the world of its peace-loving nature.

Orwell was following these developments closely, when Celia Kirwan, Koestler's sister-law and Orwell's own friend, whom he had hoped to marry a couple of years earlier, visited him in the Cranham sanatorium and confidentially told him about the work of the Information Research Department (IRD) she was now involved with. The IRD was founded in January 1948 with the aim of countering Soviet propaganda. In fact, several initiatives to do something of the kind had appeared even earlier, in 1946, but Ernest Bevin opposed them as 'too negative' and insisted on putting the emphasis on presenting 'the positive side of the new Britain'.[109] Bevin's own memorandum of 1948 combined the call for 'effective rebuttal of "Russian misinterpretations about Britain"', exposure of 'communist human rights abuses . . . and the imperialistic intent of Stalin's foreign policy'[110] with promoting the positive role of Britain and the Third Force foreign policy. This was expressed in the following passage:

> It is for us, as Europeans and as a Social Democratic Government, and not the Americans, to give the lead in spiritual, moral and political sphere [*sic*] to all democratic elements in Western Europe which are anti-Communist and at the same time, genuinely progressive and reformist, believing in freedom, planning and social justice – what one might call the 'Third Force'.[111]

The IRD had indeed appeared about six months before the corresponding Office of Policy Coordination (OPC) was established in the United States. For various reasons, the positive 'Third Force' foreign policy failed to materialize, but, according to Hugh Wilford, 'Labour had good reason to back the IRD, Third Force or no Third Force'.[112]

In any case, in March 1949, Orwell, was 'delighted to hear' about the work of the new department and 'expressed his wholehearted and enthusiastic approval of [its] aims'.[113] At Celia's request, 'he suggested various names of writers who might be enlisted to write for us',[114] she reported to the IRD. They were Darsie Gillie, *The Manchester Guardian* Paris correspondent; C. D.

---

[109] Quoted in: *IRD. Origins and Establishment of the Foreign Office Information Research Department, 1946–48* (Historians, Library and Research Department of the FCO, No. 9, August 1995), 3.

[110] Wilford, *The CIA, the British Left and the Cold War*, 50.

[111] Quoted in ibid.

[112] Ibid., 55.

[113] Celia Kirwan's Report to the IRD, 30 March 1949. CW, XX, 319.

[114] Ibid., 320.

Darlington, an ardent opponent of Lysenko's theories; and Franz Borkenau. Soon Orwell added the name of Gleb Struve, and also mentioned 'hordes of Americans, whose names can be found in the (New York) *New Leader*, the Jewish monthly paper *Commentary*,[115] and the *Partisan Review*'.[116] It was in the same letter that he suggested sending Celia 'a list of journalists & writers who in my opinion are crypto-Communists, fellow-travellers or inclined that way & *should not be trusted as propagandists*' [emphasis added].[117] On 2 May 1949 he sent Celia the list with thirty-eight names in it to be passed to the IRD. These names were extracted from his 'blue notebook' containing a list of 135 names, not intended for the IRD.[118]

Although the account of Orwell's notebook was first published in the *Sunday Telegraph* on 20 October 1991, it did not attract any attention then: the fall of the Berlin Wall, the liberation of Eastern Europe, the defeat of the August 1991 anti-*perestroika* coup in the USSR – all made supporters of Soviet communism keep quiet – unfortunately, not for very long. When just five years later, in July 1996, British papers published Orwell's letter to Celia with the offer to send her his list, all hell broke loose. In retrospect, it seems that the row that erupted said more about the people who chose to express their disgust at Orwell's conduct, than about him. Frances Stonor Saunders suggested that Orwell 'had confused the role of the intellectual with that of a policeman',[119] Tony Benn, MP, announced that he had 'given in',[120] and a Marxist historian, Christopher Hill, had, allegedly, always known that Orwell 'was two-faced. There was something fishy about [him]', he said.[121] Others, trying to defend Orwell, explained his action by his illness, by his love for Celia Kirwan or by his naiveté.

In fact, Orwell, who was not naïve at all, trusted the IRD, a government agency, not in the least because it was widely distributing *Tribune*, his paper, which, in the view of the agency, combined 'the resolute exposure of Communism and its methods with the consistent championship of those objectives which Left-wing sympathisers normally support'.[122] Many of *Tribune*'s articles were earmarked for use for IRD purposes. Why should he have been apprehensive? He was sure that the people he was naming would

---

[115] *Commentary* was founded in 1945 by the American Jewish Committee.

[116] Orwell to Kirwan, 6 April 1949, XX, 322.

[117] Ibid.

[118] See *The Lost Orwell*, 212.

[119] Saunders, *Who Paid the Piper?* 300.

[120] *Independent on Sunday*, 14 July 1996.

[121] Ibid. According to Boris Volodarsky, Hill, a friend of Peter Smollett, was himself a crypto-communist and an agent of influence; see Volodarsky, *Stalin's Agent*, 115–17.

[122] FO 1110/221:PR 442 quoted in Editorial Note 'Orwell and the Information Research Department', CW, XX, 319.

definitely not be suitable for 'the resolute exposure of Communism and its methods'. Moreover, he wrote to Celia about his list:

> It isn't very sensational and I don't suppose it will tell your friends anything they don't know. At the same time it isn't a bad idea to have the people who are probably unreliable listed. If it had been done earlier it would have stopped people like Peter Smollett worming their way into important propaganda jobs where they were probably able to do us a lot of harm.[123]

This letter contains an answer to the question many critics find confusing: why would Orwell keep a list of 135 names for himself, even before anybody asked for it? He certainly did it for the same reason that he wrote *Nineteen Eighty-Four* – he acutely felt the danger coming from the Soviet Union. He was sure that its regime was dangerous, not only for those who lived under it and had a first-hand experience of purges and the power of the state to crush an individual, but also for the whole world. The NKVD tactics in Spain, attempts of the pro-Soviet 'People's Convention' in 1940–1 to stop Britain from fighting Hitler, destruction of democracy in the countries of Eastern Europe and the nearly year-long Berlin blockade did not leave any doubt in Orwell's mind about the aggressive nature of the Soviet system. And at the same time he observed the readiness of the British intelligentsia to support it: before the war, feeling enthusiastic about the first 'socialist state'; during the war, reluctant to offend Britain's ally, and finally, after the war, gripped by anti-Americanism. He wrote:

> I think the Russian myth has done frightful harm to the leftwing movement in Britain and elsewhere, and that it is above all necessary to make people see the Russian regime for what it is (i.e. what I think it is). . . . I have no wish to interfere with the Soviet regime even if I could. I merely don't want its methods and habits of thought imitated here, and that involves fighting against the Russianisers in this country. The danger as I see it is not our being conquered by Russia, which might happen but depends chiefly on geography. The danger is that some native form of totalitarianism will be developed here, and people like Laski, Pritt, Zilliacus, the News Chronicle and the rest of them seem to me to be simply preparing the way for this.[124]

---

[123] Orwell to Kirwan, 2 May 1949, CW, XX, 103.
[124] Orwell to Sayers, 11 December 1945, *A Life in Letters*, 275.

* * *

It is difficult to get rid of a suspicion that 'the list' supplied Orwell's detractors with a long-awaited opportunity to settle old scores – when he was alive he simply did not give them a chance. At the same time, those who, on the whole, remained loyal to him as a man and a writer, still were embarrassed and felt they should disapprove of his 'inexcusable' or 'regrettable' behaviour in this particular case. And of course, nobody admired him for it. Even when more facts became available and Orwell's guesses about Peter Smollett and Tom Driberg were confirmed by the Mitrokhin Archive,[125] which stated unambiguously that the two were Soviet agents, hardly anybody praised Orwell's insight and his patriotism. Moreover, the comments he made against the names of some people in his list were condemned almost unanimously.

Even sympathetic commentators claimed that these notes betrayed 'his worst ethnic and sexual prejudices'[126] or that 'the nature of the list itself was pretty unsavoury; certainly something he should have been ashamed of'.[127] However, just as the very fact of giving IRD the list of untrustworthy people can be understood within the context of 1949, the notes like 'occasionally Homosexual' or 'Jewish'[128] should also be read within the context of Orwell's protest against any blanket attack on all communists and his refusal to apply the same yardstick to everybody.

In 'Burnham's View of the Contemporary World Struggle' he praises Burnham for his 'intellectual courage'[129] and agrees with his assessment of the situation: 'unless the signs are very deceiving, the USSR is preparing for war with Western democracies. Indeed, as Burnham rightly says, the war is already happening in a desultory way',[130] but decisively objects to Burnham's proposal to suppress communist parties in America or Britain – 'One has only to think of the people who would approve!'[131] He also protests against Burnham's approach to '"fellow-travellers", "cryptos" and sympathisers of various shades who further the aims of the Communists without having any official connections with them'.[132] Unlike Burnham, who seems to believe that these people 'will always continue in the same strain, even if the world situation deteriorates into open warfare', Orwell is sure that they can change

[125] Andrew and Mitrokhin, *The Mitrokhin Archive*, 158, 522–6.
[126] Wilford, *The CIA, the British Left and the Cold War*, 63.
[127] Newsinger, *Hope Lies in the Proles*, 125.
[128] Ibid.
[129] Orwell, CW, XIX, 99.
[130] Ibid.
[131] Ibid., 103.
[132] Ibid., 101.

their views: 'after all, the disillusioned "fellow-traveller" is a common figure, like the disillusioned Communist'.[133] He, therefore, suggests his own way:

> The important thing to do with these people – and it is extremely difficult since one has only inferential evidence – is to sort them out and determine which of them is honest and which is not.[134]

This is exactly what he was doing by keeping his 'blue notebook'. He tried to sort 'these people' out, to understand their psychological motives, to analyse why 'the quasi-religious appeal of the Communist myth'[135] worked for them. Peter Davison suggested that Orwell probably felt that, with homosexuality being illegal at the time, homosexuals were 'readily open to blackmail and easily "turned"'.[136] As far as Jews are concerned, Davison quotes an opinion that they might have been marked in the list because after the Holocaust, the Soviet Union could attract Jews by its official 'internationalism' – until of course they discovered how 'fiercely antisemitic'[137] it really was. On the other hand, both homosexuals and Jews belonged to persecuted minorities, and their particular vulnerability and insecurity could have made them more susceptible to influences, or perhaps they instinctively felt safer in a group united by a higher goal. But, naturally, it was not confined to these two groups. Numerous features of a human mindset: inability to think clearly, strong anti-Americanism, illusions about the nature of the Soviet regime, whose 'mythology is most easily swallowed by people who have not seen Russian rule at close quarters'[138] – all this might have explained the lure of communism to Americans and Brits.

Considered in this light, Orwell's comments in the list stop being 'smears' applied by him to different people, but become private pointers for the writer, who honestly, humanely and without prejudice tried to see their motives and predict their behaviour. He never forgot to mention the possibility of change in the person's views or any of his positive qualities. Being sure that '"the cryptos" and "fellow-travellers" advance the interests of the USSR against those of the democracies', he still questioned 'how many of them would continue on the same lines, if war were really imminent?'[139] Would they become traitors?

Naturally, Orwell's answer to this question was different from Burnham's. Burnham's position, as nearly always, annoyed him because it was so straightforward and crude: a communist is always a communist; to fight

---

[133] Ibid.
[134] Ibid.
[135] Ibid., 97.
[136] *The Lost Orwell*, 212.
[137] Ibid.
[138] Orwell, CW, XIX, 102.
[139] Ibid., 102.

communism we need to suppress communist parties, and so on. Even dealing with the group of 'cryptos' like Zilliacus and Pritt was not so simple, Orwell thought, despite the amount of time he had spent fighting them:

> They have undoubtedly done a great deal of mischief, especially in confusing public opinion about the nature of the puppet regimes in Eastern Europe; but one ought not hurriedly to assume that they are all equally dishonest or even that they all hold the same opinions. Probably some of them are actuated by nothing worse than stupidity.[140]

Nearly twenty years after Orwell's death, his friend Richard Rees explained that this was 'a sort of game [they] played – discovering who was a paid agent of what and estimating to what lengths of treachery our favourite bête noires would be prepared to go'.[141] And on 2 May 1949, the same day that Orwell sent his list to Celia Kirwan, he wrote to Rees how important it seemed to him 'to attempt to gauge people's *subjective* feelings':

> Suppose for example that Laski had possession of an important military secret. Would he betray it to the Russian military intelligence? I don't imagine so, because he has not actually made up his mind to be a traitor, & the nature of what he was doing would in that case be quite clear. But the real Communist would, of course, hand the secret over without any sense of guilt, & so would a real crypto, such as Pritt. The whole difficulty is to decide where each person stands, & one has to treat each case individually.[142]

This 'subjective', individual, approach to people is at least one thing that proves how absurd it is to see Orwell as one of Senator McCarthy's predecessors. He was not McCarthy, he wasn't even James Burnham. He was a writer with a rare mind that fused the political and the artistic into one whole. That is why it was and is so easy to misunderstand him.

[140] Ibid., 101.
[141] Richard Rees to Ian Angus, 10 August 1967, quoted in 'Orwell's List of Crypto-Communists and Fellow Travellers', CW, XX, 241.
[142] Orwell to Rees, 2 May 1949, CW, XX, 105.

# 7

# 'As I understand it'

*All through [Laski's] book there is apparent an unwillingness to admit that Socialism has totalitarian possibilities.[1]*

Orwell, 1943

*The basis of Socialism is humanism.[2]*

Orwell, 1946

Throughout his life Orwell wrestled with the issue of socialism and still remained split about it. There was no problem with 'belonging to the left', because, as his friend put it, 'He was very much a man who was in sympathy with the downtrodden people in this world'.[3] With socialism, however, he was fascinated with the idea, appalled by the sinister consequences of its embodiment in the USSR and Germany and horrified by the possibility that they might develop elsewhere. His late assessment of the trajectory of his own approach is worth quoting in full, because it is indicative of how his position swings – like a pendulum – back and forth:

I think I can say I was always more or less 'left'. In Wigan Pier I first tried to thrash out my ideas. I felt, as I still do, that there are huge deficiencies in the whole conception of Socialism, and I was still wondering whether there was any other way out. After having a fairly good look at British industrialism at its worst, i.e. in the mining areas, I came to the conclusion that it is a duty to work for Socialism even if one is not emotionally drawn to it, because the continuance of present conditions is simply not tolerable, and no solution except some kind of collectivism is viable, because this is what the mass of people want. About the same time I became infected with a horror of totalitarianism, which indeed I already had in the form of hostility towards the Catholic Church. I fought for six months (1936-7) in Spain on the side of the

---

[1]  Orwell, 'Review of *Reflections on the Revolution of Our Time* by Harold J. Laski', CW, XV, 270–1.
[2]  Orwell, 'What is Socialism?', CW, XVIII, 61.
[3]  Mabel Fierz in *The Orwell Tapes*, 70.

Government and had the misfortune to be mixed up in the internal struggle on the Government side, which left me with the conviction that there is not much to choose between Communism and Fascism, though for various reasons I would choose Communism if there were no other choice open.[4]

This extraordinary statement makes an important point: one has to accept socialism, because rationally there is no other way out of the present intolerable conditions. The 'least-evil' argument starts at the very beginning of the passage: 'I felt as I still do, that there are huge deficiencies in the whole conception of Socialism, and I was still wondering whether there was any other way out'; it is continued in the middle: 'no solution except some kind of collectivism is viable' and concluded in the last line: 'for various reasons I would choose Communism, if there were no other choice open'. Three times Orwell says that socialism/communism is a desperate measure, but there is nothing better. The 'positive' side does not look too exciting either: 'it is a duty to work for Socialism even if one is not emotionally drawn to it'.

Publishing the letter in 2010, Peter Davison mentioned that at one point Orwell 'had either forgotten or [was] glossing over'[5] an important fact of his political biography – his membership in the ILP. The same 'forgetting or glossing over' seems to be happening when Orwell completely ignores in this passage at least two instances of actually being 'emotionally drawn' to socialism. The first one is described in *Homage to Catalonia*; the second forms the basis of *The Lion and the Unicorn*. Both are beautiful pieces of writing.

If corroboration of Orwell's emotional attitude to socialism in Spain were needed, it is to be found in his letter to Cyril Connolly written on 8 June 1937 – after he was wounded but before the start of the terror against the POUM: 'I have seen wonderful things and at last really believe in Socialism, which I never did before.'[6] These wonderful things meant something he had long dreamt of – the equality of people belonging to different classes. He failed to find it in Wigan, where, frustratingly, the workers he met refused to treat him as an equal, but in Spain – on his arrival in Barcelona and later in the POUM militia, he did suddenly experience this exhilarating feeling. This happened in a foreign country, during the revolution and war, and in an isolated community where class distinctions did not really matter. He realized that

---

[4]  Orwell to Usborne, 26 August 1947. *A Life in Letters*, xi.
[5]  Davison, 'Introduction to *A Life in Letters*', xii.
[6]  Orwell to Connolly, 8 June 1937, CW, XI, 28.

the state of affairs was only temporary, 'but it lasted long enough to have its effect upon anyone who experienced it'. He called it 'a foretaste of Socialism':

> Up here in Aragon one was among tens of thousands of people, mainly though not entirely of working-class origin, all living at the same level and mingling on terms of equality. . . . The ordinary class-division of society had disappeared to an extent that is almost unthinkable in the money-tainted air of England. . . . One had been in a community where hope was more normal than apathy or cynicism, where the word 'comrade' stood for comradeship and not, as in most countries, for humbug. . . . I am well aware that it is now the fashion to deny that Socialism has anything to do with equality. In every country in the world a huge tribe of party-hacks and sleek little professors are busy 'proving' that Socialism means no more than a planned state-capitalism with the grab-motive left intact. But fortunately there also exists a vision of Socialism quite different from this. The thing that attracts ordinary men to Socialism and makes them willing to risk their skins for it, the 'mystique' of Socialism, is the idea of equality; to the vast majority of people Socialism means a classless society, or it means nothing at all.[7]

In *The Lion and the Unicorn*, written three and a half years later, Orwell presents the idea of equality as something that makes socialism 'irreconcilably different' from fascism: 'Socialism aims, ultimately, at a world-state of free and equal human beings. It takes the equality of human rights for granted. Nazism assumes just the opposite. The driving force behind the Nazi movement is the belief in human *inequality*, the superiority of Germans to all other races, the right of Germany to rule the world.'[8] However, a bit earlier he admits the similarity between socialism and fascism in the economic sphere, especially in the time of war:

> Fascism, at any rate the German version, is a form of capitalism that borrows from Socialism just such features as will make it efficient for war purposes. Internally, Germany has a good deal in common with a Socialist state. Ownership has never been abolished . . . But at the same time the State, which is simply the Nazi Party, is in control of everything.[9]

---

[7]    Orwell, *Homage to Catalonia*, 102.
[8]    Orwell, *The Lion and the Unicorn: Socialism and the English Genius* (London: Penguin Books, 1984), 76.
[9]    Ibid., 75–6.

Moreover, Orwell at this point is sure that 'however horrible this system may seem to us, *it works*', while 'British capitalism . . . was unequal to the strain of preparing for war'[10] and 'the same tug-of-war between private profit and public necessity is . . . still continuing'.[11] From here he logically moves on to support the idea of the revolution, which would bring in a socialist 'planned economy' and therefore ensure both Britain's war victory and a classless society after the war. 'We know very well that with its present social structure England cannot survive, and we have got to make other people see that fact and act upon it. We cannot win the war without introducing Socialism, nor establish Socialism without winning the war.'[12]

Somewhat earlier in the essay he presented the same formula, but with a specification: 'We cannot establish *anything that a Western nation would regard as Socialism* [emphasis added] without defeating Hitler; on the other hand we cannot defeat Hitler while we remain economically and socially in the nineteenth century.'[13] It seems to imply that 'anything that a Western nation would regard as Socialism' would not be its Russian or German variant. However, in his review of Franz Borkenau's book *The Totalitarian Enemy* in May 1940, Orwell actually said: 'National Socialism *is* a form of Socialism'.[14] And just a couple of months after the publication of *The Lion and the Unicorn*, in April 1941, he mocked the reluctance of the left to acknowledge it:

Since Nazism was not *what any Western European means by Socialism* [emphasis added], clearly it must be capitalism. While they reasoned thus, the official theorists of the Left were forced enormously to underrate the *strength* of Nazism. Otherwise they would have had to admit that Nazism *did* avoid the contradictions of capitalism, that it *was* a kind of socialism though a non-democratic kind.[15]

So already by this point there were at least two kinds of socialism in his mind.

Franz Borkenau, whose influence on Orwell's development as a social thinker is impossible to overestimate, did discuss in *The Totalitarian Enemy* whether the USSR and Nazi Germany were socialist countries or not. Apart from reviewing this book, as well as two previous ones, Orwell had been close to Borkenau for three years, 1937–40, and particularly so in the summer of 1940, when his diary reflects frequent meetings and their

[10]  Ibid., 77.
[11]  Ibid., 79.
[12]  Ibid., 100.
[13]  Ibid., 95–6.
[14]  Orwell, 'Review of *The Totalitarian Enemy*', CW, XII, 159.
[15]  Orwell, 'Will Freedom Die with Capitalism?', CW, XII, 461.

common conviction that a revolution in Britain was imminent ('Borkenau says England is now definitely in the first stage of the revolution,'[16] Orwell wrote triumphantly in his end of May entry). Borkenau suggested that from the position of a socialist, neither Germany nor Russia was socialist because neither had social equality and political liberty, but as far as their economies were concerned, both of them were. He was prepared to accept both approaches, but warned: 'One thing, however, is certain: it is impossible to regard one of the two countries as Socialist and the other not.'[17] At the same time he treated both countries as totalitarian and unhesitatingly declared that 'Russia is infinitely more totalitarian than Germany.'[18]

The reason for this difference, he was sure, lay 'in the degree of State interference in economic life.'[19] Obviously, in the Soviet Union it was much higher – the state interfered in everything, fully in keeping with Mussolini's 1928 formula of totalitarianism: 'Everything within the state, nothing outside the state, nothing against the state'. Orwell, who ingeniously foretold a possible appearance of fascism in place of socialism as early as in *Wigan Pier*, was well aware of the danger, and even in *The Lion and the Unicorn*, probably the most optimistic of his social predictions, did not fail to emphasize the need for 'some control over the government'. He meant the need for 'political democracy' as one of 'the necessary safeguards against the reappearance of a class system'. Without it, he warned, '"the State" may come to mean no more than a self-elected political party, and oligarchy and privilege can return, based on power rather than on money',[20] obviously hinting at the 'non-democratic', totalitarian options of Germany and Russia.

Still, he insisted on the need of 'State interference' in Britain, especially during the war and cheerfully explained in his pamphlet: 'A bombing plane, for instance, is equivalent in price to fifty small motor cars, or eighty thousand pairs of silk stockings, or a million loaves of bread. Clearly you can't have *many* bombing planes without lowering the national standard of life',[21] he added, being absolutely certain that nobody in their right mind would prefer producing bombers in peace time at the expense of loaves of bread. Sadly, anybody who lived in the Soviet Union knew only

---

[16]  *War-Time Diary*, 30 May 1940, *The Orwell Diaries*, 247. Soon after his intense discussions of the current situation with Orwell, on 26 June 1940 Borkenau was interned as an 'enemy alien' and on 10 July deported to Australia on board the notorious HMT Dunera. He came back to Britain in June 1941. He and Orwell remained friends, but less close than before, although Eileen helped to edit Borkenau's next book.

[17]  Borkenau, *The Totalitarian Enemy*, 30.

[18]  Ibid., 227.

[19]  Ibid.

[20]  Orwell, *The Lion and the Unicorn*, 75.

[21]  Ibid., 77.

too well that the living standards of the population were the last thing 'the state', preoccupied with the arms race, would care about. Moreover, Orwell continued confidently: 'It is not certain that Socialism is in all ways superior to capitalism, but it is certain that, unlike capitalism, it can solve the problems of production and consumption. . . . . The State simply calculates what goods will be needed and does its best to produce them'.[22] Again, under the Soviet kind of socialism there was, unfortunately, nothing simple about that – the problems of production and consumption were not, and probably could not be, really solved. Orwell's confusion lay in mixing up mobilization in a time of emergency and the normal existence of the economy at all other times.

Eager as ever to suggest practical solutions, Orwell even presented in his essay a six-point programme, where the first point was 'nationalisation of land, mines, railways, banks and major industries'.[23] He must have temporarily forgotten that his own clear-cut formula: 'the State, representing the whole nation, owns everything, and everyone is a State employee'[24] can lead only to the severe limitation of personal freedoms.

Borkenau had no doubt that once the economy falls under political control it can result only in totalitarianism, as it happened both in Russia and in Germany. His most striking example of the state neglecting the interests of its citizens and deliberately reducing their standard of living for the sake of its own power was the fatal decision of Stalin to bring the NEP (New Economic Policy) to a close and put the economy under the full control of the Communist Party, while other options for the country still existed:

> Economically speaking there was no objection against the development of private capitalism. It would have meant a rapid development of industry, a rapid increase of national wealth, a rise of the standard of living of both peasants and workers. But it would have meant the collapse of the regime. Political considerations pushed Russia along the road of the Five-year plan, which was a road of almost indescribable suffering, merely in the interest of the ruling political group. Economics were throughout subordinated to politics, which is one of the most distinctive features of totalitarian regime. The Five-year plan opposed the ruling group to all other groups and classes, thus creating the typical antagonism between a political gang at the top and all the economic interests of the country . . .. The year 1929, when the first Five-year plan was launched, marks the final emergence of totalitarianism in Russia.[25]

---

[22]  Ibid., 74–5.
[23]  Ibid., 104.
[24]  Ibid., 74.
[25]  Borkenau, *The Totalitarian Enemy*, 225.

Germany did the same when preparing for the war. The Nazis pushed the country to 'the mad rearmament drive',[26] but although 'all the resources . . . [were] strained beyond capacity', it did not bring about 'the increase of consumption';[27] that is, people's living standards did not rise, but rather went dramatically down. German workers had to endure 'the intolerable strain of a ten- or twelve-hour working day, while at the same time suffering from malnutrition',[28] and some categories of workers virtually became slaves, as they were not allowed 'to change their jobs, except upon orders'.[29] Even 'millions of shopkeepers and craftsmen',[30] who voted for Hitler and actually brought him to power, were crushed by the Nazi state.

In his review of Borkenau's book, Orwell stressed that he fully understood the logic of it:

> A country, and especially a poor country, which is waging or preparing for 'total' war must be in some sense socialistic. When the state has taken complete control of industry, when the so called capitalist is reduced to the status of a manager, and when consumption goods are so scarce and so strictly rationed that you cannot spend a big income even if you earn one, then the essential structure of Socialism already exists, plus the comfortless equality of war-communism. Simply in the interests of efficiency the Nazis found themselves expropriating, nationalising, destroying the very people they had set out to save. It did not bother them, because their aim was simply power and not any particular form of society.[31]

Thus, the totalitarian economy – 'socialistic' in form – was in fact the product of the drive for power of those at the top. Whether they aimed at 'any particular form of society' like Stalin or at world conquest like Hitler, it was the way for the leaders to remain in power. Was there a way to prevent this from happening, to stop the 'planned and centralized' economy from sliding into totalitarianism? This was the issue both Borkenau and Orwell kept thinking about.

---

26  Ibid., 146.
27  Ibid., 42.
28  Ibid.
29  Ibid., 50.
30  Ibid., 75–6.
31  Orwell, CW, XII, 159.

*    *    *

For both of them the return to *laissez-faire* capitalism was unthinkable. They were sure that even 'tamed and modified' it was 'inherently evil'.[32] In the same book where Borkenau competently exposed the dangers of totalitarianism, he, not less passionately, attacked supporters of the free market and capitalist competition:

> It is impossible to deny that competition, when given a free rein, is always operative in bringing about the highest technical standard obtainable. Unfortunately, the world does not consist of industrial technique and economic affairs alone. The orthodox Liberal argument far surpasses in ruthlessness anything ever conceived by Nazis and Bolsheviks. Supposing no economic unit were protected, and no doles were given to the unemployed, most of the victims of the slump would probably not find new employment before they starved. The argument is in substance identical with the Bolshevik argument that a few tens of millions of people killed in a world revolution do not matter, if only the killing brings about social progress. The only difference is that the murderous effects of unrestricted competition would be infinitely more cruel, in our present stage of industrial development, than the most cruel world revolution.[33]

The fact that Borkenau, with his prominent anti-totalitarian views, supposed that the capitalist slump might take more lives than the Bolshevik slaughter, reveals the scale of the shock that Western countries suffered during the economic crisis of the early 1930s. The conviction that only a 'centralised and planned economy' based on 'free cooperation' could save the world, and the sooner it replaced the free market the better, was deeply instilled in him and many others.

Orwell's approach to capitalism in his review of F. A. Hayek's book *The Road to Serfdom* is more philosophical but no less firm. He agrees with 'the negative part of Professor Hayek's thesis':

> By bringing the whole of life under the control of the State, Socialism necessarily gives power to an inner ring of bureaucrats, who in almost every case will be men who want power for its own sake and will stick at nothing in order to retain it.... It cannot be said too often – at any rate, it is not being said nearly often enough – that collectivism is not inherently

[32] Orwell, 'Will Freedom Die with Capitalism?' (*The Left News*, April 1941), CW, XII, 461.
[33] Borkenau, *The Totalitarian Enemy*, 78–9.

democratic, but, on the contrary, gives to a tyrannical minority such powers as the Spanish Inquisitors never dreamed of.[34]

However, Hayek's recipe: 'the only salvation lies in returning to an unplanned economy, free competition, and emphasis on liberty rather than on security'[35] makes Orwell vehemently protest:

> He doesn't see, or will not admit, that the return to 'free' competition means for the great mass of people a tyranny probably worse, because more irresponsible, then that of the State. The trouble with competitions is that somebody wins them. Professor Hayek denies that free capitalism necessarily leads to monopoly, but in practice that is where it has led, and since the vast majority of people would far rather have State regimentation than slumps and unemployment, the drift towards collectivism is bound to continue if popular opinion has any say in the matter.[36]

This being 1944, three years after writing 'The Lion and the Unicorn', Orwell is pretty pessimistic about the 'present predicament':

> Capitalism leads to dole queues, the scramble for markets, and war. Collectivism leads to concentration camps, leader-worship, and war. There is no way out of this unless a planned economy can be somehow combined with the freedom of the intellect, which can only happen if the concept of right and wrong is restored to politics.[37]

Probably because both Borkenau and Orwell did not believe that anything good would ever come out of capitalism, neither of them could imagine its future transformation: the appearance of a Welfare state and general improvement of living conditions for the majority of people, which, in the West, came into being relatively soon. Instead, they both considered the possibility of trying socialism in a developed Western country. That was their attempt to combine a socialist economy with democracy – the union, which, they hoped, would ensure a better life for the masses and preserve civil liberties.

It is not clear whose idea it originally was – it is mentioned in Orwell's correspondence as early as the very start of 1940 – before the publication of

[34] Orwell, 'Review of *The Road to Serfdom* by F. A. Hayek'; *The Mirror of the Past* by K. Zilliacus (*The Observer*, 9 April 1944), CW, XVI, 149.
[35] Ibid.
[36] Ibid.
[37] Ibid., 150.

*The Totalitarian Enemy*, but, of course, he and Borkenau were friends and could have discussed it among themselves even earlier. In any case, when on the first day of 1940, Victor Gollancz, who, after the shock of the Soviet-Nazi Pact of 1939, became much more interested in Orwell's political views than he had been previously, asked him casually, as if the issue had been debated dozens of times: 'Isn't the only thing worth doing to try to find some way of reconciling the inevitable totalitarian economics with individual freedom?'[38] Orwell replied: 'It is quite possible that freedom of thought etc. may survive in an economically totalitarian society. We can't tell until a collectivised economy has been tried out in a western country.'[39]

In Borkenau's book, the idea at first seems a purely mental experiment. Having firmly established that 'the rise of State interference threatens all democratic institutions',[40] Borkenau, towards the end of his book, suddenly suggests the reversal of this approach: 'State Socialism of the Nazi type, though not with the aims to which Nazis have made it subservient, could easily exist with a different ideology . . . . Economic collectivism . . . could be made to work for aims entirely different from those of the Nazis.'[41] True to himself, Borkenau, however, openly admits the negative consequences of the development he favours:

> Economic planning entails a great deal more bureaucratic power and centralization than was necessary and even admissible in a liberal economic system. This, far from being progress, is probably a grievous disadvantage, but it cannot be wholly avoided. *Some of the rights of the individual will have to go* [emphasis added]. In fact, the process of bureaucratisation and centralisation is proceeding in all countries irrespective of the revolutionary or non-revolutionary character of their political systems. But it is not by any means a necessity that it should acquire the characteristics of the totalitarian regimes.[42]

In Orwell's article 'Will Freedom Die with Capitalism?' – a reply to a reader of *The Left News*, who questioned the possibility of 'this new Utopia you advocate', the perspective of the socialist future is even less bright: 'It is not claimed by Socialists that the change-over to a collectivist economy will make human life happier, easier or even freer *immediately*. On the contrary, the

[38]  Gollancz to Orwell, 1 January 1940 (dated 1939 by mistake), Orwell H/1/73/3, The OA, UCL.
[39]  Orwell to Gollancz, 8 January 1940, CW, XII, 5.
[40]  Borkenau, *The Totalitarian Enemy*, 158.
[41]  Ibid., 146–7.
[42]  Ibid., 243.

transition may make life very nearly unbearable for a long period, perhaps for hundreds of years.'[43] In this article, Orwell even unexpectedly adopts a kind of Marxist determinism and claims that 'Socialism . . . is the necessary step towards communism, just as capitalism was the necessary next step after feudalism',[44] which allows him to conclude: 'It [socialism] is not in itself the final objective and I think we ought to guard against assuming that *as a system to live under* it will be greatly preferable to democratic capitalism'.[45] This sober analysis contrasts greatly with the inspired description of the idealized 'English Socialism' in *The Lion and the Unicorn*:

> It will not be doctrinaire, nor even logical. It will abolish the House of Lords, but quite probably will not abolish the monarchy. It will leave anachronisms and loose ends everywhere, the judge in his ridiculous horsehair wig and the lion and the unicorn on the soldiers cap-buttons. It will not set up any explicit class dictatorship. . . . It will never lose touch with the tradition of compromise and the belief in a law that is above the State. . . . It will crush any open revolt promptly and cruelly, but it will interfere very little with the spoken and written word.[46]

Reviewing *The Totalitarian Enemy* in 1940, Orwell was very sceptical about Borkenau's hope that it would be Britain, which would be able 'to oppose a humaner, freer form of collectivism to the purge-and-censorship variety'.[47] A better judge of his own country than an admiring foreigner, he could not 'see the present Government doing it'.[48] However, quite soon, the surge of both revolutionary and patriotic feelings made him view this romantic dream as entirely possible, and this brought forth his most 'emotional' and poetic pamphlet, one of the best examples of his prose, but not necessarily of his political vision.

By the autumn of 1944 it was obvious that the war, although not lost, had not become revolutionary and in the London Letter published in winter 1944–45, Orwell openly admitted that he had been 'grossly wrong in his analysis of the situation'[49] when he predicted a socialist revolution in Britain. Less than a year before his death, in April 1949, he asked for *The Lion and*

---

[43]　Orwell, CW, XII, 459.
[44]　Ibid.
[45]　Ibid.
[46]　Orwell, 'The Lion and the Unicorn', 113.
[47]　Orwell, CW, XII, 159.
[48]　Ibid.
[49]　Orwell, London Letter, written October (?) 1944 (*Partisan Review*, Winter 1944–45), CW, XVI, 414.

*the Unicorn* to be added to the list of his works 'NOT to be reprinted'.[50] The moment when he was 'emotionally drawn' to socialism in Britain had passed, and he probably preferred not to go back to it.

\*  \*  \*

Still he could not stop looking for a solution. In 1941, soon after the publication of *The Lion and the Unicorn*, Orwell addressed the possibility of having 'the transition to a centralised economy' in a different – not Soviet and not Nazi – form, but this time not only in Britain but in other Western states too, which 'have enough in common to be thought of as a single culture'.[51] This culture implied 'a belief in the *value* of bourgeois Democracy', and, Orwell hoped, it was not only sustained by these countries' material wealth, but by other things too: 'A hatred of civil violence and the respect for freedom of speech are definite factors in Western life, and they are not likely to vanish overnight, even if our standard of living drops to that of Eastern Europe.'[52]

When, six years later, he was invited by *Partisan Review* magazine to contribute to their series 'The Future of Socialism', he sent them his article 'Toward European Unity'. Orwell was one of a number of well-known authors who participated in the series, which was later translated into many European languages. In this very rational rather than poetic essay, Orwell proposed to make 'democratic socialism . . . work throughout some large area'[53] and suggested that this area should be Europe. This was the place where one could still find 'large numbers of people to whom the word "socialism" has some appeal and to whom it is bound up with liberty, equality, and internationalism',[54] absent, as it was already clear, from Soviet and East European socialism. This idea in his mind was naturally connected with the idea of 'a western European union'[55] which made this essay often quoted in Britain during the debate on Brexit.

Writing this article in the summer of 1947, Orwell fully realized the uncertainty of the political situation, which made any plans precarious: Will the Soviet Union get the atom bomb in the nearest future? Will the new war start before long? Will the United States remain 'capitalistic' or might 'a powerful socialist movement . . . for the first time arise' there? And 'what

[50] Orwell's Notes on His Books and Essays, CW, XX, 226.
[51] Orwell, 'Will Freedom Die with Capitalism?', CW, XII, 462.
[52] Ibid.
[53] Orwell, 'Toward European Unity' (*Partisan Review*, July–August 1947), CW, XIX, 164.
[54] Ibid.
[55] Ibid.

changes will take place in the USSR'?[56] Here Orwell predicted that although the Soviet regime

> deliberately aims at preventing the pendulum swing between generations, . . . the tendency of one generation to reject the ideas of the past is an abiding human characteristic which even the NKVD will be unable to eradicate. In that case there may by 1960 be millions of young Russians who are bored by dictatorship and loyalty parades, eager for more freedom, and friendly in their attitude toward the West.[57]

From all the forecasts contained in this article, it was this last one (apart from the creation of the European Union, of course!) that eventually came true. In 1957 Moscow hosted the Sixth World Festival of Youth and Students with 34,000 guests from 131 countries, which opened up the world at least for the Muscovites. The reason for this was not only the generational change, predicted by Orwell, but, much more importantly, a temporary liberalization of the regime – a 'thaw'.

Nikita Khrushchev's denunciation of Stalin's 'personality cult' a year earlier released thousands of political prisoners from concentration camps. This was crucial for the new generation – the 'generation of the sixties' as they soon began to be known: with prisoners coming back from the camps or internal exile, many young people saw their parents after many years of separation and this gave them some hope that the regime might grow softer or even change more radically. New literature, new theatre, new songs suddenly emerged in the Soviet Union and were not immediately crushed. The regime, however, remained the same – Khrushchev's 'thaw' was short-lived and did not impact the foundations of the system.

And still Orwell's belief that things might change for the better even in the stronghold of totalitarianism, the Soviet Union, shows that the precision of his sociological insight never cancelled out his hope for some improvement in people's lives. In the same way he considered 'a Socialist United States of Europe . . . to be the only worth-while political objective today' and, although he knew perfectly well that its success was unlikely, he still added: 'I also can't at present see any other hopeful objective'.[58]

The words 'hope, hopeful' were essential for his approach to socialism. Replying in 1944 to Noel Wilmett, who asked him whether totalitarianism in the world was expanding, Orwell tried to discriminate between two

---

[56]  Ibid., 166.
[57]  Ibid., 166–7.
[58]  Ibid., 164–6.

totalitarianisms and claimed that communism was a lesser evil than fascism. He explained his position:

> I think the USSR cannot altogether escape its past and retains enough of the original ideas of the Revolution to make it a more hopeful phenomenon than Nazi Germany. I think, and have thought ever since the war began, in 1936 or thereabouts, that our cause is the better, but we have to keep on making it the better, which involves constant criticism.[59]

He wrote this three months after finishing *Animal Farm*, where he made a point of exposing a complete post-revolutionary betrayal of revolutionary ideals in a 'fairy story' which closely followed the Soviet trajectory. Yet he still suggested that the Soviet Union had probably retained at least some of its ideals, while Germany had never had them at all. Was he trying to convince his correspondent? Or himself? Or did he mean that communism had at least *started* better than nazism? In this letter he dated the beginning of the war as 1936 – that is, he meant not the World War but the Spanish Civil War, which actually revealed for him the similarity of the conduct of communists and fascists in Spain.[60] This was also the date of his new political stance: 'Every line of serious work that I have written since 1936 has been written, directly or indirectly, *against* totalitarianism and *for* democratic Socialism, as I understand it.'[61] Qualifying the word 'socialism' twice: '*democratic* Socialism, *as I understand it*' [emphasis added], Orwell tried to specify his own approach, obviously unwilling to be seen as a supporter of the socialism to which he did not subscribe.

\*   \*   \*

An important definition of socialism is found in the cycle 'The Intellectual Revolt' that Orwell published a bit earlier than 'Why I Write' – in January–February 1946. This cycle is an attempt to present not the position of the masses, who, as Orwell repeatedly asserted, would always choose security (and therefore 'socialist regimentation') over the liberty prevalent in capitalist societies, but the perspective of intellectuals. Having said many times that 'intellectuals are more totalitarian in outlook than the common people',[62] in these four articles under a common title Orwell suddenly gives intellectuals their due and lets some of them have their say.

[59]   Orwell to Wilmett, 18 May 1944, CW, XVI, 191.
[60]   See, for example, Orwell to Charlesworth, CW, XI, 76.
[61]   Orwell, 'Why I Write', CW, XVIII, 319.
[62]   Orwell to Willmett, CW, XVI, 191.

Reviewing the viewpoints of four groups of scholars and writers – the Pessimists (Hayek, Burnham, Russell, Voigt, Drucker), the Left-Wing Socialists (Koestler, Silone, Gide, Lyons, Borkenau, Eastman), the Christian Reformers (with as unlikely bed-fellows as the Dean of Canterbury and Nicholas Berdyaev) and the Pacifists (Huxley, Read )[63] – Orwell comes to the conclusion that all of them 'hold one thing in common: opposition to the tyranny of the State'. And the very fact that 'so many minds in so many countries agree on this', brings him to the optimistic prediction that 'centralisation and bureaucratic controls . . . will not be permitted unlimited growth'.[64]

The year 1946 had started for Orwell with thinking about 'liberty and security' as he prepared the Draft of the Manifesto for a new 'League for the Rights of Man', which he sent off to Koestler on 2 January. As much as he wished to oppose 'the tyranny of the state', especially as the aim of this manifesto was to secure civil liberties, he still was reluctant to dismiss the role of the state altogether. His draft limited its functions to guaranteeing its citizens 'the equality of opportunity and a reasonable equality in income', which should protect them 'against economic exploitation' and 'against the fettering or misappropriation of [their] creative faculties and achievements'.[65] The state was also expected to ensure 'economic planning and control' and fulfil all these tasks 'with maximum efficiency and a minimum of interference'.[66]

The groups of intellectuals, which Orwell described in *The Intellectual Revolt*, differed mainly in their attitude to 'the planned society': the Pessimists completely denied its benefits, the Left-Wing Socialists 'accepted the principle of planning but [were] chiefly concerned to combine it with individual liberty',[67] while the Christian Reformers and Pacifists tried to avoid dealing with the State and its coercion altogether.

Orwell puts himself and his friends, Borkenau and Koestler, in the second group and tries – not for the first time in his life – to give a definition of socialism. He starts with talking about it as a Utopia, as 'a word evoking a dream' – this was, he says, how socialism had been thought about until the 1930s, when the results of 'testing it in the physical world' – first in Russia and then in Germany – proved to be very different from what was expected. 'Evidently it was time for the word "Socialism" to be redefined',

---

[63] Orwell, 'The Intellectual Revolt' (*Manchester Evening News*, 24, 31 January, 7, 14 February 1946), CW, XVIII, 56–71.
[64] Ibid., 71.
[65] Draft of the Manifesto, MS 2345-2.4-12.
[66] Ibid.
[67] Orwell, CW, XVIII, 57.

suggested Orwell, and asked indignantly: 'Can you have Socialism without liberty, without equality, and without internationalism? Are we still aiming at universal human brotherhood, or must we be satisfied with a new kind of caste society in which we surrender our individual rights in return for economic security?'[68] Somewhat later in the same year he wrote: 'Evidently the USSR is not Socialist and can only be called Socialist if one gives the word a meaning different from what it would have in any other context'.[69] Here again he stresses 'the monstrosity of Nazism . . . one of the most cruel and cynical regimes the world has ever seen', but seems to be more compassionate for Russian communists, who,

> in order to survive . . . were forced to abandon, at any rate temporarily, some of the dreams with which they had started out.
>
> Strict economic equality was found to be impracticable; freedom of speech, in a backward country which has passed through civil war, was too dangerous; internationalism was killed by the hostility of the capitalist powers.
>
> From about 1925 onwards Russian politics, internal and external, grew harsher and less idealistic.[70]

Russian communists are presented in this passage as victims of circumstances rather than of their own disastrous policies, and Orwell deplores here not so much their rejection of democracy but renunciation of their dreams. Again he talks not as a political thinker, but as a writer, for whom the idealism, the belief that 'the earthly paradise' is possible, that 'the human society . . . could be a great deal better than it is at present' is of primary importance. Indeed, he actually claims that a real 'Socialist or Communist' is the one 'who breaks with his own party on a point of doctrine',[71] and is 'in revolt against [the Machiavellian] tendencies'.[72]

In the ten years that had passed since Orwell wrote *The Road to Wigan Pier* he learnt to accept 'the need for planned societies and for a high level of industrial development', which he rather resented in the earlier book, but still, in exactly the same way as the 'Utopians' he describes, he still would choose 'the older conception of Socialism, which laid its stress on liberty and equality and drew its inspiration from the belief in human brotherhood'.[73]

[68]  Ibid.
[69]  Orwell, 'Second Thoughts of James Burnham' (*Polemic*, 3 May 1946), CW, XVIII, 272.
[70]  Orwell, CW, XVIII, 61–2.
[71]  Ibid., 61.
[72]  Ibid., 62.
[73]  Ibid.

Although he admits that 'at this moment it is difficult for Utopianism to take shape in a definite political movement',[74] he feels that the dream of 'the earthly paradise' is essential for anybody who hopes to change life for the better, because

> underneath it lies the belief that human nature is fairly decent to start with and is capable of indefinite development. This belief has been the main driving force of the Socialist movement, including the underground sects who prepared the way for the Russian revolution, and it could be claimed that the Utopians, at present a scattered minority, are the true upholders of Socialist tradition.[75]

This was perhaps Orwell's most open acknowledgement of the deep disappointment he experienced at the thought of the unbridgeable gap between the dream of socialism and its actual existence. He developed it in the long polemical essay on James Burnham, whose rigorous sociological analysis often infuriated Orwell, although he agreed with large parts of it. Burnham was a sociologist, Orwell was a writer with extraordinarily strong, often ingenious, sociological insights, and it was his role as a writer that made him resent what seemed to him the narrow-mindedness and even cynicism of Burnham's approach. He wrote:

> What Burnham is mainly concerned to show is that a democratic society has never existed and, so far as we can see, never will exist. Society is of its nature oligarchical, and the power of the oligarchy always rests upon force and fraud. Burnham does not deny that 'good' motives may operate in private life, but he maintains that politics consists of the struggle for power, and nothing else. All historical changes finally boil down to the replacement of one ruling class by another. All talk about democracy, liberty, equality, fraternity, all revolutionary movements, all visions of Utopia, or 'the classless society', or 'the Kingdom of Heaven on earth', are humbug (not necessarily conscious humbug) covering the ambitions of some new class which is elbowing its way into power.[76]

Orwell, naturally, strongly believed in the existence of 'good' motives in politics. Moreover, for him, these motives were the driving force of any revolution. What happened later was a separate development – if

---

[74]   Ibid.
[75]   Ibid.
[76]   Orwell, 'Second Thoughts on James Burnham', CW, XVIII, 269.

revolutionary masses proved incapable of saving the results of a revolution for themselves, they were 'thrust back into servitude'[77] by the new ruling class. This actually was what he exposed in *Animal Farm*.

He discussed the issue once again in 1948, when reviewing Oscar Wilde's *The Soul of Man Under Socialism*, originally published in 1891. He had to admit that 'Wilde's Utopia' of socialism was 'no nearer' than in its author's time, while 'Socialism, in the sense of economic collectivism, [was] conquering the earth'.[78] And yet the value of Wilde's nearly sixty-year-old book lay, according to Orwell, in its capacity 'to remind the Socialist movement of its original half-forgotten objective of human brotherhood'.[79]

'Orwell was a humanitarian – always moved by sympathy, by human love. The inconsistencies of his political opinions sprang from this fact',[80] – this was how Herbert Read described him in the posthumous review of *Nineteen Eighty-Four*. Read then gave an example of an inconsistency that was particularly close to his heart:

> Consistently he would have been a pacifist, but he could not resist the Quixotic impulse to spring to arms in defence of the weak or oppressed. It would be difficult to say what positive political ideals were left this side of his overwhelming disillusion with Communism. In his last years he saw only the menace of the totalitarian state, and he knew he had only the force left to warn us.[81]

It seems that what remained of Orwell's 'positive political ideals' was still socialism. Yes, it was a dream, a Utopia – he was perfectly aware of that, but rejecting it altogether would be for him tantamount to rejecting humanism – 'the basis of Socialism', and this he could not do.

*         *         *

In 1948, the last working year of his life, having finished the draft of *Nineteen Eighty-Four*, he finally tried to define a place for himself in the complex political situation of his day. In 'Writers and Leviathan' he decided to acknowledge publicly the uneasiness he felt about the tension between the

[77]   Ibid.
[78]   Orwell, 'Review of *The Soul of Man Under Socialism* by Oscar Wilde' (*The Observer*, 9 May 1948), CW, XIX, 333.
[79]   Ibid.
[80]   Herbert Read (*World Review*, June 1950) in: Meyers, *George Orwell: The Critical Heritage*, 285.
[81]   Ibid.

novel he was still writing and his relations with the left – both his friends and the *Tribune* colleagues, some of whom were Labour MPs. He expressed it cautiously and not without embarrassment: 'To suggest that a creative writer, in a time of conflict, must split his life into two compartments, may seem defeatist or frivolous: yet in practice I do not see what else he can do.'[82] In 'The Prevention of Literature' he said that by trying to adapt to totalitarian control the writer destroys his 'dynamo': 'If he is forced to do so, the only result is that his creative faculties will dry up.'[83] In 'Writers and Leviathan' he makes a more general statement: 'Group loyalties are necessary, and yet they are poisonous to literature, so long as literature is the product of individuals. As soon as they are allowed to have any influence, even a negative one, on creative writing, the result is not only falsification, but often the actual drying-up of the inventive faculties.'[84] So how can one stop this from happening? – 'Draw a sharper distinction than we do at present between our political and our literary loyalties', suggests Orwell, and adds: 'When a writer engages in politics he should do so as a citizen, as a human being, but not *as a writer*.'[85] As if addressing his friends and colleagues and generally those on the left, whose views he broadly shared, he tried to persuade them that he was ready to do anything for the common cause, but insisted on being allowed complete independence in his literary endeavours, because that was the only way for him to be entirely free when writing and thus to keep his integrity:

> Just as much as anyone else, he [the writer] should be prepared to deliver lectures in draughty halls, to chalk pavements, to canvas voters, to distribute leaflets, even to fight in civil wars if it seems necessary. But whatever else he does in the service of his party, he should never write for it. He should make it clear that his writing is a thing apart.[86]

These lines echo a very similar pledge of the Russian poet Sergey Esenin (not known to Orwell), who in his poem 'Soviet Russia' written in 1924, a year before his suicide, exclaimed: 'I'll give my whole soul to October and May/ But I won't give them my sweet lyre . . .',[87] where October stands for the October Revolution of 1917 and May for International Workers' Day. Orwell, however, goes further and sums up his lifelong internal divide in the

[82]  Orwell, 'Writers and Leviathan' (*Politics and Letters*, Summer 1948), CW, XIX, 292.
[83]  Orwell, CW, XVII, 375.
[84]  Orwell, 'Writers and Leviathan', CW, XIX, 291.
[85]  Ibid.
[86]  Ibid., 291–2.
[87]  *Russian Poets and the October Revolution: Alexander Blok, Sergey Yesenin, Mikhail Kuzmin and Others.* DOI: http://dx.doi.org/10.34069/AI/2020.27.03.48

following conclusion: 'Sometimes, if a writer is honest, his writings and his political activities may actually contradict one another',[88] which can only be read as an attempt to explain to his friends why the totalitarian ideology of the country he depicted in his new novel was called Ingsoc or English socialism and why he chose to explore the 'totalitarian possibilities' of socialism rather than its potential brighter sides, the dream for which he had not abandoned.

Still a row did erupt when the *New York Daily News* interpreted *Nineteen Eighty-Four* as an attack on the Labour government and Orwell had to prepare a statement, which in slightly different versions appeared in various American papers. Its main points were as follows:

> My recent novel is not intended as an attack on socialism or on the British Labour Party (of which I am a supporter) but as a show-up of the perversions to which a centralised economy is liable and which have already been partly realised in communism and fascism. (*The New York Times Book Review*)
>
> I believe also that totalitarian ideas have taken root in the minds of intellectuals everywhere, and I have tried to draw these ideas out to their logical consequences. The scene of the book is laid in Britain in order to emphasize that the English-speaking races are not innately better than anyone else and that totalitarianism, if not fought against, could triumph anywhere. (*Life*)[89]

Many years later, these statements, provoked a rather angry response from Bernard Crick, the author of the first – and arguably, the best – biography of Orwell and his ardent admirer, who wrote: 'It might have been better to have sacrificed some of the formal virtues of the novel and reached a greater clarity of intention, rather than being reduced to producing memoranda for American newspapers and press agencies after the event'.[90] It is, of course, difficult to imagine how Orwell's novel could have achieved 'a greater clarity of intention' by sacrificing some of its 'formal virtues', but Crick, as a convinced democratic socialist himself, must have been deeply disappointed by *Nineteen Eighty-Four*, which he later referred to as 'not the best thing he wrote'.[91] Still, disagreeing on this point with both the left and the right, Crick set himself the task to prove that Orwell never renounced his socialism.

---

[88]   Orwell, 'Writers and Leviathan', 292.
[89]   Orwell's Statement on *Nineteen Eighty-Four*, CW, XX, 135.
[90]   Crick, 569.
[91]   Crick, 'Introduction' to George Orwell, *Nineteen Eighty-Four. With a Critical Introduction and Annotations* (Wotton-under-Edge, Gloucestershire: Clarendon Press, 1984), 5.

The left – from Isaac Deutscher in 1955 to the new Left thinkers E. P. Thomson and Raymond Williams in the early 1970s – felt that Orwell was a traitor to socialism, an 'ex-socialist'.[92] Paul Anderson, one of the authors of *Moscow Gold? The Soviet Union and the British Left*[93] and editor of *Orwell in Tribune*,[94] who had worked with E. P. Thompson, confirms: 'Thompson . . . hated Orwell and thought that he was the first big sell-out of the Cold war . . . The idea that too vigorous a criticism of the Soviet Union undermined the democratic left in the West was very, very widespread'.[95] On the other hand, the closer the world moved to the year 1984, the more voices from the opposite side appeared which questioned Crick's assertion. The most prominent among them were the voices of two brilliant anti-communists: Norman Podhoretz, the editor of *Commentary*, and Leopold Labedz, the editor of *Soviet Survey*, who – like those in the Soviet Union and Eastern Europe – valued Orwell primarily as a fighter against communism and totalitarianism.

In his 1983 article 'If Orwell Were Alive Today', which aroused much controversy, Podhoretz, himself a neoconservative, wrote cautiously: 'I have no hesitation . . . in claiming Orwell for the neoconservative perspective on the East-West conflict [i.e., the conflict between the USSR and the USA and their supporters]. But I'm a good deal more diffident in making the same claim on the issue of socialism'.[96] Still, he put forward a number of arguments for Orwell's possible rejection of socialism, had he lived to the early 1980s.

First, the editor of *Commentary* claimed that neoconservatives of that time were 'the disillusioned former socialists',[97] who had switched to neoconservatism from democratic socialism, the belief in which they had once shared with Orwell. One of the reasons for the switch Podhoretz quoted was a statement of the philosopher William Barrett: 'Everything we observe about the behaviour of human beings in groups, everything we know about that behaviour from history, should tell us that you cannot unite political and economic power in one centre without opening the door to tyranny'.[98] In other words, as Orwell sadly admitted, 'collectivism leads to concentration

---

[92]   Raymond Williams, *Politics and Letters* (London: 1979), 390.
[93]   Paul Anderson and Kevin Davey, *Moscow Gold? The Soviet Union and the British Left* (Ipswich: Aaaargh! Press, 2014).
[94]   *Orwell in Tribune: As I Please and Other Writings 1943–47*, compiled and edited by Paul Anderson (London: Methuen Publishing, 2006).
[95]   'The Debate that Never Ends . . . ' Anderson's interview to the author in *The Orwell Society Journal* No 9, December 2016.
[96]   Norman Podhoretz, 'If Orwell Were Alive Today' (*Harper's*, January 1983), 37.
[97]   Ibid., 31.
[98]   Ibid., 37.

camps.'[99] The second argument concerned the development of both capitalist and socialist societies in the thirty-odd years after Orwell's death:

> Suppose . . . he had lived to see the wreckage through planning and centralization of one socialist economy after another, so that not even at the sacrifice of liberty could economic security be assured. Suppose . . . that he had lived to see the aims of what *he* meant by socialism realised to a very great extent under capitalism, and without either the concentration camps or the economic miseries that have been the invariable companions of socialism in practice.[100]

Podhoretz was not sure that Orwell would be convinced by these arguments, because 'nothing [had] been more difficult for intellectuals in this century that giving up on socialism',[101] but still hoped so.

For fairness' sake, it needs to be said that Orwell was dreaming of *democratic* socialism, which he expected to be free from 'either the concentration camps or the economic miseries' of the totalitarian kind. Unfortunately, this kind of socialism has never materialized, while Soviet socialism collapsed within several years after Podhoretz wrote his essay, precisely because of its economic failure. 'The idea of socialism as a planned economy, in which the commanding heights are entirely nationalised under public ownership, is something now that is very much of the past',[102] claimed Paul Anderson in 2016. A bit earlier he even wrote: 'The Orwell who advocated a planned economy and pored over Trotskyist and Anarchist polemics against Stalinism and supported the Attlee government is in some respects a figure of historical interest who does not speak to our time.'[103] Still, the way Orwell dealt with his hesitations about socialism does speak to our time. He remained split because he could not abandon either his hope for a better future of mankind, which his time had taught him to call socialism, or his capacity to see things as they are. Nobody would call him cynical and yet he refused to be deluded himself and tried to warn others against their delusions by depicting horrifying consequences of socialist dreams.

[99]  Orwell, 'Review of *The Road to Serfdom*', CW, XVI, 150.
[100]  Podhoretz, 'If Orwell Were Alive Today', 37.
[101]  Ibid.
[102]  'The Debate that Never Ends . . . ' (*The OS Journal*, No 9, December 2016).
[103]  Anderson, 'In Defence of Bernard Crick', in *George Orwell Now!*, ed. Richard Lance Keeble (New York: Peter Lang Publishing, 2015), 94.

*   *   *

One of his last articles, published in February 1948, was 'Marx and Russia', which was a review of a booklet, titled *What Is Communism?*, by John Petrov Plamenatz, an Oxford political philosopher of Montenegrin heritage. Orwell started it by noticing 'a certain ambiguity', a tension between Marx's political theory – 'the dynamo which supplies millions of adherents with faith and hence with the power to act'[104] and the 'world-wide political movement which threatens the very existence of Western civilisation'.[105]

Of course, with Marxism, the problem lay in the fact that the political movement had grown largely not out of Marx's theory but out of its distortions by the Bolsheviks: Marx did not expect 'the kind of revolution that he foresaw . . . [to] happen a backward country like Russia, where the industrial workers were a minority'. He also thought that the proletariat would govern 'democratically, through elected representatives', while Lenin, who called himself and his group to be the only 'true inheritors of the Marxist doctrine', knew very well that 'they could not stay in power democratically', so for him 'the "dictatorship of the proletariat" had to mean the dictatorship of a handful of intellectuals, ruling through terrorism'.[106]

Orwell dispassionately analysed the mechanism which ensured that Russia was 'farther from egalitarian Socialism to-day than she was 30 years ago':

> Placed as they were, the Russian communists necessarily developed into a permanent ruling caste, or oligarchy, recruited not by birth but by adoption. Since they could not risk the growth of opposition they could not permit genuine criticism, and since they silenced criticism they often made avoidable mistakes: then, because they could not admit that the mistakes were their own they had to find scapegoats, sometimes on an enormous scale.[107]

Both John Plamenatz and Orwell acutely felt the threat coming from the USSR, because aggressiveness lay in the very nature of the totalitarian regime, even though, Plamenatz hoped, the country would not at that point 'necessarily precipitate an aggressive war against the West'.[108] However, Orwell stressed, the idea of world revolution had never been abandoned: 'it has merely been modified, "revolution" tending more and more to mean "conquest"'.[109]

---

[104] 'Marx and Russia' (*The Observer*, 15 February 1948), CW, XIX, 268.
[105] Ibid., 270.
[106] Ibid., 269.
[107] Ibid.
[108] Ibid., 270.
[109] Ibid., 269.

At the end of his review, Orwell quoted the author of the Introduction to Plamenatz's booklet who said: 'If we want to combat Communism we must start by understanding it'. Orwell felt the need to take it further: 'Beyond understanding there lies the yet more difficult task of being understood, and . . . of finding some way of making our point of view known to the Russian people'.[110]

In the last years of his life, he tried to do just that – to make his point of view known to the Russian people.

[110] Ibid., 270.

# 8

# 'Over the heads of their rulers'

*One of the most important problems at the moment is to find a way of speaking to the Russian people over the heads of their rulers.*[1]

Orwell, 1947

*If translations into Slav languages were made, I should not want any money out of them myself.*[2]

Orwell, 1945

One of the very first people who felt an urge to translate *Animal Farm* was Gleb Struve. On 28 August 1945, eleven days after the book was published, he wrote to Orwell to say that he found his tale "delightful" and would like to translate it into Russian –'not for the benefit of the Russian émigrés, but for those numerous Soviet citizens, now in Europe and America, who can read the truth about their country only when outside it.'[3] Replying to this letter on 1 September, Orwell wondered 'what the procedure is. Are books in Russian published in this country, i.e. from non-official sources?'[4] 'The procedure', of course, had not yet been established – the war was barely over, but in the following years it rapidly developed in Western Europe and the United States and succeeded in making some dents in the seemingly impenetrable Iron Curtain. Orwell, who was 'naturally anxious that the book should make its way into other languages',[5] mostly worried about paying his translators, especially 'into Slav languages' and from the start was ready to forgo his own fees to 'recompense [them] for their work'.[6]

Struve, however, did not become the first translator of *Animal Farm* into a Slavonic language, but only the third one. The first was the wife of a Polish diplomat and a '"grande dame" in Italo-English literary circles',[7] Teresa Jeleńska. Five thousand copies of her translation were published at the very

[1]  Orwell, 'Burnham's View . . .', CW, XIX, 105.
[2]  Orwell to Struve, 1 September 1945, CW, XVII, 275.
[3]  Struve to Orwell, 28 August 1945, Orwell/H/2/85, The OA, UCL.
[4]  Orwell to Struve, CW, XVII, 275.
[5]  Ibid.
[6]  Ibid.
[7]  Editorial notes to Szewczenko's letter to Orwell, 11 April 1946, CW, XVIII, 237.

end of 1946 by 'Swiatpol', the League of Poles Abroad based in London. It was this edition that was the first translation of the 'fairy story' into any language.

Jeleńska corresponded with Orwell, elucidating some passages with his help,[8] and was so fascinated by the fable that she tried to organize its translation into other languages as well. Her son, Konstanty Jeleńsky,[9] who was twenty-four in 1946, had a friend of the same age, a Polish-born Ukrainian Ihor Szewczenko. At the beginning of the 1990s, Szewczenko, who had become Professor of Byzantine Studies at Harvard (and changed the spelling of his name to Ševčenko), explained to Peter Davison: 'Those post-war days ... witnessed rapprochement between left-wing or liberal Polish intellectuals and their (few) Ukrainian counterparts – for both sides realised that they had been gobbled up by the same animal'.[10] Jeleńska put Szewczenko in touch with Orwell and on 11 April 1946 he wrote to the author of *Animal Farm*: 'I was immediately seized by the idea, that a translation of the tale into Ukrainian would be of a great value to my countrymen'.[11]

Szewczenko was probably the first person to see how *Animal Farm* was affecting people from the Soviet Union, who knew only too well the historical events behind the tale. Overwhelmed by the book, he immediately started sight-translating it '*ex abrupto*'[12] (without preparation) for groups of Ukrainian DPs in the camps near Munich. Among them was his wife, the daughter of the Ukrainian poet Mykhailo Drai-Khmara, killed in one of Stalin's concentration camps in Kolyma,[13] and her mother, both sent into internal exile after the poet's arrest, and certainly many others with similar tragedies behind them. In his letter to Orwell, Szewczenko attempted – in his rich, bookish and slightly awkward English – to give the author an idea of how his book was perceived.

Soviet refugees were my listeners. The effect was striking. They approved of almost all your interpretations. They were profoundly affected by such scenes as that of animals singing 'Beasts of England' on the hill. Here I saw that apart from their attention being primarily drawn on detecting 'concordances' between the reality they lived in and the tale, they visibly reacted to the absolute values of the book, to the tale types,

---

[8]   See Krystyna Wieszczek, 'Orwell and the Poles: The Case of Animal Farm' (*The OS Journal* 8, Spring, 2016).

[9]   In 1952, Konstanty Jeleńsky, aged thirty, became Head of Central European programme of the Congress for Cultural Freedom.

[10]   Quoted in Editorial notes, CW, XVIII, 237.

[11]   Szewczenko to Orwell, 11 April 1946, CW, XVIII, 235.

[12]   Ibid., 236.

[13]   See Andrea Chalupa, *Orwell and the Refugees: The Untold Story of* Animal Farm (Amazon Digital Services, 2012), 10.

to the underlying convictions of the author and so on. Besides, the mood of the book seems to correspond with their own actual state of mind.[14]

He also informed Orwell that 'the attitude of the Western World in many recent issues roused serious doubts among our refugees', who wondered 'how it were possible that nobody "knew the truth"'.[15] 'Your book', he added, 'has solved the problem'.[16] Orwell, naturally, granted permission to publish a Ukrainian translation, and Szewczenko had it ready by autumn 1946. He then gave it to the Ukrainian publisher *Prometheus* in Munich and in early March 1947 wrote to Orwell again, this time asking him for a preface as requested by the publisher. Although 'frightfully busy'[17] Orwell did write this preface, which forever remained his most detailed explanation of the motives behind the 'fairy story'. There is no doubt that one of the reasons why he agreed to do it was Szewczenko's sociological portrait of the publishers, 'who became genuinely interested in AF':

> These are for the greater part Soviet Ukrainians (till 1939 inhabitants of the Ukr. Sov. Socialist Republic,[18] if not deported), many of them ex-members of the Bolshevik party, but afterwards inmates of the Siberian camps (ITL[19]). They formed the nucleus of a political group. They stand on the 'Soviet' platform and defend 'the acquisitions of the October revolution', but they turn against the 'counter revolutionary Bonapartism' [of] Stalin's and the Russian nationalistic exploitation of the Ukrainian people; their conviction is that the revolution will contribute to the full national development. . . . Their situation and past causes them to sympathise with trotskyites, although there are several differences between them. Their theoretical weapon is Marxism, unfortunately in a somewhat vulgarised Soviet edition. But it could not be otherwise. They are men formed within the Soviet regime.[20]

Szewczenko, who thought that these people were 'representative of what any serious potential opposition inside Soviet Russia . . . could be like', finished this passage by proudly adding: 'AF is not being published by Ukrainian

---

[14]  Szewczenko to Orwell, CW, XVIII, 236.
[15]  Ibid., 235–6.
[16]  Ibid., 236.
[17]  Orwell to Szewczenko, 13 March 1947, CW, XIX, 73.
[18]  Ukrainian Soviet Socialist Republic – Ukraine's official name between 1922, when the USSR was formed, and 1991, when it collapsed.
[19]  ITL – *Ispravitelno-trudovye lagerya* (Correctional Labour Camps).
[20]  Szewczenko to Orwell, 7 March 1947, CW, XIX, 72–3; ORWELL H//2/89, The OA, UCL.

Joneses',[21] which certainly was music to Orwell's ears. He wrote back: 'I am encouraged to learn that this type of opposition exists in the USSR'.[22] The more precise and much less optimistic way of putting it would be to say that this type of opposition was being destroyed in the USSR. After all, the people Szewczenko described were abroad and those within the country had a chance to survive only if they kept silent.

During the two years of its existence (1946–8) *Prometheus* mostly published new Ukrainian literature – it was part of the Ukrainian Art Movement (MUR), an organization of about sixty Ukrainian writers from the DP camps in Germany. *Animal Farm*, then, was a remarkable exception – a book by a contemporary foreign author with his own preface!

Szewczenko later admitted to 'an unpardonable sin against literature' – taking advantage of Orwell's permission 'to cut out as much as you wish',[23] he edited out several sentences of the author's preface, which he thought unsuitable for 'Western Ukrainians, who were Polish citizens till 1939'[24] and constituted, by his estimate, about a half of the prospective readership. It is impossible to establish exactly what 'unsuitability' he meant, because, unfortunately, Orwell's original preface has been lost and what survives today is a back translation from the Ukrainian – obviously without the passages cut by Szewczenko.

In his preface Orwell tried to build a bridge to Soviet citizens he knew little about, explaining both things too remote for them to understand – what English public schools were like or what kind of country Britain was – and his own 'attitude to the Soviet regime'.[25] He stressed not only his reluctance 'to interfere in Soviet domestic affairs', but even his refusal 'to condemn Stalin and his associates for their barbaric and undemocratic methods'.[26] Yet with the same vehemence he stated:

> It was of the utmost importance to me that people in western Europe should see the Soviet régime for what it really was. Since 1930 I had seen little evidence that the USSR was progressing towards anything that one could truly call Socialism. On the contrary, I was struck by clear signs of its transformation into a hierarchical society, in which the rulers have no more reason to give up their power than any other ruling class.

[21]  Ibid.
[22]  Orwell to Szewczenko, 13 March 1947, CW, XIX, 73.
[23]  Orwell to Szewczenko, 21 March 1947, CW, XIX, 85.
[24]  Szewczenko to Orwell, 25 March 1947, ORWELL H//2/89, The OA, UCL.
[25]  Orwell, Preface to the Ukrainian Edition, CW, XIX, 87.
[26]  Ibid.

Having explained why 'totalitarianism is completely incomprehensible . . . to the workers and intelligentsia in a country like England', Orwell named as the aim of his book 'the destruction of the Soviet myth, 'essential', he insisted, 'for a revival of the Socialist movement'.[27]

The first edition of *Animal Farm* in Ukrainian,[28] published in September 1947 with Orwell's preface, did not have a happy fate. Orwell wrote to Arthur Koestler: 'the American authorities in Munich have seized 1500 copies of it and handed them over to the Soviet repatriation people, but it appears 2000 copies got distributed among the DPs first'.[29] Whether this was the failure of an attempt planned by Ukrainians 'to smuggle some copies among the Soviet soldiers' based in Germany, which, as Szewczenko suspected from the start, involved 'risks for both sides',[30] or just an incredible naiveté on the part of the American authorities, is not known. And yet 2,000 copies reached their readers and many were carefully preserved by Ukrainian families in Germany.[31] However, despite the failure of the first endeavour, Orwell was not ready to abandon the idea of sending *Animal Farm* to the Soviet Union.

\*    \*    \*

Either at the end of June or at the beginning of July 1949, he received a letter in Russian. It was from Vladimir Gorachek, the head of the Germany-based Russian publishing firm *Possev*, representing Russian DPs. He obviously had no doubt that Orwell could read Russian. In his second letter, this time in faulty English, Gorachek apologized for his mistake and explained its origin: 'We thought that such a perfect understanding of all events occurred in our country after the revolution and of the very substance of the regime now established there could not be acquired without the knowledge of Russian language'.[32]

The Russian letter came with 'a file of papers containing a Russian translation of *Animal Farm*'.[33] It must have been a collection of cuttings – the translation at that point was being serialized in the *Possev* weekly, also printed by Gorachek. Altogether it took twenty-six issues (Nos 7–32) from

[27] Ibid., 88.
[28] Szewczenko, who published his translation under the pseudonym Ivan Cherniatynskyi, has strengthened the similarity of Orwell's tale with Soviet realities by translating its title as *Kolgosp Tvarin* (The Kolkhoz [Collective Farm] of Animals).
[29] Orwell to Koestler, 20 September 1947, CW, XIX, 206–7.
[30] Szewczenko to Orwell, 25 March 1947, ORWELL H//2/89, The OA, UCL.
[31] See Chalupa, *Orwell and the Refugees*, 8.
[32] Gorachek to Orwell, 16 July 1949, Editorial Note, CW, XX, 149. ORWELL H/2/52, The OA, UCL.
[33] Orwell to Moore, 20 July 1949, CW, XX, 148.

February to August 1949. This was not a surprise for Orwell – following his early intention to translate *Animal Farm*, Gleb Struve, together with his wife, Maria Kriger, set to work and in November 1948 asked the author for permission to publish it in *Possev* weekly, which Orwell granted, adding: 'Naturally, I do not want any money from DPs, but if they ever do produce it in book form I should like a copy or two of that'.[34]

In Gorachek's second letter to Orwell, dated 16 July 1949, the publisher suggested printing the translation in book form and distributing it *gratis* to Russian readers behind the Iron Curtain. Written on *Possev's* headed paper, Gorachek's letter combined a fan's enthusiasm (he admired, no doubt sincerely, Orwell satire – 'a weapon par excellence to combat the fear and the terrorist system'[35]) with some sharp business sense – he asked its author for 2,000 Deutschmarks (then worth about £155) to publish the book, stressing that 1,000–1,200 copies would be sold in West Germany and the proceeds would cover the expenses of sending 'the bulk of this Edition through Berlin, Vienna and other channels further East'.[36]

This was exactly what Orwell was keen to do. But as he considered financing the publication, he wanted to make sure that he could trust the publisher. On the one hand, *Possev* people could be 'just working a swindle',[37] as Orwell bluntly suggested in his letter to Moore, on the other, he worried about the publisher's political position.

In exactly the same way as he did not want to have his original *Animal Farm* brought out by a reactionary publisher, Orwell did not fancy being published in Russian by those who did not understand why the Russian Revolution had happened in the first place. That is why, on 15 July 1949, even before he received Gorachek's English letter,[38] he wrote to his recent acquaintance, a former German communist Ruth Fischer, who at that moment was going to Germany, and asked her about *Possev*: 'I suppose the editors of this paper are *bona fide* people, and also not whites?'[39]

The hope that there could be people coming from the Soviet Union who hated the Soviet regime, but had not been admirers of tsarist Russia either, was given to Orwell by Ihor Szewczenko's description of the book's Ukrainian publishers – definitely not 'Ukrainian Joneses'. After many inquiries and

[34] Orwell to Struve, 23 November 1948, XIX, 472.
[35] Gorachek to Orwell, 16 July 1949.
[36] Ibid.
[37] Orwell to Moore, 20 July 1949, CW, XX, 149.
[38] Orwell must have known the content of the Russian letter, most likely translated for him by Lydia Jackson, his Russian friend, who visited him in the Cranham sanatorium on 2 July 1949.
[39] Orwell to Ruth Fischer, 15 July 1949, CW, XX, 146. 'Whites' were opponents of the October Revolution.

attempts to involve the Information Research Department[40] into contributing to funding *Possev's* project, Orwell wrote to Leonard Moore: 'I have heard from the FO who, of course, won't help to finance the Russian translation of *A. F.* However, they confirm that the *Possev* people are known to them and are reliable'.[41]

Orwell then paid *Possev* 1,000 Deutschmarks (half of the sum asked), using his fee for serializing a German translation of *Nineteen Eighty-Four* in *Der Monat*. In his letter to Moore, he made his intention clear: 'Copies should get into the Soviet zone. It is not much use publishing it for refugees only . . . It is this that I am prepared to subsidise, up to a reasonable amount, for of course copies distributed in that manner would not be paid for'.[42] He then added: 'Of course some discretion is needed. I do not want the story of the Ukrainian translation repeated'.[43]

*Possev* published *Animal Farm* in book form in 1950. Luckily, this edition and the subsequent ones of 1967, 1971 and 1978 were not seized by the authorities and some copies managed to get into the Soviet Union. However, – although Orwell never learnt about it – in one respect the *Possev* publishers did not prove reliable at all: they censored his book.

The first person to write about this censorship was the Soviet dissident Julius Telesin, who, after emigrating from the USSR, published a letter with his own translation of omitted parts in the Russian émigré magazine *Kontinent* in 1982.[44] Within the Soviet Union, it was independently noticed by one of *Animal Farm* translators, Vladimir Pribylovsky, in 1986, although he could only publish his discovery in 2003.

The cuts were small, but 'ideological', as Pribylovsky dubbed them. They concerned Moses, the tame raven, who appeared (asleep) in Chapter 1: 'All the animals were now present except Moses, the tame raven, who slept on a perch behind the back door'[45] and then disappeared in Chapter 2, 'croaking loudly',[46] as he flapped after Mrs Jones, who was trying to escape during the Rebellion. The only other thing that remained in the *Possev* Russian text about the raven was that he was fed 'crusts of bread soaked in beer'[47] by Mr Jones. Why he was there at all, what his function was in Orwell's tightly built narrative, remained a mystery for the Russian readers of the first translation

---

[40] See Chapter 6.
[41] Orwell to Moore, 28 July 1949, CW, XX, 153.
[42] Orwell to Moore, 24 July 1949, CW, XX, 151.
[43] Ibid.
[44] Julius Telesin, *Pismo v Redaktsiyu* (A Letter to the Editor) (*Kontinent*, 1982, N34), 365–7. http://www.laban.rs/orwell/Animal_Farm/Perevod_fragmentov_YT.html.
[45] Orwell, *Animal Farm* (London: Penguin Books,1989), 3.
[46] Ibid., 12.
[47] Ibid., 11.

because two important paragraphs had been cut out of Chapters 2 and 9. To make them forget the raven altogether, the publishers even deleted him from Chapter 10, where he was mentioned in the list of animals who still remembered the Rebellion.

In the paragraphs that were purged, Orwell provided a portrait of 'Mr Jones's especial pet', as 'a spy and a tale-bearer but a clever talker', whose main function was that of a dishonest preacher, telling animals about 'a mysterious country called Sugarcandy Mountain, to which all animals went when they died'.[48] Just like the Bolsheviks, who, after killing priests and destroying church buildings, still allowed the Orthodox church to function on a limited scale, as it performed the functions they needed: informing on church-goers and promising them a better life in the next world to make them submit to the imperfections of this one, Orwell's pigs 'declared contemptuously that his [Moses's] stories about Sugarcandy Mountain were lies, and yet they allowed him to remain on the farm, not working, with an allowance of a gill of beer a day'.[49] This brought in yet another important detail about the process of restoring 'the old regime' and the pigs borrowing from the Joneses the same old tricks of subjugating the masses.

The *Possev* publishers, who enjoyed Orwell's satire on the Soviet regime, could not stomach him satirizing church and religion and the role they played in society. As Orwell had feared, they *were* 'Whites' or at least the founders of the Russian émigré organization they represented – the NTS – *Narodno-Trudovoy Soyuz rossiyskikh solidaristov* (National Labour Alliance of Russian Solidarists) – 'belonged to the younger cohorts of the White emigration'.[50] These young people, who, unlike their fathers, did not simply accept as a *fait accompli* the Bolsheviks' victory, formed their alliance in 1930 and made it 'a single and centralized political organisation', which, at least during its first decade, was 'right-radical and fascist-influenced'.[51] Moreover, during the war many NTS members collaborated with the Nazis and fought in the Russian Liberation Army (Vlasov's Army) under Nazi command. Naturally, in the post-war period they had to work hard to reinvent themselves. *Possev* publishing became one of the main vehicles for that effort.

Vladimir Gorachek, the head of *Possev* at that time, joined the NTS in 1934. Born in Russia, he lived in Prague for eighteen years until 1945, when, with the Soviet troops approaching, he took the last train to Germany. Like all the NTS leaders, he hated the Soviet regime, and *Possev* certainly did a

---

[48] Ibid., 10.
[49] Ibid., 78.
[50] Benjamin Tromly, *Cold War Exiles and the CIA: Plotting to Free Russia* (Oxford: Oxford University Press, 2019), 40.
[51] Ibid.

lot to fight it by publishing literature that could have never been published in the USSR. Being a political activist, Vladimir Gorachek, according to his son, was also a believer, a man of the church and later even a churchwarden.[52] He must have felt offended by Orwell's caricature of the Russian Orthodox church under Bolsheviks and simply censored the writer, which suggests that although *Possev* was in opposition to the Soviet régime it did not mind using the same methods – even though in their case the author paid half of the cost of the publication.

But what about that edition's translator, Gleb Struve? Struve was Orwell's sincere admirer – he rushed to translate *Animal Farm*, sure that Russian readers would appreciate it; he gave *Nineteen Eighty-Four* glowing reviews and later wrote Orwell's obituary for the Russian émigré press; he was Orwell's trusted friend and helped the writer with some important information about the USSR. And Orwell tried hard, if unsuccessfully, to help Struve with his life's work: publishing in the West several Russian authors prohibited at home, including Zamyatin and Mandelstam. Still it is difficult to imagine that the publisher made the cuts without letting the translator know about them.

Julius Telesin's letter to *Kontinent* brought the issue of censorship into the open. Struve's relations with *Possev* had not always run smoothly. And yet, on learning about Telesin's letter, he did not write an indignant letter to *Possev*. Instead, he wrote to Telesin. At that time Struve was already eighty-five years old; he had severe problems with his vision and relied on others to help him read and write. The letter he dictated on 13 July 1983 is full of repetitions and contradictions and might either reflect his old age and failing memory or his wish to make it appear so. His clearest statement on the matter is as follows: 'I have not made any cuts either in the first or in the subsequent editions . . . and have to confess that I had not noticed them in due time myself. This is my fault. If I had discovered them I would have pointed them out both to the publishers and to the public. The cuts must have been done by *Possev*'.[53] The alleged failure to notice the omissions does not look very credible as there are half a dozen letters in Struve's archive about his corrections of the translation and the publishers introducing them into later editions. One can only conclude that at this stage neither the publisher nor the translator thought it necessary to check the English original.

*Possev's* reaction to Telesin's letter was also one of denial. In September 1983, Anastasia Artemova, then an NTS senior staff member, asked Struve to respond to Telesin's charges. She added that suggesting, as Telesin had done,

[52] Olga Orlova, 'In Memory of Archbishop Agapit of Stuttgart'. https://orthochristian.com /131631.html.
[53] Struve to Telesin, 13 July 1983. Struve papers, box 34, folder 12, Hoover.

that *Possev* censored Orwell because of his anticlerical stand, was 'simply stupid!'[54]

It is important to emphasize that Gleb Struve's attitude to the Russian Revolution even at the end of 1940s was rather different from Orwell's. The Russian critic hints at their differences in the first sentence of his letter to Orwell about *Animal Farm*, where he tells the author that he found the book 'delightful, even though I do not necessarily agree with what one of the reviewers described as your "Trotskyist prejudices"'.[55] What he means becomes clearer after reading his 'Translator's preface' to the serialization in *Possev* weekly, where among numerous accolades to Orwell's book he writes: 'His [Orwell's] sympathies for Trotsky (Snowball in his satire), his Trotskyist approach as well as his idealization of the early phase of the Russian revolution are undeniable. That is why much in his outlook will be unacceptable for a large part of Russian anti-Bolsheviks.'[56] The use of the word 'Trotskyist' throughout the preface obviously betrays a certain crudeness of Struve's description – Orwell had never been a Trotskyist and was always critical of Trotsky, but this was the shorthand usage of the time to denote a pro-revolutionary yet anti-Stalinist position – Orwell used it too but, obviously, not about himself. Further in his preface Struve also makes a subtler point, but comes to the same conclusion:

Orwell's satire is wider than just a lampoon of our own revolution. This is a lampoon of revolutions in general. It's a search for an answer to the question: why, under the influence of what forces, revolutions degenerate. The author does not provide this answer, he probably did not even set out to find it, but modern Russian readers have an overall idea as to what it might be, at least as far as our own revolution is concerned, and firmly distinguish between the February revolution and the October coup. . . . That is why they will easily see all the shortcomings of the author's 'Trotskyist' position.[57]

Moreover, Struve claims that Orwell 'was once infatuated with communism' and makes it seem a reason for his fighting in Spain, saying in the next sentence: 'He took an active part in the Spanish Civil war on the "Red" side, came into close contact with Stalinists and got bitterly disappointed with

54 Anastasia Artemova to Struve, 15 September 1983. Struve papers, box 34, folder 12, Hoover.
55 Struve to Orwell, 28 August 1945.
56 Struve, *Predislovie perevodchika* (Translator's Preface), *Possev*, No. 6, 1949, 12.
57 Ibid.

them'.[58] Writing his preface for *Possev*, Struve definitely knew that some NTS members behind the publishers had fought on the side of Franco.

Orwell, who guessed correctly that the *Possev* people were 'Whites', did not seem to care about Struve being 'White' (he must have known that Struve fought against the 'Reds' in 1918), probably because, as he wrote to Stephen Spender, 'when you meet anyone in the flesh you realise immediately that he is a human being and not a sort of caricature embodying certain ideas'.[59] Struve, who admired Orwell's work immensely, was less attentive to Orwell the man, while Orwell, who liked Struve as a person, trusted him as a friend and as a translator. He wrote about *Animal Farm* in Russian: 'I know it must be a good translation, as it is by Gleb Struve, whom I know well'.[60] And he obviously could not imagine that Struve would allow any censoring of *Animal Farm*.

\* \* \*

In 1947 Struve alerted Orwell to the Soviet press attack on him. It flared up a year after the Soviet authorities admitted that *Animal Farm* had come to their attention. Arlen Blyum, a Russian expert on censorship, found in the archive of the Soviet Writers' Union an unsigned document dated 1946 and titled 'Information on the book of George Orwell *Animal Farm*', with the usual rubber stamp 'To be kept indefinitely'.[61] The document can only be described as cautious – a direct reference to the book where Comrade Stalin was depicted as a 'fierce-looking boar' would have been suicidal, so the document's author wrote just one paragraph of his own and this was not about Orwell at all but about the magazine *Horizon*:

> In its September issue of 1945 the English journal *Horizon*, known for its peculiar reputation (the journal is a vehicle for the viewpoint of a group of English writers who call for an 'above party' and apolitical literature, at the same time lending its pages to all manner of anti-Soviet opinions), published an anonymous review of George Orwell's *Animal Farm* (A Fairy Story).[62]

---

[58]  Ibid.
[59]  Orwell to Spender, 15? April 1938, CW, XI, 132.
[60]  Orwell to Moore, 24 July 1949, CW, XX, 151.
[61]  The document kept in RGALI (f.631, op.14, d.255, ll.1–4) is quoted in: Blyum, 'George Orwell in the Soviet Union', 406.
[62]  Blyum, 'George Orwell in the Soviet Union', 406.

Having put in a keyword –'anti-Soviet' – and yet relieving oneself of any responsibility, the writer proceeded to quote from the review, which, in fact, was not anonymous but signed C.C. (the initials of Cyril Connolly, *Horizon's* editor) and to give in translation nearly the whole of its first paragraph.[63] This was followed by some information on Orwell mostly quoted from the book *20th Century Authors* (New York,1942) – by far more neutral than pieces on Orwell published in the Soviet press later. It was the following year, 1947, when the attack was launched.

On 1 February 1947 *Literaturnaya gazeta* (The Literary Gazette) edited by Vladimir Yermilov, a notorious suppressor of anything that was alive in literature, carried an article by a certain Vl. Rubin, 'The Liberty of Lies and Slander', which cracked down on anti-Soviet books published in the United States and mentioned in passing that some of them were not home-grown but imported 'like, for example, a dirty little book by the Englishman Orwell'.[64] The critic stressed that publishing this work 'under the guise of pure art' and awarding it 'The Book of the Month' title could not possibly be ignored, and yet he skilfully managed to avoid saying what it was called.

On 24 May of the same year, the same *Literaturnaya gazeta* published a lengthy article by a young critic and translator Nora Gal called 'Corrupt Literature', which actually was a review of Orwell's collection of essays *Dickens, Dali and Others. Studies in Popular Culture* (New York, 1946). Nora Gal tried hard to fill her article with the anti-Western spirit, prescribed at the time, and obviously hoped to please her bosses with her 'militant demagogic style'.[65] She rather incoherently claimed that not only the subjects of Orwell's critique made her experience 'a feeling of absolute disgust and in the end despair',[66] but the critic himself. However, two days later, Mikhail Apletin, the Deputy Chair of the Foreign Commission of the Writers' Union, sent Konstantin Simonov, one of the secretaries of the Writers' Union Board, the following threatening note:

> George Orwell is an English writer, a Trotskyist. In 1936 he was in Spain in the POUM militia. . . . Orwell has close connections with the American Trotskyist journal *Partisan Review*. George Orwell is the author of a foul book on the Soviet Union in the period from 1917 to 1944 – *Animal*

[63]  See C. C (Cyril Connolly), *Horizon* in: Meyers, 199–200.
[64]  Vl. Rubin, '*Svoboda lzhi I klevety*' ('The Liberty of Lies and Slander') in *Literaturnaya gazeta*, 1 February 1947, N5 (2320), 4. https://vivaldi.nlr.ru/pn000011682/view/?#page =4.
[65]  Blyum, 'George Orwell in the Soviet Union', 408.
[66]  Nora Gal, '*Rastlennaya literatura*' ('Corrupt Literature') in *Literaturnaya Gazeta*, 24 May 1947.

*Farm*. The publication of N. Gal's article in *Literary gazette* (24.05.1947) is a serious political mistake.[67]

In 1947 the words 'serious political mistake' could make anybody tremble, and Simonov, obviously scared that he could be accused of a lack of vigilance, immediately approached another literary functionary wondering whether the issue should be discussed at the next Board meeting.

Arlen Blyum, who told this story, thought that Nora Gal's main crime was not the way she wrote about Orwell, but the fact that she wrote about him at all, while 'Soviet citizens were not supposed to know of his existence'.[68] Blyum could not find any other documents related to the episode and believed that Nora Gal must have been reprimanded but not persecuted too severely. After this episode, she gave up the career of a critic, choosing a safer path as a translator of British and American literature and ended up writing a lively book on translation.[69] Interestingly, in his private note to Simonov, Apletin was not afraid to say that *Animal Farm* described the Soviet Union 'in the period from 1917 to 1944', which he would have never dared to do publicly. It is not quite clear whether by writing to Simonov he tried to extricate himself from possible trouble or to initiate a plot against the editor Yermilov, also disliked by Simonov. In any case, despite all the efforts to make Orwell 'an unperson', his name was mentioned again in the Soviet press just six months later.

In November 1947, Ivan Anisimov, a literary critic, who later became the director of the Gorky Institute of World Literature, published in the magazine *Oktyabr* (October) an article titled 'The Degradation of Literature Today', where he assaulted both Koestler and Orwell. It was the translation of extracts from this article that Gleb Struve sent to Orwell with his letter of 1 January 1949, adding that they were 'typical of the literary xenophobia now raging in the Soviet Union'.[70] They attacked Orwell personally.

'What is this gentleman known for?' asked Anisimov and gave a crushing reply: 'A virulently anti-Soviet lampoon expanded into a full-length satirical novel, also a volume of literary sketches which serves up Zola, Dickens, pulp fiction, low-grade detective novels, the surrealistic capers of Salvador Dali and pornographic postcards in one disgustingly mixed-up pile which this insolent fellow understands to constitute "popular culture"'.[71]

---

[67]  Ibid., 407.
[68]  Ibid., 408.
[69]  Nora Gal, *Slovo zhivoe i mertvoe* (The Word Living and Dead). Various editions.
[70]  Quoted in Editor's note, CW, XX, 18.
[71]  Ivan Anisimov, '*Sovremenny literaturny raspad*' (The Degradation of Literature Today), *Oktyabr*, No. 11, 142, 1947). Translated by Antony Wood. Struve's translations seem to have been lost.

Anisimov was brave enough to mention the 'anti-Soviet lampoon' but, like his predecessor in *Literaturnaya gazeta* Vl. Rudin, did not dare to name it (he obviously meant *Animal Farm* although it was not a novel, at any rate not a 'full-length' one). However, the brunt of his attack was directed against the same book *Dickens, Dali and Others* as Nora Gal's. Orwell, who had been a great admirer of Russian literature, seems to have been seriously shocked by the regress of Soviet literary criticism. He wrote to Richard Rees: 'Gleb Struve sent me a translation of some remarks about me in a Russian magazine. They are really very annoying but disquieting in a way because the whole thing is somehow so *illiterate*'.[72]

Besides calling Orwell an 'insolent fellow', Anisimov also branded him 'a charlatan' and moved on to his biography or rather to his own idea of it:

> A policeman in Bombay, a bailiff, an agent of the PROUM police[73] in Barcelona, then a contributor to yellow journals. A shady character, an out-and-out rogue – these are the most appropriate names for a person like that. However, English literature has sunk to a level where Orwell counts as a writer. In that country rubbish is now in great demand.[74]

Enclosing the extracts sent by Struve with the letter to Richard Rees, Orwell remarked: 'Even allowing for possible unfairness in translation, doesn't it strike you that there is something queer about the *language* of the totalitarian literature – a curious mouthing sort of quality, as of someone who is choking with rage and can never quite hit on the words he wants?'[75]

The phenomenon continued to interest him and a couple of days later he informed Rees: 'I see by the way that the Russian press has just described B.R. [Bertrand Russell] as a wolf in a dinner jacket and a wild beast in philosopher's robes'.[76]

---

[72]  Orwell to Richard Rees, 18 January 1949, CW, XX, 23.
[73]  By the 'PROUM police' Anisimov means the 'POUM militia'. The fact that he misspelled POUM suggests only that he never wondered what the abbreviation stood for. Similarly, he took 'militia' to mean 'police' because '*militsiya*' was the Russian word used to denote police forces after 1917 (and till 2011!). He never suspected that it might mean 'armed men' or stopped to ask himself how or why Orwell would work for the police in Barcelona.
[74]  Anisimov, '*Sovremenny literaturny raspad*', 142.
[75]  Orwell to Rees, 28 January 1949, CW, XX, 30.
[76]  Orwell to Rees, 4 February 1949, CW, XX, 34.

\*   \*   \*

The cautious approach to *Animal Farm*, which must have scared the Soviet officials by its unambiguous personal attack on Stalin, was in sharp contrast to their knee-jerk reaction to *Nineteen Eighty-Four*. The novel was published on 8 June 1949 and on 16 June a 'Memorandum' was sent to the Foreign Commission of the Writers' Union by the All-Union Society for Cultural Relations with Foreign Countries (*VOKS*). The 'Memorandum' plainly called Orwell a Trotskyist and *Nineteen Eighty-Four* 'an unbridled libel on socialism and socialist society'.[77] *VOKS* recommended organizing 'through the Soviet press a sharp statement by a Soviet writer, exposing the libellous fabrications of Orwell'.[78] The Writers' Union, however, did not dare to do so, obviously thinking that they would be the first to blame for attracting attention to the obnoxious book.

It was only after Orwell's death that *Pravda* published an article by the indispensable Anisimov titled 'Enemies of Mankind', where Orwell was claimed to be similar to Huxley in everything, 'especially in his disrespect for the people and the wish to slander them',[79] as was obvious from his novel set in 1984, of which no title was given. Blyum, however, mentions 'secret' documents of 1949–50, where both Orwell's name and the title of his novel occurred 'fairly often'.[80] The compilers of the secret documents used – or maybe even commissioned? – articles by American and British communists. Presumably, it was the compilers' attempt to protect themselves. One of the most striking was the attack of the communist writer Jack Lindsay, a friend of Randall Swingler's, in the magazine *Arena*, which they co-edited: 'Orwell is the ideologist of the final stage of fascism, this super fascism which looks to the destruction of humanity!'[81] This was matched only by a piece a certain Thomas Spencer printed in the *Daily Worker*, which was titled 'Prisoner of Hatred'.[82] The headline seemed to be suspiciously similar to *Pravda*'s.

\*   \*   \*

It was at about the same time that *Possev* started discussing with Orwell's widow Sonia publishing *Nineteen Eighty-Four* in Russian. The publisher Vladimir Gorachek and the editor of the quarterly *Grani*, Evgeny Romanov wrote: 'It is

---

[77]   Blyum, 'George Orwell in the Soviet Union', 409.
[78]   Ibid.
[79]   Anisimov, *Vragi chelovechestva* (Enemies of Mankind), *Pravda*, 12 May 1950, 3,
[80]   Blyum, 'George Orwell in the Soviet Union', 409.
[81]   Jack Lindsay, 'The British Scene: What is Happening to Our Culture' (*Arena*, Vol. 2–5, September–October, 1950), quoted in Blyum, 410.
[82]   Thomas Spencer, 'Prisoner of Hatred' (*Daily Worker*, 19 October 1950), quoted in ibid.

impossible to overestimate the psychological impact of this book on the Russian readers behind the Iron Curtain, and thus the contribution to the struggle against the totalitarianism and for the freedom'.[83] Therefore they asked Sonia to give them permission to bring out the novel free of charge. They promised that 'the translation would be made by a competent translator, philologist'.[84]

The translation was ready about five years later and done not by one, but by two translators – both were concealed under pseudonyms: V. Andreev and N. Vitov. Not much is known about V. Andreev apart from the fact that his real name seems to have been V. Gorevoy, but it is established that N. Vitov was Nikolay Pashin, originally Paskhin (1908–76). He was indeed a philologist, as after finishing school in Moscow he went to the Literary Institute where his fellow-students were future official Soviet writers: Konstantin Simonov and Sergey Mikhalkov. But Nikolay and his younger brother Sergey Maximov (1916–67) – were arrested before the war. Nikolay seems to have escaped relatively soon, as he was drafted into the army on 20 June 1941, while Sergey spent five years (1936–41) in Stalin's camps, then both brothers were imprisoned by the Germans and after the war chose not to return to the USSR. Nikolay taught Russian in the United States and Germany and contributed to the Russian émigré press. The first ever translation of *Nineteen Eighty-Four* was published in four issues[85] of *Grani* in 1955–6. And then, according to Evgeny Romanov, Sonia gave *Possev* a substantial grant to publish this translation as a book, which was to be sent behind the Iron Curtain.[86]

As if to respond to the émigré publication, the Ideological Department of the Central Committee of the CPSU decided in 1959 to publish in Russian a 'special edition' of *Nineteen Eighty-Four* only for the upper crust of the communist rulers, 'the Inner Party', to use Orwell's term. The publishing house *Inostrannaya literatura* (Foreign Literature), which was founded after Stalin's decree of 4 May 1946, had a special task to acquaint a limited number of high-ranking officials with non-Soviet views. With this in mind, a 'special editorial team' was created in 1949. It was supervised by Mikhail Suslov, Head of the Central Committee Department for Agitation and Propaganda, and obviously by the KGB.

'Special editions' were mostly political pamphlets, which were published abroad and translated into Russian, rather than imaginative literature. Apart from Orwell's *Nineteen Eighty-Four*, only one more work of fiction –

[83] *Possev* to Sonia Orwell, 12 August 1950, The OA, UCL, Orwell/S/2/G/1.
[84] Ibid.
[85] Issues 27, 28, 30, 31.
[86] Interview with E.R. Romanov, the founder of *Grani* to mark the 40th anniversary of the quarterly in: *Grani* N141, 1986, 271–2. https://vtoraya-literatura.com/pdf/grani_141 _1986_text.pdf.

Hemingway's *For Whom the Bell Tolls* – was included in the publication list.[87] In 1962, the year when Hemingway was published, there appeared a 'special edition' of Richard Rees's *George Orwell: A Fugitive from the Camp of Victory*, a sure sign of the ever-burning interest of Soviet party bosses in its subject.

Usually between 100 and 200 copies of 'special editions' were printed and distributed in complete secrecy. First, to avoid using the title of the book it was given a specially designated number: *Nineteen Eighty-Four*, for example, was known as 21/5058. This reminds one of Zamyatin rather than of Orwell, but party bosses had not read Zamyatin. On the book's cover it said: 'Distributed according to a special list', and then the personal number of this or that party official was given. There were about 1,000 names on the list arranged not alphabetically but according to the hierarchy: it started with Politburo members, followed by candidates to the Politburo, then Central Committee members, then candidates to the Central Committee and so on.[88] A strict selection process was applied. Then books were delivered by couriers to the addressees, who were supposed to send them after reading to the so-called 'spetskhran' – special storage sections in libraries and archives. Not all of them did. For example, Mikhail Gorbachev announced publicly in 2011 that he had in his home library about 300 books received by 'special distribution' and never returned.[89]

At the end of the 1990s a photocopy of the original 1959 edition of *Nineteen Eighty-Four* resurfaced: it was handed over to Memorial, an NGO which studied political repressions in the USSR.[90] The photocopy does not have a cover with 21/5058 or the number of the book – presumably to conceal who the addressee of the special edition was. However, the title page has the year of publication and the name of the publisher. The unsigned preface explains why the edition was necessary: 'George Orwell's novel *Nineteen Eighty-Four* deserves attention because bourgeois authors – politicians and statesmen, economists, philosophers and journalists – invoke it with exceptional frequency, especially when they refer to the Soviet Union and other socialist countries. It is for the purpose of information that *Foreign Literature* directs this book to its readers'.[91] To avoid any doubt about the purpose of the publication, the preface describes the novel thus: 'The

[87] The Russian translation of *For Whom the Bell Tolls*, which was ready in 1941, was published for the general public as late as in 1968 with severe cuts, which the special edition of 1962 did not have.
[88] Yuri Pankov, *Tainye knizhki* (Secret Books). https://www.sovsekretno.ru/articles/taynye-knizhki/.
[89] Ibid.
[90] International Memorial Archive. (f.175, op.5). Memorial was closed down at the end of 2021 (see Chapter 10), and the link to its archive is no longer available.
[91] '1984', *Inostrannaya Literatura* (Foreign Literature), 1959, 4.

depiction of Communist society in the novel is false, spurious and sometimes bordering on utter nonsense. It is a vulgar slander against the camp of peace and socialism.[92]

The names of the translators (allegedly, there were two) were held in secrecy and it is only recently that one of them seems to have been established, thanks to Professor Nikolay Nikolaevich Alipov, who decided that there was no point in keeping the secret any longer. In his 2019 interview,[93] he maintained that the 'special edition' of *Nineteen Eighty-Four* had been translated by his late father, Nikolay Vasilievich Alipov (1919–86). The son was happy to share some, not very numerous, details of his father's work, as he learnt about its secret component only in his twenties, that is, in the late 1970s.

Officially, Nikolay Alipov-senior was an editor in the *Progress* Publishing House[94]; for six years he also worked in the UN in Geneva as a translator and interpreter for the World Meteorological Organization. At the same time, he was regularly doing 'special' translations of classified Western publications, including the CIA archives. According to his son, he was extremely interested in this kind of work. He translated some non-fiction books, 'officially' published in the USSR, the most well known among them being James Dugan's *Man Under the Sea*, printed in 1956 in English and in 1965 in Russian. Alipov had never translated any other fiction or poetry and, as his son supposes, 'the CPSU Central Committee was not particularly interested in Orwell's book as a work of literature'. Alipov-junior also assumes that his father's co-translator, whose name the son had never known, was not a literary translator either, because 'translating "a bomb" like *Nineteen Eighty-Four* could be commissioned only to tried and trusted people'.[95] Alipov-senior knew Orwell's book very well and, it seems, admired it, but he could not keep the English original at home – in fact, his son is not even sure whether he was allowed to translate it at home – usually translators had to go to specially allocated premises and work there. In short, there was nothing the authorities would not do to keep their work secret.

* * *

And still, despite all the efforts to stop *Nineteen Eighty-Four* from getting to ordinary Soviet readers, the novel, as well as other banned books, started slipping through the border controls and spreading around the USSR by the

[92]  Ibid.
[93]  Nikolay Nikolaevich Alipov's interview with the author on 27 October 2019.
[94]  *Progress* was founded in 1931 and in 1964 *Foreign Literature* publishers, including its 'special editorial team', were moved under its auspices.
[95]  N.N. Alipov's interview with the author.

beginning of the 1960s. This was the time when both *tamizdat* ('over there-publishing', that is, publishing abroad) and *samizdat* ('self-publishing', that is, typing at home) were coming into being and, notwithstanding extraordinary obstacles, continuing to grow for the next twenty-five years up to the time when Gorbachev's *glasnost* and then the Internet rendered them unnecessary.

In 1949 Orwell was angry with the British Foreign Office: 'They will throw millions down the drain on useless radio propaganda, but not finance books.'[96] Radio, of course, was not reduced to propaganda and, moreover, it helped to make books known: *Animal Farm*, for instance, was broadcast in Russian (in instalments) by the BBC Russian Service, while readings from the fable could also be heard in English, French, Spanish, Polish and Bulgarian – all in the period between August 1950 and April 1951.[97] Besides, the most comprehensive programmes of sending books from the West to the Eastern Block, and to the Soviet Union, in particular, originated in American radio stations, eager to send over the Iron Curtain not only radio signals but also the printed word.

Radio Liberty (RL), which was broadcasting to the Soviet Union and is still today broadcasting to Russia, and Radio Free Europe (RFE), broadcasting to Eastern Europe, started their book programmes in 1956. This was preceded by Radio Free Europe's rather eccentric attempts to send balloons launched from Germany with leaflets providing information unobtainable in Eastern Europe to Czechoslovakia and then Hungary and Poland.[98] The project would have never worked for the Soviet Union, but it was eventually thought dangerous even for the countries located much closer to Germany, where the stations were based, so it was abandoned, but the desire to send printed information and books remained.

Moving from balloons to the so-called 'blind mailings' – parcels sent by ordinary post to people whose names were taken from newspaper articles or even from telephone directories, both programmes eventually came down to 'hand-outs', that is, giving pocketbooks printed on thin paper to diplomats and ordinary Westerners travelling to 'socialist' countries in the hope that they would be able to distribute them there for free. They also were given to East European and Soviet visitors to the West. It was much more difficult for Soviet people to travel abroad than for East Europeans, and yet even

---

[96]  Orwell to Moore, 20 July 1949, CW, XX, 148.
[97]  A. M. Heath and Company Ltd to Sonia Orwell, 19 April 1951. The OA, UCL, Orwell/S/2/E/1.
[98]  Alfred A. Reisch, *Hot Books in the Cold War: The CIA-Funded Secret Western Book Distribution Programme Behind the Iron Curtain* (Budapest, New York: CEU Press, 2013), 9–10; Ivan Tolstoy, '*Platforma dlya Tamizdata* (A Platform for Tamizdat)', in *Izdatelskoe delo rossiyskogo zarubezhya 19–20 vekov (Russian Publishing Abroad in the 19–20 Centuries)* (Moscow: Dom russkogo zarubezhya, 2017), 46–60.

the Soviet Union provided a steady, if narrow, stream of thoroughly vetted citizens: sailors, performers on tour, sportsmen, participants in international conferences, etc. This 'person to person' method was a resounding success, as the books' recipients from behind the Iron Curtain had a choice: either to keep the gifts for themselves and maybe with the help of manual typewriters copy them for others, thus turning 'tamizdat' into 'samizdat', or simply to sell them at black-market prices, as demand was always high.

'These books for me are analogous to food denied to needy people by their oppressors', said one of the presidents of the Free Europe Committee.[99] Needless to say, the book programmes organized by the radio stations were secret – how could it be otherwise? As many people guessed, the funding both for them and for the radio stations, which accommodated them, came from the CIA. Even when, following the public debate in Washington in 1972,[100] the CIA had to stop financing the radios, it carried on with the book programmes.

The CIA gave money for publishing and translating books, buying books from émigré publishers, organizing mailings and hand-outs and paying their staff for doing all that. They also paid for the premises where books were stored. In response, they wanted reports as to where the funds were going. As in the case of the Congress for Cultural Freedom, they did not 'run' the programmes. A remarkable Romanian émigré, George Minden, was in charge of sending books to Eastern Europe for over thirty years, while the programme for the Soviet Union was headed for sixteen years by the former American diplomat, Isaak Patch,[101] and then effectively went under Minden's control too.

The task for those who tried to quench the thirst for books in the Soviet Union was much more difficult than for those working to help Eastern Europe: its territory was so much bigger, bans on books stricter, persecutions harsher, foreign travel much more limited, grasp of foreign languages poorer, but the need to overcome the separation from the rest of the world was as great as in other 'socialist' countries. 'How could Soviet intellectuals and writers live in mental isolation, not knowing the works of Kafka, Orwell or Camus?'[102] wondered, in her memoir, Lyudmila Thorne, who worked for the Russian language book programme between 1964 and 1975. She did not

---

[99] Quoted in Reisch, *Hot Books in the Cold War*, 520.

[100] It was initiated by Senator Fulbright's suggestion to close RFE and RL as 'cold war relics'. Since 1973 and up to now RFE and RL (which merged in 1976), have been financed directly by the US Congress.

[101] Patch published his memoir of the book programme: Isaak Patch, *Closing the Circle: A Buckalino Journey Around Our Time* (Wellesley: Wellesley College Printing Services, 1996).

[102] Lyudmila Thorne, *Books not Bombs* (Unpublished memoir. Bakhmeteff Archive), 5.

doubt that the relationship between their programme and the CIA 'could be best described as a meeting of the minds'[103] and was sure that 'in the case of the USSR' the CIA's activities 'like the book programmes and foreign radio broadcasts were positive and contributed to the democratisation of the Soviet Union'.[104] She and her colleagues felt that by opening the outside world to Soviet citizens they 'were helping in some small way to undermine the wretched regime'.[105]

The most exciting part of the work for them was publishing Western literature in translations into Russian, and more often than not commissioning these translations. During the decade that Thorne worked for the programme over two dozen books were published – maybe not too many, but what books they were! Orwell and Camus, Kafka and Joyce, Victor Serge and Ignazio Silone; books of Russian writers banned in the USSR – from 'the founder of socialist realism' Maxim Gorky, whose *Untimely Thoughts* of 1917–18 were undesirable for the Soviet regime, to Pasternak's *Doctor Zhivago* and novels by Nabokov; and there was also political non-fiction: *The Great Terror* by Robert Conquest (translated by Leonid Vladimirov, it was the most popular book of all), *Thirteen Days. A Memoir of the Cuban Missile Crisis* by Robert F. Kennedy, *The Communist Party of the Soviet Union* by Leonard Schapiro, *In Praise of Inconsistency* by Leszek Kołakowski.[106] Between 4,000 and 7,000 copies of each title were printed in Italy, Belgium, France and Canada, but the names and locations of the publishing houses adorning the covers were invented – they sounded credible and, as Thorne put it, 'romantic':[107] Paris, *Editions de la Seine*; Firenze, *Edizioni Aurora*; Napoli, *Edizioni Scientifiche Italiane*. Dates of publication were often missing as well as the names of the translators.

It was this secrecy that led to several riddles related to some of Orwell's books which are still not solved. The biggest of them is the mystery of the Russian *Homage to Catalonia*. A small grey book that would easily fit into an ordinary pocket printed by *Editions de la Seine* in Belgium does not have either the date of publication or the name of the translator. Lyudmila Thorne, who remembered a lot, did not mention it in her memoir and

---

[103] Ibid., 11.
[104] Thorne to Lloyd Salvetti, director of the Centre for the Study of Intelligence, CIA, 7 July 1999. Bakhmeteff Archive.
[105] Thorne, *Books not Bombs*, 19. A similar relationship is described in Paweł Sowiński's article 'Cold War Books: George Minden and his Field Workers, 1973–1990'. https://doi.org/10.1177/0888325419857151
[106] The list obviously is not full. These are just the titles mentioned in Thorne's memoir and in Tolstoy's *Platform for Tamizdat*.
[107] Thorne, *Books not Bombs*, 26.

actually admitted in her correspondence with Vladimir Pribylovsky[108] that she could not remember commissioning its translation or who the translator was. Her former colleague, Jack Stewart, who until 1973 worked for the book programme in Rome, also claimed recently that he had not even known that this book ever existed.[109] It is of course probable that *Homage to Catalonia* was published in Russian after 1975 when both Stewart and Thorne had left. There is some hope that after the CIA archives are declassified the name of the translator will be found there.

The other mystery concerns *Nineteen Eighty-Four*, which also has no date of publication or the translator's name. Apart from the name of the author and the title of the book, there is just one word on the cover: 'Roma'. However, there is no doubt that this is a reprint of the 1957 *Possev* edition[110] and *Possev's* correspondence with Gleb Struve helps us to surmise the date of publication.

On 5 August 1969 *Possev* publishers informed Struve that they were planning to publish his translation of *Animal Farm* and the 1957 translation of *Nineteen Eighty-Four* in one hard-cover volume with a dust-jacket. However, on 11 March 1971, they wrote to say that the plan was 'frustrated' (the word was in inverted commas) 'by our mutual acquaintance Mr Stewart, who with the help of his organisation published 7000 copies of *Nineteen Eighty-Four*'.[111] So it makes 1970 or early 1971 as the most probable date of this book's publication. The head of *Possev* publishing house at the time, Oleg Perekrestov, also told Struve that he had met Stewart at the end of 1970, when they discussed publishing the third edition of *Animal Farm* and 'his [Stewart's] bosses commissioned *Possev* to prepare 700 copies of this book'.[112] Having received this 'firm order' *Possev* decided 'to print 2,000 copies of the new edition'.[113]

These were editions of Orwell's which, among other 'ideologically harmful books', were secretly sold and bought – usually in places well known to the KGB. The copies were then either photographed, page by page, or retyped and multiplied with the help of carbon paper, which made each next version significantly paler than the previous one. The usual batch for a typewriter would hold four copies, but if particularly thin paper was used, one could get up to ten legible copies, which were then given to reliable friends, and by

---

[108] See *Dzordzh Oruell. Pamyati Catalonii.* https://www.orwell.ru/library/books/htm_file /021.

[109] Jack Stewart's message to the author on 30 July 2020.

[110] See Tolstoy, *Platforma dlya Tamizdata.*

[111] *Possev* to Struve, 11 March 1971. Struve papers, box 34, folder 12, Hoover.

[112] Ibid.

[113] Ibid.

the end of the 1960s there were enough of them to make this secret reading a prominent feature of the time.

Blyum quotes an article published in Russia in 1994, for the tenth anniversary of 'Orwell's year': 'There is something deeply symptomatic in the fact that a whole generation of Russian readers received *Nineteen Eighty-Four* "overnight". For twenty-four hours Orwell's novel took the place of sleep and at times was indistinguishable from a state of dreaming.'[114] When books in the original became available they were read in the original by those who knew English and translated by enthusiasts. The quality of translations varied[115] but avid readers were happy to get them anyway.

Dissident Julius Telesin, the same who later discovered cuts in *Possev's* edition of *Animal Farm*, was nicknamed 'the Prince of Samizdat', so passionately was he involved in typing and distributing banned books. He recounted that in the 1960s there were two translations of *Nineteen Eighty-Four* being circulated secretly, which could immediately be distinguished by the way 'Big Brother' and 'newspeak' were rendered in Russian, but neither of them had Orwell's Appendix, 'The Principles of Newspeak', which, understandably, was extremely difficult to translate.

Once Telesin came across the original English edition, he quickly found a translator who agreed to do the job. It was decided that particularly challenging neologisms coined by Orwell would stay in English. With this in mind, blanks were left in the typescript so that English words could be inserted later, by hand. By 1968 Telesin had all four copies of the translated Appendix ready. He gave two to his friends and kept two for himself. However, when the KGB operatives searched his flat in December 1968, they seized them together with the rest of Telesin's samizdat 'by force and without any record'.[116] Telesin was lucky – it had just occurred to the authorities that they could get rid of some tiresome activists by letting (or sometimes making) them leave the country. Telesin left in May 1970 and in 1976 published in *Kontinent* his own translation of Orwell's Appendix.

Many others had to face much worse consequences, as keeping a prohibited book at home and giving it to others could be easily treated as 'anti-Soviet agitation and propaganda'. Article 70 of the Soviet Criminal Code of 1960 stated that it meant not only 'agitation or propaganda

[114] S. Kuznetsov, *1994: yubilei nesluchivshegosya goda* (1994: The Anniversary of the Year that Never Was), quoted in Blyum, 411.

[115] Reportedly, one of the best early translations of *Nineteen Eighty-Four* was made by a Rostov philosopher Mikhail Petrov (1924–87) in 1968. This translation was never published, a copy of it is kept in the Bremen Archives.

[116] Telesin, 'Dzhordzh Orvell, "1984". *Glava iz romana, neizvestnaya russkomu chitatelyu* (George Orwell. *Nineteen Eighty-Four*. A Chapter from the Novel Unknown to the Russian Reader)' (*Kontinent*, No. 10, 1976), 363–4.

carried on for the purpose of subverting or weakening the Soviet regime or of committing especially dangerous crimes against the state' but also 'the [verbal] spreading for the same purpose of slanderous fabrications defaming the Soviet political and social system, or the circulation or preparation or keeping, for the same purpose, of literature of such content'.[117] In the eyes of the regime, *Nineteen Eighty-Four* obviously was a 'slanderous fabrication', and therefore, 'circulation or preparation or safekeeping' of it could be punished by 'deprivation of freedom for a term from six months up to seven years (with or without additional exile for a term of 2 to 5 years), or by exile for a term of 2 to 5 years'.[118] No wonder that on getting to the chapter where Winston Smith is reading *the book*, readers in the Soviet Union knew exactly how he felt.

\* \* \*

Meanwhile, Orwell was still hardly mentioned in the Soviet press. Arlen Blyum distinguishes between three types of Soviet experts in English literature: those who 'acted on the principle "better say nothing than lie" and avoided referring to Orwell at all; others, who placed him among the "ideologues of imperialist reaction", and still others, who attempted to "rehabilitate" Orwell, claiming that his satire was directed not against communism and the Soviet Union, but against capitalism'.[119] Neither group was very numerous, but the approach of the latter came in handy around 1984, when it became extremely difficult to pretend that Orwell's books did not exist, because of the 'flood of journal and newspaper articles written to mark "Orwell's year" by French and Italian "Eurocommunists"'.[120] On 20 January 1984 *Literaturnaya gazeta*, where the article by Nora Gal had been published in 1947, carried an article by S. Volovets called '*Tost za proshloe (Po sledam Oruella)*' – 'A Toast to the Past (In the Footsteps of Orwell)', which presented him 'practically as an ally'.[121]

The same line was chosen in 1984 for the reprinting of the 1959 'special' edition of *Nineteen Eighty-Four* by *Progress* publishers, the heirs of *Foreign Literature*. This time the book had a preface signed by Soviet diplomat and foreign affairs journalist Gennady Gerasimov, who wrote: 'conceived as a satire against communism' the novel is now being read as directed against

---

[117] See https://chronicle-of-current-events.com/article-70/.
[118] Ibid.
[119] Blyum, 'George Orwell in the Soviet Union', 413.
[120] Ibid., 415.
[121] Ibid.

the West, which 'as if in a mirror sees in Orwell's book its own features'.[122] Still, this 'positive' approach to Orwell did not of course mean that his books suddenly started being published for the general public in Russia. Ordinary readers received a chance to get to Orwell's books legally only after Gorbachev announced *perestroika*.

Both *Nineteen Eighty-Four* and *Animal Farm* were for the first time officially published in Russian in 1988. The authorities, however, were still scared of the books and of a possible sudden return to the Soviet rules and regulations, in which case they ran the risk of being held responsible for 'spreading slanderous publications'. That is why they decided to start with serializing them in small journals, and not in Moscow or Leningrad, but in the Soviet republics: *Animal Farm* (translated by I. Polotsk) was published in Latvia[123] and *Nineteen Eighty-Four* (translated by V. Nedoshivin) in Moldavia.[124]

Apart from these two 'main' books, which since 1988 have been published many times in different translations (at least half a dozen translations of *Animal Farm* and at least four of *Nineteen Eighty-Four*), some of Orwell's essays reached Russian readers in the 1990s. His first book *Down and Out in Paris in London* and the four 'realistic' novels became known in Russian in the 2000s – all translated by one translator, and the last of Orwell's books to appear in Russian – *The Road to Wigan Pier* – came out as late as in 2014. Russian publishers obviously thought that there would not be sufficient interest in post-*perestroika* Russia either in descriptions of the life of English miners or in Orwell's doubts about socialism – thus they nearly missed Orwell's most autobiographical book.

---

[122] Russian State Public Historical Library on 1984 special edition of *Nineteen Eighty-Four*. https://m.facebook.com/story.php?story_fbid=3327779247298842&id=18959904 1116894&p=10.

[123] See *Rodnik*, a journal published by the Central Committee of the CP of Latvia, March–June 1988.

[124] See *Kodry*, a journal published by the Writers' Union of Moldavia, September–December 1988, January 1989.

# 9

# 'Alone with the forbidden book'[1]

*The book fascinated him, or more exactly it reassured him. In a sense it told him nothing that was new, but that was part of the attraction. It said what he would have said, if it had been possible for him to set his scattered thoughts in order. It was the product of a mind similar to his own, but enormously more powerful, more systematic, less fear-ridden. The best books, he perceived, are those that tell you what you know already.[2]*

Orwell, *Nineteen Eighty-Four*

The main feeling readers in the Soviet Union experienced when they first encountered *Nineteen Eighty-Four* was that of recognition. Winston Smith's life had an uncanny resemblance to their own: 'a fruity voice . . . reading out a list of figures which had something to do with the production of pig-iron'; the lift that 'even at the best of times . . . was seldom working'[3]; perennial lack of this or that indispensable everyday item – razor blades, shoelaces, cooking pots; dull insipid food; obligatory attendance at official functions; 'the Ninth Three-Year Plan'[4]; the common abbreviations, like Minitrue or Miniluv, which sounded exactly like Minfin or Minzdrav.[5] These were the matches that leapt to the eye of those who lived under Brezhnev, but in Oceania they obviously lived under Stalin – with arrests that 'invariably happened at night'[6]; disappearances of people, who were not simply killed, but 'vaporized' – 'abolished, annihilated'[7] as if they had never existed; tortures in the cellars; executions; the hysterical atmosphere at the official meetings; children informing on their parents; calls for vigilance against enemies of the people; never-ending scheming of the constantly exposed and yet invincible enemy Goldstein (Trotsky) and, of course, under the invariably wise leadership of

---

[1]  Orwell, *Nineteen Eighty-Four*, 159.
[2]  Ibid., 160.
[3]  Ibid., 3.
[4]  Ibid., 4.
[5]  Minfin stood for the Ministry of Finance, Minzdrav for *Ministerstvo zdravookhraneniya*, the Ministry of Healthcare.
[6]  Orwell, *Nineteen Eighty-Four*, 18.
[7]  Ibid., 19.

the fair and powerful Big Brother (Stalin). Orwell's awareness of the minutest details of the Soviet everyday, the details, which survived for years and years – the physical drill broadcast all over the country for people to exercise at their working place (Winston, of course, has to do 'the Physical Jerks' even at home); 'voluntary work' in the evenings; ubiquitous slogans – made it difficult to believe that the author had never been in the USSR.

There, just like in Oceania, the 'bareness', 'dinginess', 'listlessness' of the ordinary life, which reduced you to 'slogging through dreary jobs, fighting for a place on the Tube, darning a worn-out sock, cadging a saccharine tablet, saving a cigarette end'[8] contrasted sharply with the ideal set up by the party – 'huge, terrible and glittering – the world of steel and concrete, of monstrous machines and terrifying weapons'.[9] Official propaganda naturally invaded the private space: the first thing that Winston heard on coming home was the telescreen (in the real world it would be the radio), and it seemed to follow you everywhere: somewhat later 'behind Winston's back the voice from telescreen was still bubbling away about pig-iron and the overfulfilment of the Ninth Three-Year Plan'.[10] In the USSR you could switch the voice off, but not in Oceania. Pig-iron production,[11] however, triumphantly compared with the amount manufactured in 1913, remained a constant trait of the Soviet economic record, an everlasting source of pride even half a century later. In his poem written in 1969, the Russian poet Joseph Brodsky used the gloomy metal as a metaphor for the unchanging character of Russian life and its regime based on violence:

> This whole realm is just static. Imagining the output of lead
> and cast iron, and shaking your stupefied head,
>         you recall bayonets, Cossack whips of old power.
> Yet the eagles land like good lodestones on the scraps.
> Even wicker chairs here are built mostly with bolts and with nuts,
>         one is bound to discover.[12]

But apart from strikingly recognizable details, there was something else, even more important, something that Soviet readers identified as their own from the very first page – the secret interior life of an individual under an oppressive

[8]   Ibid., 61.
[9]   Ibid.
[10]  Ibid., 6.
[11]  Orwell's attention may have been first attracted to the importance of pig-iron production when he was reading Lyons's *Assignment to Utopia*, where the author reflected on the 'hyperbolic' optimism of the First Five-year Plan (Lyons, 241).
[12]  Joseph Brodsky, 'The End of a Beautiful Era', trans. David Rigsbee with the author, in *Collected Poems in English* (Manchester: Carcanet Press Ltd, 2001), 38. In Russian the same word *chugun* is used both for pig-iron and cast iron.

regime. The details, after all, could be collected from books, papers, stories of those who travelled to the Soviet Union, although their selection, as in the case of 'pig-iron', required special sensitivity. Besides, Orwell obviously borrowed some particulars for the novel from his own experience in London during the war years: bombs, devastation, the short supply of necessary things – and 'the pleasures of recognition [were] roused'[13] in Britain too. On top of this, his work for the BBC in 1941–43 gave him a sense of a huge corporation, run by bureaucrats and bound by war-time censorship. But it was his decade-long thinking about totalitarianism, imagining himself in these unfamiliar circumstances, that allowed his talent, his creative sensibility, to assimilate with those he hardly ever met, to piece together their psychology. It was the inner monologue of a secret 'thought-criminal', seized by fear and yet burnt by silent protest that was so convincing and instantly impressed Orwell's readers in the Soviet Union, who, like readers of lyrical poetry, were ready to exclaim: 'Yes, this is what I feel, but I could never express it so well!' They would have been overwhelmed even if Orwell had got his details wrong. But the details were right too. It was 'about us'.

What was so incredibly similar between Winston Smith's plight in the first part of the book and the life of Soviet citizens, not necessarily dissidents, but those, perhaps a majority, who kept silent and yet looked critically or cynically at what was going on around them? The enforced duality of their lives. Eugene Lyons, whose book made a profound, if unacknowledged, impression on Orwell back in 1938, explained the peculiarities of the Russian mentality he encountered in the Soviet Union in the late 1920s to early 1930s by the historical legacy:

> The absence of a free press, the all-powerful secret service, the outlawry of all independent thoughts and feelings, the tom-tom monotony of surface slogans – all these things that have been the country's portion for a thousand years seemed to have driven the Russian people underground: their essential life seems subterranean, a life of secret thoughts, unspoken hopes, vague dreads, clandestine satisfactions.
> . . . Every Russian man and woman lives automatically a double existence, has lived it for numberless generations: one public and obviously conformist, the other private and untrammelled.[14]

The Soviet totalitarian regime undoubtedly exacerbated the tension between the two, and Winston Smith, who starts his rebellion in the worst

[13] Julian Symons, 'Review of *Nineteen Eighty-Four*'; Meyers, 253.
[14] Lyons, *Assignment in Utopia*, 604.

possible circumstances, seemed incredibly close to those who read about him in Russia. The most familiar feature of his mindset was his ingrained overwhelming fear accompanied by the knack of survival. Starting a diary, and thus his protest against the state, he tries hard not to betray himself and reveals a superb ability to distinguish between different kinds of danger. The helicopter flying next to his building 'was the police patrol, snooping into people's windows. The patrols did not matter, however. Only the Thought Police mattered'.[15] This common wisdom based on experience was almost unconsciously acquired by an individual in the Soviet Union, even in the most 'vegetarian' – as Anna Akhmatova would call them – that is, post-Stalin, times.

You would not read a forbidden book on the underground or even keep it at home without wrapping it first; mention something you heard on a foreign radio in a company you did not fully trust; say things or tell jokes that could be considered politically objectionable over the phone. When you discussed anything to do with politics or criticized the authorities you would cover the phone with a cushion or you could talk in the bathroom with the water running, or, better still, write your message on a piece of paper, let your companion read it and then simply burn it. 'You had to live – did live, from habit that became instinct – in the assumption that every sound you made was overheard, and except in darkness, every movement scrutinised.'[16] In the daytime, of course, Winston Smith never forgot to 'set his features into the expression of quiet optimism which it was advisable to wear when facing the telescreen'.[17] Eugene Lyons, who left the Soviet Union in 1934, 'knew men and women who lived in a state of constant terror, their little suitcases always packed, though they worked diligently and avoided even facial expressions which might cast doubt on their loyalty'.[18] People around you in the Soviet Union were sure to notice your 'facial expression' as fast as a telescreen – and often with the same disastrous consequences.

It is not so surprising, then, that in the Soviet Union it was rather difficult to read *Nineteen Eighty-Four* as a dystopia, prophecy or science fiction. Gleb Struve, who was the first to say it, remarked: 'Unlike Zamyatin and Aldous Huxley, Orwell put no stress in his own satire on elements of technical progress. He wrote not a utopia, but a satire and this many people have not understood and have not caught the meaning of…. [Orwell] drew his material from contemporary, and especially Soviet, reality'.[19] All the characteristics of

[15]  Orwell, *Nineteen Eighty-Four*, 6.
[16]  Ibid.
[17]  Ibid., 8.
[18]  Lyons, *Assignment in Utopia*, 346–347.
[19]  Gleb Struve, 'Telling the Russians', in *Orwell Remembered*, 261.

a dismal future invented by Orwell were metaphors or satirical exaggerations of features that already existed but were not yet drawn out 'to their logical consequences'.[20]

Orwell did not fight 'surveillance' in the technical sense, as it is commonly understood today, he did not predict the technology used now – from CCTV to computers gathering data – which can follow humans and collect information about them. He wrote about people corrupted by the idea that there is one and only one correct way of thinking and acting and therefore convinced that reporting on any 'deviations' from it is the duty of every responsible citizen. Whether it was a 'thought-crime', that is, just an intention to commit an offence (like Winston scrawling 'DOWN WITH BIG BROTHER') or an actual offence, did not matter – 'in the eyes of the Party there was no distinction between the thought and the deed'.[21] It was exactly the same in the Soviet Union, where people were arrested for possessing a book, while in Oceania 'Thought Police' materialized as a separate force, no less necessary for fighting thought-criminals than the usual police was for fighting actual crime.

The Soviet reality could not boast of telescreens, but there was bugging, line tapping and simply KGB informers, who were involved in 'active surveillance', and in Stalin's time also countless voluntary informers, who would write anonymous denunciations if they simply coveted somebody's room or job. Besides, children 'were systematically turned against their parents and taught to spy on them and report their deviations. The family had become in effect an extension of the Thought Police. It was a device by means of which everyone could be surrounded night and day by informers who knew him intimately'.[22]

Just as Orwell's telescreens were the materialization of political surveillance, there was obviously no 'Anti-Sex League' in the USSR, but love for the leader, for the party, for the Motherland or for the Communist cause had always been deemed much more important than love for your partner. That is why the final words of *Nineteen Eighty-Four* are so convincing – nothing less than love was demanded for Stalin!

The main thrust of the novel – and this was fully understood by Soviet readers – lay in the idea of human fragility under the relentless pressure of the state, 'a boot stamping on a human face – for ever'.[23] And it was not just fragility under torture, although this was well known to millions who had been in Stalin's prisons where 'confessions' were demanded, it was fragility

[20] Orwell's Statement on *Nineteen Eighty-Four*, CW, XX, 136.
[21] Orwell, *Nineteen Eighty-Four*, 192.
[22] Ibid., 109.
[23] Ibid., 212.

under the systematic endeavour of the totalitarian state to control the mind and thus destroy the individual's integrity and capacity to resist. Controlling the mind was achieved in many ways, one of which was deliberate eradication of normal emotions and feelings – trust and love among them: 'Already we are breaking down the habits of thought which have survived from before the revolution', O'Brien explains to Winston. 'No one dares trust a wife or a child or a friend any longer.'[24] And this, unfortunately, was also familiar to Orwell's readers in the Soviet Union – it was just another survival knack that a person daily surrounded by informers had to learn. 'There will be no loyalty, except loyalty towards the Party. There will be no love, except the love of Big Brother',[25] predicted O'Brien, and betrayals of loved ones were more common than one would care to mention, even not under torture.

The most common of these betrayals, and the most well known among them, was repudiating one's parents, habitually done by young people who hoped to find their own place in the new 'huge, terrible and glittering' world of party propaganda. The well-known Soviet poet Alexander Tvardovsky suffered till the end of his days because he had renounced his father, who had been deported as a 'kulak' together with the rest of the family. In his long 1968 poem *By Right of Memory* he wrote:

Proud that we did not believe in God,
But in the name of our own sanctities,
We sternly required this sacrifice:
Renounce thy father and thy mother.

Forget the family whence you came,
Remember this, and do not question:
Your love for the Father of the Peoples
By any other love is lessened.

The task is clear, sacred the cause
For the shortest way to the highest goal,
Betray your brother as you go
And stab your best friend in the back.[26]

---

[24] Ibid.
[25] Ibid.
[26] Alexander Tvardovsky, *By Right of Memory*. The part quoted here: 'The Son Does Not Answer for the Father', trans. George Saunders, can be found in the book 'An End to Silence', ed. Stephen F. Cohen (Norton, 1982). Or here https://www.latimes.com/archives/la-xpm-1987-08-31-me-3226-story.html.

This poem, written fifteen years after Stalin's death, was not published and Tvardovsky died soon after writing it, aged sixty-one. His brother, who survived the Gulag, had a rather strained relationship with him till the end of his days.

There were other cases, also reflected in literature. Lydia Chukovskaya's novella about the Great Terror, *Sofia Petrovna*,[27] written in 1939–40, is a rare example of fiction describing harrowing events at the time when they were happening. Chukovskaya has her naïve and conformist heroine, a typist in the publishing house, experience the shock of her son's arrest. After months and months of not knowing anything about her Kolya, apart from the fact that he is not even allowed to receive parcels, she receives a letter, presumably smuggled out of a prison or camp, where Kolya describes his investigator beating him up to make him confess to his alleged crimes and asks his mother to help him. Realizing that she is unable to do so and can only endanger herself by trying, Sofia Petrovna burns the letter and stamps out the ashes.

In the afterword written in 1962, during Khrushchev's thaw, when Chukovskaya had some reason to hope that her novella might be published in the Soviet Union (Solzhenitsyn's *One Day of Ivan Denisovich* was published that year), she explained:

> For my heroine I chose not a sister, not a wife, not a sweetheart, not a friend, but that symbol of devotion – a mother. My Sofia Petrovna loses her only son. I wanted to show that when people's lives are deliberately distorted, their feelings become distorted, even maternal ones. Sofia Petrovna is a widow; her son is her life. Kolya is arrested; he is sentenced to hard labour; is called an 'enemy of the people'. Sofia Petrovna, schooled to believe newspapers and officials more than herself, believes the prosecutor when he tells her that her son has 'admitted his crimes' and deserves his sentence. Sofia Petrovna knows full well that Kolya has committed no crime, that he is incapable of it, that to the depths of his being he is loyal to the party, to his factory, to Comrade Stalin personally. But if she is to believe in herself, not in the prosecutor and the newspapers, then . . . then . . . the universe will collapse, the

---

[27] The novella was first published in Russian in France in 1965 and in English in 1967 under the title *The Deserted House*, trans. Aline Worth. The translation was subsequently emended by Eliza Kellogg Klose and published by Northwestern University Press in 1988. It was in the same year that *Sofia Petrovna* was published for the first time in Russia.

earth give way beneath her feet, the spiritual comfort in which she has so comfortably lived, worked, rejoiced, turn to dust.[28]

Sofia Petrovna's betrayal does not necessarily mean that there were no examples of people refusing to renounce their family or friends – certainly there were: Chukovskaya herself was not betrayed by any of the five people she invited to her home to listen to *Sofia Petrovna* as she read it out to them in 1940. One of the characters in her book, Kolya's friend Alik, refuses to renounce Kolya and is himself arrested. However, these were rare occasions. Fear for oneself, but also reluctance to give up the 'spiritual comfort' of being at one with the party and with the country were much more common, and many ordinary people – not only scoundrels who hoped to use other people's demise for their own benefit – just carried on living their lives and keeping silent. Even today, perhaps, a large part of Russia's population would rather 'burn letters' from the Gulag – dismiss the information which reached them decades later and deny the existence of the Soviet terror altogether – all for the sake of their own spiritual comfort. This certainly confirms what Orwell predicted as early as in 1938 – the corruption of human nature: 'It may be just as possible to produce a breed of men who do not wish for liberty as to produce a breed of hornless cows',[29] he wrote and, perhaps, contemporary attitudes in Russia are still a product of the Soviet and, unfortunately, also the post-Soviet, regimes.

The case analysed by Orwell in *Nineteen Eighty-Four* is different. As 'the last man on earth' and a conscious rebel, even if subdued by fear, Winston Smith does not at all seek spiritual comfort. He preserves his freedom of thought for as long as he can and even under torture tries to argue with O'Brien and resist him. But he has one illusion – and Orwell, relentlessly drawing totalitarian 'ideas out to their logical consequences',[30] deprives him and – most importantly – the novel's readers of it.

Before Winston is arrested, he still hopes that 'they can't get inside you': 'they could not alter your feelings. . . . They could lay bare in the utmost detail everything that you had done or said or thought; but the inner heart, whose workings were mysterious even to yourself, remained impregnable.'[31] Orwell's answer to this becomes his ultimate warning: they can. They can, as O'Brian threatens Winston, 'squeeze you empty, and then . . . fill you with

---

[28]  Lydia Chukovskaya, 'Afterword to *Sofia Petrovna*'. https://anzlitlovers.com/2019/04/22/sofia-petrovna-by-lydia-chukovskaya-translated-by-aline-worth/.

[29]  Orwell, 'Review of *Russia Under the Soviet Rule*', CW, XI, 315.

[30]  Orwell's Statement on *Nineteen Eighty-Four*, CW, XX, 136.

[31]  Orwell, *Nineteen Eighty-Four*, 135.

[themselves]'.[32] The process is carefully thought through and still remains convincing for those who know that this is not an abstract speculation of a 'pessimistic' writer, but an absolutely real and possible development.

Once Winston first gets to the cellars of the Ministry of Love, he imagines Julia tortured and thinks: 'If I could save Julia by doubling my own pain, would I do it? Yes, I would'. This, however, is followed by an immediate comment by the author: 'But that was merely an intellectual decision, taken because he knew that he ought to take it. He didn't feel it'.[33] After the first blow by a truncheon, Winston realizes: 'Never, for any reason on earth, could you wish for an increase of pain. Of pain you could wish only one thing: that it should stop'.[34] His body continues to suffer, but his spirit is still intact and in his 'inner heart' he knows that he has not betrayed Julia.

In a letter to Julian Symons, who reviewed *Nineteen Eighty-Four* in the TLS, Orwell admitted: 'You are of course right about the vulgarity of the 'Room 101' business. I was aware of this while writing it, but I did not know another way of getting somewhere near the effect I wanted'.[35] Whatever the criticism or self-criticism, 'the Room 101 business' showed that human beings can be broken not only physically but also spiritually, if their torturers set it as their aim, and for every person the tool they would use would be different – the one that would seem 'the worst thing in the world'[36] to this particular individual.

In thousands of Gulag memoirs there are thousands of instances when people describe how they or the people they knew 'broke down'. Historian Mark Botvinnik, arrested in 1938 together with his fellow-students who attended a club for an in-depth study of antiquity – which, as the prosecution implied, testified to their lack of interest in the modern world – tells a story of his fellow inmate, who was naïve enough to ask his investigator: 'Please do not hit me in my liver – I have a liver condition' and, of course, they started deliberately hitting him in his liver. Botvinnik, who was then twenty-one, also told his own story of investigators extorting confessions from him:

> I resisted for as long as I could. I managed to go through the so called 'conveyor belt', which was horrible: several investigators interrogated me for a week – they came and went, without allowing me a moment of respite. I broke down later when one of them started tearing out my

[32]  Ibid., 203.
[33]  Ibid., 189.
[34]  Ibid., 190.
[35]  Orwell to Symons, 16 June 1949, CW, XX, 137.
[36]  Orwell, *Nineteen Eighty-Four*, 225.

hair – one lock after another. This stupefied me. Besides, all the accused in my case had already signed the interrogation file. And so did I.[37]

Botvinnik also writes about a tremendous sense of guilt, the darkest of depressions experienced by some people who were made to incriminate their nearest and dearest. This could have been as terrible as for Winston to betray Julia.

'Getting inside' a person was achieved by many different methods, and sometimes by several methods combined. In May 1937, the Soviet poet, Olga Bergholz, at that time a devout Communist, was expelled from the party for her connection to the 'enemy of the people', Leopold Averbach,[38] who was her lover. The expulsion and public humiliation were a severe blow for her. Later, in July, when she was seven months pregnant, she was called to the NKVD as a witness in Averbach's case and then, in December 1938, pregnant again, she was arrested on different charges and spent nearly seven months in prison.[39] Both in July 1937 and in 1938–9 she lost her unborn babies under psychological and physical torture. And even this was not all.

Bergholz was one of very few people who kept diaries during the Great Terror. The search preceding her arrest resulted in the confiscation of all her diaries (over twenty notebooks) and when she was released, they were returned to her with red markings. Remarkably, she continued to keep a diary even after she was released, although admitting that she was 'haunted by the thought: "This will be read by an investigator." The secret of the recorded soul is violated. They have broken into your mind, your heart, they defiled it, they forced it open by finding the right picklocks and jimmies'.[40]

She understood what had happened to her even earlier, when on 14 December 1939 she made the following entry:

I was arrested exactly a year ago. I feel the prison now – after five months of liberty – more acutely than when I was just released. They've taken

---

[37] Mark Botvinnik, '*Kamera No 25*' (Cell No 25) in *Vospominaniya o GULAGe I ikh avtory* (Memoirs of the Gulag and their authors). https://www.sakharov-center.ru/asfcd/auth/?t=page&num=7315.

[38] Leopold Averbach (1903–37), once the powerful head of the Russian Association of Proletarian Writers (RAPP), was arrested in April 1937, following the arrest of his brother-in-law Genrich Yagoda, the head of the NKVD between 1934 and 1936, and shot in August 1937.

[39] Bergholz was released in July 1939 as she was lucky to have her case reviewed together with a number of others after the dismissal of Nikolay Yezhov (Yagoda's successor) as the Head of the NKVD and appointment of Lavrenty Beria to this post.

[40] Diary Entry of 1 March 1940 in *Olga. Zapretny dnevnik* (Olga. The Forbidden Diary). Diaries, letters, prose and poetry by Olga Bergholz. Edited by Natalya Sokolovskaya (St Petersburg: Azbuka, 2010), 36.

out my soul, rooted through it with their stinky fingers, spat at it, defiled it, then pushed it back and said: 'Live!' . . . Will I survive? I still don't know . . . It all reminds me of a poignant tale of Shchedrin's 'Adventures of Kramolnikov': 'He realized that everything remained as it had been, only his soul was sealed.'[41]

Both Winston's and Julia's souls were 'sealed' after their torture in the Ministry of Love. Everything was 'dead inside'[42] them. Exactly as in real life, their 'inner hearts' were violated and became irresponsive. And although they were hardly watched any longer, they could not return to their former loving relationship. 'There were things, your own acts, from which you could not recover. Something was killed in your breast: burnt out, cauterized out'.[43] The last scene of Winston and Julia is one of the saddest encounters of former lovers in literature. This is, of course, no longer a satire, but the powerful ending of a psychological novel. And the book's very final sentence, echoing Tvardovsky's lines: 'Your love for the Father of the Peoples/ By any other love is lessened', brings its readers, once again, to the logical conclusion: Winston, dead inside without his love for Julia, is no longer a rebel – he becomes like everybody else and loves Big Brother.

When Orwell was working on *Nineteen Eighty-Four*, he wrote to Fredric Warburg that his book was 'in a sense a fantasy, but in the form of a naturalistic novel. That is what makes it a difficult job'.[44] Irving Howe insisted that the book 'ought to be read as a mixture of genres, mostly Menippean satire and conventional novel, but also bits of tract and a few touches of transposed romance'.[45] Today it is most commonly called a 'dystopia' or 'anti-utopia', which often raises 'false expectations'[46] and leads readers away from its main theme – a warning against a social order that destroys human beings, not necessarily by killing them.

*  *  *

There is not much doubt as to what social order Orwell meant when he was warning his readers about the danger of totalitarian ideas. There are

[41]	Diary Entry of 14 December 1939 in: Ibid., 31. Mikhail Saltykov-Shchedrin (1826–1889) was a Russian satirist.
[42]	Orwell, *Nineteen Eighty-Four*, 203.
[43]	Ibid., 230.
[44]	Orwell to Warburg, 31 May 1947, CW, XIX, 149.
[45]	Irving Howe, '1984: Enigmas of Power', in *1984 Revisited: Totalitarianism in Our Century*, ed. Irving Howe (New York, Cambridge, Philadelphia, San Francisco, London, Mexico City, Sydney: Harper & Row, 1983), 7–8.
[46]	Ibid., 8.

numerous proofs to confirm it. Peter Davison in his Introduction to the Facsimile edition of *Nineteen Eighty-Four* draws attention of the readers to one of them:

> When O' Brien describes to Winston the way martyrdom has been eliminated, he recounts previous persecutions concluding with 'the totalitarians, as they were called. There were the German Nazis and the Russian Communists'. The preliminary draft has only the Russian Communists (and probably Orwell first intended to write 'Russian Bolshevists' or Bolsheviks – for there is the trace of a scored-out 'B' before 'Communists').[47]

Orwell's spontaneous reference to the Russians is natural – at that moment he was thinking about them, rather than about Nazis. In the novel, immediately after the sentence quoted by Davison, O'Brien continues:

> The Russians persecuted heresy more cruelly than the Inquisition had done. And they imagined that they had learned from the mistakes of the past; they knew, at any rate, that one mustn't make martyrs. Before they exposed their victims to public trial, they deliberately set themselves to destroy their dignity. They wore them down by torture and solitude until they were despicable, cringing wretches, confessing what was put into their mouths, covering themselves with abuse, accusing and sheltering behind one another, whimpering for mercy. And yet after only a few years the same thing had happened over again. The dead men had become martyrs and their degradation was forgotten.[48]

O'Brien obviously aims at competing with the Russians and achieving more than them. He threatens Winston:

> Even the victim of the Russian purges could carry rebellion locked up in his skull as he walked down the passage waiting for the bullet. But we make the brain perfect before we blow it out.[49]

Having mentioned Orwell's draft version in his Introduction, Davison then quotes Tosco Fyvel, who thought that Orwell 'had something of a blind spot'

---

[47] Peter Davison, Introduction to *George Orwell: Nineteen Eighty-Four. The Facsimile of the Extant Manuscript*, ed. Peter Davison (London: Secker & Warburg, Weston, Massachusetts: M & S Press, 1984), xvii.

[48] Orwell, *Nineteen Eighty-Four*, 201.

[49] Ibid., 203.

about Hitler's Germany, because, after his experience in Spain, he was more concerned with the danger of 'the Communist enemy'.[50] It does not seem to be a matter of having a 'blind spot' – otherwise, Orwell would not have inserted 'the German Nazis'[51] into his final manuscript and would not have repeated the phrase 'the German Nazis and the Russian Communists'[52] several pages later. He obviously did not deny the existence of German totalitarianism, but nobody around him was infatuated with it either, whereas the USSR had never lost its capacity to attract people by its mendacious slogans. Moreover, in 1947–8, when Orwell was writing *Nineteen Eighty-Four*, Nazi Germany had been defeated and the Soviet Union emerged victorious and therefore much more dangerous for the present and future. Besides, as Robert Conquest, an acknowledged expert on the Soviet terror, wrote:

> The Nazis, though responsible for the most frightful mass slaughter, imposed the terror with characteristics different from those of the Soviet Union or *Nineteen Eighty-Four*. It is true that the Hitler regime was in power a comparatively short time, had not seriously attacked a number of fairly autonomous groupings like the churches and the Officers' Corps, had not gone so far into totalism as had been possible in Russia. And it is quite plausible that a victorious Nazism might have developed the same insistence on brainwashing and full control of the victim's, or citizen's, mind as was implicit in Stalinism. But at any rate it was not the model here for Orwell.[53]

Controlling the mind in Oceania starts with instilling in it the idea that 'reality is not external. Reality exists in the human mind and nowhere else',[54] which, naturally, makes the Party omnipotent – over the present and over the past. And the pivotal episode in Winston Smith's understanding of the Party's falsification of history also comes from the Soviet experience.

Orwell based Winston's discovery of an old photograph of Jones, Aaronson and Rutherford on a real episode during the Mensheviks' show trial in 1931. In the novel, the photograph from *The Times* proves irrefutably that although 'all three men confessed that on that date they had been on Eurasian soil', this could not be true as on the same date they were 'at some Party function

---

[50] Peter Davison, 'Introduction to *George Orwell: Nineteen Eighty-Four*', xvii.

[51] Orwell, *Nineteen Eighty-Four*, 201.

[52] Ibid., 209.

[53] Conquest, 'Totaliterror', in *On Nineteen Eighty-Four*, ed. Peter Stansky (New York, San Francisco: W.H. Freeman and Company, 1983), 181.

[54] Orwell, *Nineteen Eighty-Four*, 197.

in New York'[55] – which means that their confessions were lies. Orwell learnt about the 'cynical coax'[56] used at the Menshevik trial from two different sources almost simultaneously: Lyons's *Assignment in Utopia* and Borkenau's *The Communist International*, which he read and reviewed within three and a half months in 1938.

At the Menshevik trial, it was claimed that one of the Second International leaders, Rafael Abramovich,[57] who emigrated from Russia in 1920, made a secret visit to the country in 1928 'in order to form a conspiracy for the overthrow of the Soviet Government'.[58] 'The whole Menshevik plot centered around that visit, and the defendants "confessed" meetings and discussions in detail.'[59] Moreover, they 'confessed that Abramovich had acted at the direct orders of the bureau of the Second International',[60] thus implicating Léon Blum, who later became the French prime minister. 'Unfortunately for the GPU stage directors',[61] as Lyons sarcastically remarks, on the very days that Abramovich was allegedly conspiring with the Mensheviks in Russia, he was attending an International Socialist Congress in Brussels and was photographed with other delegates at the Congress. As a contemporary scholar of Russian social-democracy points out, 'even *Pravda* had reported on his activities at the congress!'[62] The Menshevik trial took place three years later and re-reading old *Pravdas* had never been recommended in the USSR. Abramovich's participation in the congress and his photographs were assumed to have been forgotten. This story, which could have helped international socialists to undermine the trial, had never become widely known in Russia but was noticed by Orwell scholars.[63]

On reading *Nineteen Eighty-Four*, Orwell's erstwhile friend, Franz Borkenau, who had meanwhile moved to Germany, wrote to him, judging the novel primarily from the point of view of 'sociological interpretation' presented in it:

[55]  Ibid., 64.
[56]  Lyons, *Assignment in Utopia*, 380.
[57]  Rafael (Rafail) Abramovich (1880–1963) was the father of Mark Rein kidnapped in Barcelona in 1937 (see Chapter 3).
[58]  Borkenau, *The Communist International*, 350.
[59]  Lyons, *Assignment in Utopia*, 380.
[60]  Borkenau, *The Communist International*, 350.
[61]  Lyons, *Assignment in Utopia*, 380.
[62]  André Liebich, *From the Other Shore: Russian Social Democracy After 1921* (Cambridge, MA and London, England: Harvard University Press, 1999), 207. See *Pravda*, 8 August 1928.
[63]  William Steinhoff, *The Road to 1984* (London: Weidenfeld and Nicolson, 1975), 189–190.

I felt that behind every detail there was a bulk of correct analysis and at the same time such an invocation of horror that it makes one doubt the value of living in this period. The problem for all of us is of course that the horrors of the totalitarian regime are such that they defy both scholarly analysis and artistic creation; therefore, we always tend to remain below the level of the actual thing and that is a help to the dictatorships. Yours is the only book which seems to me to convey fully what a totalitarian regime means in terms of the individuals living under it.[64]

\*    \*    \*

George Woodcock, another friend of Orwell's, who wrote about him and about his books with great insight, acknowledged in 1984 that 'readers of the samizdat editions of *Nineteen Eighty-Four* in the Communist countries' understood the book differently from readers in the West. 'For them, the novel is not a futurist fantasy; it is, like *Animal Farm*, an easily recognizable satire on the world they inhabit.'[65] But he stressed, '[Orwell's] aims in writing *Nineteen Eighty-Four* were considerably broader'[66] and eventually came to the following conclusion: 'I believe it would be well if we in the West also turned Orwell's satiric lens on the world we inhabit in 1984.'[67] At first glance it seems absolutely right – what world would not benefit from turning 'Orwell's satiric lens on it'? Unfortunately, in real life, turning Orwell's satiric lens on different worlds inevitably meant turning it *away* from the one he tried to attract attention to.

Robert Conquest warned that an excessively broad understanding of *Nineteen Eighty-Four* can lead to losing Orwell's aim and diluting his ideas.

> In spite of its clearly established Stalinist background, it is sometimes said that *Nineteen Eighty-Four* is intended to satirise not this Stalinist possibility in particular, but 'tendencies to totalitarianism' in all societies. In the sense that its intention is to satirise tendencies to Stalinism, or to the excusing of Stalinism, in all societies, this is true. But . . . it is not true in the sense that Orwell was writing about some supposed tendency for all societies to become totalitarian or was making some general attack on Stalinist and non-Stalinist attitudes alike.[68]

[64]  Borkenau to Orwell, 14 September 1949, The OA, UCL, ORWELL/H/1/20/3.
[65]  George Woodcock, *Orwell's Message. 1984 and the Present* (Pender Harbour, British Columbia: Harbour Publishing, 1984), 34.
[66]  Ibid.
[67]  Ibid., 39.
[68]  Conquest, 'Totaliterror', 185.

Conquest stressed that 'the West needs to defend itself against a fearful political threat, but in particular against its own misrepresentations and misunderstanding of this threat'.[69] He was happy that 'after a generation of hard work by those who have sought out and presented the real facts of the USSR in Stalin's time, delusions about it have at last almost wholly dissipated'.[70] 'But', he predicted,

> human nature, the will to be deceived, does not change, and it will be surprising if there are not many Western intellectuals who in 20 or 30 years will in turn – one trusts not too late – have to abandon delusions about similar regimes, whose legitimisation is, as ever, merely the similar hostility to the West, and their ability to project similar misapprehension about their real acts and aspirations. If the meaning of the book is distorted to deal with other targets, however deserving, Orwell's intent is lost.[71]

This was written nearly forty years ago. After the collapse of the Soviet Union, the West joyously celebrated the disappearance of 'a fearful political threat'. It celebrated its victory, marking, in particular, Orwell's victory too: the former totalitarian Russia, it was announced, had become a democracy; the crimes of communism would be explored and exposed; falsification of history, torture and lies in its domestic policy and imperial expansion in its foreign policy would never return.

They did. And as predicted by Conquest, 'many Western intellectuals' and Western governments reluctantly – and obviously 'too late' – felt they had to 'abandon delusions' about a regime that was uncannily similar to the one that had only recently – within the living memory! – existed in its place.

This, tragically, meant that 'Orwell's intent' had indeed been 'lost'. It seems now that it was lost not so much because of the number and diversity of other targets in other countries – they obviously were closer to home and easier to understand, but because of the stubborn refusal of the West to believe in the strength and tenacity of the totalitarian regime, so powerfully depicted by Orwell. 'The will to be deceived' had made Western politicians and businessmen for over thirty years happily support the slogan promoted by Russian propaganda: 'there is no longer any ideological divide between Russia and the West', especially because it was pleasantly substantiated by the lucrative prospect of making quick money in the previously closed

---

[69]  Ibid., 187.
[70]  Ibid.
[71]  Ibid.

region. Their attitude fluctuated between indifference, born out of a cynical conviction that 'Russia is a nuisance, but not a danger', and appeasement based on the naïve belief that whatever happens it would still be possible to do business. In February 2022 both these approaches crashed.

In Russia, on the other hand, Orwell's popularity went sky-high – unfortunately, for the wrong reasons: those who read him and even those who have only heard of him found themselves in the world he described all over again.

# 10

# 'To arrest the course of history . . . '[1]

*We do not plan to attack other countries, we did not attack Ukraine either.*
Sergey Lavrov, Russian foreign minister,[2] 10 March 2022

*Totalitarianism demands . . . a disbelief in the very existence*
*of objective truth.*[3]
Orwell, 1946

24 February 2022, the day Russia invaded Ukraine, shook the foundations of the world order that had existed since 1945, and finally convinced those previously unwilling to believe it that under the guise of 'post-Soviet Russia' there had emerged an aggressive totalitarian state – similar but not identical to the Soviet Union – which had now fully matured. Putin's Russia had been moving towards totalitarianism for years, but the invasion triggered the endgame, and within days the country displayed an even stronger resemblance to the absurd totalitarian monster described by Orwell.

The word 'war' was instantly banned and ordered to be replaced, on pain of prosecution, by the phrase 'a special military operation'. Those who came out into the streets with placards bearing the Oceania slogans 'War is Peace', 'Freedom is Slavery', 'Ignorance is Strength' or their variations were detained and a man who handed out free copies of Orwell's novel was charged with the administrative offence of 'discrediting Russia's armed forces'.[4] Protesters soon found that they could be arrested for holding a copy of Tolstoy's novel *War and Peace* or singing the Soviet children's anti-war song 'May There Always Be Sunshine', while the most vigilant officials even started dismantling old Soviet slogans: 'Peace to the World!', as happened in the town of Vytegra in the northwest of Russia, where huge letters still

---

[1]  Orwell, *Nineteen Eighty-Four*, 169.
[2]  'Ukraine War: Russia "Did Not Attack Ukraine" Says Lavrov After Meeting Kuleba'. Euronews with AP, AFP, 10 March 2022. https://www.euronews.com/2022/03/10/ukraine-war-russia-did-not-attack-ukraine-says-lavrov-after-meeting-kuleba.
[3]  Orwell, 'The Prevention of Literature', CW, XVII, 374.
[4]  'In Russia they opened a case against a man who gave away Orwell's novel "1984" for free', News Read online, 14 April 2022. https://newsreadonline.com/in-russia-they-opened-a-case-against-a-man-who-gave-away-orwells-novel-1984-for-free/.

adorned the roof of a residential building.[5] The brutal war, unthinkable in the twenty-first century, which killed and maimed Ukrainians, ruined their cities and brought profound grief to every Ukrainian family, to say nothing of the Russian 'cannon fodder' ruthlessly sacrificed to the ambitions of the state's rulers, was not even allowed to be called by its proper name – a metaphor for the huge delusion under which the country was living.

It became obvious that Russia had created its own closed world hostile to the rest of mankind, where citizens absorbed the state propaganda and were sure that what they were told was the only truth, while anything else was 'fake news'; where family ties were often broken as those living outside Russia tried to persuade their loved ones across the border that the reality was different, but were met with incredulity and resentment; where the majority believed that the 'preventive strike' had been necessary, otherwise 'they would have attacked us'; and where the contemporary 'special operation'[6] was deliberately linked to the war in the past, as if Putin's regime, like the regimes in Oceania, Eurasia and Eastasia, was really trying 'to arrest progress and freeze history at a chosen moment'.[7]

\* \* \*

The role of the Great Patriotic War (22 June 1941–9 May 1945) in Russia's official propaganda had been growing with each passing year. Contemporary scholars spoke about Putin's 'foundation myth' and essentially paraphrased Orwell's 'who controls the past, controls the future'[8] when they said that 'Russia exemplifies how "the politics of memory"[9] can be utilized as a political tool'.[10] This myth already existed in the Soviet time, but then it was one of many others supported by Soviet ideology. Having dismissed Marxism-Leninism and glorification of the 1917 revolution (its centenary was played down in Russia), Putin brought the war against the Nazis to the fore, as a sacred image dear to every Russian's heart.

5   Leonid Ragozin on Twitter, 8 March 2022. https://twitter.com/leonidragozin/status /1501107181990694912?lang=en-GB.
6   Even 'a partial mobilization', announced on 21 September 2022, did not make the authorities use the word 'war'.
7   Orwell, *Nineteen Eighty-Four*, 162.
8   Ibid., 31.
9   Vera Tolz, 'Modern Russian Memory of the Great War 1914–1920', quoted in Joseph Barker, 'Putin's Foundation Myth: Russian Memory and the Second World War', *New Critique*. https://newcritique.co.uk/2016/11/22/essay-putins-foundation-myth-russian -memory-and-the-second-world-war-joseph-barker/
10  Barker, 'Putin's Foundation Myth'.

The main function of this myth was to unite the country. The very idea of 'unity' is vital for Putin's regime, and it is not accidental that his party is called 'United Russia'. In democratic societies, people can agree to disagree, but minority rights will still be respected; if an undemocratic country is 'united' behind its leader, then any disagreement with the official line becomes a subversion.

The unity is at its strongest when victory is invoked – the state's triumph over its enemies. Orwell was uniquely sensitive to the role this collective triumph plays in a totalitarian country: in *Nineteen Eighty-Four*, victory is everywhere. Winston Smith lives in Victory Mansions; drinks Victory gin and Victory coffee; smokes Victory cigarettes; Trafalgar Square is renamed Victory Square and even the notion of *facecrime* is explained thus: 'In any case, to wear an improper expression on your face (to look incredulous when a victory was announced, for example) was itself a punishable offence.'[11] Moreover, Winston's final transformation – his discovery of his love for Big Brother – happens against the background of 'victory – greatest victory in human history – victory, victory, victory!'[12]

In Putin's Russia, this gushing, spluttering excitement over victory was contemptuously described by the opponents of the regime in a newly coined derogatory term *'pobedobesie'*, usually translated as 'victory frenzy'. The term first appeared in 2005 to reflect the atmosphere that surrounded the sixtieth anniversary celebrations of the victory over Nazism.[13] Since then, the obsession with the 'Great Victory' had only been growing – the feeling of superiority instilled and encouraged by the authorities grew to be nearly all-pervading.

The 'victory frenzy' acquired its own popular symbol: black and orange ribbons once attached to St George's order of the Russian Empire and in the twenty-first century, fastened to prams, ladies' bags and the antennas of foreign-made cars as a sign of patriotism and the continuity of Russian military glory. It also introduced a number of easy-to-remember slogans like 'Thanks for the Victory, Grandad!' and a rather menacing one: 'We can do it again!' With the start of the war in Ukraine, Latin letters 'Z' and 'V', either on their own or sticking out from the Cyrillic of Russian words, assumed the same aggressively triumphalist role. In February 2022, Putin was preparing to celebrate the victory over Ukraine in a matter of days.

In a chapter from Goldstein's book read by Winston Smith, Orwell stresses the 'emotional' side of war, its 'special mental atmosphere',[14] which demands and creates a certain kind of response:

---

[11]  Orwell, *Nineteen Eighty-Four*, 52.
[12]  Ibid., 235.
[13]  See *Pobedobesie*, Special Project of the website Grani.ru and Free Russia Foundation. https://pobedobesie.info/.
[14]  Orwell, *Nineteen Eighty-Four*, 159.

Even the humblest Party member is expected to be competent, industrious, and even intelligent within narrow limits, but it is also necessary that he should be a credulous and ignorant fanatic whose prevailing moods are fear, hatred, adulation and orgiastic triumph. In other words it is necessary that he should have the mentality appropriate to a state of war.[15]

In Russia, this mentality spread like wildfire eight years before the full-scale invasion of 2022: then state-sponsored television administered daily doses of fear and hysteria by telling viewers of the 'fascist junta' that had grabbed power in Ukraine after ousting the legitimate president, Victor Yanukovych. This was how the 2013 Revolution of Dignity was interpreted. Ukrainian 'fascists', the propaganda insisted, habitually committed acts of unspeakable cruelty targeting those who spoke Russian. As the very word 'fascists' conjured up for viewers images of brutal, sadistic Germans in Nazi uniforms seen in numerous Soviet films about the war, people were genuinely frightened. And then, overnight, this depressing picture transformed into the 'orgiastic triumph' of the slogan 'Crimea is Ours!'. It did not matter that the Crimean peninsula belonged to another country, that its real natives were not Russians, but Crimean Tatars, that nobody had prevented Russians from going to the Crimean Black Sea and spending their holidays there – it felt like a victory and filled hearts with a pride rarely experienced since Soviet days. The official count of those supporting the annexation was 86 per cent. In reality it must have been lower, but still covered the larger part of the population.

In 2022, when feelings of pride and triumph were on the wane – as was the Russian economy – it was deemed necessary to revive the sense of righteous indignation: 'we' were – again! – threatened by Nazis. This time the word 'Nazi' was used more often than 'fascists', and the 'denazification' of Ukraine was announced as one of the two most important aims of the war, the other being 'demilitarization'. 'Denazification', as it was soon made clear,[16] implied 'deukrainization', that is, depriving Ukraine of its sovereignty, its language and its culture. All because the country had made its choice: to be with Europe rather than with the backward-looking, isolationist Russia. This insistence of the forty-million-strong nation on its sovereignty was reframed as Nazism. But even this was not all: the concept of 'Nazis' had shifted and broadened – the word now covered not just the Ukrainians, but the Americans, NATO

---

[15] Ibid., 154.
[16] Timofey Sergeytsev, 'What Should Russia Do with Ukraine', 4 April 2022. https:// medium.com/@kravchenko_mm/what-should-russia-do-with-ukraine-translation-of -a-propaganda-article-by-a-russian-journalist-a3e92e3cb64.

and the West as a whole. This naturally required the re-writing of history, including the most sacred history of all – that of the Great Patriotic War.

In 1942 Orwell was worried: 'How will the history of the Spanish war be written?' And he predicted: '*some* kind of history will be written, and after those who actually remember the war are dead, it will be universally accepted. So for all practical purposes the lie will have become truth'.[17] People who 'actually remember' the siege of Leningrad during the Second World War are still among us; others remember what they had been taught even in Soviet schools, but on 28 April 2022, the governor of St Petersburg (formerly Leningrad), Alexander Beglov, proclaimed the following:

> We remember well who organized the siege. Leningrad was surrounded by the troops of 13 European states, exactly the same which, today, together with the USA, are trying to besiege our entire country. They arm the Nazis, supplying them with weapons in exactly the same way as their fathers and grandfathers supplied Hitler's troops. Today these weapons are directed against our soldiers, against the grandchildren of those who liberated Europe from Nazism.[18]

Thus, according to governor Beglov, it was not just Nazi Germany that had tried to starve Leningrad into submission but it was assisted by thirteen (?) European states. The Europeans did not fight Hitler, but 'together with the USA' supplied the Nazis with arms – this is how the governor of the second largest city in Russia, its cultural capital, sees history. It transpired that Beglov had expressed similar views earlier, but then there had been no war waged by Russia and no comparisons with the present day followed. 'This kind of thing is frightening to me, because it often gives me the feeling that the very concept of objective truth is fading out of the world',[19] deplored Orwell six years before he wrote a novel where 'the mutability of the past and the denial of objective reality'[20] are the main tools for manipulating human minds.

[17]  Orwell, 'Looking Back on the Spanish War', CW, XIII, 504.
[18]  Sergey Yeremeyev, *Vo vremya vystuplenia v ZakSe Beglov rasskazal o natsistah na Ukraine* (Beglov Speaks in Legislative Assembly about Nazis in Ukraine), ZAKS.RU, Politics in St Petersburg, 28 April 2022. https://www.zaks.ru/new/archive/view/225636 ?fbclid=IwAR0ZmBw6YBN9q8F-LSAr9MczYgp-JSqPTrxBMKM6mKOMMBC3LhE gwAkBzLQ.
[19]  Orwell, 'Looking Back on the Spanish War', 504.
[20]  Orwell, *Nineteen Eighty-Four*, 127.

\* \* \*

Minds were deliberately, if inconspicuously, manipulated in Russia from the very start of Putin's rule. Orwell's 1946 formula proved right: 'The organised lying practised by totalitarian states is not, as is sometimes claimed, a temporary expedient of the same nature as military deception. It is something integral to totalitarianism, something that would still continue even if concentration camps and secret police forces had ceased to be necessary.'[21]

'Concentration camps' may not have fully 'ceased to be necessary', but one of the reasons why Putin's regime was not immediately recognized as totalitarian was its different type of political terror and the comparatively limited scale of repressions, especially compared to Stalin's times. The terror was selective and sometimes seemed random in character. The number of political prisoners approached the number in the late Soviet Union, not under Stalin, but if one added political assassinations of the harshest critics of Putin; the use of criminals to beat up and maim activists; unlawful imprisonment allegedly for economic crimes; persecution of certain religious movements, like Jehovah's Witnesses[22] and Hizb ut-Tahrir,[23] whose members received eighteen- to twenty-year-long sentences; exorbitant fines for social media posts and the spread of torture in prisons and pre-trial detention centres (which was not all that common in the late Soviet period and took the country back to Stalin's practices), it became obvious that repressions were ongoing but, as Orwell predicted, less noticeable than before.

'Secret police forces', on the other hand, had only increased their influence in Russia since Soviet times, because in the past it was the Communist Party that controlled the secret services, while under Putin they started running the country, and their proficiency in organized lying was felt immediately.

The original denial of the Russian troops' presence in Crimea during the 2014 referendum, when the media spoke of 'little green men' and Putin claimed that a military uniform resembling a Russian military uniform could be easily bought in a shop,[24] was replaced a *month* later with the assertion that the Russian army *had been* in Crimea to ensure the smooth running of the

---

[21] Orwell, 'The Prevention of Literature', CW: XVII, 373.

[22] See 'More Jehovah's Witnesses Handed Lengthy Prison Terms in Russia', RFE/RL, 26 October 2021. https://www.rferl.org/a/jehovah-witnesses-russia-prison/31529981.html.

[23] Halya Coynash, 'Crimean Tatar Prisoner of Conscience Sentenced to 19 Years for Religious "Dissidence" Faces New Torment in Russian Prison', 10 November 2021. https://khpg.org/en/1608809714 The Hizb ut-Tahrir movement, illegal in Russia, is not illegal in Ukraine, so after Russia's annexation of Crimea many Crimean Tatars automatically became criminals.

[24] Steven Pifer, 'Putin, Lies and "His Little Green Men"' (*CNN*, 20 March 2015). https://edition.cnn.com/2015/03/20/opinions/pifer-putin-misleads/index.html.

referendum[25] and a *year* later with the full admission that in 2014 Russia had decided to incorporate Crimea into the Russian Federation and had sent its army there for this very purpose.[26]

Orwell describes a similar kind of lying, also within a very short period of time, but on a much smaller, domestic issue: when Winston Smith hears about the 'demonstrations to thank Big Brother for raising the chocolate ration to twenty grammes a week' he is amazed, as it was only yesterday that 'it had been announced that the ration was to be *reduced* to twenty grammes a week. Was it possible that they could swallow that, after only twenty-four hours? Yes, they swallowed it. . . . Was he, then, alone in the possession of a memory?'[27]

With Putin's propaganda it was not even so much about memory, but about a new kind of cynical impudence, which seemed to mock the very notion of truth and celebrate its own impunity. A deliberate campaign of disinformation about the Malaysian Airline Flight MH17, which was shot down by the Russians over Eastern Ukraine on 17 July 2014, killing all 298 people on board, proffered, among others, the following improbable versions:

- 'MH17 was shot down by a Ukrainian jet.'
- 'It was blown up by a missile intended for the Russian President's plane.'
- 'It was already full of dead bodies (sic!) and crashed deliberately.'
- 'It was shot down by a BUK missile but not one of Russia's.'[28]

Ben Emmerson QC, the distinguished lawyer, who represented Marina Litvinenko at the public hearing on her husband's assassination in London and is, therefore, well versed in the deceptions of official Russia, once suggested replacing the usual legal term 'plausible deniability' with the one coined specially for Putin's regime: 'implausible deniability', which would mean that the regime simply 'can't be bothered to make up believable lies.'[29] In this way the Russian leadership expressed its contempt for the West and

[25] 'Putin Admits Russian Forces Were Deployed to Crimea' (*Reuters*, 17 April 2014). https://www.reuters.com/article/russia-putin-crimea-idUKL6N0N921H20140417.

[26] 'Putin Reveals Secrets of Russia's Crimea Takeover Plot' (*BBC*, 9 March 2015). https://www.bbc.co.uk/news/world-europe-31796226.

[27] Orwell, *Nineteen Eighty-Four*, 50.

[28] Fatima Tlis, 'The Kremlin's Many Versions of the MH17 Story' (*Polygraph. Info*, 25 May 2018). https://www.polygraph.info/a/kremlins-debunked-mh17-theories/29251216.html.

[29] Jeffrey Kahn, 'Oral Argument in Georgia vs Russia (II): The Fake News Era Reaches Strasbourg'. https://www.lawfareblog.com/oral-argument-georgia-v-russia-ii-fake-news-era-reaches-strasbourg.

its institutions and hinted – to its supporters – that it was indeed behind the acts of which it was accused but could easily fool its accusers. This approach somehow gave Putin's admirers at home a peculiar sense of superiority over the West. One could hear this new cynicism during the interview with the Russian military intelligence agents, Petrov and Bashirov, suspected by Britain of carrying out an assassination attempt against Sergei Skripal and his daughter in 2018, when they talked about coming to Salisbury as tourists to see the spire of its cathedral. The Russian flag that subsequently appeared on the scaffolding near Salisbury Cathedral was a similar type of joke, cynically mocking any concern about the possible – and actual, as in the case of Dawn Sturges – loss of human life.

But there is also another, more sinister reason for producing these lies and especially for giving several alternative explanations of any one incident. The Soviet dissident Vladimir Bukovsky, who spent seventeen years in Russian prisons and psychiatric hospitals, identified it as a special feature of the KGB methods, aimed at creating in their targets a feeling of uncertainty, of the unreliability of any information.[30] It is this uncertainty that makes people exclaim helplessly: 'We will never know the truth!' And this is exactly what the totalitarian regime wants them to accept, as O'Brien tells Winston:

> You believe that reality is something objective, external, existing in its own right. You also believe that the nature of reality is self-evident. When you delude yourself into thinking that you see something, you assume that everyone else sees the same thing as you. But I tell you, Winston, that reality is not external. Reality exists in the human mind, and nowhere else. Not in the individual mind, which can make mistakes, and in any case soon perishes: only in the mind of the Party, which is collective and immortal. Whatever the Party holds to be the truth, is truth. It is impossible to see reality except by looking through the eyes of the Party.[31]

With the current war the scale of Russian organized lying has markedly increased. There is no denying that 'truth is the first casualty of any war', and yet there was something extraordinary about the Russian response to accusations of atrocities in Ukraine. About a thousand bodies of civilians – some with their hands bound behind their backs, some mutilated and burnt – discovered in the streets of the town of Bucha not far from Kyiv, after the Russian troops' withdrawal, were announced by Russian propagandists to be

[30]   Vladimir Bukovsky. Interview to the author, December 2006.
[31]   Orwell, *Nineteen Eighty-Four*, 197.

part of a 'staged provocation'[32] organized by the Ukrainians. It did not bother the propagandists that the position of the corpses in the satellite photos taken in mid-March exactly matched 'those from smartphone pictures published in early April'[33] – they simply ignored this proof obtained thanks to the revolutionary role of new technology in investigating war crimes.

What mattered was that tens of thousands of Russians readily believed the story of 'a staged provocation'. The official version protected them from the need to face the horror of what had happened. The wish to conform and to narrow personal responsibility, along with the deep-seated fear, was palpable not only in the ubiquitous clichés – 'the people in charge are no fools' and 'we can't do anything, can we?' – but also in the efforts of people to convince themselves that it is absolutely impossible to know who is right: 'I don't think that we can know the truth right now. Someday, we will find out what is really going on . . . The truth, the deep reasons, if you don't want to delve into the history, if you're not doing politics — we can't see it'.[34] But if 'the whole truth can never be known', the official account is as good as any other – at any rate you can't assert it is a lie.

\* \* \*

It is not clear how many people in Russia really support Putin's war. No polls can be conducted – or believed – if any condemnation of what the Russian army is doing in Ukraine is treated as 'discrediting the Russian armed forces' and maybe punished with ten years' imprisonment. And yet in February, when the invasion started, and in September, when mobilization was announced, thousands of people in Russian cities and towns went out to protest, knowing full well that they would be beaten, arrested and charged either with administrative or criminal offences. Unfortunately, one can't expect these courageous actions to be more numerous than they are, especially as people in Russia, with their totalitarian experience, do not particularly trust each other.[35] However, once mobilization was announced on 21 September 2022, Russian men started 'voting with their feet' and in the

[32] Alex Hern, 'Satellite Images of Corpses in Bucha Contradict Russian Claims' (*The Guardian*, 5 April 2022). https://www.theguardian.com/world/2022/apr/05/satellite-images-of-corpses-in-bucha-prove-russian-claims-wrong.

[33] Ibid.

[34] Shura Burtin, 'Feeling Around for Something Human Why Do Russians Support the War Against Ukraine?', trans. Bela Shayevich and Anne O. Fisher, *Meduza*, 3 May 2022. https://meduza.io/en/feature/2022/05/03/feeling-around-for-something-human.

[35] See Orwell, *Nineteen Eighty-Four*, 212.

first week, about 260,000 of them fled the country.[36] Again, it is impossible to know whether they had previously supported, ignored or opposed the war and whether they were simply afraid of being killed or also unwilling to kill others, but their flight was definitely an expression of disagreement with the official policy rather than compliance with it. Besides, journalists and sociologists, who have been trying to poll ordinary citizens, reported that about half of the people they approached since the start of the war, refused to reply their questions, which made some researchers suspect that these people's position was different from the official.

On the other hand, when anonymous results of the polls were obtained, they mostly revealed terribly distorted minds, more often than not displaying Orwell's *doublethink*. The ability of those polled 'to hold simultaneously two opinions which cancelled out, knowing them to be contradictory and believing in both of them'[37] struck the researchers, who desperately tried to find out what Russians were *really* thinking. People would say that they 'were against war in general and very much in favour of this particular war and didn't see any contradiction in this'.[38] Different bits of propaganda were pronounced in the same breath and the conflict between them did not bother the speakers: "'The simple folk are waiting for us to get rid of the Nazis!" – "The *khokhols*[39] have always hated us!"; "But we're one people!"– "They've never been human down there!"; "Putin did the right thing starting the war. We've needed to put things straight for a long time now!" – "America is rubbing its hands together, pitting Slavs against one another."'[40]

By September 2022, the retreat of Russian troops from the Kharkiv area made Putin urgently annex four more Ukrainian territories: Donetsk, Lugansk, Kherson[41] and Zaporizhzhia regions. This time he did not even bother to try and prove that accession to Russia was the expression of the will of the population of these regions. The occupation authorities arranged the referenda and nobody doubted that people had to vote at gunpoint. The incorporation of the Ukrainian regions into Russia, however, meant that if the Ukrainian army attacked these regions, it would be treated as an attack on Russia, which, according to Russian military doctrine, could be legitimately met with a nuclear strike. No country in the world acknowledged

---

[36] 'At Least 260,000 Russians Have Fled, Since Putin's Military Call-Up, Western Officials Believe', 28 September 2022. https://www.independent.co.uk/news/world/europe/russia-ukraine-border-exile-military-mobilisation-b2177302.html.

[37] Orwell, *Nineteen Eighty-Four*, 31.

[38] Burtin, 'Feeling Around for Something Human'.

[39] *Khokhols* is a Russian derogatory term for Ukrainians.

[40] Burtin, 'Feeling Around for Something Human'.

[41] Just over a month later, Russian troops had to withdraw from the town of Kherson.

the legitimacy of the annexation but Putin had his chance to celebrate 'the victory' with a huge concert in Moscow attended by thousands.

It was obvious that neither he, nor the people listening to his aggressive anti-Western speech in the Kremlin, nor those joining him in Red Square accepted the fact that after the collapse of the Soviet Union in 1991, Ukraine became an independent sovereign state. All of them still lived and wished to carry on living in the USSR. The attempt 'to arrest progress and freeze history at a chosen moment'[42] seemed to have succeeded.

\*   \*   \*

How did it happen? How did Russia turn into Orwell's Oceania? Why were totalitarian features not recognized when they first appeared in the country more than two decades ago? Of course, a handful of experts, journalists, human rights activists both in Russia and in the West tried to draw the attention of politicians and the public to dangerous developments in Russia, but they were not heard.

Preparation for the war, or, at least, for an even more aggressive course of the Russian government, must have started back in March 2020, when any attempts to pretend that Russia was a democracy were abandoned. All of a sudden, a constitutional amendment was proposed and promptly adopted to 'reset the counter to zero' and 'discard' all Putin's previous presidential terms so as to start afresh and enable Russia's president to retain his position till 2036. If this happens – which at the moment it still might! – Putin, who was first inaugurated in 2000, will exceed the time in power of the most long-serving Russian rulers of the last two centuries – tsar Nicholas I and Stalin. This constitutional change was followed in August 2020 with the FSB squad trying to poison Alexey Navalny – Putin's bravest critic and then, when he survived, by his arrest and long-term imprisonment. The year 2021 saw the worst clampdown against the remaining opposition since Soviet times. Navalny's nation-wide Anti-Corruption Foundation was destroyed; its leaders were either arrested or forced to leave the country. Under pressure and the toughening of anti-oppositional laws, two more well-known 'undesirable' organizations 'For Human Rights' and 'Open Russia' had to stop their activities. Numerous, mostly young, protesters against Navalny's imprisonment were detained and prosecuted all over the country.

And yet the greatest shock for those who dreamt of a better Russia – and, in retrospect, the most significant sign that something appalling was imminent – came at the very end of 2021, when the Supreme Court ordered

---

[42]   Orwell, *Nineteen Eighty-Four*, 162.

the closure of Memorial, the oldest Russian historical society and human rights centre. This marked the full circle that the country had gone through since the late 1980s when Mikhail Gorbachev's announcement of *perestroika* (restructuring) raised hopes that Russia would break with its totalitarian past and move towards becoming 'normal', that is, democratic, open, law-based and not dangerous either to its neighbours or to its own citizens.

In 1987, when the first non-governmental Memorial groups appeared, it was widely believed that only a full awareness of the enormous tragedy experienced by the Soviet Union could prevent the country from falling into the same trap again. The main aim of Memorial – as is clear from its name – was to keep the memory of the victims of Soviet political repression alive. But apart from promoting the truth about the past, the NGO was also fighting the abuse of human rights in the present. Getting ready for the invasion of Ukraine, Russia's rulers must have realized that it would be difficult to do it with the honourable NGO still around – it had to be dissolved. In court, the prosecutor denounced Memorial for projecting a false image of the USSR 'as a terrorist state' and for urging Russia's citizens to 'repent of the Soviet past, instead of remembering its glorious history'.[43]

This is not the place to discuss all the complex reasons for *perestroika's* failure – to a certain degree this has been done and hopefully will be done even more thoroughly in the future. Apart from all the errors and blunders of the reformers, who tried to implement the changes urged by Gorbachev and supported by a small section of the ruling elite, there obviously was, from the very start, a strong opposition to the transformation of the country of the other part of the rulers, unwilling to lose its power and privileges. The KGB and the Communist Party *nomenclature* must have been equally hostile to *perestroika*, but the KGB proved stronger, more active and for some time it had had a cleverer leader. Its chief, Yuri Andropov, who in 1982 replaced Brezhnev as the Communist Party general secretary, had even masterminded a policy which combined a long overdue and limited economic liberalization of the country with keeping strict political control over it.[44]

The leading Russian sociologist Lev Gudkov, head of a sociological research organization, the Levada Centre from 2006 to 2021, stresses that authoritarian tendencies appeared in the nominally 'democratic' Russian government long before Putin, by the middle of the 1990s – it is enough to remember the conflict between President Yeltsin and the Parliament in

[43] See Andrew Roth, 'Russian Court Orders Closure of Country's Oldest Human Rights Group' (*The Guardian*, 28 December 2021). https://www.theguardian.com/world/2021/dec/28/russian-court-memorial-human-rights-group-closure.

[44] Karen Dawisha, *Putin's Kleptocracy. Who Owns Russia?* (New York, London, Toronto, Sydney, New Delhi: Simon & Shuster, 2014), 26–35.

1993, the First Chechen War in 1994–6 and a campaign organized by the Russian media to ensure Yeltsin's victory in the presidential elections of 1996. However, when Putin, who in 1998–9 had been the director of the FSB (the KGB successor) and then, in 1999–2000, prime minister and acting president, became Russia's president on 7 May 2000, he embarked on restoring – slowly but consistently – its totalitarian regime. The misgivings many in the country felt when, in December 2000, he suggested bringing back the old Soviet anthem with slightly modified lyrics proved not unfounded. This process of restoration lasted for over twenty years and followed the pattern masterfully described in *Animal Farm*, that is, of a gradual departure from the principles proclaimed at the time of change.

*   *   *

Even before the war against Ukraine, hardly any critical comment within Russia about the country's sinister and farcical present could do without invoking Orwell's name – many of his Russian readers felt they were living in the absurd reality depicted by him. It has obviously been said many times that Orwell's satire is applicable in different circumstances and different countries, but because it was the Soviet Union that he primarily had in mind when writing about totalitarianism, it was striking to watch the totalitarian features he identified in 1930s and 1940s re-appearing in the 'new' Russia over eighty years later. Putin's attempts to turn the clock back were barely noticed in the West and yet now the belated realization that Russia is waging a twentieth-, if not nineteenth-century war, while most of the rest of the world lives in the twenty-first, made it clear that there had been a huge oversight. The 'restoration' would have never succeeded, had it not been permitted and partially assisted by the West. Not that it was done deliberately and the liberal democracies wanted to see the Soviet Union coming back, but mostly they did not care because they were no longer afraid of it. Tired of the international tension before Gorbachev and pleased by the changes he announced, many Western observers were once again deceived by words and failed to see totalitarianism growing in Russia.

In exactly the same way as the Western left were ready to justify everything that had been happening in the Soviet Union since 1929 because they were told that this was socialism, so in the 1990s and in the new century, the West preferred to believe that Russia had suddenly embraced both capitalism and democracy. But if socialists of the 1930s and 1940s could at least be excused by their lack of knowledge of the USSR (although Orwell did not accept this excuse!), Western politicians, business people and commentators, fifty years after Orwell's death, were happy to tolerate lies for the sake of their own greed: their countries receiving advantageous terms when buying Russian oil and gas or they personally getting some private benefits, like, for instance, lucrative positions on the boards of Russian firms. Russian human rights activists and journalists – Anna Politkovskaya is just one example – gave their lives to alert the world to what was really going on in Russia, but the West started waking up to the new reality only in 2014, when Russia blatantly breached international law with the annexation of Crimea. It is obvious today how slow and insufficient the world's reaction was. And it is difficult to dismiss the conviction that Orwell would not have missed the signals, which had been appearing for many years before that.

\*   \*   \*

The first thing that Gorbachev brought to the country was *glasnost* (openness) and this was the first thing Putin withdrew. It took some time before Orwell's definition: 'the country is considered to be totalitarian when it is governed by a one-party dictatorship which does not permit legal opposition and crushes freedom of speech and the press'[45] became fully applicable to Russia, but the attack on freedom of speech started in 2000–2001, fairly soon after Putin's coming to power and fifteen years after *glasnost* was announced. One of the first major actions of the new president was a campaign against NTV – *Nezavisimoe* (Independent) Television. A representative of the president's administration who spoke with NTV journalists demanded that from now on they should cover the Second Chechen war differently, cease investigating corruption within the Kremlin and withdraw the puppet of Putin from the programme called *Puppets* – the Russian equivalent of the *Spitting Image*. The nascent Russian civil society was shocked. Famous writers, scholars, journalists, actors, politicians (including Gorbachev), dissidents from Soviet times and others published an open letter appropriately titled: 'High Time We Started Being Concerned'.[46] This was in March 2001. And in April 2001 the channel was taken over by force. This was followed by change of management and consequently a change in programming. It did not take very long before practically all television in Russia became state-controlled.

---

[45]  Orwell, 'Notes to Swingler's article, CW, XVIII, 442. The term 'totalitarianism' had been applied to contemporary Russia even before the war, for example by Lev Gudkov, *Vozvratny totalitarizm* (Reverse Totalitarianism), Moscow: NLO, 2022 and by journalist and former dissident Alexander Podrabinek (*Rights in Russia*, 24 September 2021). https://www.rightsinrussia.org/podrabinek-2/

[46]  '*Samoe vremya nachat bespokoitsa*' ('High Time We Started Being Concerned'), a letter published on 27 March 2001. https://classic.newsru.com/ardocs/28Mar2001/pismo5 .html .

The consequences of the NTV-closure were far-reaching, as this was the station that had truly independent coverage of the First Chechen War started by Yeltsin in 1994. Trying to stop Chechnya from seceding, the Russian army acted with boundless brutality. The massacre of the village of Samashki shocked human rights activists, who tried in vain to attract international attention to it, while seeing on TV screens inhabitants of the Chechen capital Grozny – many of them Russian – left without a roof over their heads after the indiscriminate bombing did not make the war popular with ordinary viewers either. By August 1996, with the Chechens defeating federal troops, Russia had to sign a Peace Treaty (the Khasavyurt Accord), thus formally ending the conflict. The unpopularity of Yeltsin; a certain fear in the ruling elite that Yeltsin could lose his position, but, primarily, the existence of truthful media, which influenced public opinion – all worked against the war and its destructive impact.

Putin learnt this lesson and from the very start of the Second Chechen War resolved to control the work of journalists. He appointed his own spokesman to provide official information on the war to the press and TV and allowed access only to accredited journalists who were constantly supervised and saw only what they were allowed to see. The one exception to the rule was Anna Politkovskaya, who regularly travelled to Chechnya on her own. After her assassination in 2006, her friend Natalia Estemirova, a human rights activist and journalist who lived in Grozny, remained practically the only source of independent reports from Chechnya, until she was assassinated in 2009. This was how Putin won this part of the information war. The other part was presenting the war to the West – and he won that too.

Losing any interest in Russia after *perestroika* was announced, Western leaders tried to look the other way when Yeltsin unleashed the First Chechen War. Moreover, President Clinton, who came to Moscow at the height of the war in May 1995, even chose to support the Russian president and endorse the country's 'official position, that the Chechen movement for autonomy threatened the territorial integrity of Russia, and that the effort to suppress it with violence was an internal matter'.[47]

After 9/11 things got even easier for Russia's – now Putin's – propagandists. There was no problem at all to convince the West that Russia was fighting its own war on terror, and Chechens were in the forefront of international terrorism. Only a few individuals, like the French philosopher André Glucksmann, who visited Chechnya in 2000, understood the difference

---

[47]  Svetlana Savranskaya and Matthew Evangelista, 'The Massacre at Samashki and the US Response to Russia's War in Chechnya'. https://nsarchive.gwu.edu/briefing-book/russia-programs/2020-04-15/massacre-at-samashki-and-us-response-to-russias-war-in-chechnya.

between the Chechen fight for independence and international terrorism[48];
the rest, including the world leaders, accepted the situation as it was presented
to them. It was their position that enabled Putin then to continue the war and
become more and more confident of his own impunity.

*     *     *

Another important aspect of the NTV destruction was that, fully in keeping
with Orwell's assessment in 'Politics and the English Language', it was
called something else: the whole operation was described euphemistically,
in purely economic terms, as 'a conflict of business entities', and Putin,
when approached, stated that it was a legal matter and that he could not
interfere with the work of the courts. Using exactly the same method as their
Soviet predecessors, who summoned Marxist–Leninist ideology whenever
they needed to explain something the Soviet Union was doing,[49] the new
propagandists simply used the terms necessary to convince both domestic
and foreign observers that Russia was a capitalist country like any other and
Putin, a liberal and a democrat, held the rule of law in great respect. Not
everybody was deceived, but certainly only very few people in the West at
that time felt that it was high time *they* started being concerned. Some were
happy that Russia turned to capitalism, others experienced something like a
*Schadenfreude*, thinking: you should have been careful what you wished for,
but quite a few trusted the legend that it was capitalism, moreover, a rampant
capitalism typical of the 'Wild West',[50] and the NTV 'hostile takeover' was yet
another proof of that.

In real life, Russia's capitalism was rather dubious – in July 2000 the Kremlin
issued a statement promising that the president would guarantee 'his support
and comprehensive assistance to companies and banks proceeding in their
activity *guided by the government's interests*'[51] [emphasis added]. And Oleg
Deripaska, the owner of the Rusal aluminium company, surely expressed
the view of many other 'capitalists' when, in 2007, he publicly admitted his
readiness to part with his property as soon he received an instruction to do

---

48  See André Glucksmann, 'Western Leaders Betray Aslan Maskhadov' (*Prima-News*, 11
    March 2005). https://web.archive.org/web/20070927002946/http://prima-news.ru/eng/
    news/articles/2005/3/11/31434.html; Glucksmann's interview to the author, June 2000.
49  Cf 'Alliances, changes of front etc., which only make sense as part of the game of power
    politics have to be explained and justified in terms of international socialism'. Orwell,
    'Inside the Whale', CW, XII, 101.
50  On the belief that Russia went through a 'Wild West' period, see Dawisha, *Putin's
    Kleptocracy*, 17.
51  'Putin: Businesses Can Play Positive Role in Strengthening Russia' (*Interfax*, July 28,
    2000), quoted in ibid., 278.

so: 'If the state says we need to give it up, we'll give it up. I don't separate myself from the state. I have no other interests'.[52]

Toeing the line became the only acceptable way of behaviour for him and others after the start of Putin's widely publicized fight with 'oligarchs',[53] that is, businessmen who had made quick money in the late 1980s to early 1990s. Vladimir Gusinsky, the previous NTV owner, Boris Berezovsky, Putin's former supporter, and Mikhail Khodorkovsky all had to flee abroad, the latter, sadly, after serving ten years in prison. The downfall of the richest and most high-profile oligarchs was a stern warning for others that they should stay 'out of opposition politics'.[54] The other aim of this attack was to serve as a cover for the arrival of another and even more powerful group of oligarchs – the core of Putin's system, his KGB friends, who in 1996 joined him as co-founders of the *Ozero* (Lake) dacha cooperative[55] and in 2000 came with him to Moscow to rule Russia. By the end of Putin's first term and the beginning of the second, Russian Railways, Russian state-controlled energy companies Gazprom and Rosneft, the air company Aeroflot, the state arms export agency Rosoboronexport and many other major firms and banks were in the hands of Putin's friends. Boris Nemtsov, a leading opposition politician assassinated in 2015, aptly described it as 'a Chekist oligarchy'.[56]

As the years went by, the system created by Putin received different names: 'a "corporation", "Kremlin Inc", a "*systema*" or a "corporatist-kleptocratic regime"',[57] but it is worth remembering that in 1939 Orwell, in his review of Borkenau's book *The Totalitarian Enemy*, coined the term 'oligarchical collectivism' to describe the system typical of both Germany and the USSR, where a small and close-knit cabal controlled the economy.

In a way, the term 'oligarchical collectivism' is even more appropriate for Putin's cronies than for the oligarchs of the 1940s. As Orwell had in mind the leaders of the socialist and national–socialist states – oligarchs in the traditional sense of the word – he described them as 'less avaricious, less tempted by luxury, hungrier for pure power',[58] whereas the contemporary

---

[52] Catherine Belton, *Putin's People. How the KGB Took Back Russia and Then Took on the West* (London: William Collins, 2020), 362. In November 2022 the United States finally revoked Russia's market economy status granted to it in 2002.

[53] The word 'oligarch' – traditionally, a member of a small group of rulers, received a new meaning in Russia to denote people who rapidly acquired wealth during privatization. Wikipedia provides a special entry for 'Russian oligarch'.

[54] Dawisha, *Putin's Kleptocracy*, 278.

[55] A group of *dachas* (country-houses) built on a lakeshore near the border with Finland by Putin and his old KGB friends, who were also shareholders of Bank Rossiya.

[56] Neil Buckley and Arkady Ostrovsky, 'Putin's Allies are Turning Russia into a Corporate State', quoted in Belton, *Putin's People*, 311.

[57] Dawisha, *Putin's Kleptocracy*, 36.

[58] Orwell, *Nineteen Eighty-Four*, 163.

Russian rulers, in accordance with the word's new meaning, are unbelievably avaricious and mind-blowingly tempted by luxury. There is, however, one aspect common to both groups: collectivism. Basing this part of Goldstein's book on James Burnham's *Managerial Revolution*, Orwell wrote: 'It had long been realised that the only secure basis for oligarchy is collectivism. Wealth and privilege are most easily defended when they are possessed jointly'.[59]

But it was not just wealth and privilege that united Putin's oligarchs – they also shared the values and methods that the KGB taught them. Moreover, already by 2003, the Russian elites were predominantly made up of the military and the FSB – their representation in the government and Security Council was 25 per cent higher under Putin than in 1993 under Yeltsin.[60] They received even more power later. But from the very beginning, a KGB mindset manifested itself in numerous political assassinations and in the so-called 'special operations'.

Yeltsin appointed Putin as his prime minister and named him as his successor on 9 August 1999, just two days after the incursion of Chechen militants in the Southern Russian republic of Dagestan. By 14 September, Russian Federal Forces had conducted an 'anti-terrorist operation' and pushed them out of the republic. Hundreds of people were killed on both sides and 32,000 Dagestani civilians displaced. Almost simultaneously – between 4 and 16 September – a series of explosions hit four apartment blocks in Buynaksk (Dagestan), Moscow and Volgodonsk (Rostov oblast), killing 300 people and injuring more than a thousand. The explosions were blamed on the Chechens and on 23 September 1999, Putin announced the aerial bombing of the capital, Grozny, marking the start of the Second Chechen war.

Both the incursion and the apartment bombings, even at the time, were treated by many analysts with great suspicion: there were reasons to believe that they had been organized by the FSB in order to have a pretext to resume the war against Chechnya.[61]

Incredibly, the possibility of such cynical operations had also been foreseen by Orwell in his novel:

[59] Ibid., 164.
[60] Olga Kryshtanovskaya and Stephen White, 'Putin's Militocracy', quoted in Dawisha, 312.
[61] Patrick Cockburn, 'Russia "Planned Chechen War Before Bombings"', 29 January 2000, *The Independent*. http://www.independent.co.uk/news/world/europe/russia -planned-chechen-war-before-bombings-727324.html; Mike Eckel, 'Two Decades on, Smoldering Questions About the Russian President's Vault to Power', (*RFE/RL*, 7 August 2019). https://www.rferl.org/a/putin-russia-president-1999-chechnya-apartment-bombings /30097551.html; Thomas de Waal. Introduction to Anna Politkovskaya. *A Dirty War. Russian Reporter in Chechnya*, trans. and ed. John Crowfoot (London: The Harvill Press, 2001), xix–xx; David Satter, *The Less You Know, the Better You Sleep* (New Haven and London: Yale University Press, 2016).

Once when he [Winston] happened in some connexion to mention the war against Eurasia, she [Julia] startled him by saying casually that in her opinion the war was not happening. The rocket bombs which fell daily on London were probably fired by the Government of Oceania itself, 'just to keep people frightened'. This was an idea that had literally never occurred to him.[62]

Hard as it was for Winston – or for Orwell, or for anybody of a sound mind – to imagine this outrage, more and more evidence that makes a similar kind of operation plausible has been coming to the surface since 1999. Here was the government casually killing its own innocent people for the sake of frightening the rest. Of course, the Russian people *were* duly frightened. They were also grateful to the brave and business-like new prime minister who promised to kill terrorists anywhere, wherever they were discovered. His ratings went up, and six months later he was elected the president of Russia.

In the following years, at least two more horrific episodes, both involving hostage-taking, were, in all probability, 'special operations' carried out by the FSB. One of them took place in the Dubrovka theatre in Moscow in October 2002, where, apart from several hostages killed by terrorists, FSB operatives gassed 174 people who came to watch a musical, allegedly in an attempt to save them.[63] The name of the gas they used was never disclosed to the doctors, who could have found an antidote. The second happened in Beslan (North Ossetia) in September 2004, where children, parents and teachers were taken hostage in a school building on the first day of the school year, and as a result of the explosions and shooting between the terrorists and the Russian Federal forces 314 hostages died, 186 of them children. Exactly as in the apartment bombings, Putin continued to sacrifice ordinary Russians for the sake of increasing fear and hatred of the Chechens and thus justifying his war.

---

[62] Orwell, *Nineteen Eighty-Four*, 125.
[63] The allegation that the FSB had at least controlled the terrorist attack, if not masterminded it from start to finish, is supported, among other things, by Politkovskaya's interview, published by *Novaya Gazeta* on 28 April 2003, with Khanpash Terkibaev, whom she believed to be an agent planted by the special services. See also Hassan Abbas, 'Mysterious Figure Implicated in Russian Theatre Tragedy' (*North Caucasus*, Vol. 4, No. 15). https://jamestown.org/program/mysterious-figure-implicated-in-russian-theater-tragedy-2/; 'Role of Chechen Hostage-Maker Remains a Mystery' (*The Jamestown Foundation*, 8 May 2003). http://www.russialist.org/archives/7175-13.php; Amy Knight, *Putin's Killers: The Kremlin and the Art of Political Assassination* (London: Biteback Publishing, 2019), 134.

In 2002, all the world leaders, including US president George Bush[64] and British prime minister Tony Blair,[65] congratulated Putin on the successful freeing of hostages in Moscow, although the number of casualties of the alleged rescue operation was well known. As far as Beslan[66] is concerned, the European Court of Human Rights, where relatives of Beslan victims submitted a complaint in 2007, found the Russian government responsible for the massacre. This decision, however, was made in 2017 – thirteen years after the tragedy.

The ECHR had been one of the few Western institutions that consistently confirmed Russia's violations of human rights: between 2001 and 2021 it ruled against the Russian state hundreds of times. Unfortunately, Russia implemented only the easiest part of the rulings – it paid out the damages, but never tried to change the system behind these violations or punished those who had committed them. And the Court's decisions never made much of an impression on Western politicians. It did not occur to them that a merciless regime armed with nuclear weapons could soon threaten the world and should be stopped as soon as possible.

*    *    *

Relations between Russia and the West throughout Putin's years were, to put it mildly, ambiguous. On the one hand, the rulers of the country and a relatively wide layer of oligarchs just below the top enjoyed all the opportunities that the West could offer: houses and villas, yachts and planes, shopping for their wives and education for their children, meanwhile spreading corruption to the West. On the other hand, ideologically, Russia grew more and more anti-Western. It had not always been like that. Incredible as it might seem today, in Gorbachev's and the early Yeltsin's years,

> the slogans of *perestroika* – 'coming back to the global trajectory of mankind', 'Europe is our common home' and others – were shared by the majority of the population. A significant number of Russian citizens hoped that Russia would become part of the European political system;

---

[64] See Steven Lee Myers, 'Hostage Drama in Moscow: Russia Responds' (*New York Times*, 29 October 2002). https://www.nytimes.com/2002/10/29/world/hostage-drama -moscow-russia-responds-putin-vows-hunt-for-terror-cells-around.html.

[65] See Nick Paton Walsh, 'Siege Rescue Carnage as Gas Kills Hostages' (*The Guardian*, 27 October 2002). https://www.theguardian.com/world/2002/oct/27/chechnya.russia3.

[66] It is important to stress that Politkovskaya, who rushed to Beslan, hoping to help solve the crisis by negotiating with the Chechens, was poisoned on the way there. See Chris Tryhorn, 'Leading Russian Journalist "Poisoned"' (*The Guardian*, 6 September 2004). https://www.theguardian.com/media/2004/sep/06/russia.chechnya.

in the first half of the 1990s, 40-45% of those polled thought the idea of Russia joining NATO absolutely feasible and even desirable.[67]

However, the failure of the reforms, severe financial difficulties, corruption, absence of any protection on the part of the state, confusion about the incomprehensible developments in the country left people feeling despondent and vulnerable – and, as a result, more susceptible to propaganda.

In 2005 Putin called the collapse of the Soviet Union 'the greatest geo-political catastrophe of the century',[68] clearly stating what his values were. He hankered both for the empire and for strong totalitarian state. The latter led to the official refusal to analyse, criticize and eventually reject the Soviet past. The traumatic, yet uninterpreted experience of totalitarianism became part of a common national legacy, which, according to propagandists, was not in any way worse – in fact, it was implied, much better! – than the legacy of other nations. The 1990s with their freedom of speech and condemnation of Soviet rule were then reframed as the years of chaos and humiliation accepted to please the West, while Putin's path was all about the 'former glory' and 'Russia rising from its knees'. The nostalgia for the Soviet Empire became particularly acute for the Russian president when some of country's former colonies revealed their firm decision of going 'the Western way'.

Nobody was surprised when Latvia, Lithuania and Estonia chose to be with the West, although Russia tried to stop them from joining NATO in 2001, but the Orange Revolution of 2004 in Ukraine came as a bitter blow for Putin – he needed a Ukrainian president who would be loyal to Russia. Instead, Ukraine dared to be independent. It was then that Putin must have felt for the first time the dual fear that stayed with him for years to come: the fear of losing Ukraine and the fear of having a 'colour revolution' in Russia.

In both scenarios, he announced, his main enemy was the West. The first outburst of official anti-Western rhetoric occurred within Russia in 2004–5,[69] while for the West the shift became fully noticeable only a couple of years later, at the 43rd Munich Conference on security policy in February 2007,[70]

[67] Gudkov, 'Ot 'utopii Zapada' k reaktsionnoy utopuu: antizapadny resentiment v Putinskoy Rossii ('From the "Utopia of the West" to Reactionary Utopia: Anti-Western Ressentiment in Putin's Russia')', in Znamya confrontatsii: Za chto i pochemu Rossia voyuet s zapadom (The Banner of Confrontation: Why and What for Russia is Fighting the West) (Moscow: Liberal Mission Foundation, 2021), 73.

[68] 'Putin: Soviet Collapse a "Genuine Tragedy"' (NBC News, 25 April 2005). https://www.nbcnews.com/id/wbna7632057.

[69] Andreas Umland, 'Introduction to Special Issue of Forum: Anti-Western Ideological Trends in Post-Soviet Russia and their Origin, N1, 2009. https://www1.ku.de/ZIMOS/forum/inhaltruss11.html.

[70] See Rob Watson, 'Putin's Speech: Back to the Cold War?' (BBC, 10 February 2007). http://news.bbc.co.uk/1/hi/world/europe/6350847.stm.

where Putin publicly claimed that 'NATO expansion . . . represents a serious provocation that reduces the level of mutual trust'.[71] In vain did the Czech president Vaclav Havel, a former dissident, try to reason, back in 2001, that 'Russia must finally realize that NATO's mission poses no threat to it and that if NATO moves closer to Russia's borders, it brings closer stability, security, democracy and an advanced political culture, which is obviously in Russia's essential interest'.[72] Putin's idea of Russia's essential interests (even if he cared about them) would be completely different from Havel's: he, after all, was not a former dissident but a former KGB officer.

Therefore, both in 2004 and in 2013–14, when Ukraine again and again confirmed that it had chosen to move away from Russia and towards the West, Russian propaganda claimed that protesting Ukrainians were nothing more than puppets of the Americans. Exactly the same accusation had been used in winter 2011–12 in Moscow to discredit protests there. In the NTV film commissioned by the authorities,[73] Americans were accused of financing the protests, coordinating them and even rewarding protesters with cookies.

Soon afterwards, in 2012, the law against 'foreign agents' was introduced in Russia. The term, actually meaning the same as 'spy', could be used nearly as conveniently as Stalin's 'enemy of the people', but had an added value of the anti-Western thrust, and the law, which in 2012 was not yet widely applied, indicated even then that Russia was on course for a collision.

\* \* \*

Russia was set against the West, but the democracies of Europe and America were still under its spell. Once Russian propaganda chose to present Ukrainian protesters in 2014 as fascists or simply far-rightists, some Westerners would repeat it without any hesitation. The tendency to accuse opponents of being fascists dates back to Orwell's time, and Orwell was shocked not just by the tendency that revealed itself in the 'man-hunts' he witnessed in Spain but by the response to it:

> In Spain as well as in Russia the nature of the accusations (namely, conspiracy with the Fascists) was the same and as far as Spain was

---

[71] Eckel, 'Did the West Promise Moscow That NATO Would not Expand? Well, It's Complicated', (*RFE/RL*, 19 May 2021). https://www.rferl.org/a/nato-expansion-russia-mislead/31263602.html.

[72] Ibid.

[73] *The Anatomy of Protest*, NTV documentary, 15 March 2012. https://www.ntv.ru/video/296996/. The NTV by that time had become not simply pro-government but aggressively anti-oppositional channel.

concerned, I had every reason to believe that the accusations were false. To experience all this was a valuable object lesson: it taught me how easily totalitarian propaganda can control the opinion of enlightened people in democratic countries.[74]

It was nearly as easy in 2014 as it was in 1937. The Western media covered the 'Ukrainian far-right' with a mixture of curiosity and horror, and it was only when Ukrainian elections showed a drop in the popularity of all the far-right parties in 2014, and then again in 2019, which proved that the far-right in Ukraine had much fewer supporters than, for example, in France, the Ukrainian 'fascist scare' in the West almost completely stopped attracting further attention,[75] while in Russia, where they don't believe in any election results anyway, it was used and reused and reached its climax with 'denazification' in 2022.

Another example of Western support for Putin's regime was a long and loud campaign of a large part of the American and European intelligentsia against 'NATO eastward expansion'. These 'enlightened people in democratic countries' invariably blamed themselves and their leaders, sighed mournfully and regretted 'humiliating' Russia. 'NATO should not have expanded', they said. 'Russia has legitimate reasons to worry.' Critical of their own governments, certain of their balanced and objective approach, they probably did not realize that they were betraying not only the East European countries, both those who benefited and those who might still benefit from joining the Alliance, but also Russia itself – a different, democratic Russia that failed to appear after all the promise of Gorbachev's changes, the Russia that would not have felt 'humiliated' by NATO expansion.

Crucially, NATO itself betrayed the hopes of new applicants, who sought protection from their aggressive neighbour. In April 2008, at the NATO summit in Bucharest, the requests of Georgia and Ukraine to be allowed to join the Membership Action Plan (MAP) with a view of becoming members of the Alliance later, were rejected. Naturally, Putin was against them joining, and although US president Bush and Polish president Lech Kaczynski supported their applications, the Europeans – Gordon Brown, Angela Merkel and Nicolas Sarkozy, particularly reluctant to annoy Russia, pressed for a compromise, which was adopted: Georgia and Ukraine were

---

[74] Orwell, Preface to the Ukrainian edition of *Animal Farm*, CW, XIX, 87.

[75] Some continuing Western attempts to present Ukraine as a country of the extreme right were assessed in: Umland, 'How Anti-Right Wing Critique Becomes Right Wing?' (*Kyiv Post*, 2016). https://www.academia.edu/36951196/How_anti_right_wing_critique _becomes_right_wing.

welcomed to become NATO members some time in future, while the issue of joining the MAP was postponed. Sure enough, appeasing Putin did not bring any peace: Russia attacked Georgia four months later, in August 2008, and proclaimed two of the Georgian territories – South Ossetia and Abkhazia – independent. Then, in 2014, came the turn of Ukraine: Crimea was annexed and Donbass surreptitiously invaded, with Russia helping to establish on its territory two 'people's republics' – Donetsk (DPR) and Luhansk (LPR), under its own control. By the end of the so-called Minsk negotiations, which lasted nearly eight years, it was obvious that France and Germany were effectively supporting Russia, which behaved as if it were not a party to the conflict but a mediator between Ukraine and the 'people's republics' on its territory.

On the eve of war in 2022, Russia attempted to make NATO formally promise that it would never allow a former Soviet country to become another member. NATO withstood the provocation, refusing to adopt a 'closed door' policy. Moreover, once the war started and the threat of Russia's aggression became more palpable for everybody, the Alliance invited previously neutral Finland and Sweden to join, which both countries accepted.

However, the position of the West still remained ambiguous – it gave Ukraine generous moral support and much more cautious military assistance. At the end of November 2022, after nine months of fighting, it became obvious to everybody that the conflict had been turning into a quagmire, claiming more and more lives and destroying the economy. The remarkable courage and high morale of the Ukrainians, armed with Western weapons, ensured some important Ukrainian victories on the battlefield, which forced Russia to insist on its readiness for negotiations. Evidently, the invader badly needed a ceasefire to give a respite to its exhausted army, to regroup and then attack again. The idea of negotiations on Russia's terms was welcomed by many in the West, especially by those who had always thought that the road to peace lies through appeasement of the aggressor, in particular, one with nuclear weapons, although the experience of the twentieth and early twenty-first centuries should by now have convinced them that pandering to any totalitarian regime does not make it tamer. At the time of writing, in late autumn 2022, the shadow of totalitarian Russia is still hanging over Ukraine, over its neighbours and over Russia's own population.

Back in 1942, Orwell was looking for ways to stop the world from sliding into totalitarian nightmare where there is no objective truth and 'the leader' can control the past, present and future. He came up with the following solution:

Against that shifting phantasmagoric world in which black may be white tomorrow and yesterday's weather can be changed by decree, there are in reality only two safeguards. One is that however much you deny the truth, the truth goes on existing, as it were, behind your back, and you consequently can't violate it in ways that impair military efficiency. The other is that so long as some parts of the earth remain unconquered, the liberal tradition can be kept alive.[76]

These safeguards do not exist in *Nineteen Eighty-Four*, where military efficiency is not all that important and the philosophies of Oceania, Eurasia and Eastasia 'are barely distinguishable'.[77] But in today's real world, with military efficiency still relevant and some parts of the earth unconquered, it should be possible to confront the leaders who are trying to impose the shifting phantasmagoria onto the whole planet. It is just vital to keep the liberal tradition alive.

[76] Orwell, 'Looking Back on the Spanish War', 505.
[77] Orwell, *Nineteen Eighty-Four*, 157.

# Select bibliography

Anderson, Paul and Davey, Kevin. *Moscow Gold? The Soviet Union and the British Left*. Ipswitch: Aaaargh! Press, 2014.

Andrew, Christopher and Gordievsky, Oleg. *KGB: The Inside Story of Its Foreign Operations from Lenin to Gorbachev*. London, Sydney, Auckland, Toronto: Hodder & Stoughton, 1990.

Andrew, Christopher and Mitrokhin, Vasili. *The Mitrokhin Archive: The KGB in Europe and the West*. London: Penguin Books, 2000.

Applebaum, Anne. *Iron Curtain: The Crushing of Eastern Europe 1944–56*. London: Allen Lane, 2012.

Barker, Joseph. 'Putin's Foundation Myth: Russian Memory and the Second World War'. *New Critique*. https://newcritique.co.uk/2016/11/22/essay-putins -foundation-myth-russian-memory-and-the-second-world-war-joseph -barker/.

Beevor, Anthony. *The Battle for Spain: The Spanish Civil War 1936–1939*. London: Phoenix, 2006.

Belton, Catherine. *Putin's People: How the KGB Took Back Russia and Then Took on the West*. London: William Collins, 2020.

Bergholz, Olga. *Olga: Zapretny dnevnik (Olga: The Forbidden Diary)*. Edited by Natalya Sokolovskaya. St Petersburg: Azbuka, 2010.

Blyum, Arlen. 'George Orwell in the Soviet Union. A Documentary Chronicle on the Centenary of his Birth'. Translated by I. P. Foote, *The Library*, Vol. 4, No. 4, December 2003, 402–416.

Borkenau, Franz. *The Communist International*. London: Faber and Faber, 1938.

Borkenau, Franz. *The Spanish Cockpit*. London, Sydney: Pluto Press, 1986.

Borkenau, Franz. *The Totalitarian Enemy*. London: Faber and Faber,1940.

Borsboom, E. *Vivo de Lanti (A Life of Lanti)*. Paris: SAT, 1976.

Bowker, Gordon. *George Orwell*. London: Abacus, 2010.

Brinson, Charmian. '"Nothing Short of a Scandal?" Harry Peter Smolka and the British Ministry of Information'. *Journal for Intelligence, Propaganda and Security Studies*, Vol. 10, 2016, 8–20.

Brockway, Fenner. *Inside the Left*. Nottingham: Spokesman, 2010.

Bullock, Ian. *Under Siege: The Independent Labour Party in Interwar Britain*. Athabasca, AB: Athabasca University Press, 2017.

Chalupa, Andrea. *Orwell and the Refugees: The Untold Story of Animal Farm*. Amazon Digital Services, March 11, 2012.

Coleman, Peter. *The Liberal Conspiracy: The Congress for Cultural Freedom and the Struggle for the Mind of Postwar Europe*. New York: The Free Press, 1989.

Conquest, Robert. 'Totaliterror'. In *On Nineteen Eighty-Four*, edited by Peter Stansky, 177–187. New York, San Francisco: W. H. Freeman and Company, 1983.

Conquest, Robert. *The Great Terror: A Reassessment*. Oxford: Oxford University Press, 1990.

Corthorn, Paul. 'Labour, the Left, and the Stalinist Purges of the Late 1930s'. *The Historical Journal*, Vol. 48, No. 1, 2005, 179–207.

Corthorn, Paul. *In the Shadow of the Dictators: The British Left in the 1930s*. London: I.B. Tauris, 2006.

Costello, John and Tsarev, Oleg. *Deadly Illusions*. London: Century, 1993.

Courtois, Stéphane and Panné, Jean-Louis. 'The Shadow of the NKVD in Spain'. In *The Black Book of Communism: Crimes, Terror, Repression*, edited by Stéphane Courtois et al., 333–352, Cambridge, Massachusetts and London, England: Harvard University Press, 1999.

Crick, Bernard. *George Orwell: A Life*. Harmondsworth, Middlesex: Penguin Books, 1982.

Croft, Andy. *The Years of Anger: The Life of Randall Swingler*. London and New York: Routledge, 2020.

Curtis, J. A. E. *The Englishman from Lebedian: A Life of Evgeny Zamiatin*. Brighton: Academic Studies Press, 2013.

Davenport-Hines, Richard. *Enemies Within: Communists, the Cambridge Spies and the Making of Modern Britain*. London: William Collins, 2019.

Dawisha, Karen. *Putin's Kleptocracy: Who Owns Russia?* New York, London, Toronto, Sydney, New Delhi: Simon & Shuster, 2014.

de Waal, Thomas. Introduction. In: Anna Politkovskaya. *A Dirty War: Russian Reporter in Chechnya*. Translated and edited by John Crowfoot. London: The Harvill Press, 2001.

Eastman, Max. *Artists in Uniform: A Study of Literature and Bureaucratism*. London: George Allen &Unwin Ltd, 1934.

Gide, André. *Return from the USSR*. New York: Alfred A. Knopf, Borzoi Books, reprint by Lightning Source Ltd.

Goldman, Emma. *Living My Life*. New York: Dover Publications, 1970.

Goldman, Emma. *My Disillusionment in Russia*. ReadaClassic.com, 2011.

Goodway, David. *Anarchist Seeds Beneath the Snow*. Oakland, CA: PM Press, 2012.

Grogin, Robert C. *Natural Enemies: The United States and the Soviet Union in the Cold War 1917–1991*. Lanham, MD: Lexington Books, 2001.

Guiheneuf, Hervé. *10 Ans en URSS (1923–1933): L'Itinéraire d'Yvon (10 Years in the USSR (1923–1933): Yvon's Route)*. Nantes: Quest Editions, 2001.

Harman, Oren Solomon. 'C. D. Darlington and the British and American Reaction to Lysenko and the Soviet Conception of Science'. *Journal of the History of Biology*, Vol. 36, No. 2, 2003, 309–352.

Hollander, Paul. *Political Pilgrims: Travels of Western Intellectuals to the Soviet Union, China and Cuba 1928–1978*. New York: Harper Colophon Books, 1983.

Howe, Irwing. '1984: Enigmas of Power'. In *1984 Revisited: Totalitarianism in Our Century*, edited by Irving Howe, 3–18. New York, Cambridge, Philadelphia, San Francisco, London, Mexico City, Sydney: Harper & Row, 1983.

Jones, Bill. *The Russia Complex: The British Labour Party and the Soviet Union*. Manchester: Manchester University Press, 1977.

Jones, Gareth. Talk 'Soviet Russia in March 1933' given in Chatham House on 30 March 1933. https://anglorussiannetwork.wordpress.com/topics/travel/gareth-jones-a-man-of-goodwill/.

Jones, William D. 'Toward a Theory of Totalitarianism: Franz Borkenau's *Pareto*'. *Journal of the History of Ideas*, Vol. 53, No. 3, 1992, 455–466.

Koltsov, Mikhail. *Ispaniya v ogne (Spain on Fire)*. Moscow: Political Literature Publishers, 1987.

Krivitsky, Walter Germanovich. *In Stalin's Secret Service*. New York: Harper and Brothers Publishers, 1939.

Landau, Katia. 'Stalinism in Spain'. *Revolutionary History*, Vol. 1, No. 2, Summer 1988. https://www.marxists.org/history/etol/document/spain/spain08.htm.

Lanti, Eugéne. 'Tri Semajnojn en Rusio'. (Three Weeks in Russia), *Sennacieca Revuo*, November-December 1922, July 1923.

Lanti, Eugéne. *Leteroj de E. Lanti. (E.Lanti's Letters)*. Paris: SAT, 1940.

Lanti, Eugéne. 'Three Weeks in Russia'. Translated by Mitch Abidor. https://www.marxists.org/archive/lanti/1922/3-weeks.htm.

*Letters from Barcelona: An American Woman in Revolution and Civil War.* Edited by Gerd-Rainer Horn. London: Palgrave Macmillan, 2009.

Lins, Ulrich. 'Orwell's Tutor? Eugène Adam (Lanti) und die Ernüchterung der Linken'. In *Jahrbuch der Gesellschaft für Interlinguistik*, edited by Cyril Robert Brosch and Sabine Fiedler, 103–124. Leipzig: Leipziger Universitätsverlag, 2020.

Lins, Ulrich. *Dangerous Language – Esperanto and the Decline of Stalinism*. London: Palgrave, 2017.

Lins, Ulrich. *Dangerous Language – Esperanto Under Hitler and Stalin*. London: Palgrave Macmillan, 2016.

Longstaff, S. A. '"Missionary in a Dark Continent": *Der Monat* and Germany's Intellectual Regeneration, 1947-1950'. *History of European Ideas*, Vol. 19, No. 1–3, 1994, 93–99.

Lyons, Eugene. *Assignment in Utopia*. London: George G. Harrap and Co, 1938.

Martin, Marko. *Orwell, Koestler und all die anderen: Melvin J. Lasky und Der Monat (Orwell, Koestler and All the Others: Melvin J. Lasky and Der Monat)*. Asendorf: MUT-Verlag, 1999.

McGovern, John. *Terror in Spain: How the Communist International has Destroyed Working-Class Unity, Undermined the Fight Against Franco, and Suppressed the Social Revolution*. London: ILP,1938.

Meyers, Jeffrey, ed. *George Orwell: The Critical Heritage*. London and New York: Routledge, 2011.

Miner, Steven Merritt, *Stalin's Holy War: Religion, Nationalism and Alliance Politics, 1941-1945*. Chapel Hill and London: The University of North Carolina Press, 2003.

Newsinger, John. *Hope Lies in the Proles: George Orwell and the Left*. London: Pluto Press, 2018.

*Orwell Remembered*, compiled by Audrey Coppard and Bernard Crick. London: Ariel Books, BBC, 1984.

Orwell, George. *A Life in Letters*. Selected and annotated by Peter Davison. London: Penguin Books, 2011.

Orwell, George. *Animal Farm*. London: Penguin Books,1989.

Orwell, George. *Coming Up for Air*. London: Penguin Books,1962.

Orwell, George. *Down and Out in Paris and London*. London: Penguin Books, 2001.

Orwell, George. *Homage to Catalonia*. Harmondsworth, Middlesex: Penguin Books, 1985.

Orwell, George. *Keep the Aspidistra Flying In: The Penguin Complete Novels of George Orwell*. London: Penguin Books, 1983.

Orwell, George. *Nineteen Eighty-Four*. Harmondsworth, Middlesex: Penguin Books, 1987.

Orwell, George. *Nineteen Eighty-Four: The Facsimile of the Extant Manuscript*. Edited by Peter Davison. London: Secker & Warburg; Weston, Massachusetts: M & S Press, 1984.

Orwell, George. *The Complete Works of George Orwell*. Edited by Peter Davison, 20 volumes. London: Secker & Warburg, 1998.

Orwell, George. *The Lost Orwell: A Supplement to The Complete Works of George Orwell*. Compiled and annotated by Peter Davison. London: Timewell Press, 2006.

Orwell, George. *The Orwell Diaries*. Edited by Peter Davison. London: Penguin Books, 2010.

Orwell, George. *The Road to Wigan Pier*. London: Penguin Books, 2001.

Pimlott, Ben. *Labour and the Left in the 1930s*. Cambridge: Cambridge University Press,1977.

Podhoretz, Norman. 'If Orwell Were Alive Today'. *Harper's*, January 1983.

Radosh, Ronald, Habeck Mary, R. And Sevostianov, Grigory, eds., *Spain Betrayed: The Soviet Union in the Spanish Civil War*. New Haven and London: Yale University Press, 2001.

Reisch, Alfred A. *Hot Books in the Cold War: The CIA-Funded Secret Western Book Distribution Programme Behind the Iron Curtain*. Budapest-New York: CEU Press, 2013.

Rossianov, Kirill O. 'Stalin As Lysenko's Editor: Reshaping Political Discourse in Soviet Science'. *Russian History*, Vol. 21, No. 1, 1994, 49–63.

Sarnov, Benedict. *Stalin I pisateli (Stalin and Writers)*. Moscow: Eksmo, 2009.

Scammell, Michael. *Koestler: The Indispensable Intellectual*. London: Faber and Faber, 2010.

Schor, Esther. *Bridge of Words: Esperanto and the Dream of a Universal Language*. New York: Metropolitan Books, 2016.

Scott-Smith, Giles. '"A Radical Democratic Political Offensive": Melvin J. Lasky. *Der Monat*, and the Congress for Cultural Freedom'. *Journal of Contemporary History*, Vol. 35, No. 2, April 2000, 263–280.

Shafranek, Hans. *Kurt Landau*. https://www.marxists.org/history/etol/revhist/backiss/vol4/no1-2/schafra.htm.

Souvarine, Boris. *Cauchemar en URSS*. Paris: La Revue de Paris, 1 July 1937.

*Stalin-Wells Talk: The Verbatim Record and a Discussion by G. Bernard Shaw, H. G. Wells, J. M. Keynes, Ernst Toller and Others*. London: New Statesman and Nation, 1934.

Steinhoff, William. *The Road to 1984*. London: Weidenfeld and Nicolson, 1975.

Struve, Gleb. 25 *Years of Soviet Russian Literature (1918–1943)*. London: George Routledge and Sons, 1944.

Telesin, Julius. Pismo v Redaktsiyu. (A Letter to the Editor). *Kontinent*, 1982, N34. http://www.laban.rs/orwell/Animal_Farm/Perevod_fragmentov_YT .html.

*The Orwell Tapes*. Conceived and compiled by Stephen Wadhams. Vancouver: Locarno Press, 2017. Previously published as *Remembering Orwell*. Markham, ON: Penguin Books, 1984.

Thorne, Lyudmila. *Books Not Bombs*. Unpublished memoir. Bakhmeteff Archive of Russian and East European Culture at Columbia University, New York.

Tolstoy, Ivan. *Platforma dlya Tamizdata ('A Platform for Tamizdat') in: Izdatelskoe delo rossiyskogo zarubezhya 19-20 vekov (Russian Publishing Abroad in the 19-20 centuries)*. Moscow: Dom russkogo zarubezhya, 2017.

Udy, Giles. *Labour and the Gulag: Russia and the Seduction of the British Left*. London: Biteback Publishing, 2017.

*Vision on Fire: Emma Goldman on the Spanish Revolution*. Edited by David Porter. Edinburgh, Oakland, West Virginia: AK Press, 2006.

Walter, Nicholas. 'Orwell and Anarchism'. In *George Orwell at Home (And Among the Anarchists)*, 47–75. London: Freedom Press, 1998.

Wilford, Hugh. *The CIA, the British Left and the Cold War: Calling the Tune?* London and Portland, OR: Frank Cass, 2003.

Woodcock, George. *Orwell's Message: 1984 and the Present*. Pender Harbour, British Columbia: Harbour Publishing, 1984.

Wynne, Miriam. 'Biographical Details of Mrs Mary Myfanwy Westrope (nee Wynne)'. Unpublished. Mary Myfanwy Westrope file. Hull University Archives (HUA), U DLB-11-124.

# Archives

Bakhmeteff Archive of Russian and East European Culture at Columbia University, New York: Lyudmila Thorne's file.

Bernard Crick Archive, Birkbeck College Archive: Gleb Struve's letters to Crick and Angus.

Hoover Institution Library and Archives, Stanford, CA: Struve papers.

Hull University Archive: Mary Myfanwy Westrope file.

Marx Memorial Library. International Memorial Trust: Walter Tapsell's Reports.

The Orwell Archive, UCL Library Services, Special Collections: Letters to
    Orwell.
The Russian Archive of Social and Political History, Moscow: Collection 545.
University of Edinburgh Archive: Arthur Koestler's Papers. Collection 146.

# Index